BLACKSTONE'S
HUMAN RIGHTS DIGEST

BLACKSTONE'S
HUMAN RIGHTS DIGEST

Keir Starmer

with
Iain Byrne

With a foreword by Lord Irvine of Lairg
Lord Chancellor

Consultant editor: Francesca Klug

Human Rights Act Research Unit
School of Law
King's College
University of London

BLACKSTONE
PRESS LIMITED

Published by
Blackstone Press Limited
Aldine Place
London
W12 8AA
United Kingdom

Sales enquiries and orders
Telephone +44-(0)-20-8740-2277
Facsimile +44-(0)-20-8743-2292
e-mail: sales@blackstone.demon.co.uk
website: www.blackstonepress.com

ISBN 1-84174-153-1
© Keir Starmer 2001
First published 2001

British Library Cataloguing in Publication Data
A catalogue record for this book is available from the British Library

Typeset in 10½/12pt Goudy by Style Photosetting Ltd, Mayfield, East Sussex
Printed and bound in Great Britain by Antony Rowe Limited,
Chippenham and Reading

CONTENTS

FOREWORD

The Human Rights Act came into force on 2 October 2000. It is a firm expression of the Government's commitment to promoting a new culture of respect for human rights – and the responsibilities that come hand in hand with those rights – across all our institutions and ultimately the whole of our society.

We were one of the principal authors of the Convention. Yet for 50 years, British people had to go to Strasbourg to enforce their Convention rights – an expensive and time-consuming road which few took in practice. The Act allows British people to enforce their Convention rights in British courts with British judges, sensitive to the needs and standards of our administration. People in every other Western European country have had these rights in their own courts for years and their societies have only benefited.

UK governments have been complying with the ECHR for over 50 years. Significant changes to the law – for example on telephone tapping, the security and intelligence agencies, police powers, prisoners' rights – were made in the 1980s and 1990s to take account of Strasbourg court judgments. But incorporation of the Convention gave us the opportunity and the incentive to look again at how successfully we were protecting fundamental rights.

In the run up to implementation, all Government Departments examined their legislation, policies, practices and procedures to ensure compliance. They also worked with their non-departmental public bodies, including some semi-public bodies, to ensure that they too were prepared. For example, my Department organised a series of 'walk-throughs' to alert all the players in the justice system to the potential impact of the Act and to explore possible changes to policy, practice and procedure. Experienced human rights practitioners, including the author of this *Digest*, prepared and presented case studies which were then explored by judges, magistrates, defence and prosecution lawyers, policy makers and others with an interest. As a result, training programmes were refined and improvements made to policy, practice and procedure.

But it is important to emphasise that most of our laws were already compliant; that this country has as great a respect for human rights as any of our European neighbours; and that our laws and procedures generally reflect that. So Declarations of Incompatibility by the higher courts, calling for legislative change, will be very rare. What we *can* expect more of, however, is radical interpretation of legislation by the courts. This will sometimes be necessary in order to achieve compatibility with the Convention and will, in some cases, require practices and procedures to change to bring them into line with legislation interpreted in this way. But it is wrong to see successful human rights challenges as 'defeats' for the Government. On the contrary, these should be seen as manifesting a new partnership between Parliament, government and the judiciary, which the Human Rights Act marks. The Act specifically provides that judges cannot overrule Parliament, but they can point the way forward and help develop the culture of rights and responsibilities we all want to see. The Human Rights Act means that, in developing the law, judges will operate within a democratic code of values based on human rights. So, the working out of the Act should be seen, not as an obstacle to good administration, but as an essential element in the path to achieving it.

The judiciary has a major role to play in the successful implementation of the Act and it has been well prepared. A full-scale programme of training has ensured that all full- and part-time judges have been trained, as well as 30,000 lay magistrates and their legal advisers. All full-time judges also now have access to an Internet-based system allowing quick exchange of information on developing Strasbourg and ECHR case law. Judges are, as predicted, dealing very sensibly with the human rights issues brought before them. Prior to 2 October, the Court of Appeal, for example in *R v Perry* and *Daniels v Walker*, criticised lawyers for raising unmeritorious human rights points. And more recently the Privy Council gave a salutary judgment in *Procurator Fiscal for Dunfermline v Brown*. Overturning the decision of the High Court of Justiciary in Scotland, it held that s. 172 of the Road Traffic Act 1988 did not breach Article 6(1) of the Convention, since that provision is a proportionate response to the serious social problem of drink-driving.

By enabling people to enforce their Convention rights in British courts, the Act enhances access to justice and makes the law of the European Convention even more relevant to our everyday lives. Blackstone's *Human Rights Digest* does the same. It sets out in an easily accessible way the key Convention principles and underlying case law. It does so by providing a comprehensive bullet-point analysis of the case law of the European Court and Commission, along with key extracts. The Digest will provide a useful tool for those who need speedy access to human rights materials – both experts and non-experts, practitioners and non-practitioners. The aim is to provide material that is useful in court and out of court and which helps to ensure decision-making is Convention compatible without the need for litigation. It will also assist the Human Rights Act Research Unit at the Law School, King's College, to monitor and evaluate the impact of the Act. This the Government welcomes.

The Digest is accompanied by a CD-ROM containing the European Court judgments up to and including December 2000 and selected Commission decisions, together with a search engine permitting topics as well as case names and dates to be searched. This will complement HUDOC, the European Court's own website and so provide a useful addition to the growing network of readily available human rights information.

Lord Irvine of Lairg
Lord Chancellor
January 2001

PREFACE AND ACKNOWLEDGEMENTS

This *Digest* is the product of an on-going debate about the effectiveness of human rights protection in the UK. That debate took a new turn in 1995 when Francesca Klug, now academic director of the Human Rights Act Research Unit, first suggested the creation of a *Human Rights Index* to measure the UK's compliance with its international human rights obligations. The index was a set of standards drawn from the international instruments ratified by the UK, as developed by the case law of the various supervising bodies, such as the European Court of Human Rights and the UN Human Rights Committee. Having devised such an index, Francesca and I used it to 'audit' civil and political rights in the UK and published our results in *The Three Pillars of Liberty* (1996).

Things have moved on since then. Now individuals can enforce their rights under the European Convention on Human Rights in domestic law. And, as a result, the debate about human rights protection in the UK has also moved on. Where once we explored the extent to which the common law was capable of giving effect to international human rights obligations, now we are interested in how effective the Human Rights Act will be in protecting Convention rights. Accordingly, the Human Rights Incorporation Project at the Law School, King's College, has given way to the Human Rights Act Research Unit, a unit exclusively devoted to monitoring and evaluating the impact of the Human Rights Act in court and, equally importantly, elsewhere.

This *Digest* is primarily intended to provide a framework for that monitoring and evaluation by drawing together the principles underpinning Convention rights on an issue by issue (rather than Article by Article) basis and setting out the key extracts from the case law of the European Court of Human Rights. Hopefully, because it contains a comprehensive analysis of Convention case law, it will also serve as a useful tool for all those involved in human rights protection in the UK.

So far as acknowledgements are concerned, the starting point has to be Iain Byrne, who carried out much of the research for this *Digest*. He spent many months reading, extracting and writing much of the comparative material, reflecting his well-recognised commitment to effective human rights protection throughout the world. I am very grateful for his important contribution. Next there is Francesca Klug. She had the inspiration to conceive of a human rights index in the first place and the commitment to refashion it by acting as a consultant in the writing of this *Digest*.

King's College School of Law also deserves special mention. Robin Morse, the Dean, provided unfailing support for the whole project. Jenny Watson, development director, and Elena Salgado, research associate of the Human Rights Act Research Unit, provided crucial support and assistance in the later stages of the *Digest*. And, of course, none of this would have been possible without the generous support and incisive advice of the Joseph Rowntree Charitable Trust and its officers and trustees.

I am also extremely grateful to the staff at Blackstone Press, who backed this project with unswerving faith despite the many broken deadlines and unfulfilled promises. Without the enthusiasm and support of Alistair MacQueen, David Stott and Jeremy Stein, this *Digest* would never have seen the light of day.

Finally, I need to acknowledge all my friends and colleagues who I lent on and let down in equal measure during the writing of this *Digest*, particularly Julie Morris, who endured my reclusive episodes with bemused affection. I do not think anyone escaped without at least one unreturned telephone call and a cancelled appointment. I hope it was worth it.

Keir Starmer
London
January 2001

TABLE OF ECHR CASES

TABLE OF DOMESTIC CASES

TABLE OF SCOTTISH CASES

TABLE OF CANADIAN CASES

TABLE OF NEW ZEALAND CASES

TABLE OF SOUTH AFRICAN CASES

TABLE OF COMMONWEALTH CASES

TABLE OF INTERNATIONAL INSTRUMENTS

TABLE OF PRIMARY LEGISLATION

TABLE OF SECONDARY LEGISLATION

ABBREVIATIONS AND USE WITH THE CD

The following abbreviations are used throughout this book:

ECHR   European Convention on Human Rights
ECmHR   European Commission of Human Rights
ECtHR   European Court of Human Rights
EHRLR   European Human Rights Law Review
EHRR   European Human Rights Reports
HRA   Human Rights Act 1998

The CD which accompanies this work contains the full text of judgments of the European Court of Human Rights up to and including December 2000. The judgments can be searched by subject index, name or date.

The CD also contains selected decisions of the European Commission of Human Rights. Decisions which can be viewed on the CD are indicated in the text with the symbol[CD].

A STRUCTURED APPROACH TO CONVENTION RIGHTS

In many instances, Convention issues can be addressed by adopting a structured approach using the questions set out below.

General

What Convention right (if any) is engaged?
What category does it fall within?

Absolute rights:	Article 2, 3, 4(1) and 7
Special rights:	Articles 4(2), 5, 6, 9(1), 12, Protocol 1, Articles 2 and 3, Protocol 6, Article 1
Qualified rights:	The rest. In particular, Articles 8, 9 10 and 11

Absolute rights

If 'absolute', has there been any breach of the right in question?

Article 2

Is Article 2 engaged?

If so, does Article 2(2) apply?

If so, are the conditions set out in Article 2(2) fulfilled?

If not, a violation of the Convention must be found.

Article 3

Is Article 3 engaged?

If so, is the treatment/punishment in question sufficiently serious to cross the Article 3 threshold?

If so, a violation of the Convention must be found.

Article 4(1)

Does the treatment in question amount to slavery?

If so, a violation of the Convention must be found.

Article 7

Do the proceedings relate to a criminal offence or criminal penalty?

If so, has the law been applied retrospectively?

If so, does Article 7(2) apply?

If not, a violation of the Convention must be found.

Special rights

Article 5

Is Article 5 engaged (i.e., has the individual in question been detained)?

If so, what is the legal authority for his or her detention and have the procedural requirements of domestic law been complied with?

If so, is the detention permitted under Article 5(1)(a) to 5(1)(f)?

If so, were reasons given to the individual for his or her detention in accordance with Article 5(2)?

If so, is there a procedure whereby the individual can test the legality of his or her detention before a court in accordance with Article 5(4)?

In the criminal context, have the pre-trial rights in Article 5(3) been complied with (bearing in mind that bail and trial within a reasonable period are not alternatives)?

If not, does the UK derogation apply?

In all cases, is there an enforceable right to compensation for anyone detained in breach of his or her Article 5 rights?

Article 6

Do the proceedings involve the determination of a criminal charge (bearing in mind that some 'civil' matters are deemed criminal under the Convention)?

If so, have the fair trial requirements of Article 6(1) been met?

If so, has the presumption of innocence been respected as required by Article 6(2)?

If so, have the minimum requirements of Article 6(3)(a) to 6(3)(e) been met?

Are any further guarantees required to ensure a fair trial?

If the proceedings are not criminal, but civil, have the fair trial requirements of Article 6(1) been met?

Are any further guarantees required to ensure a fair trial?

Qualified rights

If 'qualified' rights are engaged, has there been any apparent breach of the right in question (or some limitation upon it)?

If so, what is the legal authority for the breach of limitation and does it correspond to the Convention rule of legality:

- does it have a proper basis in domestic law?
- if so, is the law/rule in question 'accessible' (is it in the public domain)?
- if so, is the law/rule in question reasonably precise?

If so, can the reasons for the breach or limitation be found in the second paragraph of Articles 8 to 11?

If so, is the breach or limitation both necessary and proportionate (bearing in mind that necessary does not simply mean reasonable and a restriction on a Convention right is unlikely to be proportionate if the same ends could be achieved by a less restrictive means)?

If not, a breach of the Convention must be found.

Discrimination (applicable in all cases)

Is a Convention right in issue?

If so, has there been discrimination (or differential treatment) between two individuals or groups of individuals?

If so, has it been established that the discrimination or difference in treatment had a legitimate aim or purpose?

If so, has it been established that the means employed to achieve the legitimate aim or purpose in question were proportionate?

If not, a breach of the Convention must be found (even if the actual Convention right primarily in issue is not breached).

THE RIGHTS PROTECTED

1.1 CONVENTION RIGHTS

- The rights protected by the HRA are called 'Convention rights' (s. 1(1)). They are set out in Schedule 1 to the HRA.

- In the HRA 'the Convention rights' means the rights and fundamental freedoms set out in:

  - (a) Articles 2 to 12 and 14 of the ECHR;
  - (b) Articles 1 to 3 of the First Protocol; and
  - (c) Articles 1 and 2 of the Sixth Protocol (s. 1(1)).

- The subject-matter of these rights is as follows:

  Article 2: The right to life
  Article 3: Prohibition on torture
  Article 4: Prohibition on slavery and forced labour
  Article 5: Right to liberty and security
  Article 6: Right to a fair trial
  Article 7: No punishment without law
  Article 8: Right to respect for private and family life
  Article 9: Freedom of thought, conscience and religion
  Article 10: Freedom of expression
  Article 11: Freedom of assembly and association
  Article 12: Right to marry
  Article 14: Prohibition on discrimination
  Protocol 1, Article 1: Protection of property
  Protocol 1, Article 2: Right to education
  Protocol 1, Article 3: Right to free elections
  Protocol 6, Article 1: Abolition of the death penalty
  Protocol 6, Article 2: Death penalty in times of war

- These rights are to be read with Article 16 (restrictions on political activities of aliens), Article 17 (prohibition on abuse of rights) and Article 18 (limitation on use of restrictions on rights) (s. 1(1)).

1.2 THE STATUS OF CONVENTION RIGHTS

- Convention rights are not all of equal status. The protection afforded under the ECHR and the HRA varies from right to right.

- Broadly speaking, the ECtHR recognises three categories of Convention rights:

Absolute rights
Rights which are strongly protected and which cannot be restricted even in times of war or other public emergency: Article 2 (the right to life), Article 3 (prohibition on torture), Article 4(1) (prohibition on slavery) and Article 7 (no punishment without law).

Although there are special provisions dealing with the death penalty and death caused by the use of force, in all other respects the public interest cannot justify any interference with absolute rights.

Special rights
Rights which are less strongly protected, but which can be restricted even in times of war or other public emergency: Article 4(2) and (3) (prohibition on forced labour), Article 5 (right to liberty and security), Article 6 (fair trial), Article 9(1) (freedom of thought, conscience and religion – but *not* freedom to manifest religion or belief, which is a qualified right), Article 12 (right to marry), Protocol 1, Article 2 (the right to education), Protocol 1, Article 3 (right to free elections) and Protocol 6, Article 1 (abolition of the death penalty).

The practical difference between these rights and absolute rights is that restriction in the public interest can be justified, but only on the grounds expressly provided for within the text of the Article itself: e.g., Article 4(2) prohibits forced labour, but Article 4(3) then sets out a number of exceptions; similarly, the first sentence of Article 5(1) provides for the right to liberty and security of person, but the second sentence then lists (exhaustively) all the circumstances in which that right can be restricted. Unless a restriction is expressly provided for in the text of the Article, the public interest cannot justify any interference with special rights.

Strictly speaking, Article 6 (fair trial) probably falls into a category of its own. That is because the ECtHR has read a number of implied restrictions into Article 6, e.g., to ensure the protection of victims and vulnerable witnesses within the trial process. Such restrictions are limited and must be strictly necessary and proportionate. In all other respects, the public interest cannot justify any interference with Article 6 rights.

Qualified rights
Rights which are to be balanced against the public interest and which can be restricted even in times of war or other public emergency: Article 8 (right to respect for private and family life), Article 9 (right to manifest religion or belief), Article 10 (freedom of expression), Article 11 (freedom of assembly and association), Article 14 (prohibition on discrimination) and Protocol 1, Article 1 (protection of property).

These rights are in positive form, but can be restricted where it can be shown that a restriction is:

(a) prescribed by law;
(b) legitimate;
(c) necessary and proportionate;
(d) not discriminatory.

Protocol 1, Article 1 (protection of property) also probably falls into a category of its own because it is less well protected than the other qualified rights. Where property rights are interfered with, the question will be whether a 'fair balance' has been achieved between the individual's right to property and the general public interest.

Relevant ECHR cases

Selmouni v France (1999) 29 EHRR 403, ECtHR

• Nothing can justify infringing absolute rights:

> Even in the most difficult circumstances, such as the fight against terrorism and organised crime, the Convention prohibits in absolute terms torture or inhuman or degrading treatment or punishment. (*Selmouni v France*, para. 95)

Relevant domestic cases

R v DPP, ex parte Kebilene [1999] 3 WLR 175

• Article 6, ECHR is not a qualified right:

> Any human rights instrument must represent a compromise between the rights of the individual and the rights of other individuals who collectively make up the community, society or state. But a human rights instrument such as the Convention is a measure to protect human rights and fundamental freedoms. This does not mean that all Convention rights are equal: some may be the subject of derogation by contracting states, others may not; some (such as Article 3) are expressed without any qualification, others (such as Articles 8, 9, 10 and 11) are subject to express qualifications; some rights have been recognised in the [HRA] itself as deserving enhanced protection: see sections 12 and 13. The right to a fair trial, protected by Article 6, is not a right from which a contracting state is not permitted to derogate; but nor is it a right which is in any material way qualified. I can readily conceive of circumstances in which it would be doubtful whether the presence of a certain feature (in itself undesirable) was such as to render a trial unfair, but I can conceive of no circumstances in which, having concluded that that feature rendered the trial unfair, a court would not go on to find a violation of Article 6. (*R v DPP, ex parte Kebilene, per* Lord Bingham, pp. 189D–G – *comments not disapproved on appeal*; see also the Scottish case of *Brown v Procurator Fiscal* (5 December 2000), PC; (2000) SLT 379, AC)

1.3   THE LEGALITY OF RESTRICTIONS

Key ECHR cases

Amann v Switzerland (16 February 2000), ECtHR
Baranowski v Poland (28 March 2000), ECtHR
Bronda v Italy (9 June 1998), ECtHR
Khan v UK (12 May 2000), ECtHR
Kopp v Switzerland (1998) 27 EHRR 91, ECtHR
Petra v Romania (23 September 1998), ECtHR
Rekvényi v Hungary (20 May 1999), ECtHR
Silver and others v UK (1983) 5 EHRR 347, ECtHR

Spacek v Czech Republic (9 November 1999), ECtHR
Steel and others v UK (1998) 28 EHRR 603, ECtHR
Sunday Times v UK (1979) 2 EHRR 245, ECtHR
Valenzuela Contreras v Spain (30 July 1998), ECtHR

Govell v UK [1999] EHRLR 101, ECmHR[CD]

ECHR principles

- Any restriction on Convention rights must be lawful.

- In some Articles the word 'lawful' itself is used (e.g., Article 5). In others, phrases such as 'in accordance with law' or 'prescribed by law' are used (e.g., Articles 8 and 9).

- Even where no express provision is made (e.g., Protocol 1, Article 1), any restriction on Convention rights must nonetheless be 'lawful'.

- Under the ECHR the term 'lawful' has special meaning. A restriction on Convention rights will only be 'lawful' if:

    (a)   there is an established legal basis in domestic law for the restriction, e.g., it is provided for by legislation or special rules;
    (b)   the provision in question is 'accessible', i.e. those likely to be affected by it can find out what it says;
    (c)   the provision in question is 'foreseeable', i.e. it is formulated with sufficient clarity to enable those likely to be affected by it to understand it and to regulate their conduct accordingly.

- Primary and subordinate legislation are a sufficient basis in domestic law for a restriction on Convention rights; so too is the common law:

    . . . the word 'law' in the expression 'prescribed by law' covers not only statute but also unwritten law. Accordingly, the Court does not attach importance here to the fact that contempt of court is a creature of the common law and not of legislation. It would clearly be contrary to the intention of the drafters of the Convention to hold that a restriction imposed by virtue of the common law is not 'prescribed by law' on the sole ground that it is not enunciated in legislation: this would deprive a common law State which is Party to the Convention of the protection of Article 10(2) and strikes at the very roots of that State's legal system . . . (*Sunday Times v UK*, para. 47)

- Home Office guidelines and internal police guidelines are unlikely to satisfy the requirement that provisions governing restrictions on Convention rights be accessible unless they are made publically available:

    . . . [in the present case] there is no existing statutory system to regulate the use of covert listening devices, although the Police Act 1997 [*not in force at the time*] will provide a statutory framework. The Home Office guidelines at the relevant time were neither legally binding nor were they publicly accessible . . . Consequently, . . . the interference . . . cannot be considered to be 'in accordance with law'. (*Govell v UK*, para. 62; see also *Silver and others v UK* and *Khan v UK*)

- Absolute certainty is not required for a provision to be 'foreseeable':

    . . . whilst certainty is highly desirable, it may bring in its train excessive rigidity and the law must be able to keep pace with changing circumstances. Accordingly, many laws are inevitably couched in terms which, to a greater or lesser extent are vague and whose interpretation and application are questions of practice. (*Sunday Times v UK*, para. 49)

- The degree of certainty will depend on the circumstances. In some fields of application a fairly wide degree of flexibility is acceptable:

   The level of precision required of domestic legislation – which cannot in any case provide for every eventuality – depends to a considerable degree on the content of the instrument in question, the field it is designed to cover and the number and status of those to whom it is addressed . . . Because of the general nature of constitutional provisions, the level of precision required of them may be lower than for other legislation. (*Rekvényi v Hungary*, para. 34 – *inevitable that provisions restricting the political activities of police officers cannot be defined with absolute precision*)

   Although a power vested in a court to take appropriate measures where the conduct of a parent is detrimental to a child is rather general, in this sphere of the law precision is difficult to attain and, where there is the safeguard of review by another court, such a power is capable of being 'in accordance with law'. (*Bronda v Italy*, para. 54)

- In others, a relatively high level of certainty is required:

   . . . where deprivation of liberty is concerned it is particularly important that the general principle of legal certainty be satisfied. It is therefore essential that the conditions for deprivation of liberty under domestic law be clearly defined and that the law itself be foreseeable in its application, so that it meets the standard of 'lawfulness' set out by the Convention, a standard which requires that all law be sufficiently precise to allow the person – if need be, with appropriate advice – to foresee, to a degree that is reasonable in the circumstances, the consequences which a given action may entail . . . (*Baranowski v Poland*, para. 52; citing *Steel and others v UK*)

- Prison regulations governing the interception of prisoners' correspondence which allow the authorities to retain any material 'unsuited to the process of rehabilitating a prisoner' are too vague for compliance with Article 8 (*Petra v Romania*).

- Prison regulations governing the interception of prisoners' correspondence which are unpublished breach Article 8 (*Petra v Romania*).

   . . . tapping and other forms of interception of telephone conversations constitute a serious interference with private life and correspondence and must accordingly be based on law which is particularly precise. It is essential to have clear, detailed rules on the subject, especially as the technology available for use is continually becoming more sophisticated . . . (*Amann v Switzerland*, para. 56; citing *Kopp v Switzerland*)

- The safeguards required by Article 8 should be set out in the law; it is not enough to rely on the judiciary to acquaint itself with and apply the relevant standards:

   The requirement that the 'law' be foreseeable means, in the sphere of monitoring telephone communications, that the guarantees stating the extent of the authorities' discretion and the manner in which it is to be exercised must be set out in detail in domestic law so that it has binding force which circumscribes the judges' discretion in the application of such measures. (*Valenzuela Contreras v Spain*, para. 60)

   The phrase 'in accordance with law' in Article 8 implies – when read purposively – that, in addition to clarity of the law etc., there must be legal safeguards against abuse of powers to collate, store and use private information about the individual. This is unlikely to be satisfied where the law does not regulate the circumstances in which information can be gathered, the purposes for which it can be used, the length of time it can be stored for and the point at which it should be destroyed. (*Rotaru v Romania*, para. 57)

- In very specialist fields, there is no specific requirement as to the degree of publicity to be given to a particular legal provision:

  Legislation required businesses to keep their account in accordance with prescribed accounting principles. Although the legislation was properly published as law, the principles were only published in a financial bulletin, not the Official Gazette. (*Spacek v Czech Republic*, paras 59 and 60 – *since the applicant had received the financial bulletin and had treated it as containing the applicable principles, the requirements were sufficiently accessible and foreseeable*)

Relevant Canadian cases

Committee for Cth. of Can. v Can. [1991] 1 SCR 139
Martineau v Matsqu Institution Inmate Disciplinary Board [1978] 1 SCR 118
R v Therens [1985] 1 SCR 613
Re Ontario Film and Video Appreciation Society (1983) 41 OR (2d) 583, CA

- A statute, regulation or rule of common law will satisfy the requirement that a restriction be prescribed by law (*R v Therens*).

- But directives and guidelines issued by government departments or agencies and falling outside the class of officially published delegated legislation may not (*Re Ontario Film and Video Appreciation Society* – *standards published by Ontario Board of Censors not a law because not binding on the Board*; *Committee for Cth. of Can. v Can.* – *Court divided on whether airport's internal directives were law*; *Martineau v Matsqu Institution Inmate Disciplinary Board* – *Court divided on whether departmental directives were law*).

Relevant Commonwealth cases

Abuki v Attorney General of Uganda (1998) 3 BHRC 199

- An accused's fair trial rights are violated where the offence with which he is charged is defined so vaguely as to leave him uncertain as to the nature of the conduct prohibited:

  The reasons for these requirements [of precision] are not hard to find. Firstly, it is to notify the citizens clearly of what conduct the statute prohibits. This assists a citizen to distinguish the prohibited conduct from the permissible conduct and therefore to be able to guard against violation. Secondly, in the event of a charge being levelled against him under the statute, a citizen shall be able to prepare his defence since the ingredients of the offence are known. (*Abuki v Attorney General of Uganda*, p. 214)

1.4   THE LEGITIMACY OF RESTRICTIONS

Key ECHR cases

Chassagnou and others v France (1999) 29 EHRR 615, ECtHR
Karatas v Turkey (8 July 1999), ECtHR

Serif v *Greece* (14 December 1999), ECtHR
Sidiropoulos v *Greece* (1998) 27 EHRR 633, ECtHR

ECHR principles

- Any restriction on Convention rights must be legitimate.

- For qualified rights, so long as a restriction genuinely pursues one of the aims set out in the Article itself, it will be legitimate.

- The aims set out in Articles 8 to 11 include: national security, public safety, the prevention of disorder or crime, and the protection of the rights and freedoms of others.

  > Regulation of hunting, including restrictions on the right to exclude others from land, can be legitimate because there is a general interest in avoiding unregulated hunting and encouraging rational management of game stocks. (*Chassagnou and others* v *France*, para. 79 – *challenge to law requiring applicants to allow hunting on their land as part of a municipal scheme to regulate hunting*)

  > But upholding national cultural traditions and historic and cultural symbols is not a legitimate basis for restricting freedom of association under Article 11. Exceptions to freedom of association must be narrowly interpreted; their enumeration in Article 11(2) is strictly exhaustive and the definition necessarily restrictive. (*Sidiropoulos* v *Greece*, para. 79 – *refusal to register Applicants' association on basis that it promoted the idea of a Macedonian minority in Greece*)

- Restrictions which do not recognise religious pluralism are unlikely to be legitimate (or necessary):

  > . . . the Court does not consider that, in democratic societies, the State needs to take measures to ensure that religious communities remain or are brought under a unified leadership . . .
  >   Although the Court recognises that tension is created in situations where a religious or any other community becomes divided, it considers that this is one of the unavoidable consequences of pluralism. The role of the authorities in such circumstances is not to remove the cause of tension by eliminating pluralism, but to ensure that the competing groups tolerate each other. (*Serif* v *Greece*, paras 52 and 53)

- Where the protection of the rights and freedoms of others is relied upon, an important distinction has to be made between Convention protected rights and freedoms and others' rights and freedoms:

  > If the 'rights and freedoms of others' is relied upon as the justification a distinction has to be drawn between those rights and freedoms protected by the Convention and those not so protected. Since the associations in question only protect the right to hunt, which is not a Convention protected activity, only indisputable imperatives can justify interference with [Article 11] rights. (*Chassagnou and others* v *France*, para. 113 – *challenge to law requiring applicants to allow hunting on their land as part of a municipal scheme to regulate hunting*)

- In free speech cases, the size of the target audience will be relevant to the legitimacy of the restriction:

  > The Court observes . . . that the applicant is a private individual who expressed his views through poetry – which by definition is addressed to a very small audience –

rather than through the mass media, a fact which limited their potential impact on 'national security', 'public order' and 'territorial integrity' to a substantial degree. Thus, even though some of the passages from the poems seem very aggressive in tone and to call for the use of violence, the Court considers that the fact that they were artistic in nature and of limited impact made them less a call to an uprising than an expression of deep distress in the face of a difficult political situation. (*Karatas v Turkey*, para. 52 – *conviction of poet for writing poetry which contained passages which were aggressive in tone and appeared to call for violence*)

- Any restriction on the prohibition on discrimination must also be legitimate, but, unlike Articles 8 to 11, Article 14 does not specifically list those aims deemed to be legitimate.

1.5   THE NECESSITY OF RESTRICTIONS

Key ECHR cases

Chassagnou and others v France (1999) 29 EHRR 615, ECtHR
Handyside v UK (1976) 1 EHRR 737, ECtHR
Litwa v Poland (4 April 2000), ECtHR

ECHR principles

- Any restriction on Convention rights must be necessary.

- For qualified rights, this requirement flows from the use of the phrase 'necessary in a democratic society' in Articles 8 to 11.

- Necessary is not synonymous with reasonable:

    . . . whilst the adjective 'necessary', within the meaning of Article 10(2), is not synonymous with 'indispensable', neither has it the flexibility of such expressions as 'admissible', ordinary', 'useful', 'reasonable', or 'desirable' . . . (*Handyside v UK*, para. 48)

- Neither will a restriction be necessary just because the majority are in favour of it:

    . . . in assessing the necessity of a given measure a number of principles must be observed. The term 'necessary' does not have the flexibility of such expressions as 'useful' or 'desirable'. In addition, pluralism, tolerance and broadmindedness are hallmarks of a 'democratic society'. Although individual interests must on occasion be subordinated to those of a group, democracy does not simply mean that the views of a majority must always prevail: a balance must be achieved which ensures the fair and proper treatment of minorities and avoids any abuse of a dominant position. (*Chassagnou and others v France*, para. 112)

- Detention is unlikely to be necessary where there are viable alternatives:

    The notion of 'lawfulness' runs through Article 5. As a result it is not enough simply to establish that one of the grounds for detention under Article 5(1)(a) to (f) is made out, detention must also be *necessary*. And detention will not be necessary unless the authorities can show that other measures short of detention – such as taking the individual home – were considered but rejected as insufficient. (*Litwa v Poland*, para. 78 – *blind person taken into detention to sober up after it was alleged that he was drunk in a post office*)

1.6   PROPORTIONALITY

Key ECHR cases

Handyside v UK (1976) 1 EHRR 737, ECtHR
Informationsverein Lentia v Austria (1993) 17 EHRR 93, ECtHR
Lehideux and Isorni v France (23 September 1998), ECtHR

ECHR principles

* Any restriction on Convention rights must be proportionate.

* For qualified rights, this requirement flows from the use of the phrase 'necessary in a democratic society' in Articles 8 to 11.

    . . . every 'formality', 'condition', 'restriction' or 'penalty' imposed in this sphere must be proportionate to the legitimate aim pursued. (*Handyside v UK*, para. 49)

* A restriction will be proportionate only if the objective behind the restriction justifies interference with a Convention right, there is a rational connection between the objective and the restriction in question and the means employed are not more than is necessary to achieve the objective.

* In making this assessment, the following factors are relevant:

    (a)   whether relevant and sufficient reasons have been advanced for the restriction;
    (b)   whether there was a less restrictive, but equally effective, way of achieving the same objective;
    (c)   whether sufficient regard has been paid to the rights and interests of those affected; in some cases (e.g., in family cases) those affected should be consulted;
    (d)   whether safeguards exist to guard against error or abuse (e.g., in secret surveillance cases);
    (e)   whether the restriction in question destroys the very essence of the Convention right in issue.

* Evidence from other Council of Europe countries will often be relevant to the question of whether a restriction is proportionate:

    Finally, and above all, it cannot be argued that there was no equivalent, less restrictive, solution; it is sufficient by way of example to cite the practice of certain countries which either issue licences subject to specified conditions of variable content or make provision for forms of private participation in the activities of the national corporation (*Informationsverein Lentia v Austria*, para. 39 – *public broadcasting monopoly inconsistent with Article 10*)

- The passage of time may be relevant to the question of proportionality:

  > As time passes, the appropriate response to certain types of publication changes. The lapse of time makes it inappropriate to deal with some remarks 40 years on with the same severity as 10 or 20 years previously. This forms part of the efforts that every country must make to debate its own history openly and dispassionately. (*Lehideux and Isorni v France*, para. 43 – *applicants convicted for publication of material about Marshal Petain, suggesting that his policies when head of the Vichy government might have been right, or, at least, well intentioned*)

Relevant Canadian cases

R v Edwards Books and Art [1986] 2 SCR 713
R v Oakes [1986] 1 SCR 103

- Four criteria must be satisfied before a restriction on Charter rights and freedoms can be justified:

    (a) There must be a sufficiently important objective.
    (b) There must be a rational connection between the restriction and the objective.
    (c) The restriction must impair the right in question no more than is necessary to accomplish the objective.
    (d) The restriction must not have a disproportionately severe effect on the person to whom it applies.

Although the nature of the proportionality test will vary depending on the circumstances, in each case courts will be required to balance the interests of society with those of individuals and groups. There are, in my view, three important components of a proportionality test. First, the measures adopted must be carefully designed to achieve the objective in question. They must not be arbitrary, unfair or based on irrational considerations. In short, they must be rationally connected to the objective. Second the means, even if rationally connected to the objective in the first sense, should impair 'as little as possible' the right or freedom in question . . . Third, there must be a proportionality between the *effects* of the measures which are responsible for limiting the Charter right or freedom, and the objective which has been identified as of 'sufficient importance'. (*R v Oakes*, per Dickson CJ, pp. 138–9)

. . . their effects [the limiting measures] must not so severely trench on individual or group rights that the legislative objective, albeit important, is nevertheless outweighed by the abridgement of rights. (*R v Edwards Books and Art*, per Dickson CJ, p. 768)

1.7   THE MARGIN OF APPRECIATION

Key ECHR cases

Buckley v UK (1996) 23 EHRR 101, ECtHR
Handyside v UK (1976) 1 EHRR 737, ECtHR

ECHR principles

- The doctrine of the 'margin of appreciation' is part of the jurisprudence of the ECtHR. The ECtHR has frequently acknowledged that, by reason of their direct and continuous contact with the vital forces of their countries, the national authorities (including the courts) are better placed to evaluate local needs and conditions than an international court (*Buckley* v *UK*, paras 74–75).

- Although this means that, as the ECtHR explained in *Handyside* v *UK*, 'the machinery of protection established by the Convention is subsidiary to the national systems safeguarding human rights' (para. 48), it goes hand in hand with European supervision.

- The extent of this supervision will vary according to such factors as the nature of the Convention right in issue, the importance of the right for the individual and the nature of the activities involved in the case.

Relevant domestic cases

R v *DPP, ex parte Kebilene* [1999] 3 WLR 972

- The margin of appreciation doctrine has no application in domestic law:

  The doctrine is an integral part of the supervisory jurisdiction which is exercised over state conduct by the international court. By conceding a margin of appreciation to each national system, the court has recognised that the Convention, as a living system, does not need to be applied uniformly by all states but may vary in its application according to local needs and conditions. This technique is not available to the national courts . . . (*R* v *DPP, ex parte Kebilene, per* Lord Hope pp. 993–4)

- However, the ECHR does not prevent domestic courts and tribunals from affording *some* discretion to decision-making bodies when reviewing their actions:

  . . . in the hands of the national courts . . . the Convention should be seen as an expression of fundamental principles rather than as a set of mere rules. The questions which the courts will have to decide in the application of these principles will involve questions of balance between competing interests and issues of proportionality.

  In this area difficult choices may have to be made by the executive or the legislature between the rights of the individual and the needs of society. In some circumstances it will be appropriate for the courts to recognise that there is an area of judgment within which the judiciary will defer, on democratic grounds, to the considered opinion of the elected body or person whose act or decision is said to be incompatible with the Convention. . . . It will be easier for such an area of judgment to be recognised where the Convention itself requires a balance to be struck, much less so where the right is stated in terms which are unqualified. It will be easier for it to be recognised where the issues involve questions of social or economic policy, much less so where the rights are of constitutional importance or are of a kind where the courts are especially well placed to assess the need for protection. (*R* v *DPP, ex parte Kebilene, per* Lord Hope p. 994)

1.8   POSITIVE OBLIGATIONS

Key ECHR cases

Guerra and others v *Italy* (1998) 26 EHRR 357, ECtHR
LCB v *UK* (1998) 27 EHRR 212, ECtHR

López Ostra v Spain (1994) 20 EHRR 277, ECtHR
Osman v UK (1998) 29 EHRR 245, ECtHR
Ozgur Gundem v Turkey (16 March 2000), ECtHR
Plattform "Arzte für das Leben" v Austria (1988) 13 EHRR 204, ECtHR
T v UK, V v UK (1999) 30 EHRR 121, ECtHR
X and Y v Netherlands (1985) 8 EHRR 235, ECtHR

ECHR principles

* The ECHR safeguards Convention rights by limiting the circumstances in which they can be restricted (if at all). Public authorities are under a duty to refrain from restricting Convention rights in any other circumstances.

* The ECHR also safeguards Convention rights by imposing an obligation on public authorities to adopt positive measures to protect the Convention rights of individuals:

  Genuine, effective freedom of peaceful assembly cannot . . . be reduced to a mere duty on the part of the state not to interfere; a purely negative conception would not be compatible with the object and purpose of Article 11. Like Article 8, Article 11 sometimes requires positive measures to be taken, even in the sphere of relations between individuals, if need be. (*Plattform "Arzte für das Leben" v Austria*, para. 32)

* The extent of this obligation will vary according to such factors as the nature of the Convention right in issue, the importance of the right for the individual and the nature of the activities involved in the case.

* The most onerous positive obligations arise where, by very definition, a Convention right requires the provision of resources: e.g., the right to free legal assistance in criminal cases under Article 6(3)(c), the right to education under Protocol 1, Article 2, and the duty to hold elections under Protocol 1, Article 3.

* However, the doctrine of positive obligations under the ECHR is not restricted to the provision of resources in such circumstances.

* It includes a duty on the relevant authorities to put in place a legal framework which provides effective protection for Convention rights:

  . . . the protection afforded by the civil law in the case of wrongdoing of the kind inflicted on Miss Y [sexual assault] is insufficient. This is a case where fundamental values and essential aspects of private life are at stake. Effective deterrence is indispensable in this area and it can be achieved only by criminal-law provisions; indeed, it is by such provisions that the matter is normally regulated. (*X and Y v Netherlands*, para. 27 – *state liable for failing to put in place appropriate legal framework to protect applicant's rights*)

* The doctrine of positive obligations also imposes a duty on the relevant authorities to take positive steps to prevent breaches of Convention rights. This duty is strictest where fundamental rights, such as the right to life or the prohibition on torture, are at stake:

  The Court notes that the first sentence of Article 2(1) enjoins the State not only to refrain from the intentional and unlawful taking of life, but also to take appropriate steps to safeguard the lives of those within its jurisdiction. It is common ground that the State's obligation in this respect extends beyond its primary duty to secure the right to life by putting in place effective criminal law provisions to deter the commission of offences against the person backed up by law-enforcement machinery for the prevention, suppression and sanctioning of breaches of such provisions . . . Article 2 of the Convention may also imply in certain well-defined circumstances a positive obligation on the authorities to take preventative operational measures to protect an individual whose life is at risk from the criminal acts of another individual. (*Osman v UK*, para. 115)

. . . states have a duty under the Convention to take measures for the protection of the public from violent crimes . . . (*T v UK, V v UK*, para. 98)

- However, such an obligation must be interpreted in a way which does not impose an impossible or a disproportionate burden on the authorities. Accordingly, not every claimed risk to life can entail for the authorities a Convention requirement to take operational measures to prevent that risk from materialising (*Osman v UK*, para. 116).

- Furthermore, the doctrine of positive obligations under the ECHR cannot be used as a mechanism for restricting the Convention rights of others:

  Another relevant consideration is the need to ensure that the police exercise their powers to control and prevent crime in a manner which fully respects the due process and other guarantees which legitimately place restraints on the scope of their action to investigate crime and bring offenders to justice, including the guarantees contained in Articles 5 and 8 of the Convention. (*Osman v UK*, para. 116)

- It must be established that the authorities failed to do all that could reasonably be expected of them to avoid a 'real and immediate' risk to life about which they knew or ought to have known (*Osman v UK*, para. 116).

- The doctrine of positive obligations also applies where intimate interests, such as the protection of privacy, family life and the home under Article 8, are concerned:

  . . . although the object of Article 8 is essentially that of protecting the individual against arbitrary interference by the public authorities, it does not merely compel the State to abstain from such interference: in addition to this primarily negative undertaking, there may be positive obligations inherent in effective respect for private and family life. (*Guerra and others v Italy*, para. 58 – *once the authorities became aware of dangers of pollution from a chemical factory, they failed in their obligations to those living in the neighbourhood by not providing them with assistance and support*; see also *López Ostra v Spain*)

- In certain circumstances, the relevant authorities may be under a positive obligation to provide information to those whose Convention rights are at risk:

  Where a Government engages in hazardous activities . . . which might have hidden adverse consequences on the health of those involved in such activities, respect for private and family life under Article 8 requires that an effective and accessible procedure be established which enables persons to seek all relevant and appropriate information. (*LCB v UK*, para. 101; see also *Guerra and others v Italy*, para. 60, *where risks did not emanate from the government itself*)

- The obligation also applies to freedom of expression:

  The Court has long held that, although the essential object of many provisions of the Convention is to protect the individual against arbitrary interference by public authorities, there may in addition be positive obligations inherent in an effective respect of the rights concerned.

The Court recalls the key importance of freedom of expression as one of the preconditions for a functioning democracy. Genuine, effective exercise of this freedom does not depend merely on the state's duty not to interfere, but may require positive measures of protection, even in the sphere of private relations between individuals.

In determining whether or not a positive obligation exists, regard must be had to the fair balance that has to be struck between the general interests of the community and the interests of the individual, the search for which is called for throughout the Convention. The scope of this obligation will inevitably vary, having regard to the diversity of situations obtaining in contracting states, the difficulties involved in policing modern societies and the choices which must be made in terms of priorities and resources. Nor must such an obligation be interpreted in such a way as to impose an impossible or disproportionate burden on the authorities . . .

In the present case the authorities were aware that [the applicant] and persons associated with it, had been subject to a series of violent acts and that the applicants feared that they were being targeted deliberately in efforts to prevent publication and distribution of the newspaper. No response however was given to almost all petitions and requests for protection submitted by the newspaper or its staff . . . The Court finds, having regard to the seriousness of the attacks and their widespread nature, that the government cannot rely on the investigation lodged by individual public prosecutors into specific incidents. It is not persuaded . . . that these investigations provided adequate or effective responses to the applicants' allegations that the attacks were part of a concerted campaign which was supported, or tolerated, by the authorities. (*Ozgur Gundem v Turkey*, paras 42 and 43 – *applicant, a daily newspaper, made allegations that it (and its journalists) were subject to serious attacks and harassment, which the authorities were either directly or indirectly responsible for, leading to its closure in breach of Article 10*).

Relevant Scottish cases

Brown v Procurator Fiscal, Dunfermline (Stott) (2000) SLT 379, AC
Janice Ward v Scotrail Ltd (27 November 1998), HC

- Article 8 of the ECHR put the relevant authorities under a duty to protect individuals from deliberate persecution and harassment by others (*Janice Ward v Scotrail Ltd*, p. 5 – *sexually explicit letters being sent from one employee to another*).

- The duty on the relevant authorities to preserve life under Article 2 does not require the successful prosecution of road traffic offences by negating the fair trial rights of an accused, e.g., by obtaining evidence gained in violation of the right against self-incrimination (*Brown v Procurator Fiscal, Dunfermline (Stott)* – *overturned on appeal, but not on this point* (5 December 2000, PC)).

1.9   THE APPLICATION OF THE ECHR BETWEEN PRIVATE INDIVIDUALS

Key ECHR cases

A v UK (1998) 27 EHRR 611, ECtHR
Casado Coca v Spain (1994) 18 EHRR 1, ECtHR
Costello-Roberts v UK (1993) 19 EHRR 112, ECtHR

Hoffmann v Austria (1993) 17 EHRR 293, ECtHR
X and Y v Netherlands (1985) 8 EHRR 235, ECtHR
Young, James and Webster v UK (1981) 4 EHRR 38, ECtHR

Rommelfanger v Germany (1989) 62 DR 151, ECmHR
Spencer v UK (1998) 25 EHRR CD 113, ECmHR

ECHR principles

- The mere fact that a public authority is not directly responsible for a breach of an individual's Convention rights does not render the ECHR inapplicable (e.g., *X and Y v Netherlands* – *state authorities responsible where child subjected to sexual assault by adult*; *Costello-Roberts v UK* – *corporal punishment in private schools*; *Young, James and Webster v UK* – *rules governing membership of trade unions*; *Rommelfanger v Germany* – *restrictions in private contract of employment*).

- In certain circumstances, public authorities come under a duty to protect private individuals from breaches of the ECHR by other private individuals, e.g., where a father beats his child in the privacy of his own home:

  The Court considers that the obligation on the High Contracting Parties under Article 1 of the Convention to secure to everyone within their jurisdiction the rights and freedoms defined in the Convention, taken together with Article 3, requires States to take measures designed to ensure that individuals within their jurisdiction are not subjected to torture or inhuman or degrading treatment or punishment, including such ill-treatment administered by private individuals. (*A v UK*, para. 22)

- Furthermore, a breach of the ECHR can be established where a court makes an order in litigation between private parties (e.g., *Hoffmann v Austria* – *child custody*; *Casado Coca v Spain* – *disciplinary action by Barcelona Bar Council*) or fails to provide a remedy:

  . . . the Commission would not exclude that the absence of an actionable remedy in relation to the publications of which the applicants complain could show a lack of respect for the private lives. It has regard in this respect to the duties and responsibilities that are carried with the right of freedom of expression guaranteed by Article 10 of the Convention and to the Contracting States' obligation to provide a measure of protection to the right of privacy of an individual affected by others' exercise of their freedom of expression. (*Casada Coca v Spain* – *no violation found on facts*)

Relevant domestic cases and materials

- Under the HRA, courts and tribunals must act compatibly with the ECHR whether or not a public authority is a party to the proceedings:

  We also believe that it is right as a matter of principle for the courts to have the duty of acting compatibly with the Convention not only in cases involving other public authorities but also in developing the common law in deciding cases between individuals. Why should they not? In preparing this Bill, we have taken the view that it is the other course, that of excluding Convention considerations altogether from cases between individuals which would have to be justified. We do not think that would be justifiable; nor indeed do we think that it would be practicable. (Lord Chancellor, HL Debs, col. 783, 24 November 1997)

- The same applies to the interpretation of legislation:

  Clause 3 requires the courts to interpret legislation compatibly with the Convention rights and to the fullest extent possible in all cases coming before them. (*Ibid.*)

Relevant Canadian cases

Retail, Wholesale and Department Store Union Local 580 v Dolphin Delivery (1985) 33 DLR (4th) 174

- Although aggrieved individuals cannot claim directly against other individuals for breach of their 'rights', they can claim that the courts should apply and develop existing law in the light of the principles represented by any applicable constitutional rights:

  Where private party A sues private party B relying on the common law . . . the Charter will not apply . . . However, this is a different issue from the question whether the judiciary ought to apply and develop the principles of the common law in a manner consistent with the *fundamental values* enshrined in the Constitution. The answer to that question must be in the affirmative. (*Retail, Wholesale and Department Store Union Local 580 v Dolphin Delivery*, p. 573)

1.10   RESTRICTIONS ON THE POLITICAL ACTIVITY OF ALIENS UNDER ARTICLE 16

Key ECHR cases

Piermont v France (1995) 20 EHRR 301, ECtHR

ECHR principles

- Article 16 provides that:

  Nothing in Articles 10, 11 and 14 shall be regarded as preventing the High Contracting Parties from imposing restrictions on the political activities of aliens.

- It is to be narrowly interpreted because it does not reflect contemporary attitudes to aliens in international law:

  The Commission observes that in placing this article in the Convention those who drafted it were subscribing to a concept that was then prevalent in international law, under which a general, unlimited restriction of the political activities of aliens was thought legitimate.

  The Commission reiterates, however, that the Convention is a living instrument, which must be interpreted in the light of present day conditions and the evolution of modern society. (*Piermont v France*, Commission Report, paras 58–59)

- Membership of the European Union cannot necessarily be relied upon to exclude from Article 16 those who would otherwise be aliens; but possession of the nationality of a Member State, together with some special status, e.g., being an MEP, might be enough (*Piermont v France*, Court Judgment, paras 62–64).

1.11   PROHIBITION OF ABUSE OF RIGHTS UNDER ARTICLE 17

Key ECHR cases

Lawless v Ireland (No. 3) (1961) 1 EHRR 1, ECtHR
Lehideux and Isorni v France (23 September 1998), ECtHR

De Becker v Belgium (1961) Series B, No. 4 (App. No. 214/56), ECmHR
Glimmerveen and Hagenbeek v Netherlands (1979) 18 DR 187, ECmHR
Kuhnen v Germany (1988) 56 DR 205, ECmHR[CD]

ECHR principles

- Article 17 provides that:

    Nothing in this Convention may be interpreted as implying for any state, group or person any right to engage in any activity or perform any act aimed at the destruction of any of the rights and freedoms set forth herein or at their limitation to a greater extent than is provided for in this Convention.

- Its purpose is to prevent extremists using the ECHR to destroy the rights of others:

    In the opinion of the Court the purpose of Article 17 in so far as it refers to groups or to individuals, is to make it impossible for them to derive from the Convention a right to engage or perform any act aimed at destroying in any activity any of the rights and freedoms set forth in the Convention. Therefore, no person may be able to take advantage of the provisions of the Convention to perform acts aimed at destroying the aforesaid rights and freedoms. (*Lawless v Ireland (No. 3)*, para. 7)

- Article 17 can be applied only to those rights which are capable of being exercised so as to destroy the rights of others: it cannot be used to restrict rights designed to protect the individual, such as those in Articles 5 and 6 of the ECHR:

    This provision, which is negative in scope, cannot be construed *a contrario* as depriving a physical person of the fundamental individual rights guaranteed by Articles 5 and 6 of the Convention. (*Lawless v Ireland (No. 3)*, para. 7)

    The general purpose of Article 17 is to prevent totalitarian groups from exploiting in their own interests the principles enunciated by the Convention. To achieve that purpose, it is not necessary to take away every one of the rights and freedoms guaranteed from persons found to be engaged in activities aimed at the destruction of any of those rights and freedoms. Article 17 covers essentially those rights which, if invoked, will facilitate the attempt to derive therefrom a right to engage personally in activities aimed at the destruction of any of the rights and freedoms set forth in the Convention. (*Glimmerveen and Hagenbeek v Netherlands*, p. 195)

- Any measure taken under Article 17 must be strictly proportionate to the threat to the rights of others:

  Article 17 is of somewhat limited scope; it applies only to persons who threaten the democratic system of the Contracting States and then only to an extent strictly proportionate to the seriousness and duration of such a threat, as is confirmed by Article 18. Accordingly Article 17 cannot be used to deprive an individual of his rights and freedoms permanently merely because at some given moment he displayed totalitarian convictions. (*De Becker v Belgium*, para. 279; see also *Lehideux and Isorni v France*)

1.12 LIMITATION ON RESTRICTIONS UNDER ARTICLE 18

Key ECHR cases

Kamma v Netherlands (1974) 1 DR 4, ECmHR

ECHR principles

- Article 18 provides that:

  The restrictions permitted under this Convention to the said rights and freedoms shall not be applied for any purpose other than those for which they have been prescribed.

- It is not a free-standing provision: it can be breached only in conjunction with another provision of the Convention (*Kamma v Netherlands*).

1.13 THE INTERPRETATION OF CONVENTION RIGHTS

Key ECHR cases

Artico v Italy (1980) 3 EHRR 1, ECtHR
Chassagnou and others v France (1999) 29 EHRR 615, ECtHR
Golder v UK (1975) 1 EHRR 524, ECtHR
Selmouni v France (1999) 29 EHRR 403, ECtHR
Soering v UK (1989) 11 EHRR 439, ECtHR
T v UK, V v UK (1999) 30 EHRR 121, ECtHR
Tyrer v UK (1978) 2 EHRR 1, ECtHR
Wemhoff v Germany (1968) 1 EHRR 55, ECtHR

ECHR principles

- Convention rights should be interpreted in light of their object and purpose:

  . . . given that it is a law-making treaty, it is also necessary to seek the interpretation that is most appropriate in order to realise the aim and achieve the object of the treaty, and not that which would restrict to the greatest possible degree the obligations undertaken by the parties. (*Wemhoff v Germany*, para. 8)

- The object and purpose of Convention rights are to protect individual rights, maintain the rule of law and to uphold the ideas and values of a democratic society (*Golder v UK*, para. 34; *Soering v UK*, para. 87)

- Convention rights should be interpreted in such a way as to make them 'practical and effective':

  . . . the Convention is intended to guarantee not rights that are theoretical or illusory but rights which are practical and effective . . . (*Artico v Italy*, para. 33)

  In interpreting the Convention regard must be had to its special character as a treaty for the collective enforcement of human rights and fundamental freedoms . . . Thus, the object and purpose of the Convention as a living instrument for the protection of individual human beings require that its provisions be interpreted and applied so as to make its safeguards practical and effective. (*Soering v UK*, para. 87)

- Words and phrases in the ECHR are to be given an autonomous meaning, i.e. the meaning ascribed by the ECtHR, not (necessarily) the meaning ascribed in the domestic law of the Contracting States.

- This is to prevent states undermining the efficacy of the ECHR:

  . . . the question is not so much whether in French law [the associations] are private associations, public or para-public associations, or mixed associations, but whether they are associations for the purposes of Article 11 of the Convention.
  If Contracting States were able, at their discretion, by classifying an association as 'public' or 'para-administrative', to remove it from the scope of Article 11, that would give them such latitude that it might lead to results incompatible with the object and purpose of the Convention, which is to protect rights that are not theoretical or illusory but practical and effective . . .
  The term 'association' therefore possesses an autonomous meaning; the classification in national law has relative value and constitutes no more than a starting-point. (*Chassagnou and others v France*, para. 100)

- The ECHR is a 'living instrument' requiring a dynamic, evolving interpretation:

  [the ECHR] . . . is a living instrument which . . . must be interpreted in the light of present-day conditions (*Tyrer v UK*, p. 10)

  The Court has previously examined cases in which it concluded that there had been treatment which could only be described as torture . . . However, having regard to the fact that the Convention is a 'living instrument' which must be interpreted in the light of present-day conditions . . . the Court considers that certain acts which were classified in the past as 'inhuman and degrading treatment' as opposed to 'torture' could be classified differently in future. It takes the view that the increasingly high standard being required in the area of the protection of human rights and fundamental liberties correspondingly and inevitably requires greater firmness in assessing breaches of the fundamental values of democratic societies. (*Selmouni v France*, para. 101)

  . . . since the Convention is a living instrument, it is legitimate when deciding whether a certain measure is acceptable under one of its provisions to take account of the standards prevailing amongst the member states of the Council of Europe. (*T v UK, V v UK*, para. 72 – *trial of two 11-year-old boys for murder of two-year-old child in adult Crown Court*)

Relevant domestic cases

R v DPP, ex parte Kebilene [1999] 3 WLR 972
R v Ministry of Defence, ex parte Smith [1996] QB 517

- A generous and purposive construction is to be given to Convention rights under the HRA:

  In *AG of Hong Kong v Lee Kwong-kut* [1993] AC 951, 966 Lord Woolf referred to the general approach to the interpretation of constitutions and bills of rights indicated in previous decisions of the Board, which he said were equally applicable to the Hong Kong Bill of Rights Ordinance 1991. He mentioned Lord Wilberforce's observations in *Minister of Home Affairs v Fisher* [1980] AC 319, 328 that instruments of this nature call for generous interpretation suitable to give to individuals the full measure of the fundamental rights and freedoms to which all persons in the state are to be entitled. The same approach will now have to be applied in this country when issues are raised under the Act of 1998 about the compatibility of domestic legislation and acts of public authorities with the fundamental rights and freedoms which are enshrined in the Convention. (*R v DPP, ex parte Kebilene, per* Lord Hope, pp. 988E–H)

- Like the ECHR, the incremental development of the common law also requires an evolving approach:

  . . . a belief which represented unquestioned orthodoxy in year X may become questionable by year Y and unsustainable by year Z. (*R v Ministry of Defence, ex parte Smith*, p. 554)

Relevant Commonwealth cases

Matadeen v Pointu [1999] 1 AC 98, PC
Minister of Home Affairs v Fisher [1980] AC 319

- Human rights instruments require special interpretation, taking into account moral and political values:

  It has often be said, in passages in previous opinions of the Board too familiar to need citation, that constitutions are not to be construed like commercial documents. This is because every utterance must be construed in its proper context, taking into account the historical background and the purpose for which the utterance was made. The context and purpose of a commercial contract is very different from that of a constitution. The background of a constitution is an attempt, at a particular moment in history, to lay down an enduring scheme of government in accordance with certain moral and political values. Interpretation must take these purposes into account. (*Matadeen v Pointu*, Lord Hoffmann, p. 108)

- Human rights instruments call for generous interpretation, avoiding what has been called 'the austerity of tabulated legalism' (*Minister of Home Affairs v Fisher*, pp. 23f–24f).

Relevant Canadian cases

Hunter v Southam Inc. [1984] 2 SCR 145

- Human rights provisions should be interpreted according to contemporary standards and expectations:

  A constitution . . . is drafted with an eye to the future. Its function is to provide a continuing framework for the legitimate exercise of government power and, when joined by a Bill or a Charter of Rights, for the unremitting protection of individual rights and liberties. Once enacted its provisions cannot easily be repealed or amended. It must, therefore, be capable of growth and development over time to meet new social, political and historical realities often unimagined by the framers. (*Hunter v Southam Inc.*, per Dickson J, p. 649)

1.14 THE BURDEN AND STANDARD OF PROVING A BREACH OF CONVENTION RIGHTS

Key ECHR cases

Aksoy v Turkey (1996) 23 EHRR 553, ECtHR
Jersild v Denmark (1994) 19 EHRR 1, ECtHR
Timurtas v Turkey (13 June 2000), ECtHR

ECHR principles

- It is for the complainant to show that his or her Convention rights have been infringed, but for the respondent public authority to justify any infringement established:

    The Court will look at the interference complained of in the light of the case as a whole and determine whether the reasons adduced by the national authorities to justify it are relevant and sufficient and whether the means employed were proportionate to the legitimate aim pursued. (*Jersild v Denmark*, para. 31)

- Where absolute rights are at stake, the standard of proof is high: beyond reasonable doubt. However, this can be established by the coexistence of sufficiently strong, clear and concordant inferences or similar, unrebutted presumptions of fact:

    . . . where an individual is taken into police custody in good health but is found to be injured at the time of release, it is incumbent on the State to provide a plausible explanation as to the causing of the injury, failing which a clear issue arises under Article 3 of the Convention. (*Aksoy v Turkey*, para. 61)

- Failure of the respondent to furnish information may lead to adverse inferences being drawn:

    . . . Convention proceedings do not in all cases lend themselves for rigorous application of the principle of *affirmanti incumbit probatio* (he who alleged something must prove that allegation). The Court has previously held that it is of the utmost importance for the effective operation of the system of individual petition . . . that states should furnish all necessary facilities to make possible a proper and effective examination of applications . . . Failure on a government's part to submit . . . information [capable of corroborating or refuting an allegation] . . . may . . . give rise to the drawing of inferences as to the well-foundedness of the allegations. (*Timurtas v Turkey*, para. 66)

Relevant Canadian cases

Andrews v Law Society of British Columbia (1989) 56 DLR (4th) 1
R v Cobham (1994) 118 DLR (4th) 301

R v Edwards Books and Art [1986] 2 SCR 713
R v Oakes [1986] 1 SCR 103
Retail, Wholesale and Department Store Union Local 580 v Dolphin Delivery (1985) 33 DLR (4th) 174

- At the first stage, the court must decide whether a Charter right has been infringed. At the second stage, the burden or persuasion shifts to the government (or other party) seeking to support the challenged law. It is for the government to persuade the court that the challenged law is a 'reasonable limit', and that it 'can be demonstrably justified in a free and democratic society' (*Andrews v Law Society of British Columbia*, p. 21; *R v Cobham*, p. 301; *R v Oakes*, pp. 136–7).

- The standard of proof is 'the civil standard, namely, proof by a preponderance of probability' (*R v Oakes*, p. 137).

- Evidence is usually required, but some findings will be 'self-evident' or 'obvious' without evidence (*R v Jones*, pp. 299–300; *Retail, Wholesale and Department Store Union Local 580 v Dolphin Delivery*, p. 590; *R v Edwards Books and Art*, pp. 769–70).

- The question whether a Charter right is 'prescribed by law' is a pure question of law to which no burden of proof is attached (*R v Oakes*).

1.15   WAIVER

Key ECHR cases

McGonnell v UK (8 February 2000), ECtHR
Pfeifer and Plankl v Austria (1992) 14 EHRR 692, ECtHR

Rommelfanger v Germany (1989) 62 DR 151, ECmHR[CD]

ECHR principles

- Convention rights can be waived, but only in limited circumstances:

  According to the Court's case law, the waiver of a right guaranteed by the Convention – in so far as it is permissible – must be established in an unequivocal manner. Moreover . . . in the case of procedural rights a waiver, in order to be effective for Convention purposes, requires minimum guarantees commensurate with its importance. (*Pfeifer and Plankl v Austria*, para. 37 – *waiver of right to fair trial by unrepresented defendant not valid*)

- Failure to raise an issue cannot automatically be equated with waiver:

  Failure to raise the issue is not, in itself, waiver; the key question is the reasonableness of the individual's conduct in not raising the issue. If case law is against the individual, s/he cannot be expected to have raised it. (*McGonnell v UK*, paras 44 to 46 – *in context of fair trial*)

- Individuals may contract out of their Convention rights, e.g., in the employment context:

  The Commission notes that by entering into contractual obligations *vis-à-vis* his employer the applicant accepted a duty of loyalty towards the Catholic Church which limited his freedom of expression to a certain extent. Similar obligations may also be agreed with other employees . . . In principle, the Convention permits contractual obligations of this kind if they are freely entered into by the person concerned. A violation of such obligations normally entails the legal consequences stipulated in the contract, including dismissal. Their enforcement with the assistance of the competent State authorities does not as such constitute an 'interference by public authority' with the rights guaranteed by Article 10(1) of the Convention. (*Rommelfanger* v *Germany*, p. 160)

- However, there must be a mechanism – enforceable in the courts and tribunals – to protect individual Convention rights from unreasonable demands of employers, even if the contract of employment is otherwise valid (*Rommelfanger* v *Germany*, p. 161).

- Certain Convention rights probably cannot be waived at all, e.g., absolute rights such as the right to life and the prohibition on torture and slavery, and perhaps also fair trial rights under Article 6: '. . . even supposing that the rights in question [Article 6 fair trial rights] can be waived by a defendant' (*Pfeifer and Plankl* v *Austria*, para. 39).

Relevant Scottish cases

David Millar v *Procurator Fiscal* (3 August 2000), AC
Elgin and Paul Stewart and others v *Procurator Fiscal* (13 August 2000), AC

- The right to an independent and impartial tribunal can be waived (*David Millar* v *Procurator Fiscal*; *Elgin and Paul Stewart and others* v *Procurator Fiscal*).

- But any issue of waiver, in particular in relation to the right to an independent and impartial tribunal, must be carefully scrutinised. This scrutiny will include an assessment of the reasonableness of waiver:

  Even where an express waiver is on the face of it unequivocal, it may be necessary to scrutinise the context, in order to determine matters of understanding and intention, and the overall reasonableness of treating what has been said as an abandonment of rights. When nothing has been said, and tacit waiver is alleged, it is difficult to see how silence in itself, without regard to context, could ever constitute or even imply waiver: everything will depend upon what can reasonably be inferred from background and context. (*David Millar* v *Procurator Fiscal*; *Elgin and Paul Stewart and others* v *Procurator Fiscal, per* Lord Prosser, para. 29)

- Where there is genuine waiver, a prosecutor (as a public authority) is not necessarily barred from proceeding merely because he or she is under a duty to act compatibly with the HRA (*David Millar* v *Procurator Fiscal*; *Elgin and Paul Stewart and others* v *Procurator Fiscal, per* Lord Prosser, para. 39).

Relevant Canadian cases

R v *Tran* [1994] 2 SCR 951

- Given the public interest in securing the right to a fair trial, there are situations, especially in criminal cases, when the right cannot be waived (*R* v *Tran*).

Relevant New Zealand cases

Christchurch International Airport Ltd v *Christchurch City Council* [1997] 1 NZLR 573
Martin v *Tauranga District Court* [1995] NZLR 491, HC

- Where the state relies upon the conduct of the accused or upon waiver to justify or explain delay in criminal proceedings, it is put to strict proof. Waiver cannot be presumed merely because an accused has made no protest about delays which have been occurring (*Martin* v *Tauranga District Court*, para. 506).

- However, public policy does not preclude the possibility that an individual may trade in his right to freedom of expression for some other advantage, e.g., a clause precluding complaints about noise in return for permission to build (*Christchurch International Airport Ltd* v *Christchurch City Council*, pp. 584–5).

THE INTERPRETATION OF LEGISLATION

2.1 PRIMARY LEGISLATION

- So far as it is possible to do so, primary legislation must be read and given effect in a way which is compatible with Convention rights (HRA, s. 3(1)).

- The use of the word 'possible' is intended to convey a stronger interpretative requirement than 'reasonable':

  > If we had used the word 'reasonable' we would have created a subjective test. 'Possible' is different. It means, 'What is the possible interpretation? Let us look at this set of words and the possible interpretations'. (Home Secretary, HC Debs, vol. 313, col. 421–422, 3 June 1998 – *resisting an amendment to replace 'possible' with 'reasonable'*)

- This rule of interpretation applies whenever the legislation in question was enacted (HRA, s. 3(2)(a)). To that extent, courts and tribunals will not be bound by previous interpretations of legislative provisions (White Paper, para. 2.8).

- Courts and tribunals should find that primary legislation is incompatible with Convention rights only when compatibility is impossible:

  > We want the courts to strive to find an interpretation of the legislation which is consistent with Convention rights as far as the language of the legislation allows and only in the last resort to conclude that the legislation is simply incompatible with them. (Lord Chancellor, HL Debs, col. 535, 18 November 1997)

  > [The HRA] rests upon giving the strongest jurisdiction possible to the judges to interpret Acts of Parliament so as to make them, whenever possible, compatible with the Convention. (Lord Chancellor, HL Debs, col. 795, 24 November 1997)

- This obligation applies to all courts and tribunals in all proceedings at every level.

- Nothing in the HRA affects the validity, continuing operation or enforcement of primary legislation which is incompatible with Convention rights (HRA, s. 3(2)(b)).

- But in such circumstances, higher courts may make a 'declaration of incompatibility' (see **2.2** below).

Relevant domestic cases

Litster v Forth Dry Dock Ltd [1990] 1 AC 546
Pickstone v Freemans Plc [1989] AC 66
R v DPP, ex parte Kebilene [1999] 3 WLR 972

- HRA, s. 3 enacts a strong interpretative provision (Lord Steyn, *R v DPP, ex parte Kebilene*, p. 980E).

- It may require the courts to interpret clear reverse onus provisions in criminal statutes as merely placing an evidential burden on the defence to raise a defence:

  > [Section 3] . . . is a strong adjuration. It seems distinctly possible that it may require section 16A of the [Prevention of Terrorism (Temporary Provisions) Act 1989] to be interpreted as imposing on the applicant an evidential, but not persuasive (or ultimate), burden of proof. I agree that such is not the natural or ordinary meaning . . . it is a *possible* meaning . . . (Lord Cooke, *R v DPP, ex parte Kebilene*, p. 987C)

- Section 3 applies to all legislation:

  > Unlike the constitutions of many of the countries within the Commonwealth which protect pre-existing legislation from challenge under their human rights provisions, the Act of 1998 will apply to all legislation, whatever its date, in the past as well as in the future. (Lord Hope, *R v DPP, ex parte Kebilene*, p. 991G)

- In appropriate circumstances a 'purposive' interpretation of legislative provisions can justify reading words into primary or subordinate legislation:

  > If this provision fell to be construed by reference to the ordinary rules of construction applicable to a purely domestic statute and without reference to Treaty obligations, it would, I think, be quite impermissible to regard it as having the same prohibitory effect as that attributed by the European Court to article 4 of the Directive. But it has always to be borne in mind that the purposes of the Directive and of the Regulations was and is to 'safeguard' the rights of employees on a transfer and that there is a mandatory obligation to provide remedies which are effective and not merely symbolic to which the Regulations were intended to give effect. . . . *Pickstone v Freemans Plc* [1989] AC 66 has established that the greater flexibility available to the court in applying a purposive construction to legislation designed to give effect to the United Kingdom's Treaty obligations to the Community enables the court, where necessary, to supply by implication words appropriate to comply with those obligations . . . Having regard to the manifest purpose of the Regulations, I do not, for my part, feel inhibited from making such an implication in the instant case . . . In effect this involves reading regulation 5(3) as if there were inserted after the words 'immediately before the transfer' the words 'or would have been so employed if he had not been unfairly dismissed in the circumstances described in regulation 8(1)'. For my part, I would make such an implication which is entirely consistent with the general scheme of the Regulations and which is necessary if they are effectively to fulfil the purpose for which they were made of giving effect to the provisions of the Directive. (*Litster v Forth Dry Dock Ltd*, per Lord Oliver at pp. 576F–577D – *compatibility of Transfer of Undertakings (Protection of Employment) Regulations 1981 with Council Directive (77/187/EEC)*).

Relevant Scottish cases

Brown v Procurator Fiscal, Dunfermline (Stott) (2000) SLT 379, AC
Her Majesty's Advocate v Montgomery and Coulter (14 September 1999)

- '[I]t would be wrong . . . to see the rights under the European Convention as somehow forming a wholly separate stream in our law; in truth they soak through and permeate the areas of our law in which they apply.' (*Her Majesty's Advocate* v *Montgomery and Coulter, per* Lord Justice General, p. 6)

- In determining whether a statutory provision is compatible with Convention rights the following process should be followed:

    (a) First, the court should analyse whether on an ordinary construction, the provision is compatible with the relevant Convention Article.
    (b) If not, the next question is whether it nonetheless can be read and given effect in the manner envisaged by HRA, s. 3.
    (c) If not, HRA, s. 3 does not apply.

    (*Brown* v *Procurator Fiscal, Dunfermline* (Stott) – *overturned on appeal, but not on this point* (5 December 2000, PC))

Relevant Canadian cases

Moonen v *Film and Literature Board of Review* (1999) CA 42/99

- The court should identify possible meanings of a provision said to be inconsistent with the Bill of Rights and then adopt that which would impose the 'least possible' limitation on the right or freedom in question (*Moonen* v *Film and Literature Board of Review*).

2.2   DECLARATIONS OF INCOMPATIBILITY

- Under the HRA, s. 4(2), certain courts are given the power to make declarations of incompatibility if they determine that a provision in primary legislation is incompatible with Convention rights.

- Those courts are: the House of Lords, Court of Appeal or High Court; the Judicial Committee of the Privy Council; the Courts-Martial Appeal Court; and the High Court of Justiciary (Scotland) and Court of Session (Scotland) (HRA, s. 4(5)).

- A declaration of incompatibility is intended to operate as a signal to Parliament that an incompatibility has been found and to prompt remedial action.

- It does not affect the validity, continuing operation or enforcement of the provision in question (HRA, s. 4(6)(a)).

    We expect that, in almost all cases, the courts will be able to interpret legislation compatibly with the Convention. However, we need to provide for the rare cases where it cannot be done . . . A declaration of incompatibility will not affect the continuing validity of the legislation in question. That would be contrary to the principle of the [Act]. However, it will be a clear signal to Government and Parliament that, in the court's view, a provision of legislation does not conform to the standards of the Convention . . . it is likely that the Government and Parliament would wish to respond to such a situation and would do so rapidly. (Home Secretary, HC Debs, vol. 306, col. 789, 16 February 1998)

- A declaration of incompatibility does not bind inferior courts:

    > In a judicial and political sense, the *status quo ante* would apply. Then, obviously, the Government would have to consider, and in most cases they would consider, the position pretty rapidly. (Home Secretary, HC Debs, vol. 317, col. 1306, 21 October 1998)

- Neither is it binding on the parties to the proceedings in which it is made (HRA, s. 4(6)(b)). But a remedial order may have retrospective effect (HRA, Sch. 2, para. 1(1)(b)): see **2.5** below).

- If a court is considering whether or not to make a declaration of incompatibility, the Crown has a right to be notified and can intervene (HRA, s. 5(1) and (2): see **2.4** below).

- In criminal proceedings, if any application is to be made to the Court of Appeal for a declaration of incompatibility, or any issue is to be raised which may have that effect, notice must be given in the notice of appeal and a copy of the notice served on the prosecutor (Criminal Appeal (Amendment) Rules 2000, r. 2(aa) and (ab)). The Court of Appeal must then give notice to the Crown (r. 14A).

- In civil proceedings, no declaration of incompatibility can be made unless 21 days' notice has been given to the Crown (Civil Procedure (Amendment No. 4) Rules 2000, r. 19.4A; see also the Family Proceedings (Amendment) Rules 2000, r. 10.26(4)).

Relevant domestic cases

R v DPP, ex parte Kebilene [1999] 3 WLR 972

- The HRA is intended to preserve Parliamentary sovereignty:

    > It is crystal clear that the carefully and subtly drafted Human Rights Act 1998 preserves the principle of Parliamentary sovereignty. In a case of incompatibility, which cannot be avoided by interpretation under section 3(1), the courts may not disapply the legislation. The court may merely issue a declaration of incompatibility which then gives rise to a power to take remedial action. (Lord Steyn, *R v DPP, ex parte Kebilene*, p. 981D)

2.3 SUBORDINATE LEGISLATION

- So far as it is possible to do so, subordinate legislation must be read and given effect in a way which is compatible with Convention rights (HRA, s. 3(1)).

- As with primary legislation, this rule of interpretation applies whenever the subordinate legislation in question was enacted (HRA, s. 3(2)(a): see **2.1** above).

- Unlike the position in relation to primary legislation, where subordinate legislation cannot be read and given effect in a way which is compatible with Convention rights, this *does* affect its validity, continuing operation and enforcement (HRA, s. 3(2)(b) and (c)) and it can be quashed or declared invalid by reason of incompatibility (HRA, s. 10(4)):

> The position simply is that at present subordinate legislation may be struck down by
> the courts on the same grounds as in the case of other forms of administrative action
> . . . subordinate legislation which is incompatible with the Convention rights will thus
> become susceptible to challenge on *vires* grounds in the ordinary way . . . (Lord
> Chancellor, HL Debs, vol. 583, coll. 544–545, 18 November 1997)

- The only exception is where primary legislation prevents the removal of any incompatibility (HRA, s. 3(1)(c)). In such (rare) circumstances, certain courts may make a declaration of incompatibility (HRA, s. 4(4)).

2.4   RIGHT OF CROWN TO INTERVENE

- Where a court is considering whether to make a declaration of incompatibility, the Crown is entitled to notice in accordance with rules of court (HRA, s. 5(1): see the Criminal Appeal (Amendment) Rules 2000; Civil Procedure (Amendment No. 4) Rules 2000; and the Family Proceedings (Amendment) Rules 2000).

- Where notice has been given, the Minister of the Crown (or nominee), a member of the Scottish Executive, a Northern Ireland Minister or a Northern Ireland Department is entitled, on giving notice, to be joined as a party to the proceedings (HRA, s. 5(2)).

- In criminal proceedings, once joined, any such person or body (other than in Scotland) may, with leave, appeal to the House of Lords against any declaration of incompatibility (HRA, s. 5(4)).

2.5   REMEDIAL ACTION

- Where a legislative provision is found to be incompatible with Convention rights, a remedial order may be made by a Minister of the Crown (HRA, s. 10(1) and (2)).

- The same applies where it appears to a Minister that as a result of a finding in the ECtHR, a provision of legislation is incompatible with Convention rights (HRA, s. 10(1)(b)).

- Remedial orders can be used to amend primary legislation and to amend or revoke subordinate legislation (HRA, Sch. 2, para. 1(2)).

- They are statutory instruments (HRA, s. 20(1)), subject to the procedures set out in HRA, Sch. 2, para. 3. Urgent cases are provided for in Sch. 2, para. 4.

2.6   STATEMENTS OF COMPATIBILITY

- A Minister of the Crown in charge of a Bill in either House of Parliament is under a duty to make a statement to Parliament about its compatibility with Convention rights before its Second Reading (HRA, s. 19).

- He or she must either make a statement that the provisions are compatible with Convention rights, or that the government wishes to proceed with the Bill notwithstanding that its provisions are incompatible with Convention rights (HRA, s. 19(1)).

2.7   THE COMMON LAW

- Courts and tribunals are under a duty to act in a way which is compatible with Convention rights when developing the common law:

    We also believe that it is right as a matter of principle for the courts to have the duty of acting compatibly with the Convention not only in cases involving other public authorities but also in developing the common law in cases between individuals. (Lord Chancellor, HL Debs, vol. 583, col. 783, 24 November 1997)

- This may include fashioning a right of privacy out of existing torts:

    . . . the courts will be able to adapt and develop the common law by relying on existing domestic principles in the laws of trespass, nuisance, copyright, confidence and the like, to fashion a common law right to privacy. (Lord Chancellor, HL Debs, vol. 583, col. 783, 24 November 1997)

- But it does not include creating a new and free-standing tort:

    The scheme of the [Act] is that Parliament may act to remedy a failure where the judges cannot. In my opinion, the court is not obliged to remedy the failure by legislating via the common law either where a Convention right is infringed by incompatible legislation or where, because of the absence of legislation – say privacy legislation – a Convention right is left unprotected. In my view, the courts may not act as legislators and grant new remedies for infringement of Convention rights unless the common law itself enables them to develop new rights or remedies. (Lord Chancellor, HL Debs, vol. 583, col. 785, 24 November 1997)

Relevant domestic cases

Jones and Lloyd v DPP [1999] 2 AC 40

- The ECHR requires the common law to recognise positive rights; tolerance is not enough:

    Unless the common law recognises that assembly on the public highway may be lawful the right contained in Article 11(1) of the Convention is denied. Of course the right may be subject to restrictions . . . But in my judgment our law will not comply with the Convention unless its starting point is that assembly on the highway will not necessarily be unlawful . . . The fact that the letter of the law may not always in practice be invoked is irrelevant: mere toleration does not secure a fundamental right. (*Jones and Lloyd v DPP*, per Lord Irvine)

Relevant Canadian cases

Retail, Wholesale and Department Store Union Local 580 v Dolphin Delivery (1985) 33 DLR (4th) 174

- The Canadian Charter does have an indirect effect on the common law because 'the judiciary ought to apply and develop the principles of the common law in a manner consistent with the fundamental values enshrined in the Constitution':

. . . in this sense, then, the Charter is far from irrelevant to private litigants whose disputes fall to be decided at common law. (*Retail, Wholesale and Department Store Union Local 580 v Dolphin Delivery, per* McIntyre J, p. 603)

2.8   RELEVANCE OF STRASBOURG JURISPRUDENCE

- A court or tribunal determining a question which has arisen in connection with a Convention right *must take into account* judgments of the ECtHR and decisions of the ECmHR and Committee of Ministers (HRA, s. 2(1)).

- But such judgments and decisions are not binding: the HRA is intended to provide a floor for Convention rights, but not a ceiling:

  [The HRA] will guarantee to everyone the means to enforce a set of basic civil and political rights, establishing a floor below which standards will not be allowed to fall. (Home Secretary, HL Debs, col. 769, 16 February 1998)

  . . . courts must be free to develop human rights jurisprudence by taking into account European judgments and decisions, but they must also be free to distinguish them and to move out in new directions in relation to the whole area of human rights law. (Lord Chancellor, HL Debs, vol. 583, col. 835, 24 November 1997)

  We must remember that the interpretation of the Convention develops over the years. Circumstances may therefore arise in which a judgment given by the European Court of Human Rights decades ago contains pronouncements which it would not be appropriate to apply to the letter in the circumstances of today . . . (HL Debs, vol. 583, col. 510, 18 November 1997)

- HRA, s. 2 provides a basis for domestic courts to go further than the ECtHR has done in protecting Convention rights:

  The [Act] would of course permit United Kingdom courts to depart from existing Strasbourg decisions and upon occasion it might well be appropriate for them to do so and it is possible they might give a successful lead to Strasbourg decisions where there has been no precise ruling on the matter and a commission opinion which does so has not taken into account subsequent Strasbourg court case law. (Lord Chancellor, HL Debs, vol. 583, col. 514, 18 November 1997)

- But domestic courts may not depart from clear Strasbourg case law:

  . . . where it is relevant we would of course expect our courts to apply Convention jurisprudence and its principles to the cases before them. (Lord Chancellor, HL Debs, vol. 583, col. 514, 18 November 1997)

2.9   RELEVANCE OF COMPARATIVE JURISPRUDENCE

Relevant ECHR cases

A v UK (1998) 27 EHRR 611, ECtHR
Autronic AG v Switzerland (1990) 12 EHRR 485, ECtHR
Can v Austria (1985) 8 EHRR 121, ECtHR
Costello-Roberts v UK (1993) 19 EHRR 112, ECtHR
Groppera Radio AG v Switzerland (1990) 12 EHRR 321, ECtHR

Gustafsson v Sweden (1996) 22 EHRR 409, ECtHR
Inze v Austria (1987) 10 EHRR 394, ECtHR
Jersild v Denmark (1994) 19 EHRR 1, ECtHR
Kosiek v Germany (1986) 9 EHRR 328, ECtHR
Marckx v Belgium (1979) 2 EHRR 330, ECtHR
Müller v Switzerland (1988) 13 EHRR 212, ECtHR
National Union of Belgian Police v Belgium (1975) 1 EHRR 578, ECtHR
Olsson v Sweden (No. 2) (1992) 17 EHRR 134, ECtHR
Pretto and others v Italy (1983) 6 EHRR 182, ECtHR
Schmidt and Dahlström v Sweden (1976) 1 EHRR 632, ECtHR
Soering v UK (1989) 11 EHRR 439, ECtHR
T v UK, V v UK (1999) 30 EHRR 121, ECtHR
Van der Mussele v Belgium (1983) 6 EHRR 163, ECtHR

ECHR principles

- Other international human rights instruments are relevant to the interpretation of Convention rights under the HRA, because the ECtHR is guided by these instruments when it interprets Convention rights.

- Such instruments also provide evidence of contemporary standards for the protection of human rights, relevant to the interpretation of the ECHR as a living instrument (*T v UK, V v UK*; see **1.13**).

- Relevant international instruments include:

  The European Social Charter: *National Union of Belgian Police v Belgium; Schmidt and Dahlstom v Sweden; Gustafsson v Sweden*

  The European Convention on the Status of Children Born out of Wedlock: *Marckx v Belgium; Inze v Austria*

  The European Extradition Convention: *Soering v UK*

  The European Convention on Transfrontier Television: *Autronic AG v Switzerland*

  The International Covenant on Civil and Political Rights: *Pretto and others v Italy; Can v Austria; Müller v Switzerland; Groppera Radio AG v Switzerland*

  The International Covenant on the Elimination of All Forms of Racism: *Kosiek v Germany; Jersild v Denmark*

  UN Convention Relating to the Status of Refugees: *Soering v UK*

  UN Convention Against Torture and Other Cruel, Inhuman or Degrading Treatment or Punishment: *Soering v UK*

  UN Convention on the Rights of the Child: *Olsson v Sweden (No. 2); Costello-Roberts v UK; A v UK; T v UK, V v UK*

  ILO Convention Concerning Forced or Compulsory Labour: *Van der Mussele v Belgium*

  ILO Convention Concerning the Abolition of Forced Labour: *Van der Mussele v Belgium*

  UN Standard Minimum Rules for the Treatment of Prisoners: *Can v Austria*.

Relevant Scottish cases

Brown v Procurator Fiscal, Dunfermline (Stott) (2000) SLT 379, AC

- Where ECHR jurisprudence is not extensive, it is legitimate for domestic courts to examine comparative jurisprudence:

  [E]ven though the provisions are different, the reasoning of the judges may also give pointers to the relevant international standards. (*Brown v Procurator Fiscal – cases from Canada, South Africa and the US examined*)

- But factors such as societal differences and underlying values must be kept in mind (*Brown v Procurator Fiscal – overturned on appeal, but not on this point* (5 December 2000, PC)).

Relevant Commonwealth cases

Lewis and others v AG Jamaica and others (12 September 2000), PC
Matadeen v Pointu [1999] 1 AC 98, PC

- 'It is a well recognised canon of construction that domestic legislation . . . should if possible be construed so as to conform to [international instruments to which the state is a party]'. (Lord Hoffmann, *Matadeen v Pointu*, p. 114 – *concerning the International Covenant on Civil and Political Rights*; Lord Slynn, *Lewis v AG Jamaica – concerning the American Convention on Human Rights*)

PUBLIC AUTHORITIES

3.1 DEFINITION

- The HRA does not define a 'public authority', but it does include within its meaning:

  (a) courts and tribunals; and
  (b) any person certain of whose functions are functions of a public nature (HRA, s. 6(3)).

- The inclusion of 'any person certain of whose functions are functions of a public nature' is intended to expand, not restrict, the definition of public authority:

  . . . we wanted a realistic and modern definition of the state so as to provide a correspondingly wide protection against abuse of human rights. (Home Secretary, HC Debs, col. 811, 24 November 1997)

  In developing our proposals in [s. 6] we have opted for a wide-ranging definition of public authority. We have created a correspondingly wide liability. That is because we want to provide as much protection as possible for the rights of the individual against the misuse of power by the state within the framework of the [Act] which preserves parliamentary sovereignty. (Lord Chancellor, HL Debs, col. 808, 24 November 1997)

- The definition of public authority under the HRA is intended to include all individuals and bodies for whom the state would be responsible in proceedings before the ECtHR:

  Under the Convention, the Government is answerable in Strasbourg for any acts or omissions of the state about which an individual has complaint under the Convention. The Government has a direct responsibility for core bodies, such as central Government and the police, but they also have a responsibility for other public authorities, in so far as the actions of such authorities impinge on private individuals.
  The [HRA] had to have a definition of a public authority that went at least as wide and took account of the fact that, over the last 20 years, an increasingly large number of private bodies, such as companies or charities, have come to exercise public functions that were previously exercised by public authorities . . . (Home Secretary, HC Debs, col. 775, 16 November 1998)

- But for bodies which are public authorities only because certain of their functions are functions of a public nature, purely private acts are excluded (HRA, s. 6(5)).

- The intention was to distinguish three categories:

  (a) obvious public authorities, all of whose functions are public;
  (b) organisations with a mix of public and private functions, whose public functions are subject to the HRA; and

(c) organisations with no public functions, which fall outside the scope of HRA, s. 6.

(Home Secretary, HC Debs, vol. 314, coll. 410–411, 21 October 1998)

Relevant ECHR cases

Ireland v UK (1978) 2 EHRR 25, ECtHR
López-Ostra v Spain (1994) 20 EHRR 277, ECtHR
Van der Mussele v Belgium (1983) 6 EHRR 163, ECtHR

- The mere fact that a public authority has acted *ultra vires* will not necessarily exclude liability under the ECHR (*Ireland v UK*, para. 159).

- Public authorities cannot avoid the operation of the HRA by delegating their public functions to private individuals (*Van der Mussele v Belgium*).

- Where a public authority facilitates or colludes in the acts or omissions of private individuals or bodies, it may engage the duty to act compatibly with Convention rights (*López Ostra v Spain*).

Relevant New Zealand cases

M v Palmerston North Boys' High School [1997] 2 NZLR 60, HC
Television New Zealand Ltd v Newsmonitor Services Ltd [1994] 2 NZLR 91
TV3 Network Ltd v Eveready New Zealand Ltd [1993] 3 NZLR 435

- In the context of its duties under broadcasting legislation, a television company is covered by the human rights legislation (*TV3 Network Ltd v Eveready New Zealand Ltd*, p. 441).

- But it is not necessarily so covered when it is engaged in trading activities (*Television New Zealand Ltd v Newsmonitor Services Ltd*, p. 96).

- The board of trustees of a state boarding school is not necessarily exercising public functions in the absence of a close or agency relationship with the government (*M v Palmerston North Boys' High School*, pp. 70–71).

3.2   DUTY TO ACT COMPATIBLY WITH CONVENTION RIGHTS

- HRA, s. 6(1) makes it unlawful for a public authority to act in a way which is incompatible with Convention rights.

- The only exception is where primary legislation requires a public authority to act in a way which is incompatible with Convention rights (HRA, s. 6(2)).

- In HRA, s. 6, 'act' means acts or omissions (HRA, s. 6(6)).

- For clear public authorities, there is no exemption for private acts: everything they do must be compatible with Convention rights:

     In many cases it will be obvious to the courts that they will be dealing with a public authority. In respect of government departments, for example, or police officers, or prison officers, or immigration officers, or local authorities, there can be no doubt that the body in question is a public authority. Any clear case of that kind comes under [s. 6(1)]; and it is then unlawful for the authority to act in a way which is incompatible with one or more of the Convention rights. There is no exemption for private acts such as is conferred by [s. 6(5)] in relation to [s. 6(3)(b)]. (Lord Chancellor, HL Debs, col. 811, 24 November 1997)

3.3   PARLIAMENT

- Neither House of Parliament is a public authority for the purposes of the HRA; nor is any person exercising functions in connection with proceedings in Parliament (HRA, s. 6(3)(b)).

- The House of Lords in its judicial capacity, however, is a public authority (HRA, s. 6(4)).

- Failure to introduce in, or lay before, Parliament a proposal for legislation, or a failure to make any primary legislation or remedial order, does not amount to an act or omission under HRA, s. 6 (HRA, s. 6(6)).

SECTION 4

REMEDIES

4.1 PROCEEDINGS

- A person who claims that a public authority has acted (or proposes to act) in a way which is incompatible with Convention rights may either:

    (a) bring proceedings against the authority in the appropriate court or tribunal; or
    (b) rely on his or her Convention rights in any legal proceedings (HRA, s. 7(1)).

- Legal proceedings in this context includes proceedings brought by or at the instigation of a public authority, and any appeal against the decision of a court or tribunal (HRA, s. 7(6)).

4.2 THE VICTIM REQUIREMENT

- Proceedings against a public authority can only be brought by an individual who is (or would be) a victim within the meaning of Article 34, ECHR (HRA, s. 6(1) and (7)).

- Likewise, only victims can rely on their Convention rights in legal proceedings (HRA, s. 6(1) and (7)).

- If the proceedings are brought on an application for judicial review, the applicant is taken to have a sufficient interest in relation to the unlawful act only if he or she is, or would be, a victim of that act (HRA, s. 7(3)).

Relevant ECHR cases

Agrotexim v Greece (1995) 21 EHRR 250, ECtHR
Bowman v UK (1998) 26 EHRR 1, ECtHR
Campbell and Cosans v UK (1982) 4 EHRR 293, ECtHR
Eckle v Germany (1982) 5 EHRR 1, ECtHR
Johnston and others v Ireland (1986) 9 EHRR 203, ECtHR
Laskey, Jaggard and Brown v UK (1997) 24 EHRR 39, ECtHR
Lokanov v Bulgaria (1997) 24 EHRR 121, ECtHR
Norris v Ireland (1988) 13 EHRR 186, ECtHR
Open Door and Dublin Well Woman v Ireland (1992) 15 EHRR 244, ECtHR
Rotaru v Romania (4 May 2000), ECtHR
Sutherland v UK (1 July 1997), ECtHR

Bruggemann and Scheuten v *Germany* (1976) 5 DR 103, ECmHR
Kaplan v *UK* (1982) 4 EHRR 64, ECmHR
Lindsay v *UK* (1997) 24 EHRR CD 199, ECmHR
Times Newspapers Ltd v *UK* (1990) 65 DR 307, ECmHR[CD]

ECHR principles

- Only those 'directly affected' by an act or omission can claim to be victims under the ECHR (*Lindsay* v *UK*).

- However, there is no need to show loss (*Johnston and others* v *Ireland; Eckle* v *Germany*).

- And those merely 'at risk' of being affected by a breach can claim to be victims (*Campbell and Cosans* v *UK; Norris* v *Ireland; Sutherland* v *UK; Open Door and Dublin Well Woman* v *Ireland; Bruggemann and Scheuten* v *Germany; Times Newspapers Ltd* v *UK*):

  . . . an individual may, under certain conditions, claim to be the victim of a violation occasioned by the mere existence of secret measures or of legislation permitting secret measures, without having to allege that such measures were in fact applied to him . . . Furthermore, a 'decision or measure favourable to the applicant is not in principle sufficient to deprive him of his status as a victim unless the national authorities have acknowledged, either expressly or in substance, and then afforded redress for, the breach of the Convention'. (*Rotaru* v *Romania*, para. 35)

- That includes those at risk of prosecution, even where proceedings have not been commenced against them (*Bowman* v *UK*).

- Where an applicant dies during proceedings before the ECtHR, the complaint can be pursued by a spouse or close relative so long as that person has a legitimate interest in the outcome (*Loukanov* v *Bulgaria; Laskey, Jaggard and Brown* v *UK*).

- A company and/or its directors can be a victim under the ECHR (*Agrotexim* v *Greece; Kaplan* v *UK*).

4.3 JUDICIAL REMEDIES

- In relation to any act (or proposed act) of a public authority which the court finds is (or would be) unlawful, it may grant such relief or remedy, or make such order, within its powers as it considers just and appropriate (HRA, s. 8(1)).

- What is required is an 'effective' remedy:

  I cannot conceive of any state of affairs in which an English court, having held an act to be unlawful because of an infringement of a Convention right, would under [s. 8] be disabled from giving an effective remedy. (Lord Chancellor, HL Debs, col. 479, 18 November 1997)

- The case law of the ECtHR in relation to Article 13, ECHR (not included in Sch. 1 of the HRA) will be relevant to the question of the effectiveness of remedies:

  . . . the courts may have regard to Article 13. In particular, they may wish to do so when considering the very ample provisions of [s. 8] . . . (Lord Chancellor, HL Debs, col. 477, 18 November 1997)

Relevant domestic cases

R v Broadcasting Standards Commission, ex parte BBC (6 April 2000), CA

- In some circumstances, companies can claim for abuse of their rights, but not to the same extent as individuals:

  While the intrusions into privacy of an individual which are possible are no doubt more extensive than the infringements of privacy which are possible in the case of a company, a company does have activities which need protection from unwarranted intrusion. I consider that the BSC has jurisdiction to determine the application of article 8 of the ECHR to companies. (*R v Broadcasting Standards Commission, ex parte BBC, per* Lord Woolf MR)

Relevant South African cases

S v Bhulwana [1995] 2 SACR 748, CC

- There should be a presumption in favour of relief in human rights cases, applied on an equal basis for litigants in similar positions:

  Central to a consideration of the interests of justice in a particular case is that successful litigants should obtain the relief they seek. It is only when the interests of good government outweigh the interests of the individual litigant that the Court will not grant relief to successful litigants. In principle, too, the litigants before the Court should not be singled out for the grant of relief, but relief should be afforded to all people who are in the same situation as the litigants . . . (*S v Bhulwana*, para. 32)

4.4   DAMAGES

- Damages for breach of the HRA may be awarded only by a court which has power to award damages, or to order the payment of compensation in civil proceedings (HRA, s. 8(2)).

- No award of damages is to be made unless, taking into account all the circumstances of the case, including any other relief or remedy granted, or order made, and the consequences of any court decision, the court is satisfied that the award is necessary to afford just satisfaction to the person in whose favour it is made (HRA, s. 8(3)).

- In determining whether to award damages, and if so how much, the court must take into account the principles applied by the ECtHR in relation to its awards of compensation under Article 41, ECHR (HRA, s. 8(4)).

Relevant ECHR cases

Allenet de Ribemont v France (1995) 20 EHRR 557, ECtHR
Artico v Italy (1980) 3 EHRR 1, ECtHR
Cable and others v UK (18 February 1999), ECtHR
König v Germany (1980) 2 EHRR 468, ECtHR
Lingens v Austria (1986) 8 EHRR 103, ECtHR
Oberschlick v Austria (1991) 19 EHRR 389, ECtHR

Open Door and Dublin Well Woman v Ireland (1992) 15 EHRR 244, ECtHR
Papadapoulos v Cyprus (21 March 2000), ECtHR
Piersack v Belgium (1984) 7 EHRR 251, ECtHR
Schuler-Zgraggen v Switzerland (1993) 16 EHRR 405, ECtHR
Weeks v UK (1988) 13 EHRR 435, ECtHR
Young, James and Webster v UK (1982) 5 EHRR 201, ECtHR

- In assessing compensation under the ECHR, the ECtHR proceeds from the principle that the applicant should as far as possible be put in the position he or she would have been in had the ECHR not been breached (*Piersack v Belgium* (Article 50), para. 12).

- So long as causation is established, damages will be awarded for pecuniary loss (*Young, James and Webster v UK*). This can include fines paid in domestic proceedings (*Lingens v Austria*; *Oberschlick v Austria*); loss of income (*Open Door and Dublin Well Woman v Ireland*); loss of business opportunities (*Allenet de Ribemont v France*) and interest on late payments (*Schuler-Zgraggen v Switzerland*).

- Damages will also be paid for non-pecuniary loss such as anxiety (*Konig v Germany*), confusion and neglect (*Artico v Italy*), frustration (*Weeks v UK*) and harassment, humiliation and stress (*Young, James and Webster v UK*).

- Where a breach of Article 6 did not affect the outcome, damages are unlikely to be awarded by way of just satisfaction (*Cable and others v UK*).

- But damages for anxiety and stress can be awarded where a case has been unduly delayed in breach of Article 6(1) of the Convention (*Papadapoulos v Cyprus*, para. 31).

Relevant Commonwealth cases

Odogu v AG of the Federation and others (1996) 6 NWLR (PT 456) 508

- Exemplary damages can be awarded where human rights are abused so as to reflect the abhorrence of society and the law for such abuse (*Odogu v AG of the Federation and others* – exemplary damages in loss of liberty case).

4.5   JUDICIAL ACTS

- Where individuals claim that their Convention rights have been infringed by judicial act, they must bring their claim by way of an appeal or in some other forum as may be prescribed by rules (HRA, s. 9(1)).

- But this does not expand the scope for judicial review of courts (HRA, s. 9(2)).

- 'Judicial act' in this context includes the acts of members of tribunals, justices of the peace, clerks and other officers entitled to exercise the jurisdiction of the court (HRA, s. 9(5)).

- It also includes acts done on the instructions, or on behalf, of such individuals (HRA, s. 9(5)).

- In respect of a judicial act done in good faith, damages may not be awarded otherwise than to compensate a person to the extent required by Article 5(5) of the ECHR (HRA, s. 9(3); for Article 5(5) see **22.18**).

- An award of damages in respect of a judicial act done in good faith is to be made against the Crown, but only if the Minister responsible for the court concerned, or nominated person or government department, is joined as a party (HRA, s. 9(4) and 9(5)).

4.6   LIMITATION

- Where proceedings are brought against a public authority under HRA s. 6(1), the limitation period is one year from the date on which the act complained of took place, or such longer period as the court or tribunal considers equitable having regard to all the circumstances (HRA, s. 7(5)).

- This is subject to any rule imposing a stricter time limit in relation to the procedure in question (HRA, s. 7(5)), e.g., judicial review proceedings.

4.7   RETROSPECTIVITY

- Proceedings against a public authority for breach of Convention rights can only be brought in relation to acts or omissions occurring after 2 October 2000 (HRA, s. 22(4)).

- The same applies where individuals otherwise seek to rely on their Convention rights in legal proceedings – save where proceedings are brought by or at the instigation of a public authority, in which case a breach of Convention rights can be relied upon whenever the breach took place (HRA, s. 22(4)).

Relevant domestic cases

R v DPP, ex parte Kebilene [1999] 3 WLR 175

- Where proceedings are brought by or at the instigation of a public authority, a breach of Convention rights can be relied upon whenever the breach took place (HRA, s. 22(4)):

  The applicants point out, quite correctly, that section 22(4) introduces an element of retrospectivity on which victims of acts made unlawful by the Convention may rely when section 7(1)(b) is brought into force. (*R v DPP, ex parte Kebilene*, per Lord Bingham, p. 185C – *not reversed on this point in the House of Lords*)

OTHER RIGHTS AND PROCEEDINGS

5.1 SAFEGUARD FOR EXISTING RIGHTS

- A person's reliance on a Convention right does not restrict any other right or freedom conferred on him or her by or under any law having effect in any part of the UK (HRA, s. 11(a)).

- Neither does it restrict his or her right to make any claim or bring any proceedings which he or she could make or bring apart from claims and proceedings under the HRA (HRA, s. 11(b)).

- The ECHR is, therefore, a minimum framework of rights, which can be supplemented by other provisions in domestic law:

    Convention rights are, as it were, a floor of rights; and if there are different or superior rights or freedoms conferred by or under any law having effect in the United Kingdom, this is [an Act] which only gives and does not take away. (Lord Chancellor, HL Debs, col. 510, 18 November 1997)

5.2 FREEDOM OF EXPRESSION UNDER S. 12 OF THE ACT

- HRA, s. 12 is intended to enhance the freedom of the press:

    We have taken the opportunity to enhance press freedom in a wider way than would arise simply from the incorporation of the Convention into our domestic law. (Home Secretary, HC Debs, vol. 315, col. 536, 2 July 1998)

- But this is not at the expense of privacy:

    The difficulty with that [amendment] is that it goes further than the terms of the Convention and Strasbourg case law . . . So far as we are able, in a manner consistent with the Convention and its jurisprudence, we are saying to the courts that whenever there is a clash between Article 8 rights and Article 10 rights, they must pay particular attention to the Article 10 rights. I think that is as far as we could go . . . (Home Secretary, HC Debs, vol. 315, coll. 542–543, 2 July 1998 – *rejecting an amendment to give precedence to Article 10 over Article 8 rights (to privacy)*)

- No relief should be granted in a case concerning freedom of expression under Article 10, ECHR unless the person against whom relief is sought is either present or represented; the only exceptions are where the court is satisfied that all practical steps have been taken to notify such a person, or there are compelling reasons why he or she should not be notified (HRA, s. 12(2)).

- Neither should there be any pre-trial relief in a freedom of expression case, except where the court is satisfied that the applicant is likely to establish that publication should not be allowed (HRA, s. 12(3)), i.e. that he or she would succeed at trial:

> . . . no relief is to be granted to restrain publication pending a full trial of the issues unless the court is satisfied that the applicant is likely to succeed at trial . . . the courts should consider the merits of an application when it is made and should not grant an interim injunction simply to preserve the *status quo ante* between the parties . . . (Home Secretary, HC Debs, vol. 315, col. 356, 2 July 1998)

- Where a court is considering whether to grant relief in a freedom of expression case involving journalistic, literary or artistic material, it must have particular regard to:

  (a) the extent to which the material has, or is about to, become available to the public;
  (b) the extent to which it is, or would be, in the public interest for the material to be published; and
  (c) any relevant privacy code (HRA, s. 12(4)).

- But HRA, s. 12 only covers civil, not criminal, proceedings:

> Without such an exclusion, judges wanting to impose reporting restrictions in a criminal trial would, for example, have to consider any relevant privacy code, although plainly it would not be appropriate in that context . . . had we included criminal proceedings under the new clause 13, we would have made the running of criminal trials very complicated. (Home Secretary, HC Debs, vol. 315, col. 540, 2 July 1998)

5.3   FREEDOM OF THOUGHT, CONSCIENCE AND RELIGION UNDER S. 13 OF THE ACT

- If the determination of any question arising under the HRA by a court or tribunal might affect the exercise by a religious organisation (itself or its members collectively) of the right to freedom of thought, conscience and religion, the court or tribunal must have particular regard to the importance of that right (HRA, s. 13(1)).

- This reminds courts of the status of Article 9 under the ECHR; it does not seek to alter that status:

> The Government's new clause will not provide absolute protection for churches or other religious organisations as against any claim that might possibly be made against them . . . We could not do that without violating the Convention . . . but the new clause will send a clear signal to the courts that they must pay due regard to the rights guaranteed by Article 9, including, where relevant, the right of a Church to act in accordance with religious belief. (Home Secretary, HC Debs, vol. 315, col. 1022, 2 July 1998)

- There is no definition of 'religious organisation', but it is intended to be a flexible concept:

> The key concept that we are talking about is organisations with religious objectives . . . it is flexible enough to cover cases involving religious charities where Church issues

form a backdrop to the case. (Home Secretary, HC Debs, vol. 312, col. 1021, 20 May 1998)

5.4   DEROGATIONS

- Convention rights under the HRA are subject to designated derogations (HRA, s. 1(2)).

- The UK has one derogation in place concerning pre-trial detention under the prevention of terrorism legislation and Article 5(3), ECHR. The terms of this derogation are set out in HRA, Sch. 3, Part I.

- Designated derogations cease to have effect after five years, unless renewed (HRA, s. 16).

5.5   RESERVATIONS

- Convention rights under the HRA are subject to designated reservations (HRA, s. 1(2)).

- The UK has one reservation in place concerning the right to education under Protocol 1, Article 2. The terms of this reservation are set out in HRA, Sch. 3, Part II.

- Unlike designated derogations, designated reservations do not cease to have effect after five years, unless renewed (HRA, s. 16).

THE INVESTIGATION OF CRIME

6.1 THE DUTY TO INVESTIGATE CRIME EFFECTIVELY

Key ECHR cases

Aksoy v Turkey (1996) 23 EHRR 553, ECtHR
Aydin v Turkey (1997) 25 EHRR 251, ECtHR
Kaya v Turkey (1998) 28 EHRR 1, ECtHR
Kurt v Turkey (1998) 27 EHRR 373, ECtHR
Labita v Italy (6 April 2000), ECtHR
Osman v UK (1998) 29 EHRR 245, ECtHR

ECHR principles

- In certain circumstances, the ECHR obliges law enforcement bodies, such as the police, to carry out effective investigations where serious human rights issues arise, particularly where absolute rights – such as the right to life, or the prohibition on torture and inhuman or degrading treatment – are concerned:

  > Given the fundamental importance of the prohibition of torture and the especially vulnerable position of torture victims, Article 13 imposes, without prejudice to any other remedy available under the domestic system, an obligation on states to carry out a thorough and effective investigation of incidents of torture. Accordingly, where an individual has an arguable claim that he or she has been tortured by agents of the state, the notion of an 'effective remedy' entails, in addition to the payment of compensation where appropriate, a thorough and effective investigation capable of leading to the identification and punishment of those responsible and including effective access for the complainant to the investigatory procedure. (*Aydin v Turkey*, para. 103)

  > . . . where an individual makes a credible assertion that he has suffered treatment infringing Article 3 at the hands of the police or other similar agents of the state, that provision, read in conjunction with the state's general duty under Article 1 of the Convention to 'secure' to everyone within their jurisdiction the rights and freedoms defined in . . . [the] Convention, requires by implication that there should be an effective official investigation. As with an investigation under Article 2, such investigation should be capable of leading to the identification and punishment of those responsible . . . (*Labita v Italy*, para. 131)

- Examples where the ECtHR has found that there has been a failure to conduct a thorough and effective investigation include:

- failing to ascertain possible eye-witnesses
- failing to question suspects at an early stage
- failing to search for corroborating evidence
- the adoption of an over-deferential attitude to those in authority
- failing to follow up proper complaints
- ignoring obvious evidence
- failing to carry out a proper autopsy
- failing to test gunpowder traces

(*Aksoy* v *Turkey, Aydin* v *Turkey, Kurt* v *Turkey* and *Kaya* v *Turkey*)

Other international human rights standards

UN Basic Principles on the Use of Force and Firearms by Law Enforcement Officials

- There should be thorough, prompt and impartial investigation of all suspected cases of extra-legal, arbitrary and summary executions, including cases where complaints by relatives or other reliable reports suggest unnatural death has occurred (Principle 9).

- Where the established investigative procedures are inadequate, an independent inquiry should be set up (Principle 11).

- Families of the deceased and their legal representatives should have effective access to the investigation and (if appropriate) be given an opportunity to present evidence (Principle 16).

- Families and dependants of victims are entitled to fair and adequate compensation (Principle 20).

6.2   SURVEILLANCE

Key ECHR cases

A v *France* (1993) 17 EHRR 462, ECtHR
Halford v *UK* (1997) 24 EHRR 523, ECtHR
Huvig v *France* (1990) 12 EHRR 528, ECtHR
Khan v *UK* (12 May 2000), ECtHR
Klass v *Germany* (1978) 2 EHRR 214, ECtHR
Kopp v *Switzerland* (1998) 27 EHRR 91, ECtHR
Lambert v *France* (24 August 1998), ECtHR
Malone v *UK* (1984) 7 EHRR 14, ECtHR
Valenzuela Contreras v *Spain* (30 July 1998), ECtHR

Govell v *UK* [1999] EHRLR 101, ECmHR[CD]

ECHR principles

- Secret surveillance amounts to a serious interference with an individual's private life under Article 8 (*Kopp* v *Switzerland*).

- Therefore it must be 'prescribed by law', i.e. the applicable legal rules must be accessible and formulated with sufficient precision to enable citizens to foresee – if need be with appropriate advice – the consequences of their actions.

- The activity in question must also be necessary and proportionate: police surveillance should be restricted to that which is strictly necessary to achieve the required objective. What is legitimate for the prevention and detection of serious crime may not be legitimate for less serious crime.

- Secret surveillance is tolerable under the Convention only in so far as it is strictly necessary for the protection of national security or the prevention of disorder or crime (*Klass v Germany*).

- Article 8 can be engaged where telephone calls (or other communications) are intercepted at work, even where they take place on private or internal telecommunications systems:

  > . . . telephone calls made from business premises as well as from the home may be covered by the notions of 'private life' and 'correspondence' within the meaning of Article 8(1). (*Halford v UK*, para. 46)

- The law on secret surveillance must be particularly precise and provide effective safeguards against abuse:

  > The phrase 'in accordance with the law' [in Article 8(2)] implied that there had to be a measure of legal protection in domestic law against arbitrary interferences by public authorities with the rights in Article 8.
  > . . . the law had to be sufficiently clear in its terms to give citizens an adequate indication as to the circumstances in which and the conditions on which public authorities are empowered to resort to this secret and potentially dangerous interference with the right to respect for private life and correspondence. (*Malone v UK*, paras 66 and 67; see also *Kopp v Switzerland*)

- Although there is no requirement that individuals be given prior notice of surveillance (because in most cases that would defeat its purpose), the law governing powers of secret surveillance must be clear enough to give citizens an adequate indication of the circumstances in which, and the conditions upon which, public authorities are entitled to resort to the use of such powers:

  > The expression 'in accordance with the law' not only necessitates compliance with domestic law, but also refers to the quality of that law, requiring it to be compatible with the rule of law. In the context of secret measures of surveillance or interception of communications by public authorities, because of the lack of public scrutiny and the risk of misuse of power, the domestic law must provide some protection to the individual against arbitrary interference with Article 8 rights. (*Halford v UK*, para. 49; see also *Malone v UK*)

- If the interception of communications is to be justified under Article 8, the following minimum safeguards should be set out in legislation:

  (a) a definition of the categories of people liable to have their telephones tapped;
  (b) the nature of the offences which may give rise to authorisation for telephone tapping;
  (c) a limit on the duration of telephone tapping;

(d)   a procedure for drawing up summaries of intercepted communications;

(e)   precautions designed to ensure that the intercepted material remains intact for inspection by the trial judge and the defence; and

(f)   the circumstances in which intercepted communications should be erased, in particular, where an accused person is acquitted or the charges are dropped (*Valenzuela Contreras v Spain*, para. 46).

- These safeguards should be set out in the law; it is not enough to rely on the judiciary to acquaint itself with and apply the relevant standards (*Valenzuela Contreras v Spain*).

- Failure to provide rules dealing with sensitive issues such as legal professional privilege is likely to breach Article 8 of the ECHR (*Kopp v Switzerland*, paras 72–74; see also *Huvig v France*).

- The relevant law or rules must also be available to the public; unpublished or internal rules (such as Home Office guidelines) are unacceptable:

    . . . [in the present case] there is no existing statutory system to regulate the use of covert listening devices . . . The Home Office Guidelines at the relevant time were neither legally binding nor were they publicly accessible . . . (*Govell v UK*, para. 62, see also *Khan v UK – applicant subjected to police surveillance by use of a covert listening device. At the time the only regulation of such devices was contained in secret Home Office Guidelines*)

- There must be proper methods of accountability over both the authorisation and the use of police surveillance and other information-gathering activities.

- There must be remedies for those whose privacy has been wrongly invaded; and any investigation into allegations of abuse must be independent:

    . . . the system of investigation of complaints [by the Police Complaints Authority] does not meet the requisite standards of independence needed to constitute sufficient protection against the abuse of authority and thus provide an effective remedy within the meaning of Article 13. (*Govell v UK*, para. 70)

- To deny 'third parties' (i.e., those communicating with the target individual) the right to challenge the legality of surveillance denies them the safeguards to which they are entitled under Article 8, ECHR (*Lambert v France*, para. 40).

- Any breach of the domestic law governing secret surveillance will automatically lead to a breach of Article 8 because it will not be lawful (*A v France*).

Relevant Canadian cases

R v Duarte [1990] 1 SCR 30
R v Thompson [1990] 2 SCR 1111
R v Wong [1990] 3 SCR 36

- The interception of communications breaches the reasonable expectation of privacy where it is carried out without the knowledge or consent of the participants (*R v Thompson*): it therefore requires justification.

- Even where one of the parties consents to the interception, it will still constitute an interference with the reasonable expectation of privacy (*R v Duarte*; see also *R v Wong – violation where hotel consented to filming of illegal gambling session*).

6.3   INFORMERS AND UNDERCOVER OFFICERS

Key ECHR cases

Lüdi v Switzerland (1992) 15 EHRR 173, ECtHR
Teixeira de Castro v Portugal (1998) 28 EHRR 101, ECtHR

ECHR principles

- So long as informers and undercover officers do not actively instigate criminal offences, the fact that they carry out private surveillance does not *in itself* breach Article 8, because those who engage in serious crime cannot have any reasonable expectation that their activities will not be observed:

  > . . . the use of an undercover agent did not, either alone or in combination with the telephone interception, affect private life within the meaning of Article 8 . . . [the applicant] must . . . have been aware . . . that he was engaged in a criminal act . . . and that consequently he was running the risk of encountering an undercover police officer whose task would in fact be to expose him. (*Lüdi v Switzerland*, para. 40)

- Nonetheless, the law governing the use of undercover agents must be clear and precise; it must also provide safeguards against abuse (*Teixeira de Castro v Portugal*).

- Where informers/undercover officers go beyond observation and actively incite the commission of an offence, issues of fairness under Article 6, ECHR will arise: see **6.4** below.

Relevant Canadian cases

R v Broyles [1991] 3 SCR 595
R v Herbert [1990] 2 SCR 151
R v Liew [1999] 3 SCR 227

- An individual will be considered an informer – rather than merely a witness – only where the fact of the relationship between the informer and the state alters the nature of the exchange between suspect and informer, i.e.: '[W]ould the exchange between the accused and the informer have taken place, in the form and manner in which it did take place, but for the intervention of the state or its agents?' (*R v Broyles*, p. 608).

- The right to silence, or protection from self-incrimination, cannot be invoked to exclude statements voluntarily made to informers or undercover police officers (*R v Herbert*, p. 183).

- However, in this context, the behaviour of the informer or undercover officer will be crucial: if informers and agents actively elicit answers, the right to silence and/or freedom from self-incrimination may apply:

  > A distinction must be made between the use of undercover agents to *observe* the suspect, and the use of undercover agents to *actively elicit* information in violation of the suspect's choice to remain silent. When the police use subterfuge to interrogate

an accused after he has advised them that he does not wish to speak to them, they are improperly eliciting information that they were unable to obtain by respecting the suspect's constitutional right to silence: the suspect's rights are breached because he has been deprived of his choice. However, in the absence of eliciting behaviour on the part of the police, there is no violation of the accused's right to choose whether or not to speak to the police. If the suspect speaks, it is by his or her choice, and he or she must be taken to have accepted the risk that the recipient may inform the public. (*R v Herbert*, para. 108)

- Relevant to the question of whether information was elicited will be:

  (a) the nature of the exchange between the informer/undercover officer and the suspect: did the informer/undercover officer actively seek out information akin to interrogation, or did he or she merely conduct a conversation as if he or she was the person the suspect thought him or her to be?

  (b) the nature of the relationship between the suspect and informer/ undercover officer: was the relationship exploited to extract a statement? Was it one of trust? Was the suspect obligated or vulnerable to the informer/undercover officer? Did the informer/undercover agent manipulate the suspect to bring about a mental state where the latter was more likely to talk?

  (*R v Broyles*, p. 611; see also *R v Liew*)

Relevant New Zealand cases

R v Szeto (30 September 1998), CA 240/98

- Neither the right to natural justice, nor the right to protection from self-incrimination is violated where a suspect makes incriminating statements to an informer/undercover officer who is recording him, so long as such statements are not actively elicited (*R v Szeto*).

6.4   ENTRAPMENT

Key ECHR cases

Lüdi v Switzerland (1992) 15 EHRR 173, ECtHR
Teixeira de Castro v Portugal (1998) 28 EHRR 101, ECtHR

ECHR principles

- It is unfair under Article 6 to prosecute an individual for a criminal offence incited by undercover agents, which, but for the incitement, would probably not have been committed:

  . . . the two police officers' actions went beyond those of undercover agents because they instigated the offence and there is nothing to suggest that without their intervention it would have been committed. That intervention and its use in the impugned criminal proceedings meant that right from the outset, the applicant was definitively deprived of a fair trial. (*Teixeira de Castro v Portugal*, para. 39)

- Even the public interest in the detection of serious crime cannot justify the instigation of criminal offences by undercover agents:

  > The use of undercover agents must be restricted and safeguards put in place even in cases concerning the fight against drug trafficking . . . the right to a fair administration of justice . . . holds such a prominent place that it cannot be sacrificed for the sake of expedience. The general requirements of fairness embodied in Article 6 apply to proceedings concerning all types of criminal offence. The public interest cannot justify the use of evidence obtained as a result of police incitement. (*Teixeira de Castro v Portugal*, para. 39)

- However, so long as informers and/or undercover officers keep within the reasonable limits of passive surveillance, no issue arises under Article 6 (fair trial); neither does any privacy issue arise under Article 8 (*Lüdi v Switzerland*: see **2.4**).

Relevant domestic cases

Nottingham CC v Amin [2000] 1 WLR 1071
R v Shannon (11 October 2000), CA

- Both the common law and the ECHR recognise the distinction between inciting the commission of a crime and merely providing a suspect with an opportunity to break the law:

  > On the one hand it has to be recognised as deeply offensive to ordinary notions of fairness if a defendant were to be convicted and punished for committing a crime which he only committed because he had been incited, instigated, persuaded, pressurised or wheedled into committing it by a law enforcement officer. On the other hand, it has been recognised that law enforcement agencies have a general duty to the public to enforce the law and it has been regarded as unobjectionable if a law enforcement officer gives a defendant an opportunity to break the law, of which the defendant freely takes advantage, in circumstances where it appears that the defendant would have behaved in the same way if the opportunity had been offered by anyone else. (*Nottingham CC v Amin*, per Lord Bingham, pp. 1076–77 – *taxi driver plying for hire without a licence flagged down by two plain-clothed police officers*)

- Entrapment is not sufficient, in itself, to justify the exclusion of evidence; overall fairness is the appropriate test (*R v Shannon*).

6.5   SEARCHING INDIVIDUALS

Key ECHR cases

Engel and others v Netherlands (1976) 1 EHRR 647, ECtHR
Guzzardi v Italy (1980) 3 EHRR 333, ECtHR

McVeigh, O'Neill and Evans v UK (1981) 5 EHRR 71, ECmHR

ECHR principles

- Where the exercise of stop and search powers involves any significant period of confinement, Article 5, ECHR applies.

- This prohibits arbitrary searches, or over-broad search powers; with Article 14, ECHR, it also safeguards against discrimination in the exercise of search powers.

- Although Article 5(1)(b) usually requires that an individual be given an opportunity to fulfil a specific obligation before he or she is detained, in some circumstances it can be used to justify short periods of detention while a search is carried out (*McVeigh, O'Neill and Evans v UK*).

- In most cases, Article 5 will require the authorities to show a real need for immediate detention and that no other means are available to secure the object of the search (*McVeigh, O'Neill and Evans v UK*).

Relevant Canadian cases

R v Monney [1999] 1 SCR 652

- The detention by customs officers of a suspect in a drug facility to collect drug pellets passing through his system, amounts to a search and seizure and therefore requires justification under the Charter (*R v Monney*, para. 29).

- Such action is capable of justification so long as it is reasonable and does not involve the intentional application of force (*R v Monney*, para. 29).

6.6   SEARCHING PREMISES AND VEHICLES

Key ECHR cases

Camenzind v Switzerland (1997) 28 EHRR 458, ECtHR
Chappell v UK (1989) 12 EHRR 1, ECtHR
Funke v France (1993) 16 EHRR 297, ECtHR
Niemietz v Germany (1992) 16 EHRR 97, ECtHR
Ozgur Gundem v Turkey (16 March 2000), ECtHR

ECHR principles

- Search and seizure interfere with the right to private and family life, home and correspondence protected by Article 8. Therefore, such measures must be justified in accordance with Article 8(2) of the Convention.

- Judicial authorisation is a highly relevant factor, but not determinative of the lawfulness of search and seizure under the ECHR.

- However, where there has been no judicial authorisation for a search, courts will have to be particularly vigilant to ensure that other safeguards exist to protect individuals from unnecessary intrusion into their privacy. At the very least, a proper legal framework with very strict limits on search powers will be required:

    . . . the Court must ensure that the relevant legislation and practice afford individuals 'adequate and effective safeguards against abuse'; notwithstanding the margin of appreciation which the Court recognises the Contracting States have in this sphere, it must be particularly vigilant, where . . . the authorities are empowered under national law to order and effect searches without a judicial warrant . . . a legal framework and very strict limits on such powers are called for. (*Camenzind v Switzerland*, para. 45)

- Any warrant authorising search and seizure must be clear, specific and contain safeguards against abuse. If a warrant is drawn in very broad terms or gives too much discretion to those executing it, it is likely to breach Article 8 (*Funke v France*, paras 56 and 57; see also *Niemietz v Germany*).

- A warrant which authorises a search for 'documents' without any limitation is too broad for compliance with Article 8 (*Niemietz v Germany*).

- Relevant factors when determining whether a warrant complies with Article 8 include:

  (a) whether it is to be executed by specially trained officials;
  (b) whether there are restrictions on when it can be executed (e.g., not on Sundays or during the night);
  (c) whether there is a duty on those searching to identify themselves and explain the purpose of the search;
  (d) whether a search record has to be compiled; and
  (e) whether there is any provision for an independent observer to be present (*Niemietz v Germany* and *Camenzind v Switzerland*).

- The notion of an individual's private life can be extended to his or her business and commercial premises:

  Respect for private life must also comprise to a certain degree the right to establish and develop relationships with others . . . There appears, furthermore, to be no reason of principle why . . . the notion of 'private life' should be taken to exclude activities of a professional or business nature. (*Niemietz v Germany*, para. 29 – *lawyer's offices searched by the police acting on a court warrant in order to obtain information about the identity and whereabouts of a third party who was the subject of a criminal investigation*)

- Although lawyers' premises are not immune from search, professional confidentiality must be respected:

  . . . the warrant was drawn in broad terms, in that it ordered a search for and seizure of 'documents', without any limitation . . . not accompanied by any special procedural safeguards, such as the presence of an independent observer. More importantly . . . the search impinged on professional secrecy to an extent that appears disproportionate . . . where a lawyer is involved, an encroachment on professional secrecy may have repercussions on the proper administration of justice and hence on the rights guaranteed by Article 6. (*Niemietz v Germany*, para. 37)

- Wide seizure of documents and/or blanket arrests of everyone on the premises are unlikely to be proportionate under the ECHR (*Ozgur Gundem v Turkey*).

Relevant Scottish authorities

Gordon Dickson Birse v Her Majesty's Advocate (18 April 2000)

- The mere fact that a suspect is not present or represented when the police apply for a search warrant under misuse of drugs legislation does not breach Article 8, so long as the judge is independent and takes into account all relevant circumstances before issuing a warrant (*Gordon Dickson Birse v Her Majesty's Advocate*, p. 4).

Relevant Canadian cases

Hunter v Southam Inc. [1984] 2 SCR 145
R v Beare [1988] 2 SCR 387
R v Belnavis [1997] 3 SCR 341
R v Collins [1987] 1 SCR 265
R v Duarte [1990] 1 SCR 30
R v Durette [1994] 1 SCR 469
R v Dyment [1988] 2 SCR 417
R v Edwards [1996] 1 SCR 128
R v Egger [1993] 2 SCR 451
R v Evans [1991] 1 SCR 869
R v Feeney [1997] 2 SCR 13
R v Wise [1992] 1 SCR 527

- The Charter protects against unreasonable search and seizure (*Hunter v Southam Inc.*); it also protects a reasonable expectation of privacy.

- In determining whether a reasonable expectation of privacy exists, a number of factors will be relevant, including:

  (a) presence at time of search;
  (b) possession or control over premises searched;
  (c) use of item being searched for;
  (d) ability to regulate access, including the right to admit or exclude others from the place;
  (e) subjective expectation of privacy; and
  (f) objective reasonableness of that expectation.

  (*R v Edwards*, para. 45 – *boyfriend did not have same expectation of privacy as girlfriend in relation to her apartment, being merely a visitor*)

- A search will be reasonable if it is:

  . . . authorised by law, if the law itself is reasonable and if the manner in which the search was carried out is reasonable . . . The nature of the belief [of the police] will also determine whether the manner in which the search was carried out was reasonable. (*R v Collins*)

- In this context a police officer's reasonable grounds for suspicion can be based on information received from third parties without infringing the hearsay rule (*R v Collins*).

- Obtaining a warrant for a search is not always necessary, but there must be a good reason for proceeding without a warrant:

  . . . it may not be reasonable in every instance to insist on prior authorization in order to validate governmental intrusions upon individuals' expectations of privacy. Nevertheless, where it is feasible to obtain prior authorization, [it is] a precondition for a valid search and seizure . . . (*R v Collins*)

- Where the warrant procedure is used, it must be meaningful: the person authorising the search must assess the evidence and consider whether the interests of the state clearly outweigh those of the individual. The person performing this function need not be a judge, but must be capable of acting judicially (R v Collins).

- There is no automatic right of access to the information or materials put before a court by those seeking a warrant; but where criminal proceedings ensue, access to such information or materials may be necessary to allow the accused to challenge effectively the admissibility of evidence (R v Egger, paras 44–49; R v Durette, p. 492).

- Inviting police officers into a home to communicate with a person does not amount to a waiver of a person's reasonable expectation of privacy such as to legitimise a subsequent search (R v Evans).

- Any search and seizure flowing from an unlawful arrest is a breach of privacy (R v Feeney).

- The expectation of liberty afforded in relation to cars is lower than the expectation afforded in relation to the home:

  Society requires and expects protection from drunken drivers, speeding drivers and dangerous drivers. A reasonable level of a surveillance of each and every motor vehicle is readily accepted, indeed demanded, by society to obtain this protection. All this is to set out to emphasize that, although there remains an expectation of privacy in automobile travel, it is markedly decreased relative to the expectation of privacy in one's home or office. (R v Wise, p. 534; see also R v Belnavis, p. 363)

- Nonetheless, in some clearly defined circumstances, passengers as well as drivers can have a reasonable expectation of privacy in relation to searches of a car (R v Belnavis, para. 23).

Relevant New Zealand cases

Frost v Police [1996] 2 NZLR 716
R v Briggs [1995] 1 NZLR 196, CA
R v Grayson (1996) 3 HRNZ 250, CA
R v Oldham (1994) 11 CRNZ 658
R v Wojcik (1994) 11 CRNZ 463, CA

- A reasonable expectation of privacy regulates the exercise of search powers, but:

  Reasonable expectations of privacy are lower in public places than on private property. They are higher for the home than for the surrounding land, for farm land and for land not used for residential purposes. And the nature of the activities carried on, particularly if involving public engagement or governmental oversight may affect reasonable expectations of privacy. (R v Grayson, p. 260)

- Consent to a search will not be valid unless the consent is genuine and informed, i.e. the accused is not forced to consent and knows that he or she has a right to refuse (R v Wojcik).

- Similarly, consent will not be genuine where the accused is given to understand that the search is conducted for a reason unrelated to the real purpose (*R v Oldham*).

- Forced entry where there has been no request for access and subsequent refusal will be difficult to justify (*R v Briggs*, p. 202).

- Excessive use of force, including the use of police dogs to cause injuries, can render an otherwise lawful search unlawful (*Frost v Police*, p. 725).

6.7   FINGERPRINTS, SAMPLES AND PERSONAL DATA

Key ECHR cases

Murray v UK (1994) 19 EHRR 193, ECtHR

Friedl v Austria (1995) A/305-B, ECmHR
McVeigh, O'Neill and Evans v UK (1981) 5 EHRR 71, EcmHR
Williams v UK (App. No. 19404/92), ECmHR[CD]
X v Germany (1976) 3 DR 104, ECmHR
X v Germany 9 Coll Dec 53, ECmHR

ECHR principles

- Measures such as taking personal details, photographs and samples all engage Article 8 and must be justified (*Murray v UK*).

- The prevention of crime can justify such measures, but only where they are prescribed by law, necessary and proportionate (*McVeigh v UK*).

- In some cases, the collection of personal data from those who are not under suspicion can be justified, but only in very limited circumstances, e.g., where individuals are stopped crossing a national border and the purpose of the measures in question is the prevention of terrorism (*McVeigh v UK*).

- The retention of personal data is different from their collection and must be separately justified (*X v Germany*).

- The prevention of terrorism (or other serious offences) can justify the retention of personal data, but only for so long as the retention serves that purpose (*McVeigh v UK*).

Relevant Canadian cases

R v Arp [1998] 3 SCR 339
R v Beare [1988] 2 SCR 387
R v Borden [1994] 3 SCR 145
R v Dyment [1988] 2 SCR 417

- Taking of a blood sample amounts to an invasion of privacy:

    . . . to use an individual's blood or other bodily substances confided to others for medical purposes other than these seriously violates the personal autonomy of the individual. In this particular case, the seizure infringed upon all the spheres of privacy . . . spatial, personal and informational. Under these circumstances . . . in the absence of pressing necessity, it was unreasonable for the police officer to act as he did. The needs of law enforcement are important, even beneficent, but there is danger when this goal is pursued with too much zeal. (R v Dyment – handing over of blood sample by doctor to police to check for blood-alcohol level without subject's consent)

- But the taking of a suspect's fingerprints does not:

    . . . a person who is arrested on reasonable and probable grounds that he has committed a serious crime, or a person against whom a case for issuing a summons or warrant, or confirming an appearance notice has been made out, must expect a significant loss of personal privacy. He must expect that incidental to his being taken in custody he will be subjected to observation, to physical measurement and the like. Fingerprinting is of that nature. While some may find it distasteful, it is insubstantial, of very short duration, and leaves no lasting impression. There is no penetration into the body and no substance is removed from it. (R v Beare – mandatory fingerprinting of a person charged with indictable offence)

- Any consent to the provision of bodily samples must be an informed consent, i.e. persons consenting must be aware of their rights and as far as possible of the consequences of their consent, although they need not appreciate each and every possible consequence of their consent (R v Arp, para. 87, affirming R v Borden – hair sample given in one investigation used in subsequent investigation).

- Moreover, once consent is given, there can be little expectation of privacy in the sample itself:

    It is both illogical and undesirable to suggest that when a body sample, be it hair or blood, is voluntarily surrendered to the police with full recognition that it is to be used in the course of investigation that there continues to be any expectation of privacy extending to the 'informational content' of that sample. In my view, no such expectation real or implied existed. (R v Arp, para. 87)

Relevant New Zealand cases

Police v Kohler [1993] 3 NZLR 129

- The right to consult a lawyer applies before a suspect is required to undergo a breath or blood test for alcohol (Police v Kohler, pp. 132–3).

6.8 INTERNATIONAL COOPERATION IN THE INVESTIGATION OF CRIME

Key ECHR cases

Drozd and Janousek v France and Spain (1992) 14 EHRR 475, ECtHR

Reinette v France (1989) 63 DR 189, ECmHR

ECHR principles

- The ECHR is relevant to questions of international cooperation in the investigation of crime.

- Law enforcement officers from the UK, who carry out their functions in other countries, remain subject to the ECHR. It will therefore be possible for a suspect arrested and detained abroad by UK law enforcement officers to claim a breach of Convention rights (*Reinette* v *France*).

- In addition, it would breach the ECHR if international cooperation in the investigation of crime exposed an individual to the risk of torture or ill-treatment contrary to Article 3, or interfered with his or her right to life under Article 2, e.g., through extradition or deportation (see **28.3**).

- However, there is no absolute rule that Contracting States to the ECHR should not cooperate with non-Contracting States merely because they do not comply with the standards set out in Article 6, ECHR (fair trial):

  > As the Convention does not require the Contracting Parties to impose its standards on third States or territories, France was not obliged to verify whether the proceedings which resulted in the conviction were compatible with all the requirements of Article 6 . . . To require such a review of the manner in which a court not bound by the Convention had applied the principles enshrined in Article 6 would also thwart the current trend towards strengthening international cooperation in the administration of justice, a trend which is in principle in the interests of the persons concerned. (*Drozd and Janousek* v *France and Spain*, para. 110)

- However, where there has been, or is likely to be, a flagrant denial of justice, cooperation should be refused (*Drozd and Janousek* v *France and Spain*, para. 110).

ARREST AND PRE-TRIAL DETENTION

7.1 REASONABLE SUSPICION

Key ECHR cases

Brogan and others v UK (1988) 11 EHRR 117, ECtHR
Doorson v Netherlands (1996) 22 EHRR 330, ECtHR
Fox, Campbell and Hartley v UK (1990) 13 EHRR 157, ECtHR
Guzzardi v Italy (1980) 3 EHRR 333, ECtHR
Ireland v UK (1978) 2 EHRR 25, ECtHR
Labita v Italy (6 April 2000), ECtHR
Ozgur Gundem v Turkey (16 March 2000), ECtHR

Lukanov v Bulgaria (1993) 80-A DR 108, ECmHR[CD]
Reinette v France (1989) 63 DR 189, ECmHR
X v Germany (1974) 14 Yearbook 250, ECmHR
X v Netherlands (1966) 9 Yearbook 474, ECmHR

ECHR principles

- Article 5(1)(c) authorises arrest on 'reasonable suspicion' that an individual has committed an offence. Such suspicion requires objective justification:

  The 'reasonableness' of the suspicion on which an arrest must be based forms an essential part of the safeguard against arbitrary arrest and detention . . . having a 'reasonable suspicion' presupposes the existence of facts or information which would satisfy an objective observer that the person concerned may have committed the offence. What may be regarded as 'reasonable' will however depend upon all the circumstances. (*Fox, Campbell and Hartley v UK*, para. 32)

- The honesty and good faith of a suspicion constitute indispensable elements of its reasonableness, but honest belief alone is not enough. There must be an objective basis justifying arrest and/or detention (*Fox, Campbell and Hartley v UK*).

- However, it is not necessary that there be sufficient evidence to charge before an arrest is made. So long as there is reasonable suspicion, detention is justified to further investigations (*Brogan v UK*).

- Nonetheless, the longer the deprivation of liberty, the higher the level of suspicion required (*Murray v UK*).

- Reasonable suspicion can be based on information provided by anonymous informants, even though such information may not necessarily be admissible at trial (*Doorson v Netherlands*).

- However, the authorities should be slow to base an arrest or pre-trial detention on statements made by alleged accomplices who are assisting the prosecution (*Labita v Italy*, para. 157).

- Blanket arrests of everyone at a particular premises are unlikely to be proportionate under the ECHR (*Ozgur Gundem v Turkey*, para. 49).

- Preventative detention is not permitted under Article 5; to justify an arrest there must be a reasonable suspicion that the individual in question has committed a 'concrete and specific offence' (*Ireland v UK*; *Guzzardi v Italy*).

Relevant Canadian authorities

R v Feeney [1997] 2 SCR 13

- Lack of subjective belief that a suspect has committed an offence is fatal to the lawfulness of an arrest:

  > [I]t would be inconsistent with the spirit of the Charter to permit a police officer to make an arrest without a warrant even though he or she does not believe reasonable grounds for the arrest exist. The absence of subjective belief, therefore, rendered the arrest unlawful irrespective of the existence of objective grounds for the arrest and the effect of the Charter on powers of police officers to enter a dwelling house without a warrant in order to effect an arrest. (*R v Feeney*, para. 29)

7.2   OTHER GROUNDS FOR ARREST

- Article 5(1)(b), (d), (e) and (f) provide separate bases for arrest and detention, not related to the investigation of crime. They are dealt with at **22.7**, **22.11**, **22.12**, **22.13** and **22.14** respectively.

7.3   REASONS

Key ECHR cases

Fox, Campbell and Hartley v UK (1990) 13 EHRR 157, ECtHR
Ireland v UK (1978) 2 EHRR 25, ECtHR
Murray v UK (1994) 19 EHRR 193, ECtHR

Reinette v France (1989) 63 DR 189, ECmHR
X v Germany (1974) 14 Yearbook 250, ECmHR
X v Netherlands (1966) 9 Yearbook 474, ECmHR

ECHR principles

- Article 5(2), ECHR requires that anyone arrested be informed promptly, 'in a language he understands', of 'the reasons for his arrest and of any charge against him'.

- The promptness of reasons is to be assessed in the light of all the circumstances of the case. Giving reasons within a few hours might suffice where terrorist offences are suspected:

  > Whilst this information must be conveyed 'promptly', it need not be related in its entirety by the arresting officer at the very moment of the arrest. Whether the content and promptness of the information conveyed were sufficient is to be assessed in each case according to its special features. (*Fox, Campbell and Hartley v UK; Murray v UK*, para. 40)

- The purpose of giving reasons for an arrest is to enable anyone arrested to challenge the lawfulness of his or her detention:

  > [Article 5(2)] . . . is an integral part of the scheme of protection afforded by Article 5: by virtue of paragraph 2 any person arrested must be told, in simple, non-technical language that he can understand, the essential legal and factual grounds for his arrest, so as to be able, if he sees fit, to apply to a court to challenge its lawfulness . . . (*Fox, Campbell and Hartley v UK*)

- Reasons need not be in writing (*X v Netherlands; X v Germany*).

- But merely informing an individual that he or she has been detained under emergency legislation is insufficient (*Ireland v UK*).

7.4   THE USE OF FORCE

- Force can be used to effect an arrest, but it must be necessary and proportionate. The use of fatal force is even more strictly circumscribed and subject to a stringent test of 'absolute necessity' (see **18.2**).

7.5   HANDCUFFS AND RESTRAINTS

Key ECHR cases

Raninen v Finland (1997) 26 EHRR 563, ECtHR

ECHR principles

- The use of handcuffs and restraints is not prohibited by the ECHR, but unless justified on the facts of each case may raise issues under Article 3 and Article 8:

  > . . . handcuffing does not normally give rise to an issue under Article 3 . . . where the measure has been imposed with lawful arrest and detention and does not entail use of force, or public exposure, exceeding what is reasonably considered necessary in the circumstances. In this regard, it is of importance for instance whether there is reason to believe that the person concerned would resist arrest or abscond, cause injury or damage or suppress evidence. (*Raninen v Finland*, para. 56)

7.6   ACCESS TO A LAWYER

Key ECHR cases

Averill v UK (6 June 2000), ECtHR
Imbrioscia v Switzerland (1993) 17 EHRR 4411, ECtHR
Kamasinski v Austria (1989) 13 EHRR 36, ECtHR
Magee v UK (6 June 2000), ECtHR
Murray, John v UK (1996) 22 EHRR 29, ECtHR
S v Switzerland (1991)(14 EHRR 667, ECtHR

ECHR principles

- The right to a fair trial under Article 6, ECHR normally requires that a suspect has access to a lawyer at the initial stages of a police investigation (*Imbroscia v Switzerland*, para. 36; see also *Murray, John v UK*).

- This is so particularly where steps may be taken which will impact on the defence:

    National laws may attach consequences to the attitude of an accused at the initial stages of police interrogation which are decisive for the prospects of the defence in any subsequent criminal proceedings. In such circumstances Article 6 will normally require that the accused be allowed to benefit from the assistance of a lawyer already at the initial stages of police interrogation.

    . . . the scheme contained in the [Criminal Evidence (Northern Ireland) Order 1988] is such that it is of paramount importance for the rights of the defence that an accused has access to a lawyer at the initial stages of police interrogation . . .

    To deny access to a lawyer for the first 48 hours of police questioning, in a situation where the rights of the defence may well be irretrievably prejudiced is – whatever the justification for such denial – incompatible with the rights of the accused under Article 6. (*Murray, John v UK*, paras 63, 65 and 66 – *denial of access to lawyer before questioning where adverse inference later drawn from silence*)

- However, the actual requirements of Article 6 at the pre-trial stage will vary according to the circumstances:

    . . . the manner in which Article 6(1) and (3)(c) is to be applied during the preliminary investigation depends on the special features of the proceedings involved and the circumstances of the case; in order to determine whether the aim of Article 6 – a fair trial – has been achieved, regard must be had to the entirety of the proceedings conducted in the case. (*Imbrioscia v Switzerland*, para. 38)

- The right of access to a lawyer at the early stages of a police investigation can be restricted, but only where there is good cause for doing so and not where adverse consequences may follow for the suspect (*Murray, John v UK*, para. 63).

- Communications between a suspect and his or her lawyer should be confidential:

    . . . an accused's right to communicate with his advocate out of hearing of a third person is one of the basic requirements of a fair trial in a democratic society and flows from Article 6(3)(c) of the Convention. If a lawyer were unable to confer with his client and receive confidential instructions from him without . . . surveillance, his assistance would lose much of its usefulness, whereas the Convention is intended to guarantee rights that are practical and effective. (*S v Switzerland*, para. 48)

- But in rare cases where disorder or crime is feared, it may be legitimate to intercept lawyer/client communications. However, the mere fact that a number of lawyers are coordinating their defence strategy cannot justify interference with lawyer/client confidentiality (*S v Switzerland*, para. 49).

- To deny access to a lawyer for a long period and in a situation where the rights of the defence were irretrievably prejudiced is, whatever the justification, incompatible with Article 6 (*Magee v UK*; see also *Averill v UK*).

Other relevant international human rights standards

UN Basic Principles on the Role of Lawyers (1990)

- Everybody should be informed of the right to be assisted by a lawyer upon arrest (Principle 5).

- Furthermore, everyone should be provided with adequate opportunities, time and facilities to be visited by and to communicate and consult with a lawyer, without delay, interception or censorship and in full confidentiality. Such consultations may be within sight, but not within the hearing, of law enforcement officials (Principle 8).

Relevant Canadian cases

R v Black [1989] 2 SCR 138
R v Manninen [1987] 1 SCR 1233
R v Mohl [1989] 1 SCR 1389
R v Smith [1989] 2 SCR 368

- Everyone has the right on arrest or detention to retain and instruct counsel without delay and to be informed of that right (Charter, s. 10(b)).

- If a suspect states that he or she cannot afford a lawyer, it is incumbent on the relevant authorities to inform him or her of the availability of legal aid lawyers (*R v Manninen*).

- A suspect can waive the right to a lawyer, but the authorities should exercise caution if there are grounds for suspecting that the individual in question has not appreciated the consequences of waiver, e.g., because he or she is drunk (*R v Mohl*).

- If circumstances change after a suspect has waived the right to a lawyer – e.g., a radical change in the nature of the investigation – he or she should be reminded of the right to a lawyer (*R v Black*; *R v Smith*).

Relevant New Zealand cases

Police v Kohler [1993] 3 NZLR 129
R v Brown (1995) 13 CRNZ 161
R v Lory (Ruling No. 4) (3 September 1996)
R v Mallinson [1993] 1 NZLR 528
R v Narayan [1992] 2 NZLR 145
R v Piper [1995] 3 NZLR 540, CA

- To make an informed decision whether to consult a lawyer, a suspect must understand the jeopardy he or she faces, together with the nature of the incriminating evidence held by the police (*R v Lory (Ruling No. 4)*).

- If a suspect genuinely did not understand the position when he or she waived the right to a lawyer, it is irrelevant whether the police set out to deceive or not (*R v Lory (Ruling No. 4)*).

- The essential question is whether the suspect did properly understand the position, not whether it was legitimate for the police to have formed the view that he or she did (*R v Lory (Ruling No. 4)*; *R v Mallinson*; *R v Narayan – special care to be taken where suspect did not understand English very well*).

- Moreover, the police are under a positive duty to assist a suspect to contact a lawyer: it is not enough simply to hand over a telephone book, particularly where the suspect is having trouble contacting a lawyer (*R v Brown*).

- The right to consult a lawyer implies the right that any such consultation be private and confidential: no separate request for privacy is required (*Police v Kohler*, pp. 132–2).

- This is likely to be infringed where a police officer overhears a telephone communication between a suspect and his or her lawyer (*R v Piper*, p. 543).

- But confidentiality can be refused if there are good reasons, e.g., genuine concern about disposal of drugs before a search (*R v Piper*).

Relevant Commonwealth cases

AG Trinidad and Tobago v Whiteman [1991] 2 AC 240
R v Thornhill (1974) WIR 281, PC

- The right of access to a lawyer must be effective; where the police terminate discussions between a suspect and his or her lawyer after five minutes, the right of access is breached (*R v Thornhill*, at first instance).

- Suspects must be made aware of their right to consult a lawyer:

  > [I]t is incumbent upon police officers to see that the arrested person is informed of his right in such a way that he understands . . . It is plain that the mere exhibition of notices in the police station is insufficient in itself to convey the necessary information. (*AG Trinidad and Tobago v Whiteman*, p. 248)

7.7   ACCESS TO OTHERS

Key ECHR cases

McVeigh, O'Neill and Evans v UK (1981) 5 EHRR 71, ECmHR

ECHR principles

- Suspects in custody should normally be allowed access to their families:

    Unless there is a danger of accomplices being warned, a failure to allow persons so detained to make contact with their families cannot be justified under Article 8(2) as being necessary for the prevention of crime etc. (McVeigh, O'Neill and Evans v UK, para. 239)

Other relevant international human rights standards

- In order to guarantee the effective protection of detained persons, provisions should be made for detainees to be held in officially recognised places of detention and for their names and places of detention, as well as the names of those responsible for their detention, to be made available and accessible to those concerned, including relatives and friends (UN Human Rights Committee, General Comment 20).

7.8   QUESTIONING

Key ECHR cases

Funke v France (1993) 16 EHRR 297, ECtHR
Murray, John v UK (1996) 22 EHRR 29, ECtHR
Saunders v UK (1996) 23 EHRR 313, ECtHR

G v UK (1984) 34 DR 75, ECmHR

ECHR principles

- The ECHR recognises a right to remain silent during police questioning:

    [A]lthough not specifically mentioned in Article 6 of the Convention, there can be no doubt that the right to remain silent under police questioning and the privilege against self-incrimination are generally recognised international standards which lie at the heart of the notion of a fair procedure under Article 6. (Murray, John v UK, para. 20)

- However, that does not mean that adverse inferences cannot be drawn from silence. The fairness of drawing such inferences is a matter to be determined at trial in light of all the evidence (*Murray, John v UK*; see **9.10**).

- But it does mean that the introduction into evidence in a criminal trial for the purpose of incriminating the accused of transcripts of statements made under compulsion – e.g., to non-prosecutorial inspectors – will breach Article 6 (*Saunders v UK*).

- The same applies where the authorities seek to compel a suspect to hand over incriminating documentation (*Funke v France*).

- Incriminating answers obtained by the questioning of a suspect during incommunicado detention require very close scrutiny (*G v UK*).

7.9   THE RIGHT TO BE BROUGHT PROMPTLY BEFORE A COURT

Key ECHR cases

Brogan and others v UK (1988) 11 EHRR 117, ECtHR
Ireland v UK (1978) 2 EHRR 25, ECtHR

ECHR principles

- Everyone arrested for a criminal offence has the right to be brought promptly before a judge or other officer authorised by law to exercise judicial power (Article 5(3), ECHR).

- As a result, when determining whether an arrested person has been brought promptly before a judge or judicial officer, the scope for flexibility in interpreting and applying the notion of 'promptness' is very limited (*Brogan and others v UK*, para. 62).

- A delay of four days and six hours is too long, even when an arrest is made under prevention of terrorism legislation (*Brogan and others v UK – but see the derogation subsequently entered by the UK*, at **5.4**).

- The judge or other officers before whom an arrested person is brought must have the power to order release; a power to advise that the individual be released is insufficient (*Ireland v UK*, para. 199).

7.10   BAIL: SUBSTANTIVE ISSUES

Key ECHR cases

Aquilina v Malta (1999) 29 EHRR 185, ECtHR
Clooth v Belgium (1991) 14 EHRR 717, ECtHR
Douiyeb v Netherlands (4 August 1999), ECtHR
I.A. v France (23 September 1998), ECtHR
Kemmache v France (1991) 14 EHRR 520, ECtHR
Lettellier v France (1991) 14 EHRR 83, ECtHR
Mansur v Turkey (1995) 20 EHRR 535, ECtHR
Matznetter v Austria (1979–80) 1 EHRR 198, ECtHR
Neumeister v Austria (1968) 1 EHRR 91, ECtHR
Punzelt v Czech Republic (25 April 2000), ECtHR
Ringeisen v Austria (1971) 1 EHRR 455, ECtHR
Stögmüller v Germany (1969) 1 EHRR 155, ECtHR
Tomasi v France (1992) 15 EHRR 1, ECtHR
Toth v Austria (1991) 14 EHRR 551, ECtHR
W v Switzerland (1993) 17 EHRR 60, ECtHR
Wemhoff v Germany (1968) 1 EHRR 55, ECtHR
Yagci and Sargin v Turkey (1995) 20 EHRR 505, ECtHR

Schertenlieb v Switzerland (1980) 23 DR 137, ECmHR
Schmid v Austria (1985) 44 DR 195, ECmHR

ECHR principles

- Despite its wording, Article 5(3), ECHR does not provide for trial within a reasonable period or release pending trial as alternatives: an accused person is entitled to trial within a reasonable period and release pending trial unless the prosecuting authorities advance relevant and sufficient reasons for refusing bail (*Wemhoff* v *Germany*).

- The presumption is in favour of bail:

  [The national courts] must examine all the circumstances arguing for or against the existence of a genuine requirement of the public interest justifying, with due regard to the presumption of innocence, a departure from the rule of respect for individual liberty and set them out in their decisions on the applications for release. (*Tomasi* v *France*, para. 84)

- A rule that bail will be considered only if the accused makes an application is inconsistent with Article 5(3), which requires the court to consider bail at the earliest opportunity (*Aquilina* v *Malta*).

- Grounds for refusing bail which have been approved by the ECtHR include:

  (a) fear of absconding (*Stögmüller* v *Austria*; *Neumeister* v *Austria*);
  (b) interference with the course of justice (*Wemhoff* v *Germany*; *Letellier* v *France*);
  (c) prevention of further offences (*Matznetter* v *Austria*; *Toth* v *Austria*);
  (d) the preservation of public order (*Letellier* v *France*); and
  (e) the protection of the defendant (*I.A.* v *France*).

- The mere fact that there are reasonable grounds for suspecting that a person has committed an offence is not enough (*Letellier* v *France*, para. 35).

- Fear of absconding cannot be based solely on the gravity of the offence; other factors such as character, assets and community ties are also relevant (*Letellier* v *France*, para. 35; see also *Yagci and Sargin* v *Turkey* and *Mansur* v *Turkey*).

- Where interference with the course of justice is advanced as a basis for refusing bail, it must be supported by specific allegations; generalised assertions are not enough (*Clooth* v *Belgium*, para. 44).

- Previous convictions which are dissimilar to the offence charged do not form a sufficiently sound basis for objecting to bail on the ground that the accused will commit further offences (*Clooth* v *Belgium*, para. 40).

- Where the nature of the crime alleged and the likely public reaction are such that the release of the accused may give rise to public disorder, temporary detention may be justified; but only in relation to crimes of particular gravity (*Letellier* v *France*, paras 47–51).

- Where the psychiatric disposition of an accused person is relied upon by the prosecution as a basis for refusing bail – either allied with some other ground such as the commission of further offences, or otherwise – it may be that the provision of appropriate care is needed before pre-trial detention can be justified (*Clooth* v *Belgium*, para. 40).

- Conditional bail is permitted under the ECHR and should be granted as an alternative to pre-trial detention where objections to bail can be met with conditions (*Wemhoff v Germany*).

- Permissible conditions of bail include a requirement to surrender travel documents (*Stögmüller v Austria*); the imposition of a residence requirement (*Schmid v Austria*); and the provision of a surety, which must be assessed by reference to the means of the accused. (*Wemhoff v Germany*; *Neumeister v Austria*; *Schertenleib v Switzerland*).

- However, refusal to accept the applicant's offer of a surety on the basis that such surety was insufficient guarantee that he would attend for trial is not necessarily a breach of Article 5(3) (*Punzelt v Czech Republic*, para. 86).

- A clerical error in relation to the offence charged will not invalidate pre-trial detention if all the parties knew the true basis of the proceedings (*Douiyeb v Netherlands*).

Other relevant international human rights standards

- The general presumption is that individuals awaiting trial should not be detained (UN International Covenant on Civil and Political Rights, Article 9(3)).

7.11   BAIL: PROCEDURE

Key ECHR cases

Assenov v Bulgaria (1998) 28 EHRR 652, ECtHR
Baranowski v Poland (28 March 2000), ECtHR
Bezicheri v Italy (1989) 12 EHRR 210, ECtHR
Clooth v Belgium (1991) 14 EHRR 717, ECtHR
Lamy v Belgium (1989) 11 EHRR 529, ECtHR
Nikolova v Bulgaria (25 March 1999), ECtHR
Tomasi v France (1992) 15 EHRR 1, ECtHR
Toth v Austria (1991) 14 EHRR 551, ECtHR
TW v Malta (1999) 29 EHRR 185, ECtHR

ECHR principles

- Bail proceedings must be fair and there must be equality of arms between the prosecution and the defence.

- Although all of the fair trial requirements of Article 6(1) are not necessary in relation to a review by a court of the lawfulness of detention under Article 5(4), such review must have a judicial character and provide guarantees appropriate to the kind of deprivation in question. In the case of a person awaiting criminal trial, a hearing is required, and there must be periodic review at reasonably short intervals (*Assenov v Bulgaria*, para. 162; see also *Bezicheri v Italy*).

- Where documents exist which are relevant to the bail decision, they must be disclosed to the defence *before* the bail hearing:

    Access to the documents was essential for the applicant at this crucial stage in the proceedings, when the court had to decide whether to remand him in custody or to release him. Such access would, in particular, have enabled counsel for [the applicant] to address the court on the matter of his co-defendant's statements and attitude. In the Court's view it was therefore essential to inspect the documents in question in order to challenge the lawfulness of the arrest warrant effectively . . .

Whereas Crown counsel was familiar with the whole file, the procedure did not afford the applicant an opportunity of challenging appropriately the reasons relied upon to justify a remand in custody. Since it failed to ensure equality of arms, the procedure was not truly adversarial. (*Lamy v Belgium*, para. 29; *bail hearing four days after arrest on fraud charges, affirmed in Nikolova v Bulgaria – counsel denied access to documents in the investigation file which are essential to an effective challenge to the lawfulness of detention*)

- Mere assertions by the prosecution of a general nature are an insufficiently sound basis for refusing bail; objections to bail must be supported by 'relevant' and 'sufficient' reasons for departing from the presumption of bail (*Clooth v Belgium*, para. 44; *Tomasi v France*, para. 84).

- In some circumstances evidence may be needed, e.g., where an objection to bail is being advanced on the ground of the preservation of public order (*Tomasi v France*, para. 91).

- The sufficiency of the reasons advanced by the prosecution for objecting to bail will be important because courts should give reasons for refusing bail (*Tomasi v France*).

- Delays of six weeks while reports are prepared and one month while other evidence is obtained are not acceptable under Article 5(4) (*Baranowski v Poland*, para. 73).

- There is no requirement under the ECHR to set up appeal procedures where bail is refused; but where appeal procedures exist, they too must ensure equality of arms between the prosecution and defence (*Toth v Austria*, para. 84).

Relevant Scottish cases

Burn and McQuilken v Procurator Fiscal, Glasgow (16 March 2000), AC

- In determining bail applications, the court is under a duty to consider whether according to legal criteria there are good reasons to remand a suspect in custody and not just to rely on what it is told by the prosecution:

We are satisfied that the law as laid down by Lord McCluskey in *Boyle* [1995] does not meet the requirements of Article 5(3) [ECHR] since the sheriff is directed not to seek to go behind any statement by the procurator fiscal that the Crown are continuing to make enquiries and that it is necessary for the proper pursuit of these enquiries in the public interest that the accused should remain in custody at that stage. In effect the law as there stated enjoins the sheriff not to consider the merits of the accused's continued detention for himself but to defer to the statement by the procurator fiscal. (*Burn and McQuilken v Procurator Fiscal, Glasgow*, para. 5, applying *T.W. v Malta* (1999))

- This has implications for the nature of information furnished by the prosecution:

In future the Crown must provide sufficient general information relating to the particular case to allow the sheriff to consider the merits . . . it will not be necessary for the Crown to disclose operational details. On the other hand, where, for example, the Crown oppose bail on the ground of the risk that the accused would interfere with witnesses, the procurator fiscal . . . should be in a position to explain the basis for that fear. The same would apply where opposition is based on a fear that the accused would interfere with a possible search of premises which the police wished to carry out. (*Burn and McQuilken v Procurator Fiscal, Glasgow*, para. 6)

Relevant New Zealand cases

B v Police [2000] 1 NZLR 31, CA
Gillbanks v Police [1994] 3 NZLR 61
R v Greenaway [1995] 1 NZLR 204
Whitair v Attorney-General [1996] 2 NZLR 45

- The onus is on the prosecution to demonstrate 'just cause' for refusing bail; to discharge this onus the prosecution must provide appropriate evidence in a suitable form (*Gillbanks v Police*, p. 69).

- The seriousness of the offence cannot of itself provide a justification for refusing bail. The prosecution must also show that there is some additional factor requiring detention which cannot be dealt with by way of bail conditions (*B v Police*, p. 35).

- Where the nearest bail court is not sitting at the relevant time, the police are under a duty to bring the defendant before another court, so long as it reasonably practical to do so (*Whitair v Attorney-General*).

- Where weekend sittings can be arranged, the authorities are under a duty to advise suspects of this rather than simply delaying until Monday morning:

  It is not imposing an unreasonable burden on the police or the Court authorities to insist that any requirement governing the availability of a hearing should be made known to a prisoner, to enable him or her to make an informed choice about satisfying it. (*R v Greenaway*, pp. 207–8)

7.12   CONDITIONS OF DETENTION

- Conditions of detention can raise issues under Article 3 and Article 8 of the ECHR (see **13.3**).

7.13   ILL-TREATMENT

Key ECHR cases

Aksoy v Turkey (1996) 23 EHRR 553, ECtHR
Assenov v Bulgaria (1998) 28 EHRR 652, ECtHR
Raninen v Finland (1997) 26 EHRR 563, ECtHR
Ribitsch v Austria (1995) 21 EHRR 573, ECtHR
Salman v Turkey (27 June 2000), ECtHR
Selmouni v France (1999) 29 EHRR 403, ECtHR
Tekin v Turkey (9 June 1998), ECtHR
Tomasi v France (1992) 15 EHRR 1, ECtHR

Austria v Italy (1963) 6 Yearbook 740, ECmHR

ECHR principles

- Where individuals are in police custody, any unnecessary and deliberate force is likely to breach Article 3, ECHR:

  . . . in respect of a person deprived of his liberty, any recourse to physical force which has not been made strictly necessary by his own conduct diminishes human dignity and is in principle an infringement of . . . Article 3.

  It reiterates that the requirements of an investigation and the undeniable difficulties inherent in the fight against crime cannot justify placing limits on the protection to be afforded in respect of the physical integrity of individuals. (*Ribitsch v Austria*, para. 38, affirmed in *Tekin v Turkey*)

- Slapping, kicking and punching an individual in custody can amount to inhuman and/or degrading treatment under Article 3 (*Tomasi v France*).

- Equally, the infliction of injuries such as a band-like haematoma about 5cm long and 1cm wide on the upper right arm, three band-like haematoma, each about 6cm long and 1cm wide, on the chest, a 4cm bruise on the left scapula, a haematoma 2cm in diameter on the back of the head and five grazes to the chest each about 5cm long, is sufficiently serious to amount to ill-treatment within the meaning of Article 3 (*Assenov v Bulgaria*, para. 95).

- Presumptions of fact requiring rebuttal will arise where there is clear evidence that an individual has been injured while in police custody (*Ribitsch v Austria*).

- In other words, where an individual is taken into police custody in good health but is found to be injured at the time of release, it is incumbent on the state to provide a plausible explanation for the injuries (*Aksoy v Turkey*, affirmed in *Selmouni v France* and *Salman v Turkey*).

- Evidence obtained as a result of ill-treatment must be excluded at trial (*Austria v Italy*).

- In addition, allegations of ill-treatment must be properly investigated:

  . . . where an individual raises an arguable claim that he has been seriously ill-treated by the police or other such agents of the state unlawfully and in breach of Article 3, that provision, read in conjunction with the state's general duty under Article 1 of the Convention to 'secure to everyone within their jurisdiction the rights and freedoms in [the] Convention', requires by implication that there should be an effective official investigation. This obligation, as with that under Article 2 of the Convention, should be capable of leading to the identification and punishment of those responsible . . . If this were not the case, the general legal prohibition of torture and inhuman and degrading treatment and punishment, despite its fundamental importance . . . would be ineffective in practice and it would be possible in some cases for agents of the state to abuse the rights of those within their control with virtual impunity. (*Assenov v Bulgaria*, para. 102)

- And compensation paid where appropriate:

  Where an individual has an arguable claim that he has been ill-treated in breach of Article 3, the notion of an effective remedy entails, in addition to a thorough and effective investigation of the kind also required by Article 3 . . . effective access to the investigatory procedure and the payment of compensation where appropriate . . . (*Assenov v Bulgaria*, para. 117)

FAIR TRIAL IN CRIMINAL PROCEEDINGS

Courts considering fair trial issues under Article 6, ECHR must look at the proceedings as a whole, including appeal proceedings where appropriate. In some circumstances a deficiency at trial, e.g., less than full disclosure, may not lead to a finding that Article 6 has been breached if there was full disclosure to an appeal court, which carefully considered the impact of non-disclosure on the fairness of the trial.

8.1 THE MEANING OF 'CRIMINAL' PROCEEDINGS UNDER THE ECHR

Key ECHR cases

AGOSI v UK (1986) 9 EHRR 1, ECtHR
Air Canada v UK (1995) 20 EHRR 150, ECtHR
Bendenoun v France (1994) 18 EHRR 54, ECtHR
Benham v UK (1996) 22 EHRR 293, ECtHR
Campbell and Fell v UK (1984) 7 EHRR 165, ECtHR
Kadubec v Slovakia (2 September 1998), ECtHR
Lauko v Slovakia (2 September 1998), ECtHR
Pfarrmeier v Austria, (1995) 22 EHRR 175, ECtHR
Schmautzer v Austria (1995) 21 EHRR 511, ECtHR
Umlauft v Austria (1995) 22 EHRR 76, ECtHR

Abas v Netherlands (App. No. 27943/95), ECmHR[CD]
Perin v France (1 December 1992), ECmHR

ECHR principles

- The fair trial requirements of Article 6, ECHR distinguish between criminal and civil proceedings.

- Whether proceedings are criminal or civil is to be determined according to three criteria:

  (a) the classification in domestic law – if classified as criminal, this is determinative; if classified as civil, this is a starting point, but not determinative (*Benham v UK*);

(b) the nature of the conduct in question – sanctions which apply to the population as a whole, rather than to an identifiable subclass, point toward a criminal classification (*Benham v UK*);

(c) the severity of any possible penalty – severe penalties (e.g., including those with imprisonment in default) and penalties intended to deter are pointers towards a criminal classification of proceedings (*Schmautzer v Austria; Pfarrmeier v Austria; Umlauft v Austria*).

- Prison disciplinary proceedings do involve the determination of a criminal charge (*Campbell and Fell v UK*).

- Tax proceedings usually do not (*AGOSI v UK; Air Canada v UK; Abas v Netherlands*), unless particularly severe penalties are imposed (*Perin v France – penalties of 30% and 50% of amount due; see also Bendenoun v France*).

- A scheme to regulate conduct between neighbours and which involves, among other things, the imposition of a fine may be criminal in nature, notwithstanding that it is classified as civil in domestic law (*Lauko v Slovakia*).

- Moreover, while it is legitimate to determine minor matters administratively, ultimately there must be access to a court:

  While entrusting the prosecution and punishment of minor offences to administrative authorities is not inconsistent with the Convention, it is to be stressed that the person concerned must have an opportunity to challenge any decision made against him before a tribunal that offers the guarantees of Article 6. (*Lauko v Slovakia*, para. 64)

- This principle may extend to minor public order offences dealt with by way of a fine (*Kadubec v Slovakia*).

Relevant domestic cases

R v Manchester Crown Court, ex parte McCann (22 November 2000), Divisional Court

- Proceedings by a local authority for an anti-social behaviour order under the Crime and Disorder Act 1998 are civil, not criminal proceedings (*R v Manchester Crown Court, ex parte McCann*).

8.2 THE RIGHT TO BE INFORMED OF THE CHARGE

Key ECHR cases

Brozicek v Italy (1989) 12 EHRR 371, ECtHR
Kamasinski v Austria (1989) 13 EHRR 36, ECtHR
Pélissier v France (25 March 1999), ECtHR

GSM v Austria (1983) 34 DR 119, ECmHR

ECHR principles

- Article 6(3)(a) specifically provides that everyone charged with a criminal offence has the right to be informed promptly, in a language which he or she understands and in detail, of the nature and cause of the accusation against him or her.

- The purpose of this provision is to enable the individual to begin preparing a defence (GSM v Austria).

- Where the offence is fairly specific, it may be enough to provide a brief description of the offence, the date, place and alleged victim (Brozicek v Italy).

- Otherwise, the information provided should be detailed:

  . . . the provisions of paragraph 3(a) of Article 6 point to the need for special attention to be paid to the notification of the accusation to the defendant. Particulars of the offence play a crucial role in the criminal process . . . Article 6(3)(a) of the Convention afforded the defendant the right to be informed not only of the cause of the accusation, that is to say the acts he is alleged to have committed and on which the accusation is based, but also the legal characterisation given to those acts. That information should . . . be detailed.
  . . . the provision of full, detailed information concerning the charges against the defendant, and consequently the legal characterisation that the court might adopt in the matter, is an essential prerequisite for ensuring that the proceedings are fair. (Pélissier v France, paras 51 and 52)

Other international human rights standards

- Everyone facing a criminal charge is entitled to be informed promptly and in detail, in a language which he or she understands, of the nature and cause of the charge against her or him (International Covenant on Civil and Political Rights, Article 14(3)(a)).

- This guarantee applies to all cases of criminal charges, including those persons not in detention, and arises when in the course of an investigation a court or an authority of the prosecution decides to take procedural steps against a suspect or names her or him as such. 'Promptly' requires that information is given in the manner described as soon as the charge is first made by a competent authority. The specific requirements of Article 14(3)(a) may be met by stating the charge either orally or in writing, provided that the information indicates both the law and the alleged facts on which it is based (UN Human Rights Committee, General Comment No. 13, para. 8).

Relevant Scottish cases

Gordon McLean v Her Majesty's Advocate (3 November 1999), AC

- The right to be informed promptly and in detail of the charge under Article 6 is satisfied if the period within which the offence is said to have occurred is given rather than the actual date:

  The amount of detail which is required may vary with the nature of the allegation. Obviously there will be many cases in which the Crown cannot know the precise date on which a crime was committed. (Gordon McLean v Her Majesty's Advocate, p. 3)

Relevant New Zealand cases

Jones v Police [1998] 1 NZLR 447

- The fact that a judge amends the charge against the defendant, having reviewed the evidence, does not offend the rule that those accused of criminal offences must be informed of the charge against them promptly (*Jones v Police*).

8.3   THE RIGHT TO ADEQUATE TIME AND FACILITIES TO PREPARE A DEFENCE

Key ECHR cases

Goddi v Italy (1984) 6 EHRR 457, ECtHR
Kremzow v Austria (1993) 17 EHRR 322, ECtHR

Perez Mahia v Spain (1987) 9 EHRR 91, ECmHR
X and Y v Austria (1979) 15 DR 160, ECmHR

ECHR principles

- Article 6(3)(b) specifically provides that everyone charged with a criminal offence has the right to have adequate time and facilities for the preparation of his or her defence.

- The adequate time requirement inevitably depends on the nature and complexity of the case; it cannot be determined in the abstract but only by reference to the circumstances of each case (*X and Y v Austria*, para. 3(b)).

- Where there is a late change of lawyer, an adjournment may be necessary (*Goddi v Italy*, para. 31).

- Where it is obvious that a lawyer has not had adequate time to prepare the defence properly, the court should consider adjourning the case on its own motion (*Goddi v Italy*, para. 31).

- In assessing the length of time needed to prepare a case, within limits, the workload of the lawyer is relevant:

    . . . the court must take into account not only the complexity of the case but also the usual workload of the barrister who certainly cannot be expected to change his whole programme in order to devote all his time to a legal aid case in which he has been appointed as defence counsel. On the other hand, it is not unreasonable to require a defence lawyer to arrange at least some shifts in the emphasis of his work if this is necessary in view of the special urgency of a particular case . . . If that was not possible he had to ask the Bar Council to be discharged from his duty in this case. (*X and Y v Austria*, para. 3(c))

- The facilities needed to prepare properly for trial will also depend on the circumstances; pre-trial access to relevant documents and materials is now recognised as a necessary facility under Article 6(3)(b) (see **8.5** below).

Other international human rights standards

- The accused must have adequate time and facilities for the preparation of his or her defence and to communicate with counsel of his or her choosing (International Covenant on Civil and Political Rights, Article 14(3)(b)).

- 'Adequate time' depends on the circumstances of each case, but facilities must include access to documents and other evidence which the accused requires to prepare a defence, as well as the opportunity to engage and communicate with a lawyer (Human Rights Committee, General Comment No. 13, para. 9).

8.4   LEGAL AID

Key ECHR cases

Benham v UK (1996) 22 EHRR 293, ECtHR
Croissant v Germany (1992) 16 EHRR 135, ECtHR
Granger v UK (1990) 12 EHRR 469, ECtHR
Quaranta v Switzerland (1991) A/205, ECtHR

ECHR principles

- Article 6(3)(c) specifically provides that everyone charged with a criminal offence has the right to 'defend himself in person or through legal assistance of his own choosing or, if he has not sufficient means to pay for legal assistance, to be given it free when the interests of justice so require'.

- Relevant to the 'interests of justice' test are:

    (a)   the complexity of the case;
    (b)   the ability of the defendant to understand and present the relevant arguments without assistance (a subjective test: *Quaranta v Switzerland*, para. 33);
    (c)   the severity of the possible penalty.

    (*Benham v UK*, paras 60–62; *Quaranta v Switzerland*, para. 33; *Granger v UK*, para. 47)

- The mere fact that a defendant is able to read a pre-prepared legal text to the court does not dispense with the need for legal aid if he or she does not fully comprehend the submissions being advanced and/or is not able to deal with questions from the court or submissions from the prosecution (*Granger v UK*, para. 47).

- Where deprivation of liberty is at stake, the interests of justice, in principle, call for legal aid (*Benham v UK*, paras 60–62).

- A refusal of legal aid should be kept under review (*Granger v UK*, para. 47).

- Article 6(3)(c) does not prevent the court from ordering a convicted defendant to pay costs, if at that stage he or she has sufficient means to do so (*Croissant v Germany*, para. 36 of the Commission's report).

- For legal aid in appeal proceedings, see **12.3**.

Relevant Scottish cases

Stephen Gayne v Procurator Fiscal, Glasgow (12 August 1999), AC

• Setting limits on the grant of legal aid does not automatically violate a defendant's right to a fair trial under Article 6, unless the result is such as to deny him effective legal representation (*Stephen Gayne v Procurator Fiscal, Glasgow*, pp. 3–4 – *Criminal Legal Aid (Fixed Payments) (Scotland) Regulations 1999* set limit of £500 on solicitor's costs; citing M v UK (App. No. 9728/82, (1983)).

8.5 DISCLOSURE

Key ECHR cases

Bendenoun v France (1994) 18 EHRR 54, ECtHR
Edwards v UK (1992) 15 EHRR 417, ECtHR
Fitt v UK (2000) 30 EHRR 223, ECtHR
Foucher v France (1997) 25 EHRR 234, ECtHR
Jasper v UK (2000) 30 EHRR 97, ECtHR
Kamasinski v Austria (1989) 13 EHRR 36, ECtHR
Krcmar v Czech Republic (3 March 2000), ECtHR
Kuopila v Finland (27 April 2000), ECtHR
Rowe and Davies v UK (2000) 30 EHRR 1, ECtHR

Cannon v UK (App. No. 29335/95, 17 January 1997), ECmHR[CD]
Hardiman v UK (App. No. 25935/94, 28 February 1996), ECmHR[CD]
Jespers v Belgium (1981) 27 DR 61, ECmHR
Preston v UK (App. No. 24193/94), ECmHR[CD]

ECHR principles

• Under the ECHR, a disclosure requirement is based on:

    (a)   the requirement that there be equality of arms between prosecution and defence (*Jespers v Belgium*);
    (b)   the defendant's right to adequate time and facilities to prepare a defence under Article 6(3)(b) (*Edwards v UK*); and
    (c)   the requirement in Article 6(3)(d) that there be parity of conditions for the examination of witnesses (*Edwards v UK*, Commission Report).

• The equality of arms principle imposes on prosecuting and investigating authorities an obligation to disclose any material in their possession, or to which they could gain access, which may assist the accused in exonerating himself or herself or in obtaining a reduction in sentence, including material which might undermine the credibility of a prosecution witness (*Jespers v Belgium*, paras 55–58).

• The right to adequate time and facilities to prepare a defence requires that all material evidence for or against the accused be disclosed:

. . . it is a requirement of fairness under Article 6(1) . . . that the prosecution authorities disclose to the defence all material evidence for or against the accused . . . (*Edwards v UK*, para. 36)

It is a fundamental aspect of the right to a fair trial that criminal proceedings, including the elements of such proceedings which relate to procedure, should be adversarial and that there should be equality of arms between the prosecution and defence. The right to an adversarial trial means, in a criminal case, that both prosecution and defence must be given an opportunity to have knowledge of and comment on the observations filed and the evidence adduced by the other party . . . In addition Article 6(1) requires . . . that the prosecution authorities should disclose to the defence all material evidence in their possession for or against the accused . . . (*Rowe and Davies v UK*, para. 60)

- The requirement in Article 6(3)(d) that there be parity of conditions for the examination of witnesses requires disclosure of any material relevant to the witness's testimony, including his or her credibility:

  The Commission considers that the provisions of Article 6(3)(d) of the Convention are relevant to the present application. Whilst technically it is true that the applicant was able to cross-examine the police officers concerned about his confession, the information that they withheld from the defence and the jury may have affected the conditions under which that cross-examination took place and may have been relevant to their credibility. Article 6(3)(d) refers expressly to a parity of conditions for the examination of witnesses and to this extent it is relevant to the present case. (*Edwards v UK*, Commission Report, para. 50)

- Early disclosure is important. Disclosure at trial is insufficient:

  Moreover, it is not enough that relevant documentary evidence is read out at trial: prior disclosure will generally be required.
  A party to the proceedings must have the possibility to familiarise itself with the evidence before the court, as well as the possibility to comment on its existence, contents and authenticity in an appropriate form and within an appropriate time, if need be, in a written form and in advance. (*Krcmar v Czech Republic*, para. 42)

- The fact that the prosecution does not intend to rely on a particular document does not preclude the possibility that it should be disclosed, but it may be that in such circumstances the defence should specify why the document is needed (*Bendenoun v France*).

- Anything passed to the court must be disclosed (*Kuopila v Finland*, para. 38).

- But where the product of telephone intercepts cannot be adduced by either side at trial (because of a statutory prohibition), and where such evidence has probably ceased to exist, failure to disclose it to the defence will not necessarily breach the principle of 'equality of arms', particularly if there is no prohibition on the defence giving evidence of telephone conversations to which the applicant was party (*Jasper v UK*, para. 58; *Fitt v UK*, para. 50).

- In addition, where prison psychiatric reports on a defendant are prepared in a serious case to enable the trial judge to consider issues of fitness to plead and, in a murder case, insanity and diminished responsibility, they need not be disclosed to co-defendants. The purpose of such reports is to protect the defendant (*Hardiman v UK*).

- There may be circumstances in which material need not be disclosed to the defence on grounds of public interest immunity, but they must be subject to strict control by the courts:

    . . . the entitlement to disclosure of relevant evidence is not an absolute right. In any criminal proceedings there may be competing interests, such as national security or the need to protect witnesses at risk of reprisals or keep secret police methods of investigation of crime, which must be weighed against the rights of the accused . . . In some cases it may be necessary to withhold certain evidence from the defence so as to preserve the fundamental rights of another individual or to safeguard an important public interest. However, only such measures restricting the rights of the defence which are strictly necessary are permissible under Article 6(1) . . . Moreover, in order to ensure that the accused receives a fair trial, any difficulties caused to the defence by a limitation on its rights must be sufficiently counterbalanced by the procedures followed by the judicial authorities. (*Rowe and Davies v UK*, para. 61)

- Nonetheless, hearings on an *ex parte* basis will not usually breach Article 6.

    . . . shortly before the commencement of the applicant's trial, the prosecution made an *ex parte* application to the trial judge to withhold material in its possession on the grounds of public interest immunity. The defence were notified that an application was to be made, but were not told of the category of material which the prosecution sought to withhold. They were given the opportunity to outline the defence case to the judge . . . and to request the judge to order disclosure of any evidence relating to these alleged facts. The trial judge examined the material in question and ruled that it should not be disclosed. The defence was not informed of the reasons for the judge's decision.
    The Court is satisfied that the defence were kept fully informed and permitted to make submissions and to participate in the above decision-making process as far as was possible without revealing to them the material which the prosecution sought to keep secret on public interest grounds. Whilst it is true that in a number of different contexts the United Kingdom has introduced, or is introducing, a 'special counsel' [procedure] . . . the Court does not accept that such a procedure was necessary in the present case. The Court notes, in particular, that the material which was not disclosed in the present case formed no part of the prosecution case whatever, and was never put to the jury. (*Jasper v UK; Fitt v UK*)

- The duty on the trial judge to keep disclosure under constant review is also an important safeguard:

    The fact that the need for disclosure was at all times under assessment by the trial judge provided a further, important, safeguard in that it was his duty to monitor throughout the trial the fairness or otherwise of the evidence being withheld. It has not been suggested that the judge was not independent or impartial within the meaning of Article 6(1). He was fully versed in all the evidence and issues in the case and in a position to monitor the relevance to the defence of the withheld information both before and during the trial. Moreover it can be assumed – not least because the Court of Appeal confirmed that the transcript of the *ex parte* hearing showed that he had been 'very careful to ensure and to explore whether the material was relevant, or likely to be relevant to the defence which had been indicated to him' – that the judge applied the principles which had recently been clarified by the Court of Appeal, for example that in weighing the public interest in concealment against the interests of justice, and that the judge should continue to assess the need for disclosure throughout the progress of the trial . . .

. . . Furthermore, during the appeal proceedings the Court of Appeal also considered whether or not the evidence should have been disclosed . . . providing an additional level of protection. (*Jasper v UK*, paras 54–57; *Fitt v UK*, paras 47–49)

- Where the court fails in its duties relating to non-disclosure on grounds of public interest immunity, close scrutiny by the Court of Appeal will rarely, if ever, rectify the situation (*Rowe and Davies v UK*, para. 65).

- In some circumstances disclosure to defence lawyers might be enough (*Kamasinski v Austria*; but see *Foucher v France*).

Relevant Scottish cases

Alistair McLeod v Her Majesty's Advocate (19 December 1997)

- There is no absolute right to disclosure under the ECHR:

  I find nothing in [*Edwards v UK* (1992)] which supports [the defence's] contention that an accused person is entitled to recover documents simply on the basis that they comprise statements taken in the course of an investigation which might possibly contain some material evidence. [Instead] it suggests that an accused person would be entitled to recover documents which were material to his defence to the charges against him. (*Alistair McLeod v Her Majesty's Advocate*, p. 9 – *refusal to hand over police questionnaires concerning drug taking on premises upheld*)

Relevant Canadian cases

Michaud v Quebec [1996] 3 SCR 3
R v Bramwell (1996) 106 CCC (3d) 365
R v Carosella [1997] 1 SCR 80
R v Chaplin [1995] 1 SCR 727
R v Dixon [1998] 1 SCR 244
R v Durette [1994] 1 SCR 469
R v Egger [1993] 2 SCR 451
R v Garofoli [1990] 2 SCR 1421
R v La [1997] 2 SCR 680
R v Mills [1999] 3 SCR 668
R v Stinchcombe [1991] 3 SCR 326
R v Stinchcombe (No. 2) [1995] 1 SCR 754

- The prosecution are under an obligation to disclose all relevant material – whether inculpatory or exculpatory – in their possession so long as the material is not privileged.

- In this context, material is relevant if it could reasonably be used by the defence in meeting the prosecution's case (*R v Stinchcombe*, p. 345).

- This requires a determination by the reviewing judge that production of the information can reasonably be used by the accused either in meeting the case for the prosecution, advancing a defence, or otherwise in making a decision which may affect the conduct of the defence such as whether to call evidence (*R v Egger*, p. 467).

- The duty to disclose also gives rise to an obligation to preserve relevant evidence (*R v Egger*, p. 472 – *prosecution obliged to retain blood samples beyond three-month statutory period*) and to provide an adequate explanation where it fails to do so (*R v Stinchcombe (No. 2)*).

- Since the right to disclosure is not absolute, a careful balance has to be struck between the right of the defendant to a fair trial and a victim's right to privacy. This may require that certain documents remain confidential, unless non-disclosure would harm the overall fairness of proceedings:

  Between [the] extremes of [non-disclosure and full disclosure needed to ensure equality of arms] lies a spectrum of possibilities regarding where to strike the balance between those competing rights in any particular context. The values protected by privacy rights will be most directly at stake where the confidential information contained in a record concerns aspects of one's individual identity or where the maintenance of confidentiality is crucial to a therapeutic, or other trust-like, relationship. (*R v Mills*, para. 89)

- On the appropriate balance to be struck between fair trial and protecting the interests of victims, see **14.5**.

- Where disclosure of materials put before a court in support of an application for authority to intercept communications is relevant to a challenge to that evidence at trial, it should be disclosed, with limited editing (*R v Garofoli*, p. 1460; see also *R v Durette*, p. 492, and *Michaud v Quebec*, para. 44).

Relevant New Zealand cases

R v Bevin (16 December 1996) CA 389/96

- There may be circumstances in which a defendant is entitled to a stay of proceedings because the police have intentionally destroyed or tampered with evidence, or have failed to follow a particular line of investigation (*R v Bevin –* *on the facts, police failings not proven; cf.* Canadian case of *R v Carosella* (1997) 112 CCC (3d) 289 (SCC) – *stay of proceedings granted when evidence deliberately destroyed*).

Relevant Commonwealth cases

Kwame Apata v Roberts (No. 1) (1980) 29 WIR 69

- Failure to provide the defence with the prosecution witness statements breaches the requirement that there be adequate time and facilities for preparing a defence (*Kwame Apata v Roberts (No. 1)*).

8.6   THE RIGHT TO AN INDEPENDENT AND IMPARTIAL TRIBUNAL

Key ECHR cases

Campbell and Fell v UK (1984) 7 EHRR 165, ECtHR
Delcourt v Belgium (1969) 1 EHRR 355, ECtHR
Engel and others v Netherlands (1976) 1 EHRR 647, ECtHR
Fey v Austria (1993) 16 EHRR 387, ECtHR

Gregory v *UK* (1997) 25 EHRR 577, ECtHR
Hauschildt v *Denmark* (1989) 12 EHRR 266, ECtHR
Le Compte, Van Leuven and De Meyere v *Belgium* (1981) 4 EHRR 1, ECtHR
McGonnell v *UK* (8 February 2000), ECtHR
Piersack v *Belgium* (1982) 5 EHRR 169, ECtHR
Remli v *France* (1996) 22 EHRR 253, ECtHR
Sainte Marie v *France* (1992) 16 EHRR 116, ECtHR
Sander v *UK* (9 May 2000), ECtHR

Brown v *UK* (1986) 8 EHRR 272, ECmHR
X and Y v *Ireland* (1981) 22 DR 51, ECmHR

ECHR principles

- Article 6(1), ECHR specifically provides that in the determination of any criminal charge, everyone is entitled to a fair and public hearing 'by an independent and impartial tribunal established by law'.

- Independence must be institutional and functional, but does not require trial by jury (*X and Y* v *Ireland*, p. 73).

- Relevant to the question of independence will be:

  (a) the manner of appointment and duration of office (*Le Compte, Van Leuven and De Meyere* v *Belgium*), but the mere fact that the executive appoint judges is not automatically a breach of Article 6 (*Campbell and Fell* v *UK*, para. 79); neither is there any requirement that judges be appointed for life (*Engel and others* v *Netherlands*)
  (b) protection from external influences (*Piersack* v *Belgium*, para. 27);
  (c) an appearance of independence (*Delcourt* v *Belgium*, para. 31; *Campbell and Fell* v *UK*, para. 78).

- The requirement for trial by an 'impartial tribunal' embodies the protection against actual and presumed bias, and applies equally to the judge and to the jury.

- The ECtHR has adopted a dual test:

  (a) first assessing whether there is any evidence of actual bias; here impartiality is presumed unless there is proof to the contrary (*Piersack* v *Belgium; Hauschildt* v *Denmark*);
  (b) then assessing the circumstances alleged to give rise to a risk of bias; here the question is whether there are 'ascertainable facts which may raise doubts' about the court's impartiality (*Piersack* v *Belgium; Hauschildt* v *Denmark*).

- Where a judge has taken key decisions before trial, issues of impartiality may arise; but the mere fact that a judge has previously made a bail decision based on suspicion that the defendant has committed an offence will not automatically preclude his or her participation in the trial:

  . . . the questions which the judge has to answer when taking . . . pre-trial decisions are not the same as those which are decisive for his final judgment . . . Suspicion and a formal finding of guilt are not to be treated as being the same . . . therefore, the mere fact that a trial judge or an appeal judge . . . has also made pre-trial decisions in the case, including those concerning detention on remand, cannot be held as in itself justifying fears as to his impartiality. (*Hauschildt v Denmark*, para. 50; see also *Sainte Marie v France*, para. 32)

- Neither will the fact that a judge has dealt with the accused on a previous occasion; the key issue will be the nature and character of the previous decision (*Hauschildt v Denmark – breach where trial judge previously refused bail on a high threshold test*; cf. *Brown v UK – no breach where appeal court judge refusing leave had previously been involved in restraint proceedings*; see also *Fey v Austria*).

- Although the ECHR does not require compliance with any particular doctrine of the separation of powers, where judges have played a part in the legislative process, legitimate doubts about their impartiality might arise when they are called upon to interpret the legislation in question:

  . . . any direct involvement in the passage of legislation, or of executive rules, is likely to be sufficient to cast doubt on the judicial impartiality of a person subsequently called on to determine a dispute over whether reasons exist to permit a variation from the wording of the legislation or rules at issue. (*McGonnell v UK*, para. 55)

- Allegations of impartiality must be properly investigated, unless they are manifestly devoid of merit (*Remli v France*, para. 48; *Gregory v UK*, para. 44).

- And in some circumstances, the nature of the alleged bias or impartiality will require decisive action; directions to the jury to try the case on the evidence may not suffice:

  . . . in the present case the Court is not prepared to attach very much weight to the judge's redirection to the jury. The Court considers that, generally speaking, an admonition or direction by the judge, however clear, detailed and forceful, would not change racist views overnight. Although in the present case it cannot be assumed that such views were indeed held by one or more jurors, it has been established that at least one juror had been making racist comments. In these circumstances, the Court considers that the direction given by the judge to the jury could not dispel the reasonable impression and fear of a lack of impartiality, which were based on the original note. (*Sander v UK*, para. 30 – *juror making racist jokes and comments; judge declines to discharge jury, but directs jury to come to verdict without prejudice*)

Relevant Scottish cases

Clancy v Caird (10 December 1999), Report to Inner House of Court of Session; (4 April 2000), CS
Crummock (Scotland) Ltd v Her Majesty's Advocate (16 March 2000), AC
Douglas Gibbs v Procurator Fiscal, Linlithgow (24 November 1999), AC
Hoekstra, Van Rijs and others v Her Majesty's Advocate (9 March 2000), AC
Starrs and Chalmers v Procurator Fiscal, Linlithgow (Ruxton) (2000) SLT 42

- Independence and impartiality are fundamentally compromised by the power of the executive to recall judges without good cause. Similarly, appointments for very short periods, with a discretion to reappoint, fail to provide the required security of tenure:

In the case of temporary Sheriffs, where the appointment is frequently a 'career move', the combination of a one-year appointment with liability to either recall or suspension or limited use is in my opinion wholly inconsistent with the requirement of independence. (*Starrs and Chalmers v Procurator Fiscal, Linlithgow (Ruxton)*, p. 25; see also *Clancy v Caird*, p. 9, and *Douglas Gibbs v Procurator Fiscal, Linlithgow*)

- A judge's impartiality may be compromised by comments outside of the chamber. In this context, tone and language, together with the timing, are relevant factors in determining whether the guarantee of impartiality has been breached:

  It appears to us that the article, published very shortly after the decision in the appeal, would create in the mind of an informed observer an apprehension of bias on the part of Lord McCluskey against the Convention and against the rights deriving from it ... We stress that, in reaching this conclusion, we attach particular importance to the tone of the language and the impression which the author deliberately gives. (*Hoekstra, Van Rijs and others v Her Majesty's Advocate*, paras 22 and 23 – *legitimate fear of bias on part of senior judge following highly critical article on ECHR in national paper*)

- Although judges are not barred from commenting on the law, they must be careful about how they express criticism:

  Judges, like other members of the public and other members of the legal profession, are entitled to criticise developments in our law ... But what judges cannot do with impunity is to publish either criticism or praise of such a nature or in such language as to give rise to a legitimate apprehension that, when called upon in the course of their judicial duties to apply that particular branch of the law, they will not be able to do so impartially. (*Hoekstra, Van Rijs and others v Her Majesty's Advocate*, para. 23)

8.7   THE RIGHT TO A PUBLIC HEARING

Key ECHR cases

Campbell and Fell v UK (1984) 7 EHRR 165, ECtHR
Pretto and others v Italy (1983) 6 EHRR 182, ECtHR

ECHR principles

- Article 6(1), ECHR specifically provides that in the determination of any criminal charge, everyone is entitled to a fair and public hearing.

- But the press and public may be excluded from all or part of a trial:

  (a)   in the interests of morals, public order or national security in a democratic society;
  (b)   where the interests of juveniles or the protection of the private life of the parties so require;
  (c)   to the extent strictly necessary in the opinion of the court in special circumstances where publicity would prejudice the interests of justice.

- There is a presumption that ordinary criminal proceedings should be public, even where they involve dangerous individuals; but the same does not apply to prison disciplinary hearings:

It is true that ordinary criminal proceedings nearly always take place in public [however] . . . to require that disciplinary proceedings concerning convicted prisoners should be held in public would impose a disproportionate burden on the authorities of the state. (*Campbell and Fell v UK*, para. 87)

- The requirement in Article 6(1) that 'judgment shall be pronounced publicly' has not been interpreted literally (*Pretto and others v Italy*).

Other international human rights standards

- Everyone shall be entitled to a fair and public hearing. However, the press and the public may be excluded from all or part of the trial for reasons of morals, public order or national security in a democratic society (International Covenant on Civil and Political Rights, Article 14(1)).

- The publicity of hearings is an important safeguard in the interest of the individual and of society at large. Apart from the exceptional circumstances stated, a hearing must be generally open to the public, including the press, and must not be accessible only by certain categories of persons. Moreover, even in cases where the public is excluded, the judgment, with certain strictly defined exceptions, must be made public (UN Human Rights Committee, General Comment No. 13, para. 6).

8.8   THE RIGHT TO BE PRESENT AT TRIAL

Key ECHR cases

Barberà, Messegué and Jabardo v Spain (1988) 11 EHRR 360, ECtHR
Brozicek v Italy (1989) 12 EHRR 371, ECtHR
Colozza v Italy (1985) 7 EHRR 516, ECtHR
Ekbatani v Sweden (1988) 13 EHRR 504, ECtHR
Goddi v Italy (1984) 6 EHRR 457, ECtHR
Lala v Netherlands (1994) 18 EHRR 586, ECtHR
Pelladoah v Netherlands (1994) 19 EHRR 81, ECtHR
Poitrimol v France (1993) 18 EHRR 130, ECtHR

C v Italy (1988) 56 DR 40, ECmHR
Ensslin and others v Germany (1978) 14 DR 64, ECmHR
Geyseghem v Belgium (1999), ECmHR

ECHR principles

- As a general rule, the defendant has a right to be present at trial (*Ekbatani v Sweden*, para. 25), and adducing important evidence in the absence of the defendant will usually be unfair (*Barberà, Messegué and Jabardo v Spain*, para. 89).

- Consequently, the authorities are under a duty to notify defendants about the proceedings against them (*Goddi v Italy*).

- However, the right to be present at trial is not an absolute right. Thus defendants can be excluded where they cause disruption to the proceedings, refuse to come to court, or make themselves too ill to attend, provided that their interests are protected (e.g., because their lawyers were present) (*Ensslin and others v Germany*, paras 21–22 – *applicants unable to attend trial because of ill-health induced by hunger strike*).

- In addition, a defendant may waive his or her right to be present either expressly or impliedly by failing to attend the hearing having been given effective notice (*C v Italy*). Waiver must be clear and unequivocal (*Colozza v Italy*; *Brozicek v Italy*; *Poitrimol v France*; *Lala v Netherlands*; *Pelladoah v Netherlands*).

- There may be circumstances where an absent defendant is entitled to a rehearing when he or she subsequently emerges (*Colozza v Italy*).

- Moreover, where a defendant chooses to be absent, counsel must nonetheless be permitted to attend the trial (*Poitrimol v France*; *Geyseghem v Belgium*).

8.9   THE RIGHT TO PARTICIPATE IN THE TRIAL

Key ECHR cases

Stanford v UK (1994) A/282, ECtHR
T v UK, V v UK (1999) 30 EHRR 121, ECtHR

ECHR principles

- All defendants have a right to participate effectively in the proceedings:

    . . . Article 6, read as a whole, guarantees the right of an accused to participate effectively in a criminal trial. In general this includes, inter alia, not only his right to be present, but also to hear and follow the proceedings. (*Stanford v UK*, para. 26; *T v UK, V v UK*, para. 85)

- Particular account must be taken of factors such as a defendant's age and his or her ability to comprehend the proceedings:

    . . . it is essential that a child charged with an offence is dealt with in a manner which takes full account of his age, level of maturity and intellectual and emotional capacities, and that steps are taken to promote his ability to understand and participate effectively in the proceedings.
    It follows that, in respect of a young child charged with a grave offence attracting high levels of media and public interest, it would be necessary to conduct the hearing in such a way as to reduce as far as possible his or her feelings of intimidation and inhibition. (*T v UK, V v UK*, paras 86 and 87)

Relevant Canadian cases

R v Tran [1994] 2 SCR 951

- The right of the defendant to understand what is going on in court and to be understood is not a separate right, nor a language right, but an aspect of the right to a fair hearing (*R v Tran*).

8.10   THE RIGHT TO AN INTERPRETER AND TRANSLATION

Key ECHR cases

Brozicek v Italy (1989) 12 EHRR 371, ECtHR
Kamasinski v Austria (1989) 13 EHRR 36, ECtHR
Luedicke, Belkacem and Koç v Germany (1978) 2 EHRR 149, ECtHR
Öztürk v Germany (1984) 6 EHRR 409, ECtHR

K v France (1984) 35 DR 203, ECmHR

ECHR principles

- Article 6(3)(e), ECHR specifically provides that everyone charged with a criminal offence has the right 'to have the free assistance of an interpreter if he cannot understand or speak the language'.

- The right is not subject to qualification, even if the accused is subsequently convicted; hence a convicted person cannot be ordered to pay the costs of an interpreter (*Luedicke, Belkacem and Koç v Germany*, paras 42 and 46; *Öztürk v Germany*).

- The right to interpretation extends to all documentary material disclosed before trial, but this does not necessarily mean that all translations must be in written form; in limited circumstances, some oral translation is acceptable (*Luedicke, Belkacem and Koç v Germany*; *Kamsinski v Austria*).

- The court has an obligation to ensure the quality of interpretation:

   In view of the need for the right guaranteed by paragraph (3)(e) to be practical and effective, the obligation of the competent authorities is not limited to the appointment of an interpreter but, if they are put on notice in the particular circumstances, may also extend to a degree of subsequent control over the adequacy of the interpretation provided. (*Kamsinski v Austria*, para. 74)

- Article 6(3)(e) applies only where the defendant does not understand or speak the language used in court; it does not provide a right to conduct proceedings in the language of the defendant's choice (*K v France*, para. 8 – *applicant who understood French wanted to conduct his defence in the Breton language*).

Relevant Canadian cases

R v Tran [1994] 2 SCR 951
R v Tsang (1986) 16 WCB 341, BC CA

- Once a request for assistance with interpretation or translation has been made, it should not be refused unless there is cogent and compelling evidence that an accused's request is not made in good faith (*R v Tran; R v Tsang*).

- Given the public interest in securing the right to a fair trial, there are situations, especially in criminal cases, when the right cannot be waived, e.g., in relation to interpreters (*R v Tran*).

Relevant New Zealand cases

Alwen Industries Ltd v *Collector of Customs* [1996] 3 NZLR 226, HC

- Since the right to an interpreter is grounded in notions of fairness, there can be no justification for limiting assistance to the trial itself, nor for restricting it to oral translations only. There must be flexibility (*Alwen Industries Ltd* v *Collector of Customs*, p. 232).

- However, not all documents need to be translated in writing; oral translation of some may suffice. What is important is that the defendant understands the proceedings, is able to instruct counsel fully and prepare a defence (*Alwen Industries Ltd* v *Collector of Customs*, p. 232).

8.11   THE PRESUMPTION OF INNOCENCE

Key ECHR cases

Allenet de Ribemont v *France* (1995) 20 EHRR 557, ECtHR
Barberà, Messegué and Jabardo v *Spain* (1988) 11 EHRR 360, ECtHR
Rushiti v *Austria* (21 March 2000), ECtHR

ECHR principles

- Article 6(2), ECHR specifically provides that everyone charged with a criminal offence shall be presumed innocent until proved guilty according to law:

  > It requires, *inter alia*, that when carrying out their duties, the members of a court should not start with the preconceived idea that the accused has committed the offence charged; the burden of proof is on the prosecution, and any doubt should benefit the accused. It also follows that it is for the prosecution to inform the accused of the case that will be made against him, so that he may prepare and present his defence accordingly, and to adduce evidence sufficient to convict him. (*Barberà, Messegué and Jabardo* v *Spain*, para. 77)

- The presumption of innocence can be infringed not only by a court, but also by other public authorities, e.g., unqualified public statements by the police or prosecution which refer to an individual as the perpetrator of an offence (*Allenet de Ribemont* v *France*, para. 41).

- Where compensation proceedings are linked to criminal responsibility, statements in compensation proceedings voicing suspicions about an individual's guilt are unacceptable:

  > . . . following a final acquittal, even the voicing of suspicions regarding the accused's innocence is no longer admissible . . . once an acquittal has become final – be it an acquittal giving the accused the benefit of the doubt in accordance with Article 6(2) – the voicing of any suspicions of guilt, including those expressed in the reasons for the acquittal, is incompatible with the presumption of innocence. (*Rushiti* v *Austria*, para. 31)

- As to the burden of proof, see **9.1**.

- As to costs orders when a defendant is acquitted, see **8.20**.

8.12   PRE-TRIAL PUBLICITY

Key ECHR cases

Allenet de Ribemont v France (1995) 20 EHRR 557, ECtHR
News Verlags GmbH & CoKG v Austria (11 January 2000), ECtHR
Worm v Austria (1997) 25 EHRR 454, ECtHR

Berns and Ewert v Luxembourg (1991) 68 DR 117, ECmHR
Crociani v Italy (1980) 22 DR 147, ECmHR
Ensslin and others v Germany (1978) 14 DR 64, ECmHR
Hodgson, Woolf Productions and the NUJ v UK (1987) 10 EHRR 503, ECmHR

ECHR principles

- Since pre-trial publicity can prejudice a defendant's prospects of a fair trial, it
  can be restricted without necessarily breaching Article 10, ECHR:

    > . . . the need to ensure a fair trial and to protect members of the jury from exposure
    > to prejudicial influences corresponds to a pressing social need . . . where there is a real
    > risk of prejudice the appropriate response . . . is one which must lie, in principle, with
    > the person responsible for ensuring the fairness of the trial, namely, the trial judge.
    > (*Hodgson, Woolf Productions and the NUJ v UK*, p. 509)

    > . . . the limits of permissible comment on pending criminal proceedings may not
    > extend to statements which are likely to prejudice, whether intentionally or not, the
    > chances of a person receiving a fair trial or to undermine the confidence of the public
    > in the role of the courts in the administration of justice. (*News Verlags GmbH &
    > CoKG v Austria*, para. 56)

- But prejudice will be harder to establish in a case tried by a judge than in a case
  tried by a jury (*Crociani v Italy*, para. 20; see also *Ensslin and others v Germany*,
  para. 15).

- And a proper balance between fair trial and press freedom must be maintained:

    > There is a general recognition of the fact that the courts cannot operate in a vacuum.
    > Whilst the courts are the forum for the determination of a person's guilt or innocence
    > on a criminal charge, this does not mean that there can be no prior or contempor-
    > aneous discussion of the subject-matter of criminal trials elsewhere, be it in specialised
    > journals, in the general press or amongst the public at large.
    >   Provided that it does not overstep the bounds imposed in the interests of the proper
    > administration of justice, reporting, including comment, on court proceedings contrib-
    > utes to their publicity and is thus perfectly consonant with the requirement under
    > Article 6(1) of the Convention that hearings be public. Not only do the media have
    > the task of imparting such information and ideas; the public has a right to hear them.
    > (*Worm v Austria*, para. 50)

- While there may be good reasons for prohibiting the publication of a suspect's
  picture, a blanket ban is likely to be disproportionate, especially where the real
  complaint is about the photograph coupled with accompanying text (*News
  Verlags GmbH & CoKG v Austria*, para. 59).

- As to public statements by the police and/or prosecution, see **8.11**.

Relevant Canadian cases

Phillips v NS (Weston Mine Inquiry) [1995] 2 SCR 97
R v Sherratt [1991] 1 SCR 509

- The test for prejudice resulting from pre-trial publicity is whether there is a realistic *potential* for partiality (*R v Sherratt*).

- There may be circumstances where publicity surrounding public inquiries so prejudices the prospects of a fair trial that a decision should be made whether to proceed:

    In some circumstances proceeding with the public inquiry may so jeopardize the criminal trial of a witness called at the inquiry that it may be stayed or result in important evidence being held inadmissible at the criminal trial. In those situations it is the executive branch of government which should make the decision whether to proceed with the public inquiry. That decision should not, except in rare circumstances, be set aside by a court. (*Phillips v NS (Weston Mine Inquiry)*)

8.13   EQUALITY OF ARMS

Key ECHR cases

Borgers v Belgium (1991) 15 EHRR 92, ECtHR
Delcourt v Belgium (1969) 1 EHRR 355, ECtHR
Neumeister v Austria (1968) 1 EHRR 91, ECtHR

Kaufman v Belgium (1986) 50 DR 98, ECmHR

ECHR principles

- The principle that there should be equality of arms between the parties before the court is fundamental to the notion of a fair trial under Article 6, ECHR:

    . . . [The Commission] recalls that it has repeatedly held that the right to a fair hearing, in both civil and criminal proceedings, entails that everyone who is a party to such proceedings shall have a reasonable opportunity of presenting his case to the court under conditions which do not place him at substantial disadvantage *vis-à-vis* his opponent . . . (*Kaufman v Belgium*, p. 115)

- In particular, each party must know the case being made against him or her, have an effective opportunity to challenge it and an effective opportunity to advance his or her own case.

Relevant Scottish cases

Bullock v Her Majesty's Advocate (5 May 1999), HC

- Where a defendant is unrepresented, the court is under a duty to ensure that the prosecution do not gain any unfair advantage:

While it is no part of the [judge's] function to act as defence counsel, he must ensure not merely that an unrepresented accused is given every opportunity, within reasonable limits, to bring out any points which he wishes to make, particularly in cross-examination, but also that no advantage is taken by the prosecutor, whether deliberately or unintentionally, of the fact that the accused is unrepresented. (*Bullock v Her Majesty's Advocate* p. 13 – *failure to assist accused with technical difficulties related to playing of transcripts and leading evidence*)

Relevant New Zealand cases

R v Accused (1994) 12 CRNZ 417
R v B [1995] 2 NZLR 172, CA
R v Donaldson [1995] 3 NZLR 641
Samleung International Trading Co. Ltd v Collector of Customs [1994] 3 NZLR 285, HC

- In some circumstances, the authorities are under a duty to assist the defence to obtain evidence from other jurisdictions; failure to do so may breach the principle that there be equality of arms between the parties (*Samleung International Trading Co. Ltd v Collector of Customs*, p. 291 – *request for taking of evidence from witnesses in Hong Kong*).

- Where the police or prosecution obstruct the defence, the principle of equality of arms may be breached (*R v Donaldson* – *police refused to administer blood test during defendant's detention, which could have been vital for her defence*).

- This may even extend to cases where the defence want to have prosecution witnesses medically examined (*R v Accused; R v B*, p. 177).

Relevant South African cases

Shabala v AG (29 November 1995), CC

- A blanket prohibition on defence access to prosecution witnesses before trial may breach the principle of equality of arms:

  In many cases [such preclusion] would not [amount to a fair trial violation] because the accused or his or her legal representative would have a full opportunity of canvassing with the witness during cross-examination relevant material which he or she would otherwise have wanted to canvass in consultation. But there may be circumstances where the right to a fair trial might justify a prior consultation with a State witness. An accused might wish to canvass with the witness the identity or whereabouts of some person vital to his or her alibi and there may be a real risk that the evidence would be lost if the witness is not immediately traced.
    The relevant issue is not whether or not such consultations would ordinarily be justified in order to ensure a fair trial but whether it could legitimately be said that such consultations can never be justified. If it cannot be said that such consultations are never justified, the blanket prohibition against the right of an accused to consult State witnesses (without the consent of the prosecution), regardless of the circumstances or the conditions, might indeed bear unfairly on the accused. (*Shabala v AG*, paras 63 and 64)

8.14   LEGAL REPRESENTATION

Key ECHR cases

Artico v Italy (1980) 3 EHRR 1, ECtHR
Croissant v Germany (1992) 16 EHRR 135, ECtHR
Goddi v Italy (1984) 6 EHRR 457, ECtHR
Kamasinski v Austria (1989) 13 EHRR 36, ECtHR
Lala v Netherlands (1994) 18 EHRR 586, ECtHR
Poitrimol v France (1993) 18 EHRR 130, ECtHR

App. No. 9728/82 (1983) 6 EHRR 345, ECmHR
Baegen v Netherlands (1995) A/327-B, ECmHR
Ensslin and others v Germany (1978) 14 DR 64, ECmHR
F v Switzerland (1989) 61 DR 171, ECmHR[CD]
Philis v Greece (1990) 66 DR 260, ECmHR
X v UK (1980) 21 DR 126, ECmHR

ECHR principles

- Article 6(3)(c), ECHR specifically provides that everyone charged with a criminal offence has the right to 'defend himself in person or through legal assistance of his own choosing or, if he has not sufficient means to pay for legal assistance, to be given it free when the interests of justice so require'.

- It must be interpreted so as to ensure that the right to representation is practical and effective:

  > Everyone charged with a criminal offence has the right to be defended by counsel. For this right to be practical and effective, and not merely theoretical, its exercise should not be made dependent on the fulfilment of unduly formalistic conditions: it is for the courts to ensure that a trial is fair and, accordingly, that counsel who attends trial for the apparent purpose of defending the accused in his absence, is given the opportunity to do so. (*Lala v Netherlands*, para. 34)

- Merely allocating a lawyer to the defendant is not enough if that lawyer is manifestly unable to provide effective representation:

  > . . . [Article 6(3)(c)] guarantees the right to an adequate defence either in person or through a lawyer, this right being reinforced by an obligation on the part of the State to provide free legal assistance in certain cases.
  >
  > Article 6(3) speaks of 'assistance' and not of 'nomination' . . . [M]ere nomination does not ensure effective assistance, since the lawyer appointed for legal aid purposes may die, fall seriously ill, be prevented for a protracted period from acting or shirk his duties. If they are notified of the situation, the authorities must either replace him or cause him to fulfil his obligations.
  >
  > Admittedly, a State cannot be held responsible for every shortcoming on the part of a lawyer appointed for legal aid purposes, but, in the particular circumstances, it was for the . . . authorities to take steps to ensure that the applicant enjoyed effectively the right to which they had recognised he was entitled. (*Artico v Italy*, paras 33 and 36 – *applicant's nominated legal aid lawyer refused to represent him on appeal against a fraud conviction and he was unable to secure the services of another lawyer; see also Kamasinski v Austria, para. 65; F v Switzerland*)

- However, the state will not be responsible for every failing of an appointed lawyer, since the conduct of a defence is essentially a matter between a client and his legal representative:

  It follows from the independence of the legal profession of the State that the conduct of the defence is essentially a matter between the defendant and his counsel, whether counsel be appointed under a legal aid scheme or be privately financed . . . the competent authorities are required under Article 6(3)(c) to intervene only if a failure by legal aid counsel to provide effective representation is manifest or sufficiently brought to their attention in some other way. (*Kamasinski v Austria*, para. 65 – *inadequate legal representation in foreign country*; *F v UK – new counsel on first day of trial*)

- Action should be taken (e.g., adjourning the case) where it is clear that an appointed lawyer has not been given sufficient time and facilities to prepare for the case:

  . . . the Court [has] to determine whether the Court . . . took steps to ensure that the accused had the benefit of a fair trial, including an opportunity for an adequate defence. [The officially appointed lawyer] did not have the time and facilities he would have needed to study the case file, prepare his pleadings and, if appropriate, consult his client. Short of notifying [the applicant's own lawyer] of the date of the hearing, the Court . . . should – whilst respecting the basic principle of the independence of the Bar – at least have taken measures, of a positive nature, calculated to permit the officially appointed lawyer to fulfil his obligations in the best possible conditions. It could have adjourned the hearing, as the public prosecutor's office requested, or it could have directed on its own initiative that the sitting be suspended for a sufficient period of time.

  No inference can be drawn from the fact that [the officially appointed lawyer] himself made no such request. The exceptional circumstances of the case required the Court . . . not to remain passive. (*Goddi v Italy*, para. 31; see also *F v Switzerland*, p. 175 – *pupil advocate attached to the practice of the defendant's lawyer appointed as legal aid counsel*)

- However, the right to be legally represented does not give an accused an absolute right to determine how his defence will be conducted:

  . . . an accused person cannot require counsel to disregard basic principles of his professional duty in the presentation of his defence. If such an insistence results in the accused having to conduct his own defence, any consequent 'inequality of arms' can only be attributable to his own behaviour. (*X v UK*, para. 6)

- In legal aid cases, defendants do not have an unqualified right to counsel of their choosing:

  [Article 6(3)(c)] is necessarily subject to certain limitations where free legal aid is concerned and also where . . . it is for the courts to decide whether the interests of justice require that the accused be defended by counsel appointed by them. When appointing defence counsel the national courts must certainly have regard to the defendant's wishes . . . However, they can override those wishes when there are relevant and sufficient grounds for holding that this is necessary in the interests of justice. (*Croissant v Germany*, para. 29)

- In addition, a rule requiring a defendant to be represented by a lawyer where sexual offences are alleged will not necessarily breach Article 6(3)(c):

  . . . proceedings [in cases of rape and other sexual offences] are often conceived of as an ordeal by the victim, in particular when the latter is unwillingly confronted with the defendant. In the assessment of the question whether or not in such proceedings an accused received a fair trial, account must be taken of the right to respect for the victim's private life. Therefore, the Commission accepts that in criminal proceedings concerning sexual abuse certain measures may be taken for the purpose of protecting the victim, provided that such measures can be reconciled with an adequate and effective exercise of the rights of the defence. (*Baegen v Netherlands*, para. 77)

- The regulation of the legal profession and the need for lawyers to adhere to ethical principles may also limit the right to representation where such rules require the exclusion of a particular lawyer from participation in the case:

  Refusal to accept, or the exclusion of, a defence is a . . . difficult question, both in its principle and its effects. It is a measure which may intimidate other potential defence counsel or cast discredit on the defence in general; further, a succession of defence lawyers may be damaging to the presentation of the case and introduce greater uncertainty into the barrister's role as 'the watchdog of procedural regularity'. However . . . the right to defend one's case with the assistance of defence counsel of one's choice . . . is not an absolute right: it is limited by the State's right to make the appearance of barristers before the courts subject to regulations and the obligation on defence counsel not to transgress certain principles of professional ethics. (*Ensslin and others v Germany*, para. 20 – *defence lawyers prevented from defending applicants because they were themselves heavily implicated in criminal association of the applicants and subject to criminal proceedings*)

- As to legal aid, see **8.4**.

Other international human rights standards

- In the determination of any criminal charge against a person, he or she is guaranteed the right to legal assistance and to be informed of this right and to be assigned legal assistance in any case where the interests of justice so require, and without payment if he or she does not have sufficient means to pay for it (International Covenant on Civil and Political Rights, Article 14(3)(d)).

Relevant Scottish cases

Bullock v Her Majesty's Advocate (5 May 1999), HC
Venters v Her Majesty's Advocate (28 April 1999), HC

- Where an unrepresented defendant changes his or her mind during a trial about having legal representation, his or her application should not be dismissed out of hand but considered in the light of all the circumstances (*Bullock v Her Majesty's Advocate*, p. 12).

- A defendant in conflict with his or her lawyer should be given sufficient opportunity to brief another lawyer, not forced to proceed unrepresented (*Venters v Her Majesty's Advocate*, p. 6).

Relevant New Zealand cases

R v Shaw [1992] 1 NZLR 652, CA

- Expedition of court business is not a good reason for restricting legal representation (*R v Shaw*, pp. 653–4 – *defendant forced to conduct own defence after withdrawal of lawyer due to clash of trial dates*).

8.15   THE RIGHT TO AN ADVERSARIAL HEARING

Key ECHR cases

Krcmar v Czech Republic (3 March 2000), ECtHR
Ruiz-Mateos v Spain (1993) 16 EHRR 505, ECtHR
Van Orshoven v Belgium (1997) 26 EHRR 55, ECtHR

ECHR principles

- All evidence and submissions should be made in the presence of the defendant and in circumstances in which he or she has an opportunity to comment upon them:

   The right to an adversarial trial means the opportunity for the parties to have knowledge of and comment on the observations filed or evidence adduced by the other party. (*Ruiz-Mateos v Spain*, para. 63; see also *Krcmar v Czech Republic*, para. 40)

- This applies even where submissions are made by an independent party – such as an *amicus* lawyer – and are wholly objective:

   Although it is objective and reasoned in law, the opinion [of the *procureur général*] is nevertheless intended to advise and accordingly influence [the court] . . . the fact that it was impossible for the applicant to reply to [the *procureur général's* submissions] before the end of the hearing infringed his right to adversarial proceedings. (*Van Orshoven v Belgium*, paras 39–42)

8.16   REASONS

Key ECHR cases

De Moor v Belgium (1994) 18 EHRR 372, ECtHR
Hadjianastassiou v Greece (1992) 16 EHRR 219, ECtHR
Helle v Finland (1997) 26 EHRR 159, ECtHR
Hiro Balani v Spain (1994) 19 EHRR 566, ECtHR
Ruiz Torija v Spain (1994) 19 EHRR 553, ECtHR
Van de Hurk v Netherlands (1994) 18 EHRR 481, ECtHR

Saric v Denmark (2 February 1999), ECmHR

ECHR principles

- Article 6(1), ECHR obliges domestic courts to give reasons for the judgments:

   The Court reiterates that Article 6(1) obliges the courts to give reasons for their judgments, but cannot be understood as requiring a detailed answer to every argument. The extent to which this duty to give reasons applies may vary according to the nature of the decision. It is moreover necessary to take account, *inter alia*, of the diversity of the submissions that a litigant may bring before the courts and the differences existing in the Contracting States with regard to statutory provisions, customary rules, legal opinion and the presentation and drafting of judgments. That is why the question whether a court has failed to fulfil the obligation to state reasons, derived from Article 6 of the Convention, can only be determined in the light of the circumstances of the case. (*Hiro Balani v Spain*, para. 27)

The national courts must . . . indicate with sufficient clarity the grounds on which they based their decision. It is this, *inter alia*, which makes it possible for the accused to exercise usefully the rights of appeal available to him. (*Hadjianastassiou v Greece*, para. 33)

- But reasons are not needed in jury cases (*Saric v Denmark*).

Relevant domestic law

Stefan v General Medical Council [1999] 1 WLR 1293

- Article 6(1) may require a reappraisal of the duty to give reasons at common law:

  The provisions of Article 6(1) of the Convention on Human Rights . . . will require closer attention to be paid to the duty to give reasons, at least in relation to those cases where a person's civil rights and obligations are being determined (*Stefan v General Medical Council, per* Lord Clyde, p. 1299)

8.17   TRIAL WITHIN A REASONABLE PERIOD

Key ECHR cases

B v Austria (1990) 13 EHRR 20, ECtHR
Corigliano v Italy (1982) 5 EHRR 334, ECtHR
Eckle v Germany (1982) 5 EHRR 1, ECtHR
Foti v Italy (1982) 5 EHRR 313, ECtHR
Girolami v Italy (1991) A/196E, ECtHR
König v Germany (1978) 2 EHRR 170, ECtHR
Ledonne (No. 1) v Italy (12 May 1999), ECtHR
Ledonne (No. 2) v Italy (12 May 1999), ECtHR
Majaric v Slovenia (8 February 2000), ECtHR

Ewing v UK (1988) 10 EHRR 141, ECmHR[CD]
Orchin v UK (1981) 6 EHRR 391, ECmHR
X v UK (1979) 14 DR 26, ECmHR
X v UK (1980) 17 DR 122, ECmHR

ECHR principles

- The right to trial within a reasonable period is guaranteed under Article 5(3), ECHR for those in pre-trial detention, and more generally for anyone facing criminal proceedings under Article 6(1), ECHR.

- Since it is primarily concerned with those in pre-trial detention, the standards under Article 5(3) are more exacting than those under Article 6(1) (*Abdoella v Netherlands* (1995) 20 EHRR 585).

- Time begins to run under Article 5(3) and Article 6(1) when an individual is 'charged'. This may stretch back to arrest, rather than formal charge (*Eckle v Germany*, para. 73; *Ewing v UK*, p.143).

- Time ends for Article 5(3) purposes with the finding of guilt or innocence (*B v Austria*); time ends for Article 6(1) purposes when the proceedings are over, including any appeal.

- Neither the court nor the prosecution are responsible for delays attributable to the applicant or his or her lawyers (*Konig v Germany*).

- However, a defendant is perfectly entitled to take legitimate points, if necessary, by way of appeal:

  . . . Article 6 does not require accused persons actively to cooperate with the judicial authorities. Neither can any reproach be levelled against them for making full use of the remedies available under domestic law. Nonetheless, such conduct constitutes an objective fact, not capable of being attributed to the respondent state, which is to be taken into account when determining whether or not proceedings exceeded a reasonable time. (*Ledonne (No. 1) v Italy*, para. 25 – *applicant twice sought adjournment and twice challenged validity of summons issued against him. However, prosecuting authorities could not provide good reason for two periods of delay (18 months and 16 months) totalling two years and ten months, and on that basis breach of Article 6(1) found*)

- Periods spent at large are discounted (*Girolami v Italy*).

- The workload of the court is not a good reason for delay (and in any event should be supported with evidence of steps taken to alleviate the position (*Majaric v Slovenia*, para. 39)) neither is a shortage of resources. Article 6(1) imposes on Contracting States the duty to organise their judicial systems in such a way that their courts can meet the requirement to hear a case within a reasonable time (*Ledonne (No. 2) v Italy*, para. 23).

- Although the authorities cannot be held responsible for delay caused by a lawyers' strike, their efforts to reduce any resultant delays will affect the overall question of trial within a reasonable period (*Ledonne (No. 2) v Italy*).

- In a straightforward case, a period of inactivity of one year is unduly long (*Ledonne (No. 2) v Italy*).

Relevant Scottish cases

Caroline McNab v Her Majesty's Advocate (2 September 1999), AC
Crummock (Scotland) Ltd v Her Majesty's Advocate (16 March 2000), AC
Frank Docherty v Her Majesty's Advocate (14 January 2000), AC
Her Majesty's Advocate v James Hynd (9 May 2000), HC
Her Majesty's Advocate v William Maxwell Little (17 June 1999), HC

- The longer the period between charge and trial, the greater the likelihood that the presumption that the accused is innocent will be undermined:

  The introduction of [a right to trial within a reasonable time] must be welcomed by those interested in the rights of persons who face serious criminal charges in a society which prides itself in the presumption of innocence as a fundamental element of criminal trial procedure. (*Her Majesty's Advocate v James Hynd*, p. 2)

- It is not necessary for a defendant to show prejudice before he or she can rely upon the right under the ECHR to trial within a reasonable period (*Caroline*

McNab v Her Majesty's Advocate, p. 4; see also *Her Majesty's Advocate v William Maxwell Little*, p. 10).

- Since bodies such as the social services have no power to initiate criminal investigations, any period of initial investigations by them should not be included in the time to be taken into account between charge and trial (*Gordon McLean v Her Majesty's Advocate*, p. 4 – *attempted murder of child first brought to attention of social services*).

Relevant Canadian cases

R v Gardiner [1982] 2 SCR 368
R v Macdougall [1998] 3 SCR 45
R v Morin [1992] 1 SCR 771
R v Sander (1995) 7 BCLR (3d) 189, CA

- Any delay attributable to the state which results from an inadequate investigation of the facts or a mistaken view of the law may be unreasonable even where the authorities acted in good faith (*R v Sander*).

- As a result, there is always an onus on the prosecution to provide timely disclosure (*R v Morin*).

- The right to be tried within a reasonable time extends to sentence:

  Crime and punishment are inextricably linked. It would appear well established that the sentencing process is merely a phase of the trial process. Upon conviction the accused is not abruptly deprived of all procedural rights existing at trial: he has a right to counsel, a right to call evidence and cross-examine prosecution witnesses, a right to give evidence himself and to address the court . . . (*R v Gardiner*, p. 415)

  . . . Anxiety about the eventual punishment pending sentencing is normal and unavoidable. But when sentencing is unduly delayed, this anxiety may be suffered for a longer period of time than justified . . .
  Evidence is important in sentencing proceedings. The convicted person may wish to call character witnesses or expert witnesses. The passage of time may adversely affect the ability to do so. (*R v Macdougall*, paras 33–35)

Relevant New Zealand cases

Martin v Tauranga District Court [1995] 1 NZLR 491, HC

- Where delay extends beyond the period within which most cases are disposed of, the burden is on the prosecution to justify the delay and show, on the balance of probabilities, that it is not undue delay (*Martin v Tauranga District Court*, p. 506).

- Prejudice by reason of delay is not just measured in terms of the fairness of the trial itself: it includes anxiety about the pending proceedings and damage to reputation (*Martin v Tauranga District Court*).

Relevant South African cases

Sanderson v AG (Eastern Cape) (2 December 1997), CC

- The more serious the prejudice that a defendant may suffer – e.g., pre-trial detention, restrictive bail conditions, trial prejudice, and even anxiety – the shorter should be the period before trial (*Sanderson v AG*, para. 31).

- Systematic delay – e.g., because of resource constraints or court congestion – may be more excusable than individual failing, but:

   [T]here must come a time when systematic causes can no longer be regarded as exculpatory. The bill of rights is not a set of (aspirational) directive principles of state policy – it is intended that the state should make whatever arrangements are necessary to avoid rights violations . . . Even if one does accept that systematic factors justify delay, as one must at the present, they can only do so for a certain period of time. (*Sanderson v AG*, para. 35)

- And there must always be proportionality between the maximum sentence and the length of pre-trial detention (*Sanderson v AG*, para. 34).

8.18   RETROACTIVE OFFENCES

Key ECHR cases

SW and CR v UK (1995) 21 EHRR 363, ECtHR

X Ltd and Y v UK (1982) 28 DR 77, ECmHR

ECHR principles

- Article 7, ECHR protects individuals from being convicted of criminal offences which did not exist at the time the act was committed, and prohibits the imposition of a more severe penalty for an offence than that which applied at the time the offence was committed.

- It prohibits not only the creation of retroactive offences by legislation, but also the retroactive application of existing criminal offences through the development of the common law (*X Ltd and Y v UK*; *SW and CR v UK*).

- The War Crimes Act 1991, which gives courts retroactive jurisdiction in relation to a number of offences committed in Germany or a place under German occupation during the Second World War, is protected from challenge under Article 7(1) by the qualification in Article 7(2):

   This Article shall not prejudice the trial and punishment of any person for any act or omission which, at the time when it was committed, was criminal according to the general principles of law recognised by civilised nations.

8.19   DOUBLE JEOPARDY

Key ECHR cases

S v Germany (1983) 39 DR 43, ECmHR
X v Austria (1970) 35 EHRR CD 151, ECmHR

ECHR principles

- Double jeopardy is dealt with in Protocol 7 of the ECHR. The UK has not ratified this yet.

- Limited protection from double jeopardy may also be provided for under Article 6, ECHR (*X v Austria*; *S v Germany*).

8.20   COSTS

Key ECHR cases

Lutz v Germany (1987) 10 EHRR 182, ECtHR
Minelli v Switzerland (1983) 5 EHRR 554, ECtHR
Sekanina v Austria (1993) 17 EHRR 221, ECtHR

Byrne v UK [1998] EHRLR 628, ECmHR[CD]
X and Y v Austria (1979) 15 DR 160, ECmHR

ECHR principles

- There is no right to costs for a defendant under the ECHR:

  . . . neither Article 6(2) nor any other provision of the Convention gives a person 'charged with a criminal offence' a right to reimbursement of his costs where proceedings against him are discontinued. The refusal to reimburse [the applicant] for his necessary costs and expenses accordingly does not in itself offend the presumption of innocence. (*Lutz v Germany*, para. 59 – *court refused to reimburse costs after proceedings against applicant for road traffic offences were discontinued*)

- However, where the court has a discretion to order costs, it must respect the presumption of innocence:

  . . . the presumption of innocence will be violated if, without the accused's having previously been proved guilty according to law and, notably, without his having had the opportunity of exercising his rights of defence, a judicial decision concerning him reflects an opinion that he is guilty. This may be so even in the absence of any formal finding; it suffices that there is some reasoning suggesting that the court regards the accused as guilty. (*Minelli v Switzerland*, para. 37)

  The voicing of suspicions regarding an accused's innocence is conceivable as long as the conclusion of criminal proceedings has not resulted in a decision on the merits of the accusation. However, it is no longer admissible to rely on such suspicions once an acquittal has become final. (*Sekanina v Austria*, para. 30 – *despite acquittal for wife's murder defendant was denied reimbursement of costs and compensation on basis that there was still considerable suspicion that he was guilty*)

- The presumption of innocence will not necessarily be infringed where costs are not awarded where, by not disclosing her defence, the defendant prolonged the proceedings against her (*Byrne v UK*).

- Costs ordered against a lawyer are 'contributions' within the meaning of Protocol 1, Article 1 (the right to property) (*X and Y v Austria*, para. 4).

SECTION 9

EVIDENCE

9.1 THE BURDEN OF PROOF

Key ECHR cases

Barberà, Messegué and Jabardo v Spain (1988) 11 EHRR 360, ECtHR
Salabiaku v France (1988) 13 EHRR 379, ECtHR

Austria v Italy (1963) 6 Yearbook 740, ECmHR
Lingens v Austria (1981) 26 DR 171, ECmHR

ECHR principles

- As a general rule the presumption of innocence imposes the burden of proving guilt on the prosecution:

  [Article 6(2)] embodies the principle of the presumption of innocence. It requires, *inter alia*, that when carrying out their duties, the members of a court should not start with the preconceived idea that the accused has committed the offence charged; the burden of proof is on the prosecution . . .' (*Barberà, Messegué and Jabardo v Spain*, para. 77; see also *Austria v Italy*, p. 782)

- However, where the prosecution has proved an offence, the burden of avoiding criminal liability can, within reasonable limits, pass to the defendant:

  [Shifting the burden of proof to the defence as regards the truth of the statement] in no way means that the accused has to prove his innocence because he can only be considered as innocent if he has not committed the offence. The offence as conceived in the applicable provisions of the Penal Code . . . can even be committed by a true statement: What exculpates is not the objective truth of a defamatory statement, but the ability to prove its truth. In this way the law intends to compel the author of such statements to make sure in advance that what is being said can also be proven as true . . . (*Lingens v Austria*, para. 4 – *criminal prosecution of journalists for writing a defamatory article about a senior politician – burden on accused to prove truth of statement for successful defence*)

- Equally, not all presumptions of law and/or fact will offend the presumption of innocence: the question is whether such presumptions remain within reasonable limits:

  Presumptions of fact or of law operate in every legal system. Clearly, the Convention does not prohibit such presumptions in principle. It does, however, require . . . States to remain within certain limits . . .

Article 6(2) does not . . . regard presumptions of fact or of law provided for in the criminal law with indifference. It requires States to confine them within reasonable limits which take into account the importance of what is at stake and maintain the rights of the defence. (*Salabiaku v France*, para. 28)

Relevant domestic cases

R v Lambert (5 September 2000)

- Presumptions relating to the defence of diminished responsibility in murder cases and knowledge in drugs cases do not necessarily breach Article 6 (*R v Lambert*).

Relevant Canadian cases

Mills v The Queen [1986] 21 CRR 76
Oakes v The Queen [1986] 1 SCR 103
R v Arp [1998] 3 SCR 339
R v Audet [1996] 2 SCR 171
R v Chaplin [1995] 1 SCR 727
R v Daviault [1994] 3 SCR 63
R v Downey [1992] 2 SCR 10
R v Ellis-Don [1992] 1 SCR 840
R v Laba [1994] 3 SCR 965
R v Martin [1992] 1 SCR 838
R v Osolin [1993] 4 SCR 595
R v Richard [1996] 3 SCR 525
R v Robinson [1996] 1 SCR 683
R v Rose [1998] 3 SCR 328
R v Wholesale Travel Group Inc. [1991] 3 SCR 154
R v Whyte [1988] 2 SCR 3

- Any person charged with an offence has the right to be presumed innocent until proven guilty according to law in a fair and public hearing by an independent and impartial tribunal (Charter, section 11(d)).

- The presumption of innocence comprises elements all of which must be satisfied to fulfil the purpose of the presumption:

   (a) the state must bear the burden of proof;
   (b) proof must be proved beyond a reasonable doubt;
   (c) prosecutions must accord with lawful procedures and fairness (*Oakes v Queen*).

- In relation to the burden, where proof of one fact automatically requires a judge to presume another fact and the presumed fact does *not* inexorably flow from proof of the first fact, the presumption of innocence can be violated (*R v Downey*; *R v Audet*) unless reasonable justification can be established.

- Reasonable justification can be established where the accused only needs to rebut the presumed fact by raising a reasonable doubt about it. It is much more difficult to establish where a persuasive burden is imposed on the accused to rebut the presumed fact (*R v Downey*; *R v Laba*; *Oakes v The Queen*; *R v Whyte*).

- But there is no automatic breach of the presumption of innocence where an accused is merely required to raise sufficient evidence to justify leaving a defence to a jury (*R v Osolin*).

Relevant South African cases

S v Bhulwan a [1995] 2 SACR 748, CC
S v Coetzee (6 March 1997), CC
S v Mbatha [1996] 2 SA 464, CC
S v Mello and Botolo (28 May 1998), CC
S v Ntsele [1997] 2 SACR 740, CC

- The presumption of innocence is a fundamental element of the right to a fair trial which should not be tampered with lightly (*S v Mello and Botolo* – *drugs found in immediate vicinity of accused created presumption that he was in possession of drugs which he had to rebut*; see also *S v Bhulwana* – *where in possession of quantity of drugs, presumed that dealing*).

- Presumptions which expose a defendant to a real risk of conviction despite the existence of a reasonable doubt about guilt are inconsistent with the fundamental values underpinning the criminal legal system (*S v Coetzee*, para. 14).

- To justify reversing the burden it must first be clearly demonstrated that it furthers a specific and legitimate law enforcement aim:

    Although the need to suppress illicit drug trafficking is an urgent and pressing one, it is not clear how, if at all, the presumption furthers such an objective. In addition, there appears to be no logical connection between the fact proved (possession) and the fact presumed (dealing). (*S v Bhulwana*, para. 24)

- And even where a specific and legitimate aim can be established, the reversal of the onus of proof must be proportionate (*S v Bhulwana*, para. 24).

9.2   STRICT LIABILITY OFFENCES

Key ECHR cases

Salabiaku v France (1988) 13 EHRR 379, ECtHR

ECHR principles

- Strict liability offences do not necessarily breach Article 6, but should be kept within reasonable limits:

    . . . Contracting states may, under certain conditions, penalise a simple or objective fact as such, irrespective of whether it results from criminal intent or from negligence. (*Salabiaku v France*, para. 27)

- But strict liability offences for conduct protected by Articles 8 to 11 would be hard to justify as necessary and proportionate.

Relevant Canadian cases

R v Audet [1996] 2 SCR 171
R v Ellis-Don [1992] 1 SCR 840
R v Martin [1992] 1 SCR 838
R v Wholesale Travel Group Inc. [1991] 3 SCR 154

- Strict liability offences can only be justified where there is no risk of imprisonment (*R v Wholesale Travel Group Inc.*).

- In addition, other limitations apply (*R v Wholesale Travel Group Inc.*; *R v Martin*; *R v Ellis-Don*).

9.3   THE STANDARD OF PROOF

Key ECHR cases

Barberà, Messegué and Jabardo v Spain (1988) 11 EHRR 360, ECtHR

Austria v Italy (1963) 6 Yearbook 740, ECmHR
Goodman International and Goodman v Ireland (1993) 16 EHRR CD 26, ECmHR[CD]

ECHR principles

- Any doubt in criminal cases must be resolved in favour of the accused (*Austria v Italy*, p. 784; *Barberà, Messegué and Jabardo v Spain*, para. 77).

Other international human rights standards

- Everyone charged with a criminal offence shall have the right to be presumed innocent until proved guilty according to law (International Covenant on Civil and Political Rights, Article 14(2)).

- The presumption of innocence entails that the burden of proving the charge is on the prosecution and the accused has the benefit of doubt. No guilt can be presumed until the charge has been proved beyond reasonable doubt (UN Human Rights Committee, General Comment No. 13, para. 7).

9.4   THE RIGHT TO CALL AND EXAMINE WITNESSES

Key ECHR cases

Barberà, Messegué and Jabardo v Spain (1988) 11 EHRR 360, ECtHR
Krcmar v Czech Republic (3 March 2000), ECtHR

Kaufman v Belgium (1986) 50 DR 98, ECmHR

ECHR principles

- Article 6(3)(d), ECHR specifically provides that everyone charged with a criminal offence has the right 'to examine or have examined witnesses against him and to obtain the attendance and examination of witnesses on his behalf under the same conditions as witnesses against him'.

- This rule has not been applied inflexibly and there are certain circumstances in which hearsay evidence is permitted under the ECHR (see **9.5**).

- Nonetheless, Article 6(3)(d) does embody the principle that there should be equality of arms between the parties before the court:

    . . . [The Commission] recalls that it has repeatedly held that the right to a fair hearing, in both civil and criminal proceedings, entails that everyone who is a party to such proceedings shall have a reasonable opportunity of presenting his case to the court under conditions which do not place him at substantial disadvantage *vis-à-vis* his opponent . . . (*Kaufman v Belgium*, p. 115)

- And this includes the right to advance and to challenge evidence:

    . . . the concept of a fair hearing also implies the right to adversarial proceedings, according to which the parties must have the opportunity not only to make known any evidence needed for their claims to succeed, but also to have knowledge of, and comment on, all evidence adduced or observations filed, with a view to influencing the courts' decision . . . (*Krcmar v Czech Republic*, para. 40)

- In addition, Article 6 requires positive steps to be taken to ensure that the defendant can confront and call witnesses (*Barberà, Messegué and Jabardo v Spain*, para. 78).

9.5   HEARSAY EVIDENCE

9.5.1   *General principles*

Key ECHR cases

Artner v Austria (1991) A/242-A, ECtHR
Asch v Austria (1991) 15 EHRR 597, ECtHR
Barberà, Messegué and Jabardo v Spain (1988) 11 EHRR 360, ECtHR
Bricmont v Belgium (1989) 12 EHRR 217, ECtHR
Delta v France (1990) 16 EHRR 574, ECtHR
Isgrò v Italy (19 February 1991), ECtHR
Kostovski v Netherlands (1989) 12 EHRR 434, ECtHR
Lüdi v Switzerland (1992) 15 EHRR 173, ECtHR
Saïdi v France (1993) 17 EHRR 251, ECtHR
Unterpertinger v Austria (1986) 13 EHRR 175, ECtHR
Van Mechelen and others v Netherlands (1997) 25 EHRR 647, ECtHR
Windisch v Austria (1990) 13 EHRR 281, ECtHR

Blastland v UK (1987) 52 DR 273 (App. No. 12045/86), ECmHR
Trivedi v UK (1997) 89A DR 136, ECmHR[CD]

ECHR principles

- As a general rule, all the evidence should be produced in the presence of the accused at a public hearing.

- However, there are exceptions and reliance on hearsay evidence does not necessarily breach the ECHR, e.g., where there is some opportunity to challenge the evidence at an earlier committal hearing (*Kostovski v Netherlands*, para. 41; *Trivedi v UK*).

- But hearsay evidence must be kept within strict limits:

  > Having regard to the place that the right to a fair administration of justice holds in a democratic society, any measures restricting the rights of the defence should be strictly necessary. If a less restrictive measure can suffice then that measure should be applied. (*Van Mechelen and others v Netherlands*, para. 59)

- The question in each case is whether there has been overall fairness (*Unterpertinger v Austria*; *Kostovski v Netherlands*; *Windisch v Austria*; *Lüdi v Switzerland*; *Barberà, Messegué and Jabardo v Spain*; *Bricmont v Belgium*; *Delta v France*; *Saïdi v France*; *Asch v Austria*; *Artner v Austria*; *Isgrò v Italy*).

- There is no obligation under the ECHR to admit hearsay evidence which purports to exonerate the defendant (*Blastland v UK*).

9.5.2   *Non-compellable witnesses*

Key ECHR cases

Artner v Austria (1991) A/242-A, ECtHR
Asch v Austria (1991) 15 EHRR 597, ECtHR
Doorson v Netherlands (1996) 22 EHRR 330, ECtHR
Unterpertinger v Austria (1986) 13 EHRR 175, ECtHR

ECHR principles

- Hearsay evidence of non-compellable witnesses – such as close relatives/partners – can be relied upon (*Unterpertinger v Austria*, para. 30; *Asch v Austria*, para. 28).

- But this is subject to strict limits: such evidence should not be the sole or decisive evidence upon which conviction is based (*Asch v Austria*, para. 30).

9.5.3   *Illness and death*

Key ECHR cases

Bricmont v Belgium (1989) 12 EHRR 217, ECtHR
Ferrantelli and Santengelo v Italy (1996) 23 EHRR 288, ECtHR

MK v Austria (1997) 24 EHRR CD 59, ECmHR[CD]
Trivedi v UK (1997) 89A DR 136, ECmHR[CD]

ECHR principles

- Hearsay evidence of witnesses who are too ill to attend court or who have died can be relied upon (*Ferrantelli and Santengelo v Italy*; *Bricmont v Belgium*; *Trivedi v UK*; *MK v Austria*).

- Provided that there are counterbalancing factors to protect the defendant (*Ferrantelli and Santengelo v Italy*).

- But before resorting to hearsay evidence, the court must conduct a careful inquiry:

  [In finding there had been a fair trial] the Commission laid particular emphasis on the actions of the trial judge in conducting a detailed inquiry into [the witness's] condition, including his memory at the time. [It] also emphasised that [his] statements were not the only evidence in the case to show that the applicant had claimed for visits . . . which had not occurred. Defence counsel had a full opportunity to comment on the statements of [the witness] to the jury and in his summing-up the judge expressly warned the jury they should attach less weight to the statements. (*Trivedi v UK*, p. 522)

- And where measures less restrictive of defence rights than reliance on hearsay evidence are available, they should be taken:

  In the circumstances of the case, the exercise of the rights of the defence – an essential part of the right to a fair trial – required in principle that the applicants should have an opportunity to challenge any aspect of the complainant's account during a confrontation or an examination, either in public or, if necessary, at his home. (*Bricmont v Belgium*, para. 81)

- Corroborating evidence will be important in an assessment of overall fairness where the hearsay evidence of an ill or dead witness is relied upon:

  . . . even though the judicial authorities did not, as would have been preferable, organise a confrontation between all the accused during the 20 months preceding [the witness's] tragic death, they cannot be held responsible for the latter event. Furthermore . . . the Court . . . found the witness's statements to be corroborated by a series of other items of evidence . . . (*Ferrantelli and Santengelo v Italy*, para. 52 – *no possibility for defendants to confront hostile witness who had committed suicide in prison*)

Relevant Scottish cases

McKenna v Her Majesty's Advocate (30 December 1999), AC

- Provided that there are safeguards at trial, reliance on the statements of a hostile witness who has died does not necessarily breach the fair trial requirements of the ECHR (*McKenna v Her Majesty's Advocate*).

9.5.4   *Absconding witnesses*

Key ECHR cases

Delta v France (1990) 16 EHRR 574, ECtHR
Doorson v Netherlands (1996) 22 EHRR 330, ECtHR

ECHR principles

- Hearsay evidence from witnesses who simply fail to appear at trial should rarely be relied upon (*Delta v France*).

- However, the ECHR will not necessarily be breached where the relevant authorities can show that they have made extensive efforts to locate the witness and that his or her evidence is corroborated (*Doorson v Netherlands*).

9.5.5   *Fear of reprisals*

Key ECHR cases

Doorson v Netherlands (1996) 22 EHRR 330, ECtHR
Saïdi v France (1993) 17 EHRR 251, ECtHR
Van Mechelen and others v Netherlands (1997) 25 EHRR 647, ECtHR
Windisch v Austria (1990) 13 EHRR 282, ECtHR

ECHR principles

- Hearsay evidence of witnesses who genuinely fear reprisals if they attend court to give evidence can be relied upon.

- Provided that there are counterbalancing factors to protect the defendant.

- And it will generally be unfair to base a conviction solely or mainly on the hearsay evidence of such a witness:

    > The collaboration of the public is undoubtedly of great importance for the police in their struggle against crime. In this connection . . . the Convention does not preclude reliance, at the investigation stage, on sources such as anonymous informants. However, the subsequent use of their statements by the trial court to found a conviction is another matter. The right to a fair administration of justice holds so prominent a place in a democratic society that it cannot be sacrificed. (*Windisch v Austria*, para. 30 – *conviction for burglary on the basis of statements made by two anonymous witnesses*)

- Even for serious offences:

    > . . . in convicting the applicant the two courts which tried him referred to no evidence other than the statements obtained prior to the trial . . . The testimony therefore constituted the sole basis for the applicant's conviction, after having been the only ground for his committal for trial. Yet neither at the stage of the investigation nor during the trial was the applicant able to examine or have examined the witnesses concerned. The lack of any confrontation deprived him in certain respects of a fair trial. The Court is fully aware of the undeniable difficulties of the fight against drug-trafficking – in particular with regard to obtaining and producing evidence – and of the ravages caused to society by the drug problem, but such considerations cannot justify restricting to this extent the rights of the defence of 'everyone charged with a criminal offence'. (*Saïdi v France*, para. 44)

- As a general rule, the fear of reprisals need not be linked to a specific threat:

    > Regard must be had to the fact, as established by the domestic courts and not contested by the applicant, that drug dealers frequently resorted to threats or actual violence against persons who gave evidence against them. (*Doorson v Netherlands*, para. 71)

- The same may not be true in relation to law enforcement officers, where stronger evidence of threats will be needed before hearsay evidence can be relied upon (*Van Mechelen and others v Netherlands*, para. 61).

9.6   ANONYMOUS WITNESSES

Key ECHR cases

Cardot v France (1991) 13 EHRR 853, ECtHR
Doorson v Netherlands (1996) 22 EHRR 330, ECtHR
Isgrò v Italy (19 February 1991), ECtHR
Kostovski v Netherlands (1989) 12 EHRR 434, ECtHR
Van Mechelen and others v Netherlands (1997) 25 EHRR 647, ECtHR

X v UK (1992) 15 EHRR CD 113, ECmHR

ECHR principles

- Evidence from anonymous witnesses should be treated with caution under Article 6, ECHR:

    > If the defence is unaware of the identity of the person it seeks to question, it may be deprived of the very particulars enabling it to demonstrate that he or she is prejudiced, hostile or unreliable. Testimony or other declarations inculpating an accused may well be designedly untruthful or simply erroneous and the defence will scarcely be able to bring this to light if it lacks the information permitting it to test the author's reliability or cast doubt on his credibility.
    >
    > Although the growth in organised crime doubtless demands the introduction of appropriate measures, the Government's submissions appear . . . to lay insufficient weight on . . . 'the interest of everybody in a civilised society in a controllable and fair judicial procedure.' The right to a fair administration of justice holds so prominent a place in a democratic society that it cannot be sacrificed to expediency. The Convention does not preclude reliance at the investigation stage of criminal proceedings, on sources such as anonymous informants. However, the subsequent use of anonymous statements as sufficient evidence to found a conviction . . . is a different matter. (*Kostovski v Netherlands*, paras 42 and 44)

- But such evidence can be relied upon, where justified, so long as there are counterbalancing factors to protect the defendant:

    > . . . the 'counterbalancing procedure followed . . . must be considered sufficient to have enabled the defence to challenge the evidence of the anonymous witnesses and attempt to cast doubt on the reliability of their statements . . . (*Doorson v Netherlands*, para. 75)

- Cogent and specific evidence will be needed before anonymous evidence from law enforcement officers can be relied upon (*Van Mechelen and others v Netherlands*, para. 61).

Relevant Canadian cases

R v Garofoli [1990] 2 SCR 1421

- Although there is a general rule that a defendant must be given access to materials used to support a search warrant, the identities of confidential police informants may be edited out if there are risks to their lives or safety (*R v Garofoli*).

9.7   ACCOMPLICE EVIDENCE

Key ECHR cases

Baragiola v Switzerland (1993) 75 DR 76, ECmHR
MH v UK (1997) EHRLR 279, ECmHR[CD]
X v Austria (App. No. 1599/62), ECmHR
X v UK (1976) 7 DR 115, ECmHR

ECHR principles

- Reliance on the evidence of an accomplice is not prohibited under the ECHR:

  . . . nothing in the Convention precludes a court from hearing as a witness for the prosecution a person who is guilty of the same offence alleged against the accused . . . (*X v Austria*)

- But it may put in doubt the fairness of the proceedings if there are insufficient safeguards to protect the defendant. Close scrutiny and control are called for:

  . . . the sentences imposed on the co-defendants who had given evidence for the prosecution were considerably reduced and alleviated . . . As they ran the risk of losing the advantages they had been given if they went back on their previous statements or retracted their confessions, their statements were open to question. It was therefore necessary for the . . . courts to adopt a critical approach in assessing the statements. (*Baragiola v Switzerland*; *X v UK*, p. 118)

- Effective cross-examination is a minimum requirement (*MH v UK*, pp. 279–80 – *defendant unable to cross-examine former accomplice witness on his guilty plea which had been admitted in evidence against him*).

9.8   THE EVIDENCE OF INFORMERS AND UNDERCOVER OFFICERS

Key ECHR cases

Lüdi v Switzerland (1992) 15 EHRR 173, ECtHR
Teixeira de Castro v Portugal (1998) 28 EHRR 101, ECtHR

X v Germany (1989) 11 EHRR 84, ECmHR

ECHR principles

- Reliance on the evidence of informers and undercover officers is not prohibited under the ECHR, but safeguards are necessary to protect the rights of the defence (*Lüdi v Switzerland*; see also *X v Germany* – *evidence obtained by ruse when undercover officer posed as remand prisoner*).

- The defence must have the opportunity to challenge the evidence:

  . . . neither the investigating judge nor the trial courts were able or willing to hear [the undercover agent] as a witness and carry out a confrontation which would enable

[his] statements to be contrasted with [the defendant's] allegations; moreover, neither [the defendant] nor his counsel at any time during the proceedings had an opportunity to question him and cast doubt on his credibility. Yet it would have been possible to do this in a way which took into account the legitimate interest of the police authorities in a drug trafficking case in preserving the anonymity of their agent, so that they could protect him and also make use of him again in the future. (*Lüdi v Switzerland*, para. 49 – *conviction for drug trafficking following entrapment by undercover agent who was not called as a trial witness*)

- And the proceedings as a whole will be unfair if the informer or undercover officer incited the commission of an offence which would not otherwise have been committed (*Teixeira de Castro v Portugal*).

- See further **6.3**.

9.9   UNLAWFULLY OBTAINED EVIDENCE

Key ECHR cases

Khan v UK (12 May 2000), ECtHR
Schenk v Switzerland (1988) 13 EHRR 242, ECtHR

Austria v Italy (1963) 6 Yearbook 740, ECmHR
Wischnewski v France (1988) 58 DR 106, ECmHR

ECHR principles

- Evidence obtained in breach of absolute rights, such as Article 3, ECHR, must always be excluded from trial (*Austria v Italy*).

- Otherwise, the mere fact that evidence has been obtained in breach of qualified rights under the ECHR does not automatically lead to its exclusion:

   The question which must be answered is whether the proceedings as a whole, including the way in which the evidence was obtained, were fair. This involves an examination of the 'unlawfulness' in question and, where violation of another Convention right is concerned, the nature of the violation found. (*Khan v UK*, para. 34; *Schenk v Switzerland*)

- The central question under Article 6 will be fairness, relevant to which are the following factors:

   (a)   whether there was a breach of domestic law as well as of the ECHR:

      The Court notes at the outset that, in contrast to the position . . . in . . . *Schenk v Switzerland* . . . the fixing of the listening device and the recording of the applicant's conversation were not unlawful in the sense of being contrary to domestic criminal law. (*Khan v UK*, para. 36)

   (b)   whether the breach of Convention rights was in good faith or not:

      . . . as was further noted, there was no suggestion that, in fixing the device, the police had operated otherwise than in accordance with the Home Office Guidelines . . .

The 'unlawfulness' of which complaint is made in the present case relates exclusively to the fact that there was no statutory authority for the interference with the applicant's right to respect for private life and accordingly such interference was not 'in accordance with law' as that phrase has been interpreted in Article 8(2) of the Convention. (*Khan v UK*, para. 36)

(c) whether there was any element of entrapment or inducement:

. . . the admissions made by the applicant during the conversation with B were made voluntarily, there being no entrapment and the applicant being under no inducement to make such admissions. (*Khan v UK*, para. 36)

- Whether the unlawfully obtained evidence is the only evidence against the defendant will also be relevant, but not determinative:

The Court . . . notes that the contested material in the present case was in effect the only evidence against the applicant and that the applicant's plea of guilty was tendered only on the basis of the judge's ruling that the evidence should be admitted. However, the relevance of the existence of evidence other than the contested matter depends on the circumstances of the case. In the present circumstances, where there was no risk of it being unreliable, the need for supporting evidence is correspondingly weaker. (*Khan v UK*, para. 37)

Relevant Canadian cases

R v Collins [1987] 1 SCR 265
R v Plant [1993] 3 SCR 281

- Evidence obtained in breach of a Charter right must be excluded if 'having regard to all the circumstances, the admission of it in proceedings would bring the administration of justice into disrepute' (Charter, section 24(2)).

- Three factors are relevant:

   (a) whether the admission of the evidence affects the fairness of the trial;
   (b) whether the breach of Charter rights is serious or in good faith;
   (c) whether the effect of exclusion might itself bring the administration of justice into disrepute, particularly if a serious charge is jeopardised by a non-serious Charter breach (*R v Collins*).

- Whether the material exists independent of the Charter violation will also be important (*R v Plant*).

Relevant New Zealand cases

R v Grayson and Taylor [1997] 1 NZLR 399
R v Kirifi [1992] 2 NZLR 8
R v Te Kira [1993] 3 NZLR 257
R v Wilson [1994] 3 NZLR 285
Simpson v AG [1994] 3 NZLR 667

- Violations of constitutional rights should attract a strong response:

. . . it would be inconsistent with the concept of a Bill of Rights to relegate them to matters to be given some weight in the exercise of judicial discretion. (*Te Kira*)

- A rule of prima facie exclusion therefore applies:

  > . . . a rule of prima facie exclusion of evidence obtained in consequence of a breach'
  > is justifiable 'to preserve the integrity of the administration of justice'. (*Simpson v AG*)

- However, public interest considerations are relevant (*R v Grayson and Taylor*).

- When considering whether to exclude evidence on the grounds of unfairness, breach of a third party's constitutional rights is relevant (*R v Wilson*, p. 259).

Relevant South African cases

State v Melani [1995] 2 SACR 141
State v Motloutsi [1996] 1 SACR 78

- Breach of a constitutional right does not lead to automatic exclusion (*State v Melani; State v Motloutsi*).

- But a strict approach should be taken to breaches of constitutional rights:

  > . . . a finding that there was a conscious and deliberate violation of the accused's
  > constitutional rights had to lead to a ruling to the effect that the evidence tendered
  > was inadmissible. (*State v Motloutsi*)

- In such cases evidence should be admitted only in 'extraordinary excusing circumstances' such as the imminent destruction of vital evidence, the need to rescue a victim in peril, or when the evidence was obtained by a 'search incidental to and contemporaneous with a lawful arrest although made without a valid search warrant. (*State v Motloutsi*).

9.10   THE PROTECTION AGAINST SELF-INCRIMINATION

Key ECHR cases

Averill v UK (6 June 2000), ECtHR
Condron v UK (2 May 2000), ECtHR
Funke v France (1993) 16 EHRR 297, ECtHR
Heaney and McGuinness v Ireland (21 December 2000), ECtHR
IJL and others v UK (19 September 2000), ECtHR
Murray, John v UK (1996) 22 EHRR 29, ECtHR
Saunders v UK (1996) 23 EHRR 313, ECtHR

Abas v Netherlands (App. No. 27943/95), ECmHR[CD]
D.N. v Netherlands (26 May 1975), ECmHR
J.P., K.R. and G.G. v Austria (App. No. 6070/73, App. Nos 15135/89, 15136/89 and 15137/89, 5 September 1989), ECmHR
K v Austria (1993) A/255-B, ECmHR
Tora Tolmos v Spain (App. No. 23816/94, 17 May 1995), ECmHR

ECHR principles

- The right to a fair trial includes 'the right of anyone charged with a criminal offence . . . to remain silent and not to contribute to incriminating himself' (*Funke v France*).

- It is implied in Article 6, ECHR:

  . . . although not specifically mentioned in Article 6 of the Convention, the right to silence and the right not to incriminate oneself, are generally recognised international standards which lie at the heart of the notion of a fair procedure under Article 6. Their rationale lies, *inter alia*, in the protection of the accused against improper compulsion by the authorities thereby contributing to the avoidance of miscarriages of justice and to the fulfilment of the aims of Article 6. The right not to incriminate oneself, in particular, presupposes that the prosecution in a criminal case seek to prove their case against the accused without resort to evidence obtained through methods of coercion or oppression in defiance of the will of the accused. In this sense the right is closely linked to the presumption of innocence contained in Article 6(2) . . . (*Saunders v UK*, para. 68 – *DTI powers of compulsory questioning concerning charges of false accounting and conspiracy*)

- The right not to incriminate onseself is violated where use is made of statements compelled under statute and made to the Department of Trade and Industry (*IJL and others v UK*).

- The protection against self-incrimination applies to criminal proceedings in respect of all types of criminal cases without distinction, from the most simple to the most complex (*Saunders v UK*, para. 74).

- Neither is it confined to statements of admission of wrongdoing nor to remarks which are directly incriminating (*Saunders v UK*, para. 71; see also *Heaney and McGuinness v Ireland* – *accounting for one's movements*).

- But it is not clear that the protection from self-incrimination is absolute:

  Nor does the Court find it necessary . . . to decide whether the right not to incriminate oneself is absolute or whether infringements of it may be justified in particular circumstances. (*Saunders v UK*, para. 74)

- A presumption that the owner of a car is responsible for speeding and parking offences does not necessarily breach the protection against self-incrimination (*Tora Tolmos v Spain*; *D.N. v Netherlands*; *J.P., K.R. and G.G. v Austria*).

- Moreover, it is not the compulsory questioning as such that infringes the ECHR; it is the use in criminal proceedings of answers elicited as a result of compulsion to incriminate a defendant (*Saunders v UK*, para. 67; *Abas v Netherlands*).

- Permitting the court to draw adverse inferences from silence does not equate with compulsory questioning and is permitted within limits:

  On the one hand, it is self-evident that it is incompatible with the immunities under consideration to base a conviction solely or mainly on the accused's silence or on a refusal to answer questions or to give evidence himself. On the other hand, the Court deems it equally obvious that these immunities cannot and should not prevent that the accused's silence, in situations which clearly call for an explanation from him, be taken into account in assessing the persuasiveness of the evidence adduced by the prosecution . . . it follows from this understanding of the 'right to silence' that the question whether the right is absolute must be answered in the negative . . . (*John Murray v UK*, paras 46–52; *Condron v UK*)

- However, where a scheme permits inferences to be drawn from a defendant's silence during police interview, it is essential that the defendant should have access to a lawyer before interview (*Murray v UK*, para. 66).

- And caution should be exercised where a defendant remains silent as a result of legal advice:

  . . . the very fact that an accused is advised by his lawyer to maintain his silence must also be given appropriate weight by the domestic court . . . (*Condron* v *UK*, paras 60–62 – *breach found where judge gave insufficient direction to jury*)

  . . . the extent to which adverse inferences can be drawn from an accused's failure to respond to questioning must necessarily be limited . . . Particularly where a defendant has been denied access to a lawyer; even where s/he is later allowed to consult a lawyer but maintains silence. (*Averill* v *UK*, para. 47)

- Where the directions to the jury at trial do not conform to the requirement of the ECHR, it is unlikely that this defect can be remedied at the appeal stage:

  The Court does not agree with the government's submission that the fairness of the applicant's trial was secured in view of the appeal proceedings. Admittedly defects occurring at a trial may be remedied by a subsequent procedure before a court of appeal and with reference to the fairness of the proceedings as a whole (see *Edwards* v *UK* (1992) 15 EHRR 417). However . . . the Court of Appeal had no means of ascertaining whether or not the applicants' silence played a significant role in the jury's decision to convict. The Court of Appeal had regard to the weight of the evidence against the applicants. However, it was in no position to assess properly whether the jury considered this to be conclusive of their guilt. (*Condron* v *UK*, para. 63)

Other international human rights standards

- Everyone facing a criminal charge is entitled not to be compelled to testify against himself or to confess his guilt (International Covenant on Civil and Political Rights, Article 14(3)(g)).

Relevant domestic cases

Official Receiver v *Stern and another* (2 February 2000)

- The use in disqualification proceedings of statements obtained under compulsory questioning powers does not necessarily breach Article 6, ECHR:

  In our judgment [it is right to reject the argument] that use in disqualification proceedings of statements obtained under s. 235 must necessarily involve a breach of Article 6(1). The issue of fair trial is one that must be considered in the round, having regard to all relevant factors. The relevant factors include (but are not limited to) (i) that disqualification proceedings are not criminal proceedings, and are primarily for the protection of the public, but do nevertheless often involve serious allegations and almost always carry a degree of stigma for anyone who is disqualified; (ii) that there are degrees of coercion involved in different investigative procedures available in corporate insolvency, and these differences may be reflected in different degrees of prejudice involved in the admission, in disqualification proceedings, of statements obtained by such procedures; and (iii) that in this field as in most other fields, it is generally best for issues of fairness or unfairness to be decided by the trial judge, either at a pre-trial review or in the course of the trial. (*Official Receiver* v *Stern and another*)

Relevant Scottish cases

Brown v *Procurator Fiscal* (5 December 2000), PC

- The protection against self-incrimination does not prevent the prosecution relying on answers given under compulsion in subsequent criminal proceedings in road traffic cases:

  > The jurisprudence of the European Court very clearly establishes that while the overall fairness of a criminal trial cannot be compromised, the constituent rights comprised, whether expressly or implicitly within Article 6 are not themselves absolute. (*Brown v Procurator Fiscal, per* Lord Bingham)

Relevant Canadian cases

British Columbia Securities Commission v Branch [1995] 2 SCR 3
Donald v Law Society of British Columbia (1984) 7 CRR, BC CA
Phillips v Nova Scotia [1995] 2 SCR 97
R v Dubois [1985] 2 SCR 350
R v Fitzpatrick [1995] 4 SCR 154
R v Primeau [1995] 2 SCR 60
R v White [1999] 2 SCR 417

- A witness who testifies in any proceedings has the right not to have any incriminating evidence so given used to incriminate that witness in any other proceedings, except in a prosecution for perjury or for giving of contradictory evidence (Charter, section 13).

- The protection against self-incrimination extends to the situation where a witness is compelled to give evidence against another person (*Phillips v Nova Scotia*).

- But it is not absolute: where the predominant purpose is to obtain evidence to incriminate the witness, he or she should not be compelled to testify unless such infringement of his or her rights can be justified (*British Columbia Securities Commission v Branch; R v Primeau*).

- '[A]ny other proceedings' in section 13 of the Charter covers proceedings with penal consequences – both criminal and quasi-criminal – and those where an individual is exposed to a penalty or forfeiture; but not those involving civil liability or disciplinary matters (*Donald v Law Society of British Columbia; R v Primeau*).

  To qualify for protection the evidence or testimony need not be incriminating at the first proceedings. It is the use the prosecution seek to make of the evidence at the second proceedings that is important (*R v Dubois*).

- But protection from self-incrimination is not absolute. It falls to be assessed in the light of the particular circumstances against which the right is asserted:

  > The principle against self-incrimination demands different things at different times, with the task in every case being to determine exactly what the principle demands, if anything within the particular context at issue. (*R v White*, para. 45 – *accused leaving scene of road traffic accident*)

- And it does not extend to information that an individual is obliged to return as part of his or her employment regulation which is later used as the basis for prosecuting a regulatory offence (*R v Fitzpatrick*).

9.11   INTIMATE SAMPLES

Key ECHR cases

Saunders v UK (1996) 23 EHRR 313, ECtHR

ECHR principles

* The protection against self-incrimination does not prevent the use in criminal proceedings of intimate body samples obtained by compulsion:

  > [the right not to incriminate oneself] does not extend to the use in criminal proceedings of material which may be obtained from the accused through the use of compulsory powers but which has an existence independent of the will of the suspect such as, *inter alia*, documents acquired pursuant to a warrant, breath, blood and urine samples and bodily tissues for the purpose of DNA testing. (*Saunders v UK*, para. 69)

9.12   EXPERT EVIDENCE

Key ECHR cases

Bönisch v Austria (1985) 9 EHRR 191, ECtHR
Brandstetter v Austria (1991) 15 EHRR 378, ECtHR

ECHR principles

* The principle that there must be equality between prosecution and defence applies in relation to expert witnesses (*Bönisch v Austria*).

* But the mere fact that a court-appointed expert works at the same institute as the expert relied upon by the prosecution does not automatically breach Article 6, ECHR (*Brandstetter v Austria*).

SECTION 10

SENTENCE

10.1   FAIR TRIAL GUARANTEES IN SENTENCING

Key ECHR cases

Albert and le Compte v Belgium (1983) 5 EHRR 533; (1983) 13 EHRR 415, ECtHR
Engel and others v Netherlands (1976) 1 EHRR 647, ECtHR

ECHR principles

- The fair trial requirements of Article 6, ECHR do not cease to apply at the sentencing stage; but they do not apply in the same way.

- The presumption of innocence ceases to apply (*Engel v Netherlands*, para. 90).

- Evidence which would have been inadmissible at trial can be relied upon (*Engel v Netherlands*, para. 90).

- And previous convictions are relevant (*Albert and le Compte v Belgium*).

Relevant Canadian cases

R v Gardiner (1982) 2 SCR 368

- Procedural fairness applies at the sentencing stage:

  > Crime and punishment are inextricably linked. It would appear well established that the sentencing process is merely a phase of the trial process. Upon conviction the accused is not abruptly deprived of all procedural rights existing at trial: he has a right to counsel, a right to call evidence and cross-examine prosecution witnesses, a right to give evidence himself and to address the court. (*R v Gardiner*, p. 415)

Relevant Commonwealth cases

Browne v Queen [2000] 1 AC 45, PC: St. Christopher and Nevis
Mohammed Ali Muktar v Queen [1992] 2 AC 93, PC: Mauritius

- Sentencing is an integral part of the administration of justice and should not be left to the executive (*Browne v Queen*).

- This principle is breached where the DPP can select the potential penalty by choosing which court to bring proceedings in (*Mohammed Ali Muktar v Queen*).

10.2   RETROACTIVE PENALTIES

Key ECHR cases

Welch v UK (1995) 20 EHRR 247, ECtHR

Ibbotson v UK [1999] EHRLR 218, ECmHR
Taylor v UK (1998) (App. No. 31209/96), ECmHR[CD]

ECHR principles

- Article 7, ECHR protects individuals from being convicted of criminal offences which did not exist at the time the act was committed and prohibits the imposition of a more severe penalty for an offence than that which applied at the time the offence was committed.

- The concept of a 'penalty' autonomous: to render the protection offered by Article 7 effective, courts must be free to go behind appearances and assess for themselves whether a particular measure amounts in substance to a penalty (*Welch v UK*).

- Factors relevant to this assessment are whether the measure in question was imposed following conviction through criminal offence, the nature and purpose of the measure in question, its characterisation under national law, the procedure involved in the making and implementation of the measure and its severity.

- A requirement to register under the Sex Offenders Act 1997 is not a penalty within the meaning of Article 7, ECHR (*Ibbotson v UK*).

- Confiscation proceedings which permit courts to seize assets acquired before legislation came into force will not breach Article 7, ECHR so long as the legislation was in place before the offence giving rise to the confiscation proceedings was committed (*Welch v UK*; *Taylor v UK*).

- See also **10.8**.

10.3   LIFE SENTENCES

Key ECHR cases

Curley v UK (28 March 2000), ECtHR
Singh and Hussain v UK (1996) 22 EHRR 1, ECtHR
T v UK, V v UK (1999) 30 EHRR 121, ECtHR

Dhoest v Belgium (1988) 55 DR 5, ECmHR
Hogben v United Kingdom (1986) 46 DR 231, ECmHR[CD]
Kotalla v Netherlands (1978) 14 DR 238, ECmHR
McFeeley v UK (1981) 3 EHRR 161, ECmHR
Ryan v UK (1998) (App. No. 32875/96), ECmHR

ECHR principles

- The ECHR does not prohibit states from subjecting a child or young person convicted of a serious crime to an indeterminate sentence allowing for the offender's continued detention or recall to detention following release where necessary for the protection of the public (*T v UK, V v UK*, para. 98).

- Unjustifiable and persistent failure to fix a tariff, leaving a detainee in uncertainty for many years, might give rise to an issue under Article 3 of the Convention (*T v UK, V v UK*, para. 100; but see *Curley v UK – failure to set tariff for 10 years*).

- Equally, imposing a life sentence on children aged between 10 and 18 might breach Article 3 if no regard is paid to the changes in their character as they mature (*Singh and Hussain v UK*, para. 53 – *detention during Her Majesty's Pleasure for murder*) although not where they are young adults aged 18 to 21 (*Ryan v UK*).

- Otherwise, although desirable, there is no strict ECHR requirement to review a life sentence either under Article 3 or under another ECHR provision (*Kotalla v Netherlands*, p. 240 – *failure to provide a mechanism to limit duration of life sentence did not equate to inhuman or degrading treatment; cf Dhoest v Belgium*, p. 23 – *left open whether detention in a mental hospital without prospect of release engaged Article 3*).

- This is the case even when policy changes result in life sentence prisoners being required to serve a minimum period (e.g. 20 years) on the basis of deterrence and retribution, and thus serving a much longer period then they originally expected. (*Hogben v United Kingdom*, p. 237 – *transfer back to closed from open conditions after serving 13 years – disappointed hopes of convict did not amount to inhuman treatment*).

- Similarly, there is no breach of the ECHR where a prisoner loses remission after being disciplined (*McFeeley v UK*, para. 47 – *relevant in a case of repeated loss of remission for persistent refusal to wear prison clothes that lost remission could be restored after a period of good conduct*).

10.4   PROPORTIONALITY IN SENTENCING

Key ECHR cases

Arrowsmith v UK (1978) 19 DR 5, ECmHR

ECHR principles

- Where an individual is sentenced for conduct protected as a qualified right under the ECHR, any punishment must be proportionate:

  > Having in mind that one of the principles characterising a 'democratic society', according to the European Court of Human Rights, is that every 'penalty imposed in this sphere must be proportionate to the legitimate aim pursued', the Commission must

finally consider the severity of the sentence . . . the sentence which the applicant finally received and served (seven months' imprisonment) although admittedly severe, was not in the circumstances so clearly out of proportion to the legitimate aims pursued that this severity in itself could render unjustifiable such an interference . . . (*Arrowsmith v UK*, para. 99 – *sentence for sedition by disseminating pacifist literature to soldiers*).

Relevant domestic cases

R v Offen (2000) *The Times*, 9 November, CA

- The imposition of a mandatory life sentence under the Crime (Sentences) Act 1997 on an individual who poses no risk to the public is disproportionate and a breach of the ECHR.

10.5 PREVENTATIVE SENTENCES

Singh and Hussain v UK (1996) 22 EHRR 1, ECtHR
T v UK, V v UK (1999) 30 EHRR 121, ECtHR
Thynne, Wilson and Gunnell v UK (1990) 13 EHRR 666, ECtHR
Van Droogenbroeck v Belgium (1982) 4 EHRR 443, ECtHR
Weeks v UK (1987) 10 EHRR 293, ECtHR
Wynne v UK (1994) 19 EHRR 333, ECtHR
X v UK (1982) 4 EHRR 188, ECtHR

John Ryan v UK (1998) (App. No. 32875/96), ECmHR[CD]
Watson v UK (1997) EHRLR 181, ECmHR

ECHR principles

- Article 5(4), ECHR specifically provides that, 'Everyone who is deprived of his liberty by arrest or detention shall be entitled to take proceedings by which the lawfulness of his detention shall be decided speedily by a court and his release ordered if the detention is not lawful.'

- Where individuals are sentenced solely for the purposes of retribution, deterrence or protection of the public, as soon as the punitive part of the sentence is served and the preventative component begins, Article 5(4) is engaged.

- The key question at that stage is whether the prisoner's dangerousness continues to justify his or her detention.

- In this context both discretionary life sentences and sentences of detention at Her Majesty's Pleasure imposed on child murderers under English law are subject to judicial control (*Singh and Hussein v UK*, para. 54 – *two sets of sentences assimilated by ECtHR, s. 28 of Crime (Sentences) Act 1997 passed in response which provides oral hearings once every two years for both*; see also *X v UK*; *Van Droogenbroeck v Belgium*; *Weeks v UK*, para. 68 – *Parole Board lacked sufficient power of decision-making to constitute judicial control regarding discretionary life sentences (subsequently remedied)*; and *Thynne, Wilson and Gunnell v UK*, para. 80).

- Consequently, fixing of the tariff for child murderers by the Home Secretary violates not just Article 5(4) but also Article 6(1), ECHR (*T v UK, V v UK*; see also *Watson v UK*, p. 182).

- By contrast the mandatory life sentence imposed on adult murderers has traditionally been considered to be wholly punitive and thus not to attract Article 5(4) protection once sentencing has been carried out (*Wynne v UK*, paras 35 and 36).

- A similar approach has been taken on life sentences imposed on adult murderers aged between 18 and 21 (*John Ryan v UK*).

Relevant Scottish cases

John O'Neill v Her Majesty's Advocate (9 March 1999), HC
Murray, Hartley and Simpson v Her Majesty's Advocate (10 September 1999), AC

- Since a discretionary life sentence has both a security component and a punitive component, it is clear that the latter covers both retribution and deterrence. (*Murray, Hartley and Simpson v Her Majesty's Advocate*, p. 5 – *interpreting Thynne, Wilson and Gemmill v UK* (1990) – *appeal against sentence for murder*).

- In this regard the designated punitive component should not take into account the need to protect the public; the Parole Board should determine when the defendant should be released (*John O'Neill v Her Majesty's Advocate*, p. 5).

Relevant New Zealand cases

R v Leitch (1998) 1 NZLR 420

- It remains open to question whether a sentence of preventive detention *per se* breaches the right not to be subjected to disproportionately severe treatment or punishment (Bill of Rights Act, s. 9).

- However, as a general rule, a finite sentence is to be preferred to a preventive sentence unless the protection of the public demands otherwise (*R v Leitch*, p. 431 – *sentence of preventive detention following conviction for indecent assault manifestly excessive and replaced by detention for eight years*).

10.6   CHALLENGING THE LAWFULNESS OF DETENTION

- See **22.17**.

10.7   DEPORTATION

- Deportation raises a number of issues under Articles 3 and 8 of the ECHR: see **28.3**.

10.8   CONFISCATION AND FORFEITURE

Key ECHR cases

Soumare v *France* (24 August 1998), ECtHR

ECHR principles

- Where a court passes a sentence and imposes forfeiture/fine with further detention in default, that second period (unlike the first) is subject to review under Article 5(4), ECHR (*Soumare* v *France*). For Article 5(4) review: see **22.17**.

- For retrospective penalties: see **10.2**.

Relevant domestic cases

R v *Benjafield, Leal, Rezvi and Milford* (21 December 2000), CA

- Article 6 applies to confiscation and forfeiture procedures (*R* v *Benjafield, Leal, Rezvi and Milford*).

Relevant New Zealand cases

Lyall v *Solicitor-General* (1997) 2 NZLR 641

- Forfeiture of a defendant's interests in property after conviction is not necessarily disproportionately severe punishment where the property is instrumental in the commission of a serious offence (*Lyall* v *Solicitor-General*, p. 647).

SECTION 11

YOUTH JUSTICE

11.1   RELEVANCE OF INTERNATIONAL STANDARDS

Key ECHR cases

T v UK, V v UK (1999) 30 EHRR 121, ECtHR

ECHR principles

- Other international human rights instruments, such as the UN Standard Minimum Rules for the Administration of Juvenile Justice (the Beijing Rules), the UN Convention on the Rights of the Child 1989, the International Covenant on Civil and Political Rights 1966 and the Committee of Ministers of the Council of Europe Recommendation No. R(87)20, are relevant to the determination of issues under the ECHR concerning the rights of children (*T v UK, V v UK*, para. 77).

- Where such instruments demonstrate a trend in the way a particular right is protected, that is a relevant factor for the Court to take into account (but not determinative) (*T v UK, V v UK*, para. 77).

Other international human rights standards

- Juveniles must enjoy at least the same guarantees and protection as are accorded to adults under the International Covenant on Civil and Political Rights (UN Human Rights Committee, General Comment No. 13, para. 16).

11.2   THE AGE OF CRIMINAL RESPONSIBILITY

Key ECHR cases

T v UK, V v UK (1999) 30 EHRR 121, ECtHR

ECHR principles

- The trial of a child of age 11 does not, in itself, breach Article 3, ECHR.

    There is not (yet) any clear common standard in Europe as to the minimum age of criminal responsibility. And since the position in England and Wales does not differ disproportionately from the age-limit in other European states, it cannot be said to breach Article 3 of the Convention. (*T v UK, V v UK*, para. 74)

- Neither does it, in itself, breach Article 6, ECHR (*T v UK, V v UK*, para. 86).

Other international human rights standards

- A juvenile justice system must set out the minimum age at which juveniles can be charged with a criminal offence, the maximum age at which a person is still considered a juvenile and employ special courts and procedures (UN Human Rights Committee, General Comment No. 13, para. 16).

11.3   FAIR TRIAL RIGHTS

Key ECHR cases

Nortier v Netherlands (1993) 17 EHRR 273, ECtHR

ECHR principles

- Children enjoy the same fair trial rights under Articles 5 and 6, ECHR as adults:

  Juveniles facing criminal charges are as fully entitled as adults to benefit from all the Convention requirements for a fair trial. Great care must always be taken to ensure that this entitlement is not diluted by considerations of rehabilitation or of reform. These are considerations which should be in addition to all the procedural predictions available. Fair trial and proper proof of guilt are absolute conditions precedent. (*Nortier v Netherlands*, p. 290, concurring opinion of Judge Walsh – *15-year-old found guilty of attempted rape*)

- But the special status of children requires that the relevant standards be applied differently so as to offer additional protection beyond the general ECHR guarantees:

  . . . minors are as entitled to the same protection of their fundamental rights as adults but . . . the developing state of their personality – and consequently their limited social responsibility – should be taken into account in applying Article 6 of the Convention. In particular, the right of everyone charged with a criminal offence to be judged by an impartial tribunal should not be incompatible with the protective treatment of juvenile offenders. Under Article 25 of the Universal Declaration of Human Rights, childhood is entitled to special care and assistance. (*Nortier v Netherlands*, p. 291, concurring opinion of Judge Morenilla)

- The criminal justice system should accordingly offer:

  '. . . the necessary protection and assistance so that they can fully assume their responsibilities within the community' and prepare them 'to live an individual life in society', by promoting 'the establishment of laws, procedures, authorities and institutions applicable to children alleged as, accused of, or recognised as having infringed the criminal law.' (*Nortier v Netherlands*, p. 291, concurring opinion of Judge Morenilla; quoting the Preamble and Article 40(3) of the Convention on the Rights of the Child)

Other international human rights standards

- Juveniles must enjoy at least the same guarantees and protection as are accorded adults under the International Covenant on Civil and Political Rights (UN Human Rights Committee, General Comment No. 13, para. 16).

11.4   PROCEDURAL IMPLICATIONS

Key ECHR cases

T v UK, V v UK (1999) 30 EHRR 121, ECtHR

ECHR principles

- Adaptations to the criminal justice system are needed when children are on trial:

  . . . it is essential that a child charged with an offence is dealt with in a manner which takes full account of his age, level of maturity and intellectual and emotional capacities, and that steps are taken to promote his ability to understand and participate effectively in the proceedings. (*T v UK, V v UK*, para. 86)

- Particularly if there is considerable media attention:

  . . . in respect of a young child charged with a grave offence attracting high levels of media and public interest, it would be necessary to conduct the hearing in such a way as to reduce as far as possible his or her feelings of intimidation and inhibition. (*T v UK, V v UK*, para. 87)

- And failure to make appropriate adaptations when children are on trial will breach Article 6, ECHR:

  Although in the particular case some measures had been taken because of the applicant's age, the formality and ritual of the court must have seemed incomprehensible and intimidating, the raised dock (designed to enable the applicant to see what was going on) had adverse effects and the high levels of interest from the press and public considerably intensified the atmosphere inside the court room. Where in such circumstances there is evidence to suggest that a defendant is suffering the post-traumatic effects of what s/he has done and is unable to even think about the events in question without extreme distress, such that s/he cannot give instructions or evidence, Article 6 is likely to be breached. (*T v UK, V v UK* paras 88 and 89)

Other international human rights standards

- Accused juvenile persons shall be separated from adults and brought as speedily as possible for adjudication (International Covenant on Civil and Political Rights, Article 10(2)(b)).

- In the case of juveniles, the procedure (for determining any criminal charge) shall be such as will take account of their age and the desirability of promoting their rehabilitation (International Covenant on Civil and Political Rights, Article 14(4)).

- States Parties recognise the right of every child alleged as, accused of, or recognised as having infringed the penal law to be treated in a manner consistent with the promotion of the child's sense of dignity and worth, which reinforces the child's respect for the human rights and fundamental freedoms of others and which takes into account the child's age and the desirability of promoting the child's reintegration and the child's assuming a constructive role in society (UN Covenant on the Rights of the Child, Article 40(1)).

- Proceedings against children should be expeditious (UN Covenant on the Rights of the Child, Article 40(2)(b)(iii)).

11.5   PRIVACY

Key ECHR cases

T v UK, V v UK (1999) 30 EHRR 121, ECtHR

ECHR principles

- Although Article 6, ECHR permits courts to sit in private when hearing cases against children, it does not *require* that such proceedings be private:

  Any inquiry into serious criminal offences committed by children is likely to provoke feelings of guilt, distress, anguish and fear in those tried and, while the public nature of any such inquiry might exacerbate such feelings, it cannot be said to have caused additional suffering going beyond that which would inevitably be engendered by any attempt by the authorities to deal with child offenders. (*T v UK, V v UK*, para. 79)

Other international human rights standards

- There should be an exception to the general rule that judgments be made public when the interests of juveniles so require (International Covenant on Civil and Political Rights, Article 14(1)).

- Proceedings against children should be in private (UN Covenant on the Rights of the Child, Article 40(2)(b)(vii)).

- Protection of a child's privacy is paramount at all stages of criminal proceedings against him or her: 'In principle, no information that may lead to the identification of a juvenile offender shall be published' (Standard Minimum Rules for the Administration of Juvenile Justice (or 'Beijing Rules'), rule 8.2), including any records concerning the case which should be kept strictly confidential (Beijing Rules, rule 21).

Relevant New Zealand cases

R v F (22 June 1999), HC Auckland

- The protection afforded by the Convention on the Rights of the Child should be taken into account when determining where the balance should be struck between the child's right to privacy and the media's reporting freedoms (*R v F*).

11.6   SENTENCE

Key ECHR cases

Singh and Hussain v *UK* (1996) 22 EHRR 1, ECtHR
T v *UK*, V v *UK* (1999) 30 EHRR 121, ECtHR

ECHR principles

- The ECHR does not prohibit states from subjecting a child or young person convicted of serious crime to an indeterminate sentence allowing for the offender's continued detention or recall to detention following release where necessary to protect the public (*T* v *UK*, *V* v *UK*, para. 98).

- But imposing a true life sentence on children, even where convicted of murder, would be difficult to justify under Article 3, ECHR and could only be legitimate if it was genuinely for the protection of the public (*Singh* v *UK*, para. 61; *Hussain* v *UK*, para. 53).

- And unjustifiable and persistent failure to fix a tariff for many years might also raise issues under Article 3 (*T* v *UK*, *V* v *UK*, para. 100).

SECTION 12

APPEALS

12.1 FAIR TRIAL GUARANTEES

Key ECHR cases

Delcourt v Belgium (1969) 1 EHRR 355, ECtHR
Monnell & Morris v UK (1987) 10 EHRR 205, ECtHR
Pélissier v France (25 March 1999), ECtHR
Vacher v France (1996) 24 EHRR 482, ECtHR

Bricmont v Belgium (1986) 48 DR 106, ECmHR

ECHR principles

- There is no requirement under the ECHR to set up an appeal procedure.

- Limitations can therefore be placed on the right to appeal, including time limits, so long as they are reasonable and proportionate (*Bricmont v Belgium*, p. 151).

- In addition, if time limits for appealing are imposed, the relevant authorities are under a duty to inform the defendant of these limits:

    . . . States must ensure that everyone charged with a criminal offence benefits from the safeguards provided by Article 6(3). Putting the onus on convicted appellants to find out when an allotted period of time starts to run or expires is not compatible with the 'diligence' which the Contracting States must exercise to ensure that the rights guaranteed by Article 6 are enjoyed in an effective manner. (*Vacher v France*, para. 28)

- Where an appeal procedure is set up, it must conform to Article 6 principles:

    A criminal charge is not really 'determined' as long as the verdict of acquittal or conviction had not become final. Criminal proceedings form an entity and must, in the ordinary way, terminate in an enforceable decision . . .
    The Convention does not, it is true, compel the Contracting States to set up courts of appeal or of cassation. Nevertheless, a State which does institute such courts is required to ensure that persons amenable to the law shall enjoy before these courts the fundamental guarantees in Article 6. (*Delcourt v Belgium*, para. 25)

- Inevitably, the way in which these principles are applied will not be the same as at trial and will depend upon the special features of appeal proceedings:

    The manner in which paragraph 1, as well as paragraph 3(c), of Article 6 is to be applied in relation to appellate or cassation courts depends upon the special features of the proceedings involved. Account must be taken of the entirety of the proceedings conducted in the domestic legal order and of the role of the appellate or cassation court therein. (*Monnell & Morris v UK*, para. 56)

- Where a court, including a court of appeal, has power to substitute a conviction for an offence other than that with which an individual is actually charged, the defence must be afforded an opportunity to deal with the alternative charge (*Pélissier v France – substitution of aiding and abetting for principal offence by the court of appeal*). This is particularly so where it is conceivable that the defence would have been different.

Other international human rights standards

- Everyone convicted of a crime has the right to have his or her conviction and sentence reviewed by a higher tribunal according to law (International Covenant on Civil and Political Rights, Article 14(5)).

- This guarantee is broad and not confined to the most serious offences (UN Human Rights Committee, General Comment No. 13, para. 17).

12.2   LEAVE TO APPEAL

Key ECHR cases

Monnell & Morris v UK (1987) 10 EHRR 205, ECtHR

Webb v UK (1997) 24 EHRR CD 73, ECmHR[CD]

ECHR principles

- Article 6, ECHR applies to leave proceedings since these constitute part of the determination of the criminal charge:

  No one contested that the consideration of the applications for leave to appeal . . . constituted part of the determination of the criminal charges brought against them. Moreover, it is in accordance with the case law of the Court that Article 6 is applicable in the present case. (*Monnell & Morris v UK*, para. 54)

- However, the limited nature of proceedings for leave to appeal may not require a full public hearing:

  On an application for leave to appeal, the Court of Appeal does not re-hear the case on the facts, and no witnesses are called, even though the grounds of appeal involve questions of fact as opposed to questions of law alone. The issue for decision in such proceedings is whether the applicant has demonstrated the existence of arguable grounds which would justify hearing an appeal. If the grounds pleaded are in law legitimate grounds for appeal and if they merit further argument or consideration, leave will be given; if one or other of these conditions is lacking, leave will be refused.
  . . . as a general principle paragraph 1 of Article 6 requires that a person charged with a criminal offence be entitled to take part in the trial hearing . . . The limited nature of the subsequent issue of the grant or refusal of leave to appeal did not in itself call for oral argument at a public hearing or the personal appearance of the two men before the Court of Appeal. (*Monnell & Morris v UK*, paras 57–58)

- Similarly, full reasons may not be needed at the leave stage:

  . . . special leave to appeal to the Privy Council will only be given where a case raises a point of 'great and general importance' or in cases of 'grave injustice'. In the context of appeals to the Privy Council, where there has been a full appeal before the Court of Appeal, it must be apparent to litigants who have been refused leave that they have failed to satisfy the Privy Council that their case involves [such a point] . . . (*Webb* v *UK*, p. 74)

12.3   LEGAL AID AND LEGAL REPRESENTATION

Key ECHR cases

Boner v *UK* (1994) 19 EHRR 246, ECtHR
Granger v *UK* (1990) 12 EHRR 469, ECtHR
Maxwell v *UK* (1994) 19 EHRR 97, ECtHR
Monnell & Morris v *UK* (1987) 10 EHRR 205, ECtHR

ECHR principles

- The interests of justice require that an appellant be granted legal aid where the case is a complex one and/or there are serious consequences at stake (*Granger* v *UK*, paras 46–47 – *refusal of legal aid in appeal against conviction for perjury*).

- The ability of the accused to understand the proceedings and effectively participate will be relevant in determining whether he or she requires legal assistance:

  . . . the applicant . . . was not in a position fully to comprehend the pre-prepared speeches he read out or the opposing arguments submitted to the court. It is also clear that, had the occasion arisen, he would not have been able to make an effective reply to those arguments or to questions from the bench.
      . . . in all the circumstances of the case it would have been in the interests of justice for free legal assistance to be given to the applicant . . . Such a course would in the first place have served the interests of justice and fairness by enabling the applicant to make an effective contribution to the proceedings. (*Granger* v *UK*, para. 47 – *refusal of legal aid in appeal against a conviction for perjury*)

- This applies even where the issues are not particularly complex:

  The legal issues in this case may not have been particularly complex. Nevertheless, that [the applicant] had himself formulated the grounds for his appeal and that counsel was not prepared to represent him does not alter the fact that without the services of a legal practitioner he was unable competently to address the court on these legal issues and thus to defend himself effectively.
      Moreover, the appeal court . . . had wide powers to dispose of his appeal and its decision was final. Of even greater relevance, however, the applicant had been sentenced to five years' imprisonment. For [the applicant] therefore the issue at stake was an extremely important one. (*Maxwell* v *UK*, para. 38)

- The more severe the potential penalty if the appeal is unsuccessful, the greater the need for representation (*Maxwell* v *UK*, paras 38 and 40 – *request for legal aid to conduct an appeal against conviction for assault refused by Legal Aid Board on basis that not satisfied that had substantial grounds for appeal*).

- But the prospects of success are important:

    Under paragraph 3(c) [the applicants] were guaranteed the right to be given legal assistance free only so far as the interests of justice so required. The interests of justice cannot, however, be taken to require an automatic grant of legal aid whenever a convicted person, with no objective likelihood of success, wishes to appeal after having received a fair trial at first instance in accordance with Article 6. Each applicant . . . benefited from free legal assistance both at his trial and in being advised as to whether he had any arguable grounds of appeal. (*Monnell & Morris v UK*, para. 67)

- Decisions about legal aid should be kept under review:

    The question whether the interests of justice required a grant of legal aid must be determined in the light of the case as a whole. In that respect not only the situation obtaining at the time the decision on the application for legal aid was handed down but also that obtaining at the time the appeal was heard are material. (*Granger v UK*, para. 46)

12.4   THE RIGHT TO A HEARING

Key ECHR cases

Andersson, Jan-Ake v Sweden (1991) 15 EHRR 218, ECtHR
Axen v Germany (1983) 6 EHRR 195, ECtHR
Ekbatani v Sweden (1988) 13 EHRR 504, ECtHR
Fejde v Sweden (1991) 17 EHRR 14, ECtHR
Helmers v Sweden (1991) 15 EHRR 285, ECtHR
Kamasinski v Austria (1989) 13 EHRR 36, ECtHR
Kremzow v Austria (1993) 17 EHRR 322, ECtHR
Sutter v Switzerland (1984) 6 EHRR 272, ECtHR
Weber v Switzerland (1990) 12 EHRR 508, ECtHR

ECHR principles

- The right to a public hearing does not automatically extend to every stage of the proceedings, provided the process viewed as a whole has been fair.

- The nature of the appellate stage will determine whether a hearing is required (*Axen v Germany*, para. 28).

- Where the appeal court is merely required to assess points of law which do not require oral argument the need for a rehearing can be dispensed with (*Axen v Germany*).

- In contrast, where the court is having to determine the appellant's guilt or innocence based upon examination of law and the facts there is a greater need for a full hearing (*Ekbatani v Sweden*, para. 32).

12.5   THE RIGHT TO BE PRESENT

Key ECHR cases

Belziuk v Poland (25 March 1998), ECtHR
Cooke v Austria (8 February 2000), ECtHR
Kamasinski v Austria (1989) 13 EHRR 36, ECtHR
Prinz v Austria (8 February 2000), ECtHR

ECHR principles

- There is no absolute rule that an appellant must be present during appellate proceedings; it depends what issues are being considered:

   The Court recalls that a person charged with a criminal offence should, as a general principle based on the notion of a fair trial, be entitled to be present at the first-instance hearing. However, the personal attendance of the defendant does not necessarily take on the same significance for an appeal hearing . . . even where an appellate court has full jurisdiction to review the case on questions both of fact and law, Article 6 does not always entail rights to a public hearing and to be present in person. Regard must be had in assessing this question to, *inter alia*, the special features of the proceedings involved and the manner in which the defence's interests are presented and protected before the appellate court, particularly in the light of the issues to be decided by it and their importance for the applicant. (*Prinz v Austria*, para. 34; see also *Belziuk v Poland*)

- Where on appeal the court is simply reviewing the findings of fact below, no new facts are adduced and there is no prospect of the sentence being increased, there is no duty on the authorities to ensure that the defendant is present, particularly where he or she is represented (*Prinz v Austria*, para. 44).

- But where an assessment of factors, or more particularly the applicant's mental state, is in issue, he or she should be present:

   . . . taking into account what was at stake for the applicant – a possible increase in sentence to life imprisonment – [the Court] does not consider that his case could have been properly examined without gaining a personal impression of the applicant. It was, therefore, essential to the fairness of the proceedings that he be present at the hearing of the appeals and afforded the opportunity to participate, together with his defence counsel. (*Cooke v Austria*, para. 42 – *since applicant's sentence could have been increased and the determination of this issue involved a fresh assessment of his mental state at the time of the killing, the presence of the applicant was essential*; see also *Kamasinski v Austria*, paras 106–107)

12.6   PENALTIES FOR APPEALING

Key ECHR cases

De Salvador Torres v Spain (1996) 23 EHRR 601, ECtHR
Monnell & Morris v UK (1987) 10 EHRR 205, ECtHR

ECHR principles

- Loss of time as a penalty for appealing will not necessarily breach the ECHR:

  . . . the power of the Court of Appeal to order loss of time, as it is actually exercised, is a component of the machinery existing under English law to ensure that criminal appeals are considered within a reasonable time and, in particular, to reduce the time spent in custody by those with meritorious grounds waiting for their appeal to be heard . . . it is a power exercised to discourage abuse of the court's own procedures. As such it is an inherent part of the criminal appeal process following conviction of an offender and pursues a legitimate aim under sub-paragraph (a) of Article 5(1). (*Monnell & Morris v UK*, para. 46)

- Neither will an increase in sentence which reflects an appeal court's re-assessment of the facts of the offence and any aggravating features necessarily breach the ECHR (*De Salvador Torres v Spain*).

12.7   THE EXTENT TO WHICH THE APPEAL COURT CAN REMEDY TRIAL DEFECTS

Key ECHR cases

Condron v UK (2 May 2000), ECtHR
Edwards v UK (1992) 15 EHRR 417, ECtHR
Rowe and Davies v UK (2000) 30 EHRR 1, ECtHR

ECHR principles

- As a general rule, the whole of the proceedings, including any appeal, is relevant to an assessment of Article 6 fairness (*Edwards v UK – non-disclosure at first instance*).

- However, in some respects, an appeal court will not be able to rectify fairness problems that arose at trial, e.g., where a trial judge misdirects the jury on the question of adverse inferences:

  The Court does not agree with the government's submission that the fairness of the applicant's trial was secured in view of the appeal proceedings. Admittedly defects occurring at a trial may be remedied by a subsequent procedure before a court of appeal and with reference to the fairness of the proceedings as a whole (see *Edwards v UK* (1992) 15 EHRR 417). However . . . the Court of Appeal had not means of ascertaining whether or not the applicants' silence played a significant role in the jury's decision to convict. The Court of Appeal had regard to the weight of the evidence against the applicants. However, it was in no position to assess properly whether the jury considered this to be conclusive of their guilt. (*Condron v UK*, para. 63; see further **9.10**)

- Neither can an appeal court provide the required scrutiny in cases where material is not disclosed on grounds of public interest immunity:

  . . . the Court does not consider that [the] procedure before the appeal court was sufficient to remedy the unfairness caused at the trial by the absence of any scrutiny of the withheld information by the trial judge. Unlike the latter, who saw the witnesses give their testimony and was fully versed in all the evidence and issues in the case, the judges in the Court of Appeal were dependent for their understanding of the possible relevance of the undisclosed material on transcripts of the Crown Court hearings and on the account of the issues given to them by prosecuting counsel. In addition, the first instance judge would have been in a position to monitor the need for disclosure throughout the trial, assessing the importance of the undisclosed evidence at a stage when new issues were emerging, when it might have been possible through cross-examination seriously to undermine the credibility of key witnesses and when the defence case was still open to take a number of different directions or emphases. In contrast, the Court of Appeal was obliged to carry out its appraisal *ex post facto* and may even, to a certain extent, have unconsciously been influenced by the jury's verdict of guilty into underestimating the significance of the undisclosed evidence. (*Rowe and Davies v UK*, para. 65)

Relevant domestic cases

R v Davis, Rowe and Johnson (25 July 2000), CA

- Where material irregularities occur, in breach of Article 6, ECHR, a conviction is likely to be 'unsafe' (*R v Davis, Rowe and Johnson*).

12.8   REASONS IN APPEAL CASES

Key ECHR cases

Webb v UK (1997) 24 EHRR CD 73, ECmHR[CD]
X v Germany (1981) 25 DR 240, ECmHR

ECHR principles

- As a general rule, reasons should be given in appeal hearings.

- However, full reasons need not necessarily be given at the leave stage (*Webb v UK*; *X v Germany*).

12.9   NEW EVIDENCE

Key ECHR cases

Callaghan v UK (1989) 60 DR 296, ECmHR
X v Austria (1962) 9 EHRR CD 17, ECmHR

ECHR principles

- Once a person has been convicted and is therefore no longer 'charged with a criminal offence', establishing a duty on the relevant authorities to review the case in the light of new evidence is difficult (*X v Austria*, p. 21).

- However, where a procedure already exists for an appeal court to examine new evidence and determine whether it warrants a retrial, Article 6 will apply (*Callaghan v UK*).

- Failure to order a new trial will constitute a breach of the right to fair trial only if the appeal court declines to assess the new evidence:

  > . . . no right to a retrial is as such included among the rights and freedoms guaranteed by the Convention. Having regard to the exceptional character of the reference proceedings which ended [13 years previously], the Commission finds no indication that the assessment of the new evidence by the Court of Appeal itself and its failure to direct a fresh trial before a jury to hear this evidence deprived the applicants of a fair hearing as required by Article 6, para. 1 . . . The Commission notes in this regard the Court of Appeal's opinion that it would be impracticable to order a new trial thirteen years after the events in question and that, if there was the least doubt that the verdicts were safe or satisfactory, the Court would quash the convictions. (*Callaghan v UK*, pp. 300–2)

12.10   MISCARRIAGES OF JUSTICE

Other international human rights standards

- Everybody who is a victim of a proven miscarriage of justice and been punished as a result is entitled to compensation unless he was responsible for the non-disclosure of the relevant facts at the time (International Covenant on Civil and Political Rights, Article 14(6)).

PRISONERS

13.1 MEDICAL TREATMENT

Key ECHR cases

App. No. 6181/73 (1974) CD 46 188, ECmHR
Ayala v Portugal (1996) 87-B DR 38, ECmHR
B v Germany (1988) 55 DR 271, ECmHR[CD]
Bonnechaux v Switzerland (1980) 18 DR 100, ECmHR
Chartier v Italy (1983) 33 DR 41, ECmHR
De Varga-Hirsch v France (1983) 33 DR 158, ECmHR
Herczegfalvy v Austria (1994) 77-A DR 75, ECmHR
Jastrzebski v Poland (1995) 20 EHRR CD 126, ECmHR[CD]
Jeznach v Poland (App. No. 27850/95), ECmHR
Kudla v Poland (1998) EHRLR 630, ECmHR[CD]
Lockwood v UK (1993) 15 EHRR CD 48, ECmHR
Lukanov v Bulgaria (1993) 80-A DR 108, ECmHR[CD]
McFeeley v UK (1981) 3 EHRR 161, ECmHR
Remer v Germany (1995) 82-A DR 117, ECmHR[CD]
X v Italy (1982) 27 DR 200, ECmHR

ECHR principles

- There is a general duty on the relevant authorities to safeguard the health and well-being of prisoners, within the confinements of imprisonment (*McFeeley v UK*).

- Failure to provide adequate medical treatment to a prisoner raises issues under Article 3, ECHR, but will be difficult to establish (*Jastrzebski v Poland*, p. 129; *Ayala v Portugal*, p. 43; *Jeznach v Poland*; *Remer v Germany*, p. 123; *Bonnechaux v Switzerland*, p. 148; *Kudla v Poland*, pp. 630–31).

- The question in most cases is whether the state has taken reasonable and necessary measures to treat the prisoner.

- Obtaining medical reports and acting upon them will usually satisfy these requirements (*Chartier v Italy*, p. 57; *Bonnechaux v Switzerland*, p. 148; *De Varga-Hirsch v France*, p. 213; *Lockwood v UK*, p. 48).

- Imprisoning an individual with a severe disability also raises issues under Article 3, but again will be difficult to establish, particularly where medical treatment is available (*Chartier v Italy*; *Lukanov v Bulgaria*; *Bonnechaux v Switzerland*; *De Varga-Hirsch v France*).

Relevant Canadian cases

R v Monney [1999] 1 SCR 652

- Where there is reasonable cause to fear for the health of a detainee, reasonable steps should be taken to monitor his or her medical condition and to offer him or her access to medical care as required.

- Beyond this the state is not under an obligation to force medical care on a reluctant prisoner (*R v Monney*).

13.2   FORCE FEEDING

Key ECHR cases

X v Germany (1985) 7 EHRR 152, ECmHR

ECHR principles

- Force feeding may amount to inhuman or degrading treatment under Article 3, ECHR, but not where it is carried out pursuant to the state's positive obligation to protect life (*X v Germany*).

13.3   CONDITIONS OF DETENTION

Key ECHR cases

Cyprus v Turkey (1976) 4 EHRR 482, ECmHR
Eggs v Switzerland (1977) 6 DR 170, ECmHR
Greek Case, the (1969) 12 Yearbook 1, ECmHR
Hilton v UK (1981) 3 EHRR 104, ECmHR
McFeeley v UK (1981) 3 EHRR 161, ECmHR
X v UK (1980) 21 DR 95, ECmHR

ECHR principles

- Article 3 protects all citizens, including prisoners, against torture, inhuman and degrading treatment.

- In the prison context, the threshold is fairly high: the question is whether the conditions of confinement fall below the standards evolving in Europe.

- The following fall below the threshold:

    (a)   severe overcrowding (*The Greek Case*);
    (b)   inadequate toilet facilities, heating or recreation (*The Greek Case*);
    (c)   deprivation of food, water and medical treatment (*Cyprus v Turkey*).

- When assessing conditions of imprisonment, the Council of Europe Minimum Rules for the Treatment of Prisoners are relevant; but breach of the rules will not automatically lead to a breach of Article 3 (*Eggs v Switzerland; X v Germany*).

- The fact that appalling conditions are brought about by a prisoner's own conduct is relevant but will not absolve the authorities of all responsibility (*McFeeley v UK; Hilton v UK*).

13.4   SOLITARY CONFINEMENT

Key ECHR cases

Bonzi v Switzerland (1978) 12 DR 185, ECmHR
Dhoest v Belgium (1988) 55 DR 5, ECmHR
Ensslin and others v Germany (1978) 14 DR 64, ECmHR
Krause v Switzerland (1979) 13 DR 73, ECmHR
Krocher and Moller v Switzerland (1983) 34 DR 24, ECmHR
M v UK (1987) 52 DR 269, ECmHR[CD]
R v Denmark (1985) 41 DR 149, ECmHR
Reed v UK (1983) 19 DR 113, ECmHR
Treholdt v Norway (1991) 71 DR 168, ECmHR[CD]
Windsor v UK (App. No. 18942/91, 6 April 1991), ECmHR
X v Denmark (1982) 27 DR 50, ECmHR
X v UK (1976) 3 DR 5, ECmHR
X v UK (1980) 21 DR 95, ECmHR
X v UK (1985) 7 EHRR 140, ECmHR

ECHR principles

- Segregation is undesirable under the ECHR (*X v UK* (1976)).

- But so long as it can be justified on grounds of security, order, discipline or the prevention of crime, solitary confinement does not, in itself, breach Article 3, ECHR (*X v Denmark; R v Denmark; M v UK; Dhoest v Belgium; Treholdt v Norway; Bonzi v Switzerland; Krause v Switzerland*).

- However, complete sensory isolation coupled with complete social isolation are unjustifiable on any grounds (*Ensslin and others v Germany*).

13.5   DEATHS IN CUSTODY

Key ECHR cases

McCann and others v UK (1995) 21 EHRR 97, ECtHR
Naddaf v Germany (1987) 9 EHRR 561, ECtHR
Osman v UK (1998) 29 EHRR 245, ECtHR

Keenan v UK (App. No. 27229/95, 22 June 1998), ECmHR[CD]
Rebai v France (1997) 88-B DR 72, ECmHR
X v Germany (1985) 7 EHRR 152, ECmHR

ECHR principles

- The positive obligation on the state to protect life under Article 2, ECHR applies in prison.

- This applies even if it involves treatment which potentially violates other rights of the prisoner (*X v Germany*, p. 153 – *force feeding*; *Rebai v France*, p. 81 – *death from fire in cell after previous attempts at suicide*).

- The extent of this obligation to prevent death varies. But failure to take appropriate preventative steps in the face of an immediate and foreseeable threat to a prisoner may result in a violation of the right to life under Article 2 (*Osman v UK*, p. 230; *Keenan v UK*).

- Where death does occur, Article 2 requires an effective investigation (see **18.3**).

13.6   INTIMATE SEARCHES

Key ECHR cases

A, B v Switzerland (1995) 80-B DR 66, ECmHR
Galloway v UK [1999] EHRLR 119, ECmHR[CD]
McFeeley v UK (1981) 3 EHRR 161, ECmHR

ECHR principles

- Intimate searches require clear justification; where no such justification is established, Article 3 will probably be breached (*McFeeley v UK*).

- Requiring a prisoner to provide a urine sample for drug testing does not, in itself, attain the necessary degree of severity to breach Article 3 (*A, B v Switzerland*; *Galloway v UK*).

13.7   HANDCUFFS AND RESTRAINTS

Key ECHR cases

Raninen v Finland (1997) 26 EHRR 563, ECtHR

ECHR principles

- Using handcuffs while transporting prisoners to or from custody will not breach Article 3, ECHR where their use is necessary and reasonable, unless there is clear intention physically to harm and/or humiliate (*Raninen v Finland*, p. 345).

13.8   ILL-TREATMENT

- Ill-treatment in custody raises issues under Article 3 and Article 8, ECHR (see **7.13**).

13.9   FORCED LABOUR

Key ECHR cases

De Wilde, Ooms and Versyp v Belgium (1971) 1 EHRR 373, ECtHR

21 detained persons v Germany (1968) 11 Yearbook 528, ECmHR
X v Switzerland (1980) 18 DR 238, ECmHR

ECHR principles

- Article 4(2), ECHR specifically provides that 'No one shall be required to perform forced or compulsory labour'.

- However, Article 4(3)(a) excludes from the definition of forced labour, 'any work required to be done in the ordinary course of detention imposed according to the provisions of Article 5 of this Convention or during conditional release from such detention'.

- This applies to convicted and remand prisoners (*X v Switzerland*, p. 248 – *juvenile required to work during his placement under observation in a closed institution did not go beyond 'ordinary limits' of Article 4(3)(a)*).

- Prison work need not be remunerated (*21 detained persons v Germany*).

- It can cover work carried out for private contractors (*21 detained persons v Germany*).

- But prison work which has no rehabilitative element whatsoever may breach Article 4(2) (*De Wilde, Ooms and Versyp v Belgium*).

13.10   CATEGORISATION

Key ECHR cases

Ashingdane v UK (1985) 7 EHRR 528, ECtHR

Brady v UK (App. No. 85752/97), ECmHR
Togher v UK [1998] EHRLR 637, ECmHR
X v UK (1980) 20 DR 202, ECmHR
X v UK (1980) 21 DR 95, ECmHR

ECHR principles

- A decision to classify a prisoner as category A is not the determination of a criminal charge within the meaning of Article 6, ECHR (*X v UK* (1980) 20).

- Neither is it the determination of civil rights or obligations (*Brady v UK*).

- Stricter conditions of confinement resulting from a high-security categorisation do not automatically breach Article 3 (*X v UK* (1980) 21).

- Neither does imprisonment become unlawful under Article 5 by reason of a prisoner's security categorisation (*Ashingdane v UK*).

13.11   DISCIPLINARY PROCEEDINGS

Key ECHR cases

Campbell and Fell v UK (1984) 7 EHRR 165, ECtHR

ECHR principles

- Prison disciplinary proceedings amount to the determination of a criminal charge and therefore attract the Article 6, ECHR fair trial safeguards (*Campbell and Fell v UK*).

- Although the right to a public hearing is one aspect of a fair trial under Article 6, it does not apply rigidly to prison disciplinary proceedings (*Campbell and Fell v UK*).

- But an award of loss of remission does not technically constitute detention (*Campbell and Fell v UK*).

13.12   ACCESS TO COURT

Key ECHR cases

Ashingdane v UK (1985) 7 EHRR 528, ECtHR
Campbell and Fell v UK (1984) 7 EHRR 165, ECtHR
Golder v UK (1975) 1 EHRR 524, ECtHR

Associacion de Aviadores de la Republica, Mata et al. v Spain (1984) 41 DR 211, ECmHR
Brady v UK (App. No. 85752/97), ECmHR
Campbell v UK (1988) 57 DR 148, ECmHR[CD]
Grace v UK (1989) 62 DR 22, ECmHR
Kiss v UK (1977) 7 DR 55, ECmHR

ECHR principles

- Many decisions which affect prisoners are purely administrative; they fall outside the scope of Article 6(1), ECHR, which focuses on civil rights and obligations (*Brady v UK; Associacion de Aviadores de la Republica, Mata et al. v Spain*).

- But prisoners do not lose their right of access to the courts under Article 6 simply by reason of their imprisonment (*Golder v UK*).

- As a result, the authorities should not obstruct – and in some cases should assist – prisoners communicating with their lawyers so that they can gain effective access to a court (*Campbell and Fell v UK – right to private communication with a lawyer is ancillary to the right of access to courts*).

- Some restrictions may be necessary on grounds of security (*Campbell and Fell v UK*, para. 113); but legal privilege should be respected (see **13.14.2**).

13.13   PRIVACY AND FAMILY LIFE

Key ECHR cases

Boyle and Rice v UK (1988) 10 EHRR 425, ECtHR
Silver and others v UK (1983) 5 EHRR 347, ECtHR

A, B v Switzerland (1995) 80-B DR 66, ECmHR
App. No. 3603/68 (1970) Coll 31 p. 48, ECmHR
App. No. 7455/76 (13 December 1976), ECmHR
App. No. 7647/76 (1977), ECmHR
Campbell and Fell v UK (App. No. 7819/77), ECmHR
ELH and PBH v UK [1998] EHRLR 231, ECmHR[CD]
Galloway v UK [1999] EHRLR 119, ECmHR[CD]
Hacisuleymanoglu v Italy (1994) 79-B DR 121, ECmHR
Lant v UK (1986) 45 DR 236, ECmHR
McCotter v UK (1993) 15 EHRR CD 98, ECmHR[CD]
McFeeley v UK (1981) 3 EHRR 161, ECmHR
Ouinas v France (1988) 65 DR 265, ECmHR
S v UK (1993) 15 EHRR CD 106, ECmHR
TV v Finland (1994) 18 EHRR CD 179, ECmHR
Wakefield v UK (1990) 66 DR 251, ECmHR[CD]
X v Iceland (1976) 5 DR 86, ECmHR
X v UK (1975) 2 DR 105, ECmHR
X v UK (1979) 14 DR 246, ECmHR
X v UK (1982) 30 DR 113, ECmHR
X v UK (1983) 5 EHRR 260, ECmHR
X and Y v Switzerland (1979) 13 DR 241, ECmHR

ECHR principles

- On the basis that Article 8, ECHR includes the right to nurture and develop relationships, unless there are legitimate security grounds for segregation, prisoners are entitled to associate with one another (*McFeeley v UK*).

- Equally, access to family and friends should be permitted, within the confines of imprisonment (*X v UK* (1983); *McCotter v UK*).

- However, obligations to transfer prisoners to other locations to fulfil this aspect of Article 8 are very limited (*Campbell and Fell v UK; Ouinas v France; Wakefield v UK; S v UK*; for transfer between countries, see *Hacisuleymanoglu v Italy*).

- Limited visits do not necessarily breach Article 8 (*Boyle and Rice v UK*); neither do closed visits, if justified (*X v UK* (1979)).

13.14   CORRESPONDENCE

13.14.1   *General correspondence*

Key ECHR cases

Campbell v *UK* (1992) 15 EHRR 137, ECtHR
Domenichini v *Italy* [1997] EHRLR 192, ECtHR
McCallum v *UK* (1990) 13 EHRR 596, ECtHR
Petra v *Romania* (23 September 1998), ECtHR
Pfeifer and Plankl v *Austria* (1992) 14 EHRR 692, ECtHR
Silver and others v *UK* (1983) 5 EHRR 347, ECtHR

Chester v *UK* (1991) 68 DR 65, ECmHR[CD]
Farrant v *UK* (1987) 50 DR 5, ECmHR
Grace v *UK* (1989) 62 DR 22, ECmHR

ECHR principles

- The right to correspond with the outside world is fundamental to prisoners and is protected by Article 8, ECHR.

- As a result, the relevant authorities are under a duty to ensure the effective dispatch and receipt of authorised correspondence (*Grace* v *UK*).

- This right does not prohibit restrictions imposed on legitimate grounds – such as security or the prevention of crime – so long as the restriction is both necessary and proportionate (*Silver and others* v *UK*).

- Rules prohibiting correspondence that makes criticism or complaint of the prison regime on the basis that such matters should first be raised within the prison are not acceptable (*Silver and others* v *UK*).

- Neither are rules prohibiting correspondence which is calculated to hold the prison authorities up to contempt (*Silver and others* v *UK*; *Pfeifer and Plankl* v *Austria*).

- Even correspondence containing grossly improper language should not be stopped as a matter of course; in principle, freedom of speech includes speech which is vulgar, controversial, shocking or offensive (*Silver and others* v *UK*).

- Restrictions on correspondence containing threats of violence, or obscene or coded messages can be justified in the interests of security, good order and discipline (*Grace* v *UK*).

- Restrictions on correspondence must be set out in clear, accessible rules. Prison regulations which allow the authorities to retain any material 'unsuited to the process of rehabilitating a prisoner' are too vague (*Petra* v *Romania*).

13.14.2   *Legal correspondence*

Key ECHR cases

Campbell v *UK* (1992) 15 EHRR 137, ECtHR
Silver and others v *UK* (1983) 5 EHRR 347, ECtHR

Grace v *UK* (1989) 62 DR 22, ECmHR

ECHR principles

- Prisoners' correspondence with lawyers is privileged and protected by Article 8, ECHR (*Silver and others v UK*).

- It may be opened only where the prison authorities have good cause to believe that it contains an illicit enclosure which the normal means of detection have failed to disclose (*Campbell v UK*).

- Even when opened, save in exceptional circumstances, such correspondence should not be read. Exceptional circumstances might arise where the prison authorities have good cause for believing that legal privilege is being abused, or that the contents of the correspondence endanger prison security or the safety of others or otherwise are of a criminal nature (*Campbell v UK*).

13.15   MARRIAGE

Key ECHR cases

Draper v UK (1981) 24 DR 72, ECmHR
Hamer v UK (1982) 4 EHRR 139, ECmHR
X v UK (1975) 2 DR 105, ECmHR

ECHR principles

- Prisoners are entitled to marry, but the ceremony may have to be conducted in prison (*Hamer v UK; Draper v UK*, p. 82 – *life sentence prisoner wrongly prevented from marrying unless given a provisional release date or purpose was to legitimise a child*).

13.16   CONJUGAL VISITS

Key ECHR cases

ELH and PBH v UK [1998] EHRLR 231, ECmHR[CD]
X v UK (1975) 2 DR 105, ECmHR
X and Y v Switzerland (1978) 13 DR 241, ECmHR

ECHR principles

- A right to conjugal visits for prisoners cannot (yet) be read into Article 8, ECHR (*X v UK*). But the ECmHR has noted:

   . . . the reformative movement in several European countries as regards an improvement of the conditions of imprisonment with the possibility for detained persons of continuing their conjugal life to a limited extent. (*X and Y v Switzerland*, p. 243)

- At present, conjugal visits are not a right even where the prisoner and his partner are practising Catholics unable to avail themselves of facilities for artificial insemination (*ELH and PBH v UK*).

Relevant domestic cases

R v Secretary of State for the Home Department, ex parte Mellor (31 July 2000), HL

- A prisoner does not have the right of access to artificial insemination facilities (*R v Secretary of State for the Home Department, ex parte Mellor*).

13.17 FREEDOM OF THOUGHT, CONSCIENCE AND RELIGION

Key ECHR cases

Chester v UK (App. No. 14747/89, 1 October 1990), ECmHR
H v UK (1993) 16 EHRR CD 44, ECmHR
Islam v UK (1996) 22 EHRR CD 215, ECmHR[CD]
McFeeley v UK (1980) 20 DR 44, ECmHR
Vereniging Rechtswinkels Utrecht v Netherlands (1986) 46 DR 200, ECmHR
X v UK (1963) Coll Dec 16, p. 20, ECmHR
X v UK (1976) 5 DR 100, ECmHR

ECHR principles

- Freedom of thought, conscience and religion cannot be restricted.

- However, *manifesting* a religion or belief can be restricted.

- The health and rights of other prisoners, the prevention of crime and prison security are all legitimate grounds for restricting the manifestation of religion or beliefs by prisoners, so long as such restrictions are necessary and proportionate (*X v UK* (1976) – *requirement that Sikh sweep floor in cell contrary to his caste position justifiable; X v UK* (1963) – *no violation where religious and philosophical book withheld on the ground that it contained a section on martial arts*).

- Freedom of religion does not guarantee special 'political prisoner' status, neither can it be extended to a right for prisoners to wear their own clothes (*McFeeley v UK*, paras 27–30).

- A group providing legal advice to prisoners cannot invoke their beliefs as a ground for protecting their contact with prisoners (*Vereniging Rechtswinkels Utrecht v Netherlands*).

13.18 FREEDOM OF EXPRESSION

Key ECHR cases

Bamber v UK (1998) EHRLR 110, ECmHR[CD]
Haider v Austria (1995) 83-A DR 66, ECmHR[CD]
T v UK (1986) 49 DR 5, ECmHR

ECHR principles

- Prisoners are free to exercise their right to freedom of expression under Article 10, ECHR, within the constraints of imprisonment.

- They cannot claim a general right of access to broadcasting time to put across their views, but restrictions on access to the media which would otherwise be available must be both necessary and proportionate (*Haider v Austria; Bamber v UK – ban on life sentence prisoner's telephone communications with the media infringed Article 10*).

Relevant domestic cases

R v Secretary of State for the Home Department, ex parte Simms and O'Brien [1999] 3 WLR 328

- Prisoners must not be denied access to journalists without justification (*R v Secretary of State for the Home Department, ex parte Simms and O'Brien*).

13.19 FREEDOM OF INFORMATION

Key ECHR cases

Lowes v UK (1988) 59 DR 244, ECmHR[CD]
McFeeley v UK (1980) 20 DR 44, ECmHR
X v UK (1980) 20 DR 202, ECmHR

ECHR principles

- Prisoners are free to exercise their right to receive and impart information under Article 10, ECHR, within the constraints of imprisonment.

- In principle, prisoners can receive newspapers and journals, unless restrictions on specific publications can be justified under Article 10(2) (*Lowes v UK – withholding issue of a magazine containing anti-Semitic material justified*).

- Depriving a prisoner of reading and writing materials as a punishment will be justified only if there is a causal link between their use and the restriction, e.g., they were the tools of ill-discipline (*McFeeley v UK; T v UK*).

13.20 FREEDOM OF ASSOCIATION

Key ECHR cases

X v UK (1981) 24 DR 57, ECmHR
X v UK (1983) 5 EHRR 260, ECmHR

ECHR principles

- Prisoners are free to exercise their right to freedom of association under Article 11, ECHR, within the constraints of imprisonment.

- They are free to join trade unions; but the relevant authorities are not necessarily under a duty to protect their rights as trade unionists (*X v UK* (1981)).

- Freedom of association does not mean freedom to associate with others in the sense of enjoying their personal company (*X v UK* (1983)).

13.21   PROPERTY RIGHTS

Key ECHR cases

Davis v UK (1997) App. No. 27042/95, ECmHR
Szrabjer and Clarke v UK [1998] EHRLR 230, ECmHR

ECHR principles

- Prisoners retain their right to peaceful enjoyment of possessions under Protocol 1, Article 1, within the constraints of imprisonment.

- The deduction of a sum from prisoners' earnings to provide for entertainment does not necessarily breach this right (*Davis v UK*).

- Neither does a rule suspending state pensions during incarceration (*Szrabjer and Clarke v UK*).

13.22   EDUCATION

ECHR principles

- Protocol 1, Article 1, provides that no one shall be deprived of the right to education.

- However, it only confers the right for prisoners to avail themselves of the means of instruction existing at the time.

- It is also primarily directed towards elementary education and not advanced studies such as technology (see **38.5**).

VICTIMS OF CRIME

14.1 PROTECTION FROM CRIME

Key ECHR cases

Çakici v Turkey (8 July 1999), ECtHR
Osman v UK (1998) 29 EHRR 245, ECtHR
Stubbings and others v UK (1996) 23 EHRR 213, ECtHR
X and Y v Netherlands (1985) 8 EHRR 235, ECtHR

McCourt v UK (1993) 15 EHRR CD 110, ECmHR[CD]

ECHR principles

- There is a general duty on the relevant authorities under the ECHR to protect Convention rights, including, in particular, the right to life (Article 2), the prohibition on inhuman and degrading treatment (Article 3), the protection of physical integrity and privacy (Article 8) and the protection of property (Protocol 1, Article 1).

- The mere fact that crimes are carried out by private individuals and not by the authorities defines, but does not diminish, this obligation (X and Y v Netherlands; Stubbings v UK).

- No particular scheme for protecting these rights is prescribed by the ECHR, but the fundamental requirement of whatever scheme is put in place is that it should be effective. For investigation and prosecution, see **6.1, 18.3** and **19.5**).

- Where absolute rights – such as the right to life and the prohibition on inhuman and degrading treatment – are at stake, there is a duty to put in place criminal laws to deter offenders, and a duty to investigate serious offences and prosecute where appropriate: relying on civil remedies is insufficient:

    . . . the protection afforded by the civil law in the case [of the sexual assault] inflicted on [the applicant] is insufficient. This is a case where fundamental values and essential aspects of private life are at stake. Effective deterrence is indispensable in this area and it can be achieved only by criminal-law provisions; indeed, it is by such provisions that the matter is normally regulated. (X and Y v Netherlands, para. 27)

- Certain victims are entitled to special protection:

    . . . sexual abuse is unquestionably an abhorrent type of wrongdoing, with debilitating effects on its victim. Children and other vulnerable individuals are entitled to State protection, in the form of effective deterrents, from such grave types of interference with essential aspects of their private lives. (Stubbings and others v UK, para. 62)

- However, that does not mean that where criminal laws are already in place there must also be unlimited access to civil remedies:

    . . . Article 8 does not necessarily require that States fulfil their positive obligation to secure respect for private life by the provision of unlimited civil remedies in circumstances where criminal law sanctions are in operation. (*Stubbings and others v UK*, para. 64)

- Neither does it entitle a victim to participate in the sentencing process (*McCourt v UK*).

- There is no general principle that family members of those who 'disappear' or are otherwise subjected to violations of Articles 2 and 3 are, on that basis alone, themselves victims of treatment contrary to the ECHR. However, special factors, such as a close family tie, witnessing some or all of the conduct in question, or being subjected to alternating hope and despair by the way in which the authorities react to the issue, may be sufficient (*Çakici v Turkey*, para. 98).

14.2   PREVENTATIVE MEASURES

Key ECHR cases

Osman v UK (1998) 29 EHRR 245, ECtHR
T v UK, V v UK (1999) 30 EHRR 121, ECtHR

W v UK (1983) 32 DR 190, ECmHR
X v Ireland (1973) 16 Yearbook 388, ECmHR

ECHR principles

- Where identifiable individuals are at risk of serious crime, the obligation on the authorities to protect their ECHR rights can extend to a duty to take preventative action, particularly where there is an immediate threat to fundamental rights:

    It is common ground that the State's obligation [under Article 2] . . . extends beyond its primary duty to secure the right to life by putting in place effective criminal law provisions to deter the commission of offences against the person backed up by law-enforcement machinery for the prevention, suppression and sanctioning of breaches of such provisions. It is thus accepted . . . that Article 2 . . . may also imply in certain well-defined circumstances a positive obligation on the authorities to take preventive operational measures to protect an individual whose life is at risk from the criminal acts of another individual. The scope of the obligation is a matter of dispute. (*Osman v UK*, para. 115 – *failure of police to prevent infatuated teacher from attacking applicant and killing his father: no breach on facts*)

    . . . states have a duty under the Convention to take measures for the protection of the public from violent crimes . . . (*T v UK, V v UK*, para. 98)

- However, such an obligation must be interpreted in a way which does not impose an impossible or a disproportionate burden on the authorities. Accordingly, not every claimed risk to life can entail for the authorities a Convention requirement to take operational measures to prevent that risk from materialising (*Osman v UK*, para. 116).

- Furthermore, the duty to take preventative measures cannot be used as a mechanism for restricting the Convention rights of others:

  Another relevant consideration is the need to ensure that the police exercise their powers to control and prevent crime in a manner which fully respects the due process and other guarantees which legitimately place restraints on the scope of their action to investigate crime and bring offenders to justice, including the guarantees contained in Articles 5 and 8 of the Convention. (*Osman v UK*, para. 116)

- It must be established that the authorities failed to do all that could reasonably be expected of them to avoid a 'real and immediate' risk to life about which they knew or ought to have known (*Osman v UK*, para. 116).

- Where an identifiable individual is at risk of paramilitary attack, there may be a duty to provide protection; but not for an indefinite period:

  Article 2 cannot be interpreted as imposing a duty on a state to give protection of this nature, at least not for an indefinite period. (*X v Ireland*, p. 392)

  . . . a positive obligation to exclude any possible violence could not be read into Article 2. (*W v UK*, p. 200)

- For other cases involving the right to life, see further **18.1**.

14.3   DOMESTIC VIOLENCE

Key ECHR cases

Airey v Ireland (1979) 2 EHRR 305, ECtHR

Whiteside v UK (1994) 76-A DR 80, ECmHR[CD]

ECHR principles

- The relevant authorities are under a duty to provide effective protection against domestic violence (*Airey v Ireland; Whiteside v UK*).

- This includes effective access to the courts for the victims of domestic violence (*Airey v Ireland*).

- And effective remedies (*Whiteside v UK – no breach on the facts*).

Relevant Scottish cases

Janice Ward v Scotrail Ltd (27 November 1998), HC

- Article 8 obliges the relevant authorities to protect individuals at work from deliberate persecution and harassment (*Janice Ward v Scotrail Ltd*, p. 5 – *unwanted sexual letters sent from one employee to another*).

Relevant New Zealand cases

Whitair v Attorney-General [1996] 2 NZLR 45

- Although victims of domestic violence must be effectively protected by law, a policy of automatically denying bail to those charged in domestic violence cases is unlawful (*Whitair v Attorney-General*, p. 51).

14.4   INVESTIGATION AND PROSECUTION OF OFFENDERS

Key ECHR cases

Aksoy v Turkey (1996) 23 EHRR 553, ECtHR
Aydin v Turkey (1997) 25 EHRR 251, ECtHR
Kaya v Turkey (1998) 28 EHRR 1, ECtHR
Kurt v Turkey (1998) 27 EHRR 373, ECtHR
McCann and others v UK (1995) 21 EHRR 97, ECtHR

Dujardin v France (App. No. 16734/90), ECmHR
Taylor, Crampton, Gibson and King v UK (1994) 79-A DR 127, ECmHR[CD]

ECHR principles

- When serious crime is alleged and it affects fundamental rights – such as the right to life or the prohibition on inhuman and degrading treatment – there is a duty on the relevant authorities to respond diligently and effectively: this requires timely and efficient investigations, backed up by criminal prosecutions where appropriate:

  > [What is required is] a thorough and effective investigation capable of leading to the identification and punishment of those responsible and including effective access for the relatives to the investigatory procedure. (*Aksoy v Turkey*, para. 98; *Aydin v Turkey*, para. 103; *Kaya v Turkey*, para. 107; *Kurt v Turkey*, para. 140)

- This duty is particularly acute where state agents or officials have been involved in an incident affecting fundamental rights: what is required is 'some form of official investigation' (*McCann v UK*, para. 161).

- The duty to carry out a 'thorough and effective investigation' will not be fulfilled where the investigating authorities fail to ascertain possible eye-witnesses, fail to question suspects at a sufficiently early stage of the inquiry, fail to search for corroborating evidence or adopt an over-deferential attitude to authority (*Aksoy v Turkey*, paras 104–109).

- Other failings can include not following up the victim's complaints (*Kurt v Turkey*, para. 141), ignoring obvious evidence (*Aksoy v Turkey*, ref), not carrying out a proper autopsy and not testing for gunpowder traces (*Kaya v Turkey*, para. 89).

- However, granting an amnesty to those convicted or suspected of homicide will not necessarily breach the ECHR, so long as there is a legitimate basis for it and a proper balance is struck between the competing interests (*Dujardin v France*).

- For the wider duty to investigate suspicious deaths, see further **18.3**.

14.5   PROTECTION IN THE COURT ROOM

Key ECHR cases

Doorson v Netherlands (1996) 22 EHRR 330, ECtHR
Van Mechelen v Netherlands (1997) 25 EHRR 647, ECtHR

Baegen v Netherlands (1995) A/327-B, ECmHR
X v UK (1992) 15 EHRR CD 113, ECmHR

ECHR principles

- Although Article 6, ECHR deals primarily with the rights of defendants in criminal proceedings, the interests of victims and vulnerable witnesses can be taken into account in its interpretation:

  > It is true that Article 6 does not explicitly require the interests of witnesses in general, and those of victims called upon to testify in particular, to be taken into consideration. However, their life, liberty or security of person may be at stake, as may interests coming generally within the ambit of Article 8 of the Convention. Such interests of witnesses and victims are in principle protected by other, substantive provisions of the Convention, which imply that Contracting States should organise their criminal proceedings in such a way that those interests are not unjustifiably imperilled. Against this background, principles of fair trial also require that in appropriate cases the interests of the defence are balanced against those of witnesses or victims called upon to testify. (*Doorson v Netherlands*, para. 70)

- The interests of victims and vulnerable witnesses are particularly important where the proceedings might be seen as an ordeal in themselves, e.g., in cases involving sexual offences:

  > . . . [there is a need to have regard to] the special features of criminal proceedings concerning rape and other sexual offences. Such proceedings are often conceived of as an ordeal by the victim, in particular when the latter is unwillingly confronted with the defendant. In the assessment of the question whether or not in such proceedings an accused received a fair trial account must be taken of the right to respect for the victim's private life. Therefore the Commission accepts that in criminal proceedings concerning sexual abuse certain measures may be taken for the purpose of protecting the victim, provided that such measures can be reconciled with an adequate and effective exercise of the rights of the defence. (*Baegen v Netherlands*, para. 77; *victim in rape case remaining anonymous*)

- Where necessary, screens and other equipment can be used in court to protect vulnerable witnesses (*X v UK*), subject always to the *Van Mechelen* principle that:

  > Having regard to the place that the right to a fair administration of justice holds in a democratic society, any measures restricting the rights of the defence should be strictly necessary. If a less restrictive measure can suffice then that measure should be applied. (*Van Mechelen v Netherlands*, para. 58)

Relevant Scottish cases

Her Majesty's Advocate v Gilbert Nulty (17 February 2000)

- Since fairness of the proceedings should be considered as a whole, it is not necessarily unfair to prevent the accused cross-examining a vulnerable witness (even where the latter is the complainant), provided there are other evidential safeguards in place (*Her Majesty's Advocate v Gilbert Douglas Nulty* – *requirement of corroboration and directions from judge sufficient to counter inability of defendant to cross-examine mentally unfit teenage victim of rape*).

Relevant New Zealand cases

R v O [1999] 1 NZLR 347
TNZ Ltd v R [1996] 3 NZLR 393

- Judges who deal with victims should treat them with courtesy, compassion and respect for their personal dignity and privacy (*TNZ Ltd v R*, p. 395).

- A request by a victim for an adjournment in criminal proceedings should be considered by the court where there are good reasons for it (e.g., where an allegation is made by a defendant against a victim during the proceedings):

  > The unfairness to a victim of crime in denying him or her the ability to make an explanation related to the crime is readily apparent. In considering the exercising of its protective function the Court must take into account the need for fairness not only to the defendant but also to the complainant and the community. (*R v O*, p. 351 – *not abuse of process to adjourn in sodomy and indecent assault case*)

14.6   FEAR OF REPRISALS

- Where there is a genuine fear of reprisals, witnesses can remain anonymous and hearsay evidence can be relied upon (see **9.5** to **9.8**).

14.7   SAFEGUARDING PRIVACY

Key ECHR cases

Z v Finland (1997) 25 EHRR 371, ECtHR

ECHR principles

- The right to privacy afforded to victims and witnesses should be taken into account in criminal proceedings.

- Where intimate information has to be disclosed in the interests of prosecuting crime or ensuring a fair trial, safeguards should be put in place to protect the individual in question:

  > . . . the protection of personal data, not least medical data, is of fundamental importance to a person's enjoyment of his or her right to respect for private and family life as guaranteed by Article 8 . . . Respecting the confidentiality of health data is a vital principle in the legal systems of all the Contracting Parties . . . It is crucial not only to respect the sense of privacy of a patient but also to preserve his or her confidence in the medical profession and in the health services in general.
  >   The above considerations are especially valid as regards protection of the confidentiality of information about a person's HIV infection . . . The interests in protecting the confidentiality of such information will therefore weigh heavily in the balance in determining whether the interference was proportionate to the legitimate aim pursued.

Such interference cannot be compatible with Article 8 unless it is justified by an overriding requirement in the public interest . . . any state measures compelling communication or disclosure of such information without the consent of the patient call for the most careful scrutiny on the part of the Court as do the safeguards designed to secure an effective protection.

At the same time, the Court accepts that the interests of a patient and the community as a whole in protecting the confidentiality of medical data may be outweighed by the interest in investigation and prosecution of crime and in the publicity of court proceedings. (*Z v Finland*, paras 95–97 – *identity and sensitive medical data of innocent third party – wife of HIV positive man charged with attempted manslaughter following number of sexual offences – disclosed during trial following refusal of defendant to give evidence himself: insufficient safeguards*)

Relevant Canadian cases

M(A) v Ryan [1997] 1 SCR 157
R v Mills [1999] 3 SCR 668

- Since the right to disclosure is not absolute, a balance may have to be struck in sensitive cases between the defendant's fair trial rights and a victim's right to privacy:

  Between [the] extremes of [non-disclosure due to irrelevance and full disclosure needed to ensure equality of arms] lies a spectrum of possibilities regarding where to strike the balance between these competing rights in any particular context. The values protected by privacy rights will be most directly at stake where the confidential information contained in a record concerns aspects of one's individual identity or where the maintenance of confidentiality is crucial to a therapeutic, or other trust-like, relationship. (*R v Mills*, para. 89)

- This need for privacy safeguards is most acute in cases involving sexual offences, and rules of automatic disclosure require careful scrutiny:

  A rule of privilege which fails to protect confidential doctor/patient communications in the context of an action arising out of sexual assault perpetuates the disadvantage felt by victims of sexual assault, often women. The intimate nature of sexual assault heightens the privacy concerns of the victim and may increase, if automatic disclosure is the rule, the difficulty of obtaining redress for the wrong. (*M(A) v Ryan*, para. 30)

Relevant New Zealand cases

TNZ Ltd v R [1996] 3 NZLR 393
TV3 Network Services Ltd v R [1993] 3 NZLR 421

- A victim's right to privacy may be outweighed by the public's right to know where information is already in the public domain (*TNZ Ltd v R*, p. 397; but see also *TV3 Network Services Ltd v R*).

14.8 REMEDIES

Key ECHR cases

Aydin v Turkey (1997) 25 EHRR 251, ECtHR

ECHR principles

- Article 13, ECHR – the right to an effective remedy – requires that a range of remedies be available to victims of serious crime.

- In addition to the payment of compensation where appropriate, victims have the right to an effective investigation and the prosecution of alleged offenders (*Aydin* v *Turkey*, para. 103).

Other international human rights standards

- Victims should be treated with compassion and respect for their dignity. Moreover, they are entitled to access to the mechanisms of justice and to prompt redress, as provided for by national legislation, for the harm that they have suffered (Declaration of Basic Principles of Justice for Victims of Crime and Abuse of Power (1985), para. 4).

- Judicial and administrative mechanisms should be established and strengthened where necessary to enable victims to obtain redress through formal or informal procedures that are expeditious, fair, inexpensive and accessible. Victims should be informed of their rights in seeking redress through such mechanisms (Declaration of Basic Principles of Justice for Victims of Crime and Abuse of Power (1985), para. 5).

- When compensation is not fully available from the offender or other sources, states should endeavour to provide financial compensation to:

  (a) victims who have sustained significant bodily injury or impairment of physical or mental health as a result of serious crimes;
  (b) the family, in particular dependants of persons who have died or become physically or mentally incapacitated as a result of such victimisation.

  (Declaration of Basic Principles of Justice for Victims of Crime and Abuse of Power (1985), para. 12)

CIVIL RIGHTS AND OBLIGATIONS

15.1 THE MEANING OF CIVIL RIGHTS AND OBLIGATIONS

Key ECHR cases

Abenavoli v Italy (2 September 1997), ECtHR
Baraona v Portugal (1987) 13 EHRR 329, ECtHR
Benkessiour v France (24 August 1998), ECtHR
Cazenave de la Roche v France (9 June 1998), ECtHR
Deumeland v Germany (1986) 8 EHRR 448, ECtHR
Feldbrugge v Netherlands (1986) 8 EHRR 425, ECtHR
Frydlender v France (27 June 2000), ECtHR
Greek Refineries Stran and Stratis Andreadis v Greece (1994) 19 EHRR 293, ECtHR
GS v Austria (21 December 1999), ECtHR
Hornsby v Greece (1997) 24 EHRR 250, ECtHR
König v Germany (1978) 2 EHRR 170, ECtHR
Lapalorcia v Italy (2 September 1997), ECtHR
Le Calvez v France (29 July 1998), ECtHR
Lombardo v Italy (1992) 21 EHRR 188, ECtHR
Massa v Italy (1993) 18 EHRR 266, ECtHR
Nicodemo v Italy (2 September 1997), ECtHR
Ringeisen v Austria (1971) 1 EHRR 455, ECtHR
Robins v UK (1997) 26 EHRR 527, ECtHR
Ruiz-Mateos v Spain (1993) 16 EHRR 505, ECtHR
Rushiti v Austria (21 March 2000), ECtHR
Silva Pontes v Portugal (1994) 18 EHRR 156, ECtHR

Adams and Benn v UK (1996) 23 EHRR CD 160, ECmHR[CD]
X v Greece (11 January 1995), ECmHR

ECHR principles

- Article 6(1), ECHR applies to the determination of 'civil rights and obligations'.

- Civil rights and obligations are determined in any proceedings 'the result of which is decisive for private rights and obligations':

  Article 6(1) applies irrespective of the status of the parties, of the nature of the legislation which governs the manner in which the dispute is to be determined and of the character of the authority which has jurisdiction in the matter; it is enough that the outcome of the proceedings should be decisive for private rights and obligations. (*Greek Refineries Stran and Stratis Andreadis v Greece*, para. 39; see also *Ringeisen v Austria* para. 94)

- This includes all types of private litigation between individuals, up to and including the assessment of damages and enforcement of judgments (e.g., *Silva Pontes v Portugal*, paras 30 and 36; *Robins v UK*, para. 29; *Hornsby v Greece*).

- It also includes some, but not all, decisions of a public law character (*Ringeisen v Austria*, para. 94 – *decision by a public authority not to approve the transfer of certain plots of land to an individual directly affected the private law relationship between him and the vendor*).

- It is the impact of the proceedings on the parties rather than their classification in domestic law which is crucial:

    Whether or not a right is to be regarded as civil . . . must be determined by reference to the substantive contents and effects of the right – and not its legal classification – under the domestic law of the State concerned. (*König v Germany*, para. 89 – *authorisation to practise medicine and run a clinic withdrawn*)

- If the case is borderline, the existence of a 'uniform European notion' with regard to the right in issue will be relevant to the applicability of Article 6(1) (*Feldbrugge v Netherlands; Deumeland v Germany*).

- As a general rule, the following proceedings usually *do* determine civil rights and obligations:

    (a) property disputes (*Ringeisen v Austria; Hakansson and Sturesson v Sweden; Zander v Sweden; Sporrong and Lonroth v Sweden; Raimondo v Italy; Oerlemans v Netherlands; Gillow v UK; Beumartin v France*);
    (b) licensing decisions which affect a profession, calling or the right to engage in commercial activity (*Konig v Germany; X v Belgium; Benthem v Netherlands; Pudas v Sweden; Jorbedo Foundation of Christian Schools v Sweden; GS v Austria*);
    (c) disciplinary proceedings which have an impact on an individual's right to practise a profession (*Konig v Germany; Guchez v Belgium; H v Belgium; Ginikanwa v UK; De Moor v Belgium*);
    (d) family proceedings (*W v UK; Olsson v Sweden; Eriksson v Sweden; Keegan v Ireland*);
    (e) claims of right for compensation (*X v France; H v France; Baraona v Portugal; Greek Refineries Stran and Stratis Andreadis v Greece; Rushiti v Austria*);
    (f) claims for welfare benefits (*Feldbrugge v Netherlands; Deumeland v Germany; Minniti v Italy; Schuler-Zgraggen v Switzerland; Lo Giacco v Italy; Kerojavi v Finland; Salesi v Italy; Schouten and Meldrum v Netherlands; Machatova v Slovak Republic*).

- On the other hand, as a general rule, the following proceedings usually *do not* determine civil rights and obligations:

(a) tax proceedings (*X v Germany; X v France; Company S and T v Sweden; X v Austria*; but see *Editions Periscope v France; National & Provincial Building Society and others v UK*);

(b) discretionary or *ex gratia* payments (*Masson and van Zon v Netherlands; B v Netherlands; Nordh v Sweden; Machatova v Slovak Republic*; but see *Gustafson v Sweden*);

(c) immigration and nationality cases (*Agee v UK; Omkaranda and the Divine Light Zentrum v Switzerland; P v UK; S v Switzerland*);

(d) education disputes (*Simpson v UK; A v Germany*);

(e) election rights (*Pierre-Bloch v France*).

- Disputes relating to the recruitment, careers and termination of service of public servants are as a general rule outside the scope of Article 6(1), except where the claim in issue relates to:

(a) a 'purely economic' right, such as the payment of salary (*Lapalorcia v Italy* and *Abenavoli v Italy*) or pension (*Lombardo v Italy; Massa v Italy*); or

(b) an 'essentially economic one' (see *Nicodemo v Italy*).

(*Benkessiour v France*, para. 29 – *decision to refuse sick pay and reduce salary essentially economic*; see also *Le Calvez v France; Cazenave de la Roche v France*)

- But the test for public servants is now a functional test (*Frydlender v France*). See **37.6.2**.

15.2 THE NEED FOR A BASIS IN DOMESTIC LAW

Key ECHR cases

H v Belgium (1987) 10 EHRR 339, ECtHR
James v UK (1986) 8 EHRR 123, ECtHR
Osman v UK (1998) 29 EHRR 245, ECtHR
Powell and Rayner v UK (1990) 12 EHRR 355, ECtHR

ECHR principles

- Article 6(1), ECHR is intended to regulate the form and conduct of proceedings relating to rights and obligations which are recognised in domestic law.

- It does not require a state to provide legal remedies where none already exists:

Article 6(1) extends only to contestations (disputes) over (civil) rights and obligations which can be said, at least on arguable grounds, to be recognised under domestic law; it does not in itself guarantee any particular content for (civil) 'rights and obligations' in the substantive law of the contracting states. (*H v Belgium*, para. 40)

- Where the effect of a restriction, immunity or privilege is to extinguish a right in domestic law, Article 6(1) will have no application (*Powell and Rayner v UK*, para. 36).

- Where, on the other hand, the effect of a restriction, immunity or privilege is to limit but not extinguish a right in domestic law, Article 6(1) will apply (*Osman v UK*).

- The distinction between restrictions, immunities and privileges is dealt with more fully at **16.3**.

15.3   THE NEED FOR A DISPUTE

Key ECHR cases

Agrotexim v Greece (1995) 21 EHRR 250, ECtHR
Albert and Le Compte v Belgium (1983) 5 EHRR 533, ECtHR
Athanassoglou v Switzerland (6 April 2000), ECtHR
Balmer-Schafroth v Switzerland (1997) 25 EHRR 598
Benthem v Netherlands (1985) 8 EHRR 1, ECtHR
Hornsby v Greece (1997) 24 EHRR 250, ECtHR
Le Compte, Van Leuven and De Meyere v Belgium (1981) 4 EHRR 1, ECtHR
Pudas v Sweden (1987) 10 EHRR 380, ECtHR
Robins v UK (1997) 26 EHRR 527, ECtHR
Rolf Gustafson v Sweden (1997) 25 EHRR 623, ECtHR
Van Marle v Netherlands (1986) 8 EHRR 483, ECtHR

Porter v UK (1987) 54 DR 207, ECmHR

ECHR principles

- Article 6(1) applies to any genuine dispute over the existence, scope or manner of exercise of civil rights or obligations which can be said, at least on arguable grounds, to be recognised in domestic law (*Bentham v Netherlands; Van Marle v Netherlands; Pudas v Sweden*).

- The subject-matter of the proceedings must be a *right* rather than a discretionary benefit or an *ex gratia* payment; and a right is involved where a person who fulfils the eligibility criteria for a benefit will have an enforceable claim (*Rolf Gustafson v Sweden*).

- Where eligibility for a benefit depends on matters of expert judgment, e.g., an evaluation of knowledge and experience by a professional registration body, a *right* is not usually in issue; where it depends on ascertainable facts, a *right* usually is in issue (*Van Marle v Netherlands*).

- If the purpose of the proceedings in question is to determine civil rights and obligations, there is undoubtedly a dispute for Article 6(1) purposes (*Bentham v Netherlands*).

- But in addition Article 6(1) will also apply where, although the primary purpose of the proceedings in question is not to determine civil rights and obligations, the outcome is bound to have that effect.

- What is excluded are proceedings which only have a tenuous connection with civil rights and obligations:

    . . . [the applicants] did not . . . establish a direct link between the operating conditions of the power station which were contested by them and their right to protection of their physical integrity, as they failed to show that the operation of [the] power station exposed them personally to a danger that was not only serious but also specific and, above all, imminent. (*Balmer-Schafroth v Switzerland*, para. 40 – *objector opposing extension of operating licence for a nuclear power station*; confirmed in *Athanassoglou v Switzerland*, para. 54; see also *Agrotexim v Greece*; *Le Compte, Van Leuven and De Meyere v Belgium*; *Albert and Le Compte v Belgium*)

- Costs proceedings and enforcement proceedings are determinative of civil rights and obligations (*Robins v UK*; *Hornsby v Greece*); but an application for leave to appeal is not (*Porter v UK*).

Relevant domestic cases

R v Secretary of State for Health, ex parte C [2000] 1 FLR 627

- Placing an individual on a Consultancy Service Index as a result of proven child abuse allegations, is not 'determinative' of civil rights and obligations:

  Quite apart from the issue of whether there is indeed a 'civil right' involved, inclusion on the list is not determinative of the appellant's civil rights and obligations: see *Fayed v UK* (1994) 18 EHRR 393, at paras 56 and 61–62, applying the test adopted in *Le Compte, Van Leuven and De Meyere v Belgium* (1982) 4 EHRR 1. (*R v Secretary of State for Health, ex parte C*, p. 634)

15.4   ADMINISTRATIVE AND DISCIPLINARY HEARINGS

Key ECHR cases

Albert and Le Compte v Belgium (1983) 5 EHRR 533, ECtHR
Bryan v UK (1995) 21 EHRR 342, ECtHR
De Moor v Belgium (1994) 18 EHRR 372, ECtHR
Engel and others v Netherlands (1976) 1 EHRR 647, ECtHR
Ettl v Austria (1987) 10 EHRR 255, ECtHR
H v Belgium (1987) 10 EHRR 339, ECtHR
Kingsley v UK (7 November 2000), ECtHR
Le Compte, Van Leuven and De Meyere v Belgium (1981) 4 EHRR 1, ECtHR
Stallinger and Kuso v Austria (1997) 26 EHRR 81, ECtHR
WR v Austria (21 December 1999), ECtHR

Ginikanwa v UK (1988) 55 DR 251, ECmHR[CD]
Guchez v Belgium (1984) 40 DR 100, ECmHR
H.A.R. v Austria (1998) 27 EHRR CD 330, ECmHR
Stefan v UK (1997) 25 EHRR CD 130, ECmHR

ECHR principles

- Disciplinary proceedings do not normally determine civil rights and obligations (*Engel and others v Netherlands (No. 1)*; *Le Compte, Van Leuven and De Meyere v Belgium*).

- But where disciplinary proceedings affect the right of individuals to pursue their professional activities, Article 6(1) will apply.

- The fair trial requirements of Article 6(1) have therefore been read into:

  (a) proceedings before the equivalent of the Bar Council and the Law Society (*H v Belgium*; *Ginikanwa v UK*; *De Moor v Belgium*; *H.A.R. v Austria*);
  (b) medical disciplinary proceedings (*Le Compte, Van Leuven and De Meyere v Belgium*; *Stefan v UK*); and
  (c) proceedings before the Board of Appeals of the Architects Association in Belgium (*Guchez v Belgium*).

- The severity of any penalty or sanction is also important, a distinction being drawn between:

  (a) sanctions which truly affect the ability of individuals to continue with their professional activities, such as expulsion or striking off the professional list, suspension (even for short periods: *Le Compte, Van Leuven and De Meyere v Belgium* – *applicants were suspended for periods of between 15 days and three months*; see also *WR v Austria*, para. 30) and possibly even a heavy fine (*H.A.R. v Austria*); and
  (b) lesser measures, such as warnings and reprimands, which are by their very nature less serious in their consequences (see the ECtHR's observations in *Le Compte, Van Leuven and De Meyere v Belgium*).

- The fact that disciplinary proceedings against professionals are determined by a body which includes members of the same profession does not *in itself* offend the requirement of 'independence' in Article 6(1) of the Convention:

  There is no indication in the case law of the European Court of Human Rights that the mere fact that disciplinary proceedings against professional persons are determined by members of the profession amounts to a lack of 'independence', even where the professional body concerned regulates a number of functions of the profession. (*Stefan v UK*, p. 134; see also *H v Belgium*)

- And a panel which includes judges – even if only at the appeal stage – is more likely to comply with Article 6(1):

  The presence . . . of judges making up half the membership, including the Chairman with a casting vote . . . provides a definite assurance of impartiality and the method of election of the medical members cannot suffice to bear out a charge of bias. (*Le Compte, Van Leuven and De Meyere v Belgium*, para. 58; see also *Ettl v Austria*; *Stallinger and Kuso v Austria*; *H.A.R. v Austria*)

- Hearings need not be in public, if the parties consent:

  . . . the person subject to disciplinary proceedings may, if he so wishes, waive his right to a public hearing, for it is likely to be in the future professional interests of the person concerned to maintain the confidentiality of such proceedings, to reduce any unwarranted damage to reputation which might otherwise occur, whether or not they result in an acquittal or a disciplinary sanction. (*Ginikanwa v UK*, p. 260)

- Moreover, nothing in the Convention requires that every stage of disciplinary proceedings be conducted before a body or tribunal meeting the full requirements of Article 6(1):

Demands of flexibility and efficiency, which are fully compatible with the protection of human rights, may justify the prior intervention of administrative or professional bodies and, *a fortiori*, of judicial bodies which do not satisfy the said requirements in every respect; the legal tradition of many members of the member States of the Council of Europe may be invoked in support of such a system. (*Le Compte, Van Leuven and De Meyere v Belgium*, para. 51)

- But where proceedings do take place before a body or tribunal that does not satisfy the full requirements of Article 6(1), there must be scope for an aggrieved individual to appeal to a further body, tribunal or court that does.

- And in some circumstances, the appeal body, tribunal or court may have to examine the facts (*Albert and Le Compte v Belgium; W v UK*, para. 82; but see also *Bryan v UK*).

- Where a decision of the Gaming Board as to whether an individual is a fit and proper person for a gaming certificate is tainted by impartiality, the powers of the High Court on judicial review may be too restrictive to satisfy Article 6 (*Kingsley v UK*).

Relevant domestic cases

Brabazon-Drenning v UK Central Council for Nursing, Midwifery and Health Visiting (31 October 2000).

- Failure to hear from applicant before excluding her from the Register of Nurses was not a fair procedure (*Brabazon-Drenning v UK Central Council for Nursing, Midwifery and Health Visiting*).

Relevant Commonwealth cases

Holland v Minister of the Public Services (1997) 2 BHRC 478

- A decision to suspend an individual's membership of an executive committee of an association may be determinative of civil rights and therefore subject to fair trial guarantees:

  . . . the act of suspension was based on a determination made by the minister that the applicants were unfit to remain in office as members of the executive committee . . .
  By removing their entitlement to function as members of the executive committee, the minister effectively determined the extent of their civil rights and obligations . . . (*Holland v Minister of the Public Services*, p. 481 – *members of the National Councils of Women's Clubs did not receive a fair hearing when majority did not have the opportunity to express their views at meeting where decision taken*)

15.5   INQUIRIES

Key ECHR cases

Fayed v UK (1994) 18 EHRR 393, ECtHR

ECHR principles

- Official investigations and/or inquiries may not come within the scope of Article 6(1), ECHR; particularly where there is no 'disposition of legal rights and duties':

  Acceptance of the applicants' argument would entail that a body carrying out preparatory investigations at the instance of regulatory or other authorities should always be subject to the guarantees of a judicial procedure set forth in Article 6(1) by reason of the fact that publication of its findings is liable to damage the reputation of the individuals whose conduct is being investigated. Such an interpretation of Article 6(1) would in practice unduly hamper the effective regulation in the public interest of complex financial and commercial activities . . . [therefore] investigative proceedings of the kind in issue in the present case fall outside the ambit and intendment of Article 6(1). (*Fayed v UK*, para. 62 – *finding of dishonesty after fraud inspection not covered on the basis of need to distinguish between adjudication (within Article 6(1)) and investigation*)

ACCESS TO A COURT IN CIVIL PROCEEDINGS

16.1 THE RIGHT OF ACCESS TO A COURT

Key ECHR cases

Ashingdane v UK (1985) 7 EHRR 528, ECtHR
Golder v UK (1975) 1 EHRR 524, ECtHR
Lithgow v UK (1986) 8 EHRR 329, ECtHR

H v UK (1985) 45 DR 281, ECmHR
M v UK (1987) 52 DR 269, ECmHR[CD]

ECHR principles

- Although Article 6(1), ECHR does not expressly refer to a right of access to a court, this right has been read into it to give effect to the notion of a fair trial:

  > In civil matters one can scarcely conceive of the rule of law without there being a possibility of access to the courts . . . The principle whereby a civil claim must be capable of being submitted to a judge ranks as one of the universally recognised fundamental principles of law; the same is true of the principle of international law which forbids the denial of justice. Article 6(1) must be read in light of these principles. (*Golder v UK*, paras 35–45 – *prisoner prevented under Prison Rules from consulting a solicitor about defamation proceedings against prison officer*)

- However, it is not an absolute right: restrictions on the right of access to a court are permitted, but only in so far as they pursue a legitimate aim and are proportionate:

  > . . . by its very nature [the right of access to a court] calls for regulation by the State, regulation which may vary in time and in place according to the needs and resources of the community and of individuals . . . [but such regulation must not] . . . restrict or reduce the access left to the individual in such a way or to such an extent that the very essence of the right is impaired.
  >
  > Furthermore, a limitation will not be compatible with Article 6(1) if it does not pursue a legitimate aim and if there is not a reasonable relationship of proportionality between the means employed and the aim sought to be achieved. (*Lithgow v UK*, para. 194)

- Restrictions on rights of access to a court for children (*M v UK*), bankrupts (*M v UK*), those suffering from mental illness (*Ashingdane v UK*) and vexatious litigants (*H v UK*) are legitimate in principle, subject to proportionality.

16.2   ARBITRATION CLAUSES

Key ECHR cases

Deweer v Belgium (1980) 2 EHRR 439, ECtHR

Malmstrom v Sweden (1983) 38 DR 18, ECmHR
R v Switzerland (1987) 51 DR 83, ECmHR

ECHR principles

- Individuals are free to waive their right of access to a court by agreeing to arbitration:

  > In the Contracting States' domestic legal systems a waiver of this kind is frequently encountered . . . in civil matters, notably in the shape of arbitration clauses in contracts . . . the waiver, which has undeniable advantages for the individual concerned as well as for the administration of justice, does not in principle offend against the Convention. (*Deweer v Belgium*, para. 49; *R v Switzerland*, pp. 100–1)

- However, arbitration agreements must be genuinely voluntary; alternatively, the arbitration tribunal itself must offer fair trial safeguards:

  > . . . a distinction must be drawn between voluntary arbitration and compulsory arbitration. Normally Article 6 poses no problem where arbitration is entered into voluntarily . . . If, on the other hand, arbitration is compulsory in the sense of being required by law, as is this case, the parties have no option but to refer their dispute to an arbitration Board, and the Board must offer their guarantees set forth in Article 6(1). (*Malmstrom v Sweden*, para. 30)

16.3   IMMUNITIES AND DISABILITIES

Key ECHR cases

Ashingdane v UK (1985) 7 EHRR 528, ECtHR
Beer and Regan v Germany (18 February 1999), ECtHR
Chahal v UK (1996) 23 EHRR 413, ECtHR
Fayed v UK (1994) 18 EHRR 393, ECtHR
Osman v UK (1998) 29 EHRR 245, ECtHR
Powell and Rayner v UK (1990) 12 EHRR 355, ECtHR
Tinnelly and Sons Ltd & McElduff and others v UK (1998) 27 EHRR 249, ECtHR
Waite and Kennedy v Germany (1999) 30 EHRR 261, ECtHR

Dyer v UK (1984) 39 DR 246, 7 EHRR 469, ECmHR
Ketterick v UK (1983) 5 EHRR 465, ECmHR
Pinder v UK (1984) 7 EHRR 464, ECmHR

ECHR principles

Where an immunity or disability is broad based and strictly applied, the effect may be that no 'right' in domestic law truly exists, and Article 6(1) has no application:

. . . the effect of [the statutory provision] is to exclude liability in nuisance with regard to the flight of aircraft in certain circumstances, with the result that the applicants cannot claim to have a substantive right under English law to obtain relief for exposure to aircraft noise in those circumstances. To this extent there is no 'civil right' recognised under domestic law to attract the application of Article 6(1). (*Powell and Rayner v UK*, para. 36 – *statutory exclusion of liability in trespass and nuisance for aircraft under the Civil Aviation Act 1982*)

• Much more common are immunities or disabilities which, while restricting access to a court, do not extinguish the 'right' in question:

Whether a person has an actionable domestic claim may depend not only on the substantive content, properly speaking, of the relevant civil right as defined under national law but also on the existence of procedural bars preventing or limiting the possibilities of bringing potential claims to court. In the latter kind of case Article 6(1) may have a degree of applicability. Certainly the Convention enforcement bodies may not create by way of interpretation of Article 6(1) a substantive civil right which has no legal basis in the State concerned. However, it would not be consistent with the rule of law in a democratic society or with the basic principle underlying Article 6(1) – namely that civil claims must be capable of being submitted to a judge for adjudication – if, for example, a State could, without restraint or control by the Convention enforcement bodies, remove from the jurisdiction of the courts a whole range of civil claims or confer immunities from civil liability on large groups or categories of persons. (*Fayed v UK*, para. 65 – *effect of qualified privilege rule of government inspector's report on defamation proceedings*)

• This principle extends to immunity from suit afforded to some bodies, such as international organisations set up by Treaty:

. . . where states establish international organisations in order to pursue or strengthen their cooperation in certain fields of activities, and where they attribute to these organisations certain competencies and accord them immunities, there may be implications as to the protection of human rights. It would be incompatible with the purpose and object of the Convention, however, if the contracting states were thereby absolved from their responsibility under the Convention in relation to the field of activity covered by such attribution. (*Waite and Kennedy v Germany*, para. 67)

• The question in such cases will be whether the immunity or disability in question is legitimate and proportionate (*Osman v UK* – *immunity of police in negligence proceedings too broad*).

• The immunity from suit afforded to international organisations established between states is legitimate (*Waite and Kennedy v Germany*, para. 63).

• Proportionality will depend on a number of facts, the availability and effectiveness of alternative remedies always being relevant (*Waite and Kennedy v Germany* – *immunity of European Space Agency proportionate because applicants had alternative remedy to determine their rights as employees*).

Relevant domestic cases

Arthur J.S. Hall & Co. (a firm) v Simons; Barratt v Ansell & others (trading as Woolf Seddon (a firm)); Harris v Scholfield Roberts & Hill (a firm) [2000] 3 WLR 543
Barrett v Enfield London Borough Council [1999] 3 WLR 79

Darker v Chief Constable of the West Midlands Police (27 July 2000)
Holland v Lampen-Wolfe [2000] 1 WLR 1573
S v Gloucestershire County Council; L v Tower Hamlets Borough Council and another
[2000] 1 FLR 825

- Restrictions on a child bringing proceedings against a local authority for negligent decisions said to have resulted in sex abuse no longer apply:

  [T]he Strasbourg court held that there was in the *Osman* case a breach of [the] right of access to the English court, such breach lying in the application of a blanket exclusionary rule which excludes all claims against the police for negligent failure to investigate or protect from crime. If this is not done then it is impossible to determine whether the public interest in an efficient police force is or is not proportionate to the seriousness of the harm suffered by the plaintiff in the individual case. (*Barrett v Enfield London Borough Council*, per Lord Browne-Wilkinson, p. 84)

- But this does not preclude any claim to immunity:

  . . . the court will need to be satisfied that upon [all substantial facts relevant to the allegations of negligence], there is no real prospect of the claim in negligence succeeding and that there is no other reason why the case should be disposed of at trial. If by this process the court does so conclude and gives summary judgment, there will, in my view, have been proper judicial scrutiny of the detailed facts of the particular case such as to constitute a fair hearing in accordance with Article 6 of the Convention. (*S v Gloucestershire County Council; L v Tower Hamlets Borough Council and another*, p. 853)

- Solicitors' immunity from suit requires close scrutiny:

  It is clear from the passage I have quoted from Lord Reid's speech in *Rondel v Worsley* [1969] 1 AC 191, 228 that under the common law the presumption is strongly in favour of the right of the individual to a remedy. Any immunity from suit must therefore be clearly justifiable. In terms of human rights law it will only be justifiable if it is designed to pursue a legitimate aim and then only if it satisfies the test of proportionality. If the restriction which the immunity imposes on the right of the individual is disproportionate to the aim sought to be achieved on the grounds of public policy it will be incompatible with the right secured to the individual by Article 6(1) of the Convention. Although the common law and human rights law tests are expressed in different language, they are both directed to the same essential point of principle that an immunity from suit is a derogation from a fundamental right which requires to be justified. (*Arthur J.S. Hall & Co. (a firm) v Simons; Barratt v Ansell & others (trading as Woolf Seddon (a firm)); Harris v Scholfield Roberts & Hill (a firm)*, per Lord Hope)

- But claims to state immunity may survive challenge:

  Article 6 requires contracting states to maintain fair and public judicial processes and forbids them to deny individuals access to those processes for the determination of their civil rights. It presupposes that the contracting states have the powers of adjudication necessary to resolve the issue in dispute. But it does not confer on contracting states adjudicative powers which they do not possess. State immunity, as I have explained, is a creature of customary international law and derives from the equality of sovereign states. It is not a self-imposed restriction on the jurisdiction of its courts which the United Kingdom has chosen to adopt. It is a limitation imposed from without upon the sovereignty of the United Kingdom itself.

The immunity in question in the present case belongs to the United States. The United States has not waived its immunity. It is not a party to the Convention. The Convention derives its binding force from the consent of the contracting states. The United Kingdom cannot by its own act of acceding to a Convention and without the consent of the United States obtain a power of adjudication over the United States which international law denies. (*Holland v Lampen-Wolfe*, per Lord Millett p. 1588)

- As might the absolute immunity afforded to witnesses (*Darker v Chief Constable of the West Midlands Police*).

Relevant Scottish cases

Gordon McLean v Her Majesty's Advocate (3 November 1999), AC

- In the light of the ECtHR's judgment in *Osman v UK*, a blanket immunity for the police from actions for negligence is no longer tenable:

  It was not disputed that the police enjoy no immunity on public policy grounds in respect of the manner in which a constable drives his police vehicle or his motor cycle on the public roads. There would likewise be no immunity, in my view, in respect of the manner in which a constable in charge of directing traffic on such a road performed that function. Likewise, there is no immunity . . . in respect of the manner in which other civil road safety operational tasks are carried out by police officers where there is no inherent problem of conflict with instructions issued by superior officers or with their duties owed to other persons. (*Gordon McLean v Her Majesty's Advocate*, p. 13)

16.4   LIMITATION PERIODS AND TIME LIMITS

Key ECHR cases

Pérez de Rada Cavanilles v Spain (1998) 29 EHRR 245, ECtHR
Stubbings and others v UK (1996) 23 EHRR 213, ECtHR

Dobbie v UK [1997] EHRLR 166, ECmHR[CD]
Stedman v UK (1997) 23 EHRR CD 168, ECmHR[CD]

ECHR principles

- Limitation periods and time limits are a legitimate means of ensuring the effectiveness of any legal system:

  . . . limitation periods in personal injury cases are a common feature of the domestic legal systems of the Contracting States. They serve important purposes, namely to ensure legal certainty and finality, to protect potential defendants from stale claims which might be difficult to counter, and to prevent the injustice which might arise if courts were required to decide upon events which took place in the distant past on the basis of evidence which might have become unreliable and incomplete because of the passage of time. (*Stubbings and others v UK*, para. 49 – *inflexible six-year limitation period in civil proceedings for assault barred applicants from bringing action for sexual abuse when children*)

- But they must not be so short – or so strictly applied – as unduly to hinder access to justice (*Perez de Rada Cavanilles v Spain*; see also *Stedman v UK* – *two-year qualifying period in unfair dismissal and redundancy claims justified*).

Relevant South African cases

Mohlomi v Minister of Defence (26 September 1996), CC

- Although it is in the interests of justice to lay down time limits on pursuing litigation, these must not be so strict that they violate the right of everyone to have justiciable disputes determined by the judicial system (*Mohlomi v Minister of Defence*, para. 12).

- And the reasonableness of time periods has to be seen in the context of the ability of the litigant(s) in question to access the judicial system (*Mohlomi v Minister of Defence*, para. 14).

16.5   SECURITY FOR COSTS

Key ECHR cases

Aït-Mouhoub v France [1999] EHRLR 215, ECtHR
Tolstoy Miloslavsky v UK (1995) 20 EHRR 442, ECtHR

Grepne v UK (1990) 66 DR 268, ECmHR[CD]
X v Sweden (1979) 17 DR 74, ECmHR

ECHR principles

- Security for costs orders can operate as a restriction on access to a court and therefore must be both legitimate and proportionate.

- Most security for costs orders will be legitimate on the basis that they are intended to protect successful parties from unrecoverable costs.

- Factors relevant to proportionality will be:
    (a) the means of the applicant (*Aït-Mouhoub v France* – *excessive order made against applicant before he could pursue claim against the police*);
    (b) the prospects of success (*Tolstoy Miloslavsky v UK*); and
    (c) the stage at which an order is made, orders at first instance being much harder to justify than orders on appeal when prospects of success can be more easily gauged.

16.6   PUBLIC INTEREST IMMUNITY

Key ECHR cases

Tinnelly and Sons Ltd & McElduff and others v UK (1998) 27 EHRR 249, ECtHR

ECHR principles

- Public interest immunity certificates can operate as a restriction on access to a court and therefore must be both legitimate and proportionate.

- The protection of national security is a legitimate basis for asserting public interest immunity; but any regulatory scheme that does not provide for independent judicial scrutiny of public interest immunity certificates is unlikely to be proportionate:

    The right guaranteed to an applicant under Article 6(1) of the Convention to submit a dispute to a court or tribunal in order to have a determination on questions of both fact and law cannot be displaced by the *ipse dixit* of the executive. (*Tinnelly and Sons Ltd & McElduff and others* v *UK*, para. 77)

16.7   RETROSPECTIVE INTERFERENCE WITH CIVIL RIGHTS AND OBLIGATIONS

Key ECHR cases

Greek Refineries Stran and Stratis Andreadis v *Greece* (1994) 19 EHRR 293, ECtHR
National and Provincial Building Society, the Leeds Permanent Building Society and the Yorkshire Building Society v *UK* (1997) 25 EHRR 127, ECtHR
Pressos Compania Naviera SA v *Belgium* (1995) 21 EHRR 301, ECtHR

ECHR principles

- Retrospective interference with civil rights and obligations is not incompatible with the ECHR, but it will be subjected to very close scrutiny:

    Respect for the rule of law and the notion of fair trial require that the reasons adduced to justify such measures be treated with the greatest possible degree of circumspection. (*National and Provincial Building Society, the Leeds Permanent Building Society and the Yorkshire Building Society* v *UK*, para. 112)

- This applies particularly where such interference affects ongoing litigation to which the government is a party (*Pressos Compania Naviera SA* v *Belgium* – *retrospective legislation extinguishing negligence claims*; *Greek Refineries Stran and Stratis Andreadis* v *Greece*, para. 49; *National and Provincial Building Society, the Leeds Permanent Building Society and the Yorkshire Building Society* v *UK*).

Relevant domestic cases

Heil v *Rankin* [2000] 3 All ER 138, paras 49–51

16.8   SETTLEMENT

Key ECHR cases

Bellet v *France* (1995) A/333-B, ECtHR
F.E. v *France* (30 October 1998), ECtHR

Taylor v *UK* (1997) 23 EHRR CD 132, ECmHR

ECHR principles

- Settlement restricts (further) access to the courts, but will be legitimate if voluntary and clear.

- Confusing rules for settling multi-party claims may fall short of this requirement (*Bellet v France; F.E. v France – confusing rules relating to special fund proceedings set up to deal with individuals infected with HIV during blood transfusion*).

- But where a scheme is set up to deal with multi-party litigation, Article 6(1) is not breached when one party has to withdraw from the litigation because he or she fails to meet the agreed criteria for participation in the scheme; provided that the individual agreed to the scheme, the scheme is reasonable and proceedings can be brought outside the scheme (albeit with financial implications) (*Taylor v UK*).

FAIR TRIAL IN CIVIL PROCEEDINGS

17.1 THE RIGHT TO AN INDEPENDENT AND IMPARTIAL TRIBUNAL

Key ECHR cases

Benthem v Netherlands (1985) 8 EHRR 1, ECtHR
Campbell and Fell v UK (1984) 7 EHRR 165, ECtHR
Engel and others v Netherlands (1976) 1 EHRR 647, ECtHR
Ettl v Austria (1987) 10 EHRR 255, ECtHR
H v Belgium (1987) 10 EHRR 339, ECtHR
Langborger v Sweden (1989) 12 EHRR 416, ECtHR
Le Compte, Van Leuven and De Meyere v Belgium (1981) 4 EHRR 1, ECtHR
McGonnell v UK (8 February 2000), ECtHR
Van de Hurk v Netherlands (1994) 18 EHRR 481, ECtHR

Stefan v UK (1997) 25 EHRR CD 130, ECmHR

ECHR principles

- The reference to a 'tribunal established by law' in Article 6(1), ECHR means a body with judicial functions and fair procedures, capable of taking binding decisions (*Benthem v Netherlands*).

- A power to make recommendations or give advice is not enough (*Van de Hurk v Netherlands*, para. 54).

- A tribunal classified as 'administrative' is capable of satisfying these requirements, so long as it is independent and impartial (*Campbell and Fell v UK – in criminal context, prison Board of Visitors constituted tribunal for Article 6(1) purposes*).

- Independence means independence from the executive, the parties and from Parliament. Relevant factors are:
  (a) the manner of appointment;
  (b) safeguards against external pressure; and
  (c) the appearance of independence.

- The appointment of professional judges is not the only means of ensuring independence, e.g., the mere fact that a professional disciplinary body includes members of the profession does not *of itself* offend the requirement of independence (*H v Belgium; Stefan v UK*; but see *Langborger v Sweden – lay members of Housing and Tenancy Court too closely linked with associations*), but it is usually powerful evidence of independence:

> The presence . . . of judges making up half the membership, including the Chairman with a casting vote . . . provides a definite assurance of impartiality . . . (*Le Compte, Van Leuven and De Meyere v Belgium*, para. 58)

- If members of a tribunal are appointed on terms which are *ad hoc* or short, there is at least a risk that they will feel (or be perceived to be) under pressure to act in a manner which reflects the position of those with power to remove or reappoint them (*Stefan v UK*).

- Although the ECHR does not require compliance with any particular doctrine of the separation of powers, where judges have played a part in the legislative process, legitimate doubts about their impartiality might arise when they are called upon to interpret the legislation in question:

> . . . any direct involvement in the passage of legislation, or of executive rules, is likely to be sufficient to cast doubt on the judicial impartiality of a person subsequently called on to determine a dispute over whether reasons exist to permit a variation from the wording of the legislation or rules at issue. (*McGonnell v UK*, para. 55)

- For disciplinary proceedings, see **15.4**.

Relevant Scottish cases

- These are set out at **8.6**.

17.2   PUBLIC HEARINGS

Key ECHR cases

Axen v Germany (1983) 6 EHRR 195, ECtHR
Campbell and Fell v UK (1984) 7 EHRR 165, ECtHR
Diennet v France (1995) 21 EHRR 554, ECtHR
Ekbatani v Sweden (1988) 13 EHRR 504, ECtHR
H v Belgium (1987) 10 EHRR 339, ECtHR
Håkansson and Sturesson v Sweden (1990) 13 EHRR 1, ECtHR
Le Compte, Van Leuven and De Meyere v Belgium (1981) 4 EHRR 1, ECtHR
Pretto and others v Italy (1983) 6 EHRR 182, ECtHR
Scarth v UK [1999] EHRLR 332, ECtHR
Schuler-Zgraggen v Switzerland (1993) 16 EHRR 405, ECtHR
Zumtobel v Austria (1993) 17 EHRR 116, ECtHR

Ginikanwa v UK (1988) 55 DR 251, ECmHR[CD]
Guenoun v France (1990) 66 DR 181, ECmHR
Imbrechts v Belgium (1991) 69 DR 312, ECmHR
X v Austria (1965) 2 Digest 438, ECmHR
X v UK (1970) 30 CD 70, ECmHR
X v UK (1977) 2 Digest 452, ECmHR

ECHR principles

- In principle, the determination of civil rights and obligations under Article 6(1) should take place in public.

- However, Article 6(1) specifically provides that the press and public may be excluded from all or part of the trial:

  (a) in the interests of morals, public order or national security in a democratic society;
  (b) where the interests of juveniles or the protection of the private life of the parties so require; or
  (c) to the extent strictly necessary in the opinion of the court in special circumstances where publicity would prejudice the interests of justice.

- On that basis, restrictions have been approved in cases concerning sexual offences against children (*X v Austria*), divorce (*X v UK*) and in medical disciplinary proceedings to protect patients' privacy (*Guenoun v France*, p. 187).

- In addition, the parties to the proceedings may waive their right to a public hearing provided that:

  [waiver] is made in an unequivocal manner and [does] . . . not run counter to any important public interest. (*Schuler-Zgraggen v Switzerland*, para. 58; *Le Compte, Van Leuven and De Meyere v Belgium*, para. 59; *Ginikanwa v UK*, p. 260)

- Waiver can sometimes be implied in the absence of a request for a public hearing (*Hakansson and Sturesson v Sweden*, para. 66; *Zumtobel v Austria*, para. 34)

- The presumption, nonetheless, is in favour of public hearings and, unless there is waiver, exceptions have to be justified as necessary and proportionate (*Schuler-Zgraggen v Switzerland*).

- The proper approach is to sit in public until a legitimate reason for privacy arises (*Diennet v France*).

- A rule that arbitration hearings should be in private breaches Article 6(1) (*Scarth v UK*).

- There is some support for the proposition that interlocutory (interim) hearings need not be in public because they do not 'determine' civil rights and obligations (*X v UK*).

- The public hearing requirement in Article 6(1) is not applied strictly in appeal proceedings, particularly where the only issue is one of law (*Axen v Germany*, para. 28).

- Judgment should be given publicly, but that does not mean it must be read out in its entirety; depositing a copy with the court registry, or handing it down, will suffice (*Pretto v Italy*).

17.3   THE RIGHT TO BE PRESENT AND TO PARTICIPATE

Key ECHR cases

Muyldermans v Belgium (1991) A/214-A, ECmHR
X v Austria (1983) 31 DR 66, ECmHR

X v *Germany* (1963) 6 Yearbook 520, ECmHR
X v *Sweden* (1959) 2 Yearbook 354, ECmHR

ECHR principles

- Fairness requires that the parties are present when civil rights and obligations are determined, particularly when issues of a factual or personal nature need to be resolved (*X* v *Sweden; Muyldermans* v *Belgium; X* v *Germany*).

- However, exceptions to this general requirement do not necessarily breach Article 6(1), so long as they are legitimate and proportionate:

  > Since . . . the purpose of the hearing [was] to find out with [which] of the parents [the children] preferred to stay, it may indeed have been the proper course to exclude the influence of the interested parties and to hear the children in the absence of both parents. (*X* v *Austria*, p. 68 – *custody of children in divorce case*)

17.4   LEGAL AID AND REPRESENTATION

Key ECHR cases

Aerts v *Belgium* (1998) 29 EHRR 50, ECtHR
Airey v *Ireland* (1979) 2 EHRR 305, ECtHR
Andronicou and Constantinou v *Cyprus* (1997) 25 EHRR 491, ECtHR

Munro v *UK* (1987) 52 DR 158, ECmHR[CD]
Winer v *UK* (1986) 48 DR 154, ECmHR[CD]
X v *UK* (1980) 21 DR 95, ECmHR

ECHR principles

- Unlike the position in criminal proceedings, there is no absolute requirement under Article 6(1) that legal aid be made available to those without means in civil proceedings where the interests of justice so require (*Winer* v *UK*, p. 171).

- Effective access to the court is the touchstone; and this does not necessarily require states to set up a comprehensive legal aid scheme (*Airey* v *Ireland*).

- However, where the assistance of a lawyer is 'indispensable for effective access to court', either because legal representation is compulsory or because of the 'complexity of the procedure or of the case', lack of legal aid might breach Article 6(1) (*Airey* v *Ireland*, para. 26).

- This is more likely where intimate, rather than objective, issues are at stake (*Airey* v *Ireland; Winer* v *UK*).

- A refusal of legal aid in proceedings which have no prospect of success will not breach Article 6(1) (*X* v *UK*), unless the parties are required as a matter of law to be represented (*Aerts* v *Belgium*).

- Where the parties are required to be represented on an appeal, the legal aid authorities should not refuse legal aid on the basis that the prospects of success are low; that is a question for the court. Otherwise, the very essence of the right to appeal is destroyed (*Aerts v Belgium*, para. 60 – *in context of Article 5(4) appeal*).

- Reasonable contribution arrangements do not violate Article 6(1) (*X v UK*).

- And *ad hoc* arrangements for assistance with legal representation can be enough for Article 6(1) (*Andronicou and Constantinou v Cyprus*).

Relevant Scottish cases

Stephen Gayne v Procurator Fiscal, Glasgow (12 August 1999), AC

- In a criminal context setting limits on the grant of legal aid does not automatically violate a defendant's right to a fair trial under Article 6, unless the result is such as to deny him or her effective legal representation (*Stephen Gayne v Procurator Fiscal, Glasgow – Criminal Legal Aid (Fixed Payments) (Scotland) Regulations 1999 set limit of £500 on solicitor's costs*; citing *M v UK* (1983) (App. No. 9728/82)).

Relevant Canadian cases

New Brunswick (Minister of Health) v J.G. [1999] 3 SCR 46

- Where a child custody case is of sufficient importance and complexity, the parents are entitled to legal representation if they cannot afford it:

  The interests at stake in the custody hearing are unquestionably of the highest order. Few state actions can have more profound effect on the lives of both parents and child. Not only is the parent's right to security of person at stake, the child as well . . .

  . . . In proceedings as serious and complex as these, an unrepresented parent will ordinarily need to possess superior intelligence or education, communication skills, composure, and familiarity with the legal system in order to effectively present his case. (*New Brunswick (Minister of Health) v J.G.*, paras 76 and 80)

17.5   EQUALITY OF ARMS

Key ECHR cases

Delcourt v Belgium (1969) 1 EHRR 355, ECtHR
Dombo Beheer BV v Netherlands (1993) 18 EHRR 213, ECtHR
Kraska v Switzerland (1993) 18 EHRR 188, ECtHR
Lobo Machado v Portugal (1997) 23 EHRR 79, ECtHR
Nideröst-Huber v Switzerland (1997) 25 EHRR 709, ECtHR
Vermeulen v Belgium (20 February 1996), ECtHR

Crociani v Italy (1980) 22 DR 147, ECmHR

ECHR principles

- Equality of arms is fundamental to the concept of a fair trial under the ECHR and should not be restrictively interpreted:

In a democratic society, within the meaning of the Convention, the right to a fair administration of justice holds such a prominent place that a restrictive interpretation of Article 6(1) would not correspond to the aim and the purpose of that provision. (*Delcourt v Belgium*, para. 25).

- However, the requirements of fairness in civil proceedings are not as exacting as those in criminal proceedings (*Dombo Beheer BV v Netherlands*, para. 32).

- Nonetheless, it is a minimum requirement that:

  . . . each party must be afforded a reasonable opportunity to present his case – including his evidence – under conditions that do not place him at a substantial disadvantage *vis-à-vis* his opponent. (*Dombo Beheer BV v Netherlands*, para. 33)

- The tribunal is then under a duty to conduct a proper examination of the submissions, arguments and evidence adduced by the parties (*Kraska v Switzerland*, para. 30).

Relevant domestic cases

Re J (Abduction: Wrongful Removal) [2000] 1 FLR 78

- An *ex parte* (without notice) hearing does not of itself breach Article 6(1), so long as there is an effective mechanism for challenge:

  It is always open to an opposing party against whom an *ex parte* order has been made to apply to the court to have it set aside. It is certainly possible that there might be a breach of Article 6 if no opportunity was provided by the law to challenge an *ex parte* order that is made. (*Re J (Abduction: Wrongful Removal*, p. 81)

Relevant Canadian cases

Baker v Minister of Citizenship and Immigration [1999] 2 SCR 817

- Procedural fairness requires that any administrative process adheres to the following principles:

  Underlying [the procedural rights that the duty of fairness requires] is the notion that the purpose of the participatory rights contained within the duty of procedural fairness is to ensure that administrative decisions are made using a fair and open procedure, appropriate to the decision being made and its statutory, institutional, and social context, with an opportunity for those affected by the decision to put forward their views and evidence fully and have them considered by the decision-maker. (*Baker v Minister of Citizenship and Immigration*, p. 837)

17.6   THE RIGHT TO AN ADVERSARIAL HEARING

Key ECHR cases

Dombo Beheer BV v Netherlands (1993) 18 EHRR 213, ECtHR
Feldbrugge v Netherlands (1986) 8 EHRR 425, ECtHR
Krcmar v Czech Republic (3 March 2000), ECtHR
Nideröst-Huber v Switzerland (1997) 25 EHRR 709, ECtHR
Van Orshoven v Belgium (1997) 26 EHRR 55, EctHR

ECHR principles

- Proceedings which determine civil rights and obligations should be adversarial (*Krcmar v Czech Republic*, para. 40; see also *Feldbrugge v Netherlands; Van Orshoven v Belgium; Nideröst-Huber v Switzerland*, para. 29).

- Disclosure, the opportunity to call and challenge evidence and to address the court or tribunal are minimum requirements of an adversarial process:

  > . . . the concept of a fair hearing . . . implies the right to adversarial proceedings, according to which the parties must have the opportunity not only to make known any evidence needed for their claims to succeed, but also to have knowledge of, and comment on, all evidence adduced or observations filed, with a view to influencing the courts' decision . . . (*Krcmar v Czech Republic*, para. 40; *Van Orshoven v Belgium; Niderost-Huber v Switzerland*, para. 29)

17.7   DISCLOSURE

Key ECHR cases

Feldbrugge v Netherlands (1986) 8 EHRR 425, ECtHR
Kerojärvi v Finland (19 July 1995) A/328, noted at [1996] EHRLR 66, ECtHR
Krcmar v Czech Republic (3 March 2000), ECtHR
McGinley and Egan v UK (1998) 27 EHRR 1, ECtHR
McMichael v UK (1995) 20 EHRR 205, ECtHR
Ruiz-Mateos v Spain (1993) 16 EHRR 505, ECtHR
Van Orshoven v Belgium (1997) 26 EHRR 55, ECtHR

ECHR principles

- Disclosure of all relevant documents to all parties in civil proceedings is a requirement of Article 6(1), ECHR (*Feldbrugge v Netherlands; McMichael v UK; Kerojärvi v Finland; McGinley and Egan v UK*).

- Documents which would assist one party to establish its case are relevant:

  > . . . if it were the case that the respondent State had, without good cause, prevented the applicants from gaining access to, or falsely denied the existence of, documents in its possession which would have assisted them in establishing before the Pensions Appeal Tribunal that they had been exposed to dangerous levels of radiation, this would have been to deny them a fair hearing in violation of Article 6(1). (*McGinley and Egan v UK*, para. 86)

- Moreover, disclosure should take place prior to the hearing:

  > A party to the proceedings must have the possibility to familiarise itself with the evidence before the court, as well as the possibility to comment on its existence, contents and authenticity in an appropriate form and within an appropriate time, if need be, in written form and in advance. (*Krcmar v Czech Republic*, para. 42)

- Where third parties are involved in the proceedings – even if their only role is to give the court independent legal advice – their submissions must be disclosed to the parties, and an opportunity provided for comment (*Ruiz-Mateos v Spain; Van Orshoven v Belgium*, para. 39).

17.8   THE RIGHT TO CALL AND CHALLENGE EVIDENCE

Key ECHR cases

Dombo Beheer BV v Netherlands (1993) 18 EHRR 213, ECtHR

G v France (1988) 57 DR 100, ECmHR
X v Austria (1972) 42 EHRR CD 145, ECmHR

ECHR principles

- Although Article 6(1) does not specifically set out a right to call and examine witnesses (cf. Article 6(3)(d) in the criminal context), it is clear that in the determination of civil rights and obligations the parties must be given a proper opportunity to present their case, including the evidence. (*Dombo Beheer BV v Netherlands*, para. 33).

- This includes the right to cross-examine witnesses (*X v Austria*).

- The ECHR does not lay down any rules about the burden and standard of proof in civil cases, but domestic rules should not create an imbalance between the parties (G v France p. 140 – *statutory presumption did not offend Article 6(1)*).

17.9   EXPERT EVIDENCE

Key ECHR cases

H v France (1989) 12 EHRR 74, ECtHR
Mantovanelli v France (1997) 24 EHRR 370, ECtHR
Martins Moreira v Portugal (1988) 13 EHRR 577, ECtHR

ECHR principles

- Where expert evidence is indispensable to a fair trial, the court should call it, or it should permit the parties to (*Mantovanelli v France; H v France*).

- This may require the provision of resources (*Martins Moreira v Portugal*).

- Court-appointed experts do not necessarily breach the adversarial principle, so long as all the parties have the opportunity to give instructions to the expert and to examine him/her at trial (*Mantovanelli v France*).

17.10   REASONS

Key ECHR cases

De Moor v Belgium (1994) 18 EHRR 372, ECtHR
Hadjianastassiou v Greece (1992) 16 EHRR 219, ECtHR
Hiro Balani v Spain (1994) 19 EHRR 566, ECtHR
Van de Hurk v Netherlands (1994) 18 EHRR 481, ECtHR

X v Germany (1981) 25 DR 240, ECmHR

ECHR principles

- Article 6(1) obliges domestic courts to give reasons for their judgments:

> The Court reiterates that Article 6(1) obliges the courts to give reasons for their judgments, but cannot be understood as requiring a detailed answer to every argument. The extent to which this duty to give reasons applies may vary according to the nature of the decision. It is moreover necessary to take account, *inter alia*, of the diversity of the submissions that a litigant may bring before the courts and the differences existing in the Contracting States with regard to statutory provisions, customary rules, legal opinion and the presentation and drafting of judgments. That is why the question whether a court has failed to fulfil the obligation to state reasons, derived from Article 6 of the Convention, can only be determined in the light of the circumstances of the case. (*Hiro Balani v Spain*, para. 27)

> The national courts must . . . indicate with sufficient clarity the grounds on which they based their decision. It is this, *inter alia*, which makes it possible for the accused to exercise usefully the rights of appeal available to him. (*Hadjianastassiou v Greece*, para. 33)

Relevant domestic cases

Stefan v General Medical Council [1999] 1 WLR 1293

- Article 6(1), ECHR may require a reappraisal of the duty to give reasons at common law:

> The provisions of Article 6(1) of the Convention on Human Rights . . . will require closer attention to be paid to the duty to give reasons, at least in relation to those cases where a person's civil rights and obligations are being determined (*Stefan v General Medical Council, per* Lord Clyde, p. 1299)

17.11   CIVIL APPEALS

Key ECHR cases

Ekbatani v Sweden (1988) 13 EHRR 504, ECtHR
Helmers v Sweden (1991) 15 EHRR 285, ECtHR

ECHR principles

- There is no right of appeal under the ECHR.

- However, where a right of appeal is provided for in domestic law, Article 6(1) applies, with appropriate modifications to reflect the fact that appeal hearings are different in nature to first instance hearings.

- An oral public hearing may not be required, unless factual issues require determination (*Ekbatani v Sweden*; *Helmers v Sweden*).

17.12   COSTS

Key ECHR cases

Robins v UK (1997) 26 EHRR 527, ECtHR

B v UK (1984) 38 DR 213, ECmHR
Grepne v UK (1990) 66 DR 268, ECmHR^{CD}
X v Germany (1978) 14 DR 60, ECmHR

ECHR principles

- There is no *right* to costs in civil proceedings under Article 6(1), ECHR.

- But costs are an integral part of the determination of civil rights and obligations, and their allocation should be fair (*Robins v UK*, para. 35).

- A rule requiring the losing party to pay costs is fair *Grepne v UK*, p. 270).

- The recovery of costs is included in the overall assessment of whether there has been trial within a reasonable period (*Robins v UK*, para. 35).

- Wasted costs orders do not determine civil rights and obligations (*B v UK*, p. 215), neither do they raise property issues under Article 1 of Protocol 1 (*X v Germany*, p. 61).

17.13   THE ENFORCEMENT OF JUDGMENTS

Key ECHR cases

Di Pede v Italy (26 September 1996), ECtHR
Hornsby v Greece (1997) 24 EHRR 250, ECtHR
Iatridis v Greece (1999) 30 EHRR 97, ECtHR
Saffi v Italy (28 July 1999), ECtHR
Silva Pontes v Portugal (1994) 18 EHRR 156, ECtHR
Zappia v Italy (26 September 1996), ECtHR

ECHR principles

- The determination of civil rights and obligations includes the enforcement of judgments (*Hornsby v Greece*).

- The period taken to enforce a judgment therefore comes within the requirement that there be trial within a reasonable period:

  > . . . the [right to a court] would be 'illusory', if a Contracting State's domestic legal system allowed a final, binding judicial decision to remain inoperative to the detriment of one party. It would be inconceivable that Article 6 should describe in detail procedural guarantees afforded to litigants – proceedings that are fair, public and expeditious – without protecting the implementation of judicial decisions. (*Hornsby v Greece*, para. 40; see also *Saffi v Italy*, para. 63)

- A stay of execution for such period as is strictly necessary to facilitate a satisfactory solution to legitimate problems may be justified in exceptional circumstances; but the consequence should not be that execution is prevented, invalidated or unduly delayed, still less that the substance of the decision is undermined (*Saffi v Italy*, paras 69 and 74 – *suspended eviction order*).

- Public authorities are under a special duty to comply with court orders and judgments (*Iatridis v Greece*, para. 66).

17.14   TRIAL WITHIN A REASONABLE PERIOD

Key ECHR cases

Agga v Greece (25 January 2000), ECtHR
Dewicka v Poland (4 April 2000), ECtHR
Golder v UK (1975) 1 EHRR 524, ECtHR
Guincho v Portugal (1984) 7 EHRR 223, ECtHR
H v UK (1987) 10 EHRR 95, ECtHR
Hokkanen v Finland (1994) 19 EHRR 139, ECtHR
Hornsby v Greece (1997) 24 EHRR 250, ECtHR
Kiefer v Switzerland (28 March 2000), ECtHR
Nibbio v Italy (1992) A/228-A, ECtHR
Obermeier v Austria (1990) 13 EHRR 290, ECtHR
Robins v UK (1997) 26 EHRR 527, ECtHR
Silva Pontes v Portugal (1994) 18 EHRR 156, ECtHR

ECHR principles

- Article 6(1), ECHR specifically provides that civil rights and obligations should be determined within a reasonable period.

- Time runs from the initiation of proceedings (*Guincho v Portugal*; but see also *Golder v UK*) and ends with the enforcement of judgment (*Hornsby v Greece*).

- Relevant factors in the overall assessment are:
  - (a)   the complexity of the case;
  - (b)   what is at stake for the applicant;
  - (c)   the conduct of the relevant authorities, including the courts; and
  - (d)   the conduct of the applicant.

- Where delay in court proceedings is caused by industrial action by court staff, it may be that the state is not responsible under the Convention, but only if the relevant authorities provide clear evidence of the causal link to the particular case in issue (*Agga v Greece*, para. 25).

- The following cases call for particular diligence:
  - (a)   child care cases (*H v UK; Hokkanen v Finland*);
  - (b)   serious personal injury cases or cases involving the old and infirm (*Silva Pontes v Portugal; Kiefer v Switzerland; Dewicka v Poland*);
  - (c)   employment disputes (*Obermeier v Austria; Nibbio v Italy*); and
  - (d)   cases with a particular quality of irreversibility.

THE RIGHT TO LIFE

18.1 LEGAL PROTECTION OF LIFE

Key ECHR cases

Andronicou and Constantinou v Cyprus (1997) 25 EHRR 491, ECtHR
LCB v UK (1998) 27 EHRR 212, ECtHR
Mahmut Kaya v Turkey (28 March 2000), ECtHR
McCann and others v UK (1995) 21 EHRR 97, ECtHR
Osman v UK (1998) 29 EHRR 245, ECtHR

Barrett v UK (1997) 23 EHRR CD 185, ECmHR[CD]
Keenan v UK (App. No. 27229/95, 22 June 1998), ECmHR[CD]
W v UK (1983) 32 DR 190, ECmHR
X v Germany (1971) 14 Yearbook 698, ECmHR
X v Ireland (1973) 16 Yearbook 388, ECmHR

ECHR principles

- Article 2(1), ECHR enjoins the state not only to refrain from the intentional and unlawful taking of life, but also to take appropriate steps to safeguard the lives of those within its jurisdiction (*Mahmut Kaya v Turkey*, para. 85; *LCB v UK*).

- This can extend in appropriate circumstances to a positive obligation on the authorities to take preventative operational measures to protect an individual or individuals whose life or lives is or are at risk from the criminal acts of another individual (*Mahmut Kaya v Turkey*, para. 85, citing *Osman v UK*).

- The scope of the obligation must not impose an impossible or disproportionate burden on the authorities (*Mahmut Kaya v Turkey*, para. 86, citing *Osman v UK*).

- For a positive obligation to arise, it must be shown that the authorities knew or ought to have known of a real and immediate risk to the life of an identified individual from the criminal acts of a third party (*Mahmut Kaya v Turkey*, para. 86, citing *Osman v UK*).

- The obligation is then to take such measures, within their powers, as were reasonable to avoid that risk (*Mahmut Kaya v Turkey*, para. 86, citing *Osman v UK*).

- This can extend to an obligation to take reasonable steps to prevent self-inflicted deaths in custody (*Keenan v UK*, paras 79–80).

- Where an identifiable individual is at risk of paramilitary attack, there may be a duty to provide protection, but not for an indefinite period:

Article 2 cannot be interpreted as imposing a duty on a state to give protection of this nature, at least not for an indefinite period. (*X v Ireland*, p. 392)

. . . a positive obligation to exclude any possible violence could not be read into Article 2. (*W v UK*, p. 200)

Relevant domestic cases

In Re A (Minors) (Conjoined Twins) (22 September 2000), CA

18.2   THE USE OF FORCE

Key ECHR cases

Andronicou and Constantinou v Cyprus (1997) 25 EHRR 491, ECtHR
McCann and others v UK (1995) 21 EHRR 97, ECtHR

Aytekin v Turkey (18 September 1997), ECmHR^{CD}
Diaz Ruano v Spain (1994) A/285-B, ECmHR
Farrell v UK (1982) 30 DR 96 and (1984) 38 DR 44, ECmHR
Kelly v UK (1993) (App. No. 17579/90), ECmHR^{CD}
Stewart v UK (1984) 39 DR 162, ECmHR
Wolfgram v Germany (1986) 49 DR 213, ECmHR
X v Belgium (1969) 12 Yearbook 174, ECmHR

ECHR principles

- Lethal force may be used under Article 2(2), ECHR, but only when it is 'absolutely necessary'.

- The only legitimate purposes for using such force are:

  (a) self-defence or defence of others (*Wolfgram v Germany*, p. 216; *Diaz Ruano v Spain*, para. 51);

  (b) to effect an arrest or prevent escape (*Farrell v UK*, pp. 47–8; *Kelly v UK*; *Aytekin v Turkey*);

  (c) to quash a riot or insurrection (*Stewart v UK*, pp. 172–3; *X v Belgium*).

- The test of 'absolute necessity' under Article 2 is much stricter than the test of 'necessity' under Articles 8 to 11.

- It involves a determination of whether the use of force was 'strictly proportionate' (*McCann and others v UK*, para. 194; *Andronicou and Constantinou v Cyprus*, para. 171).

- It also involves an assessment of the organisation and planning (if any) of the operation during which lethal force was used: the training, instructions and communications of those who used lethal force and those who lay behind the operation are relevant to this determination (*McCann and others v UK*, para. 194; *Aytekin v Turkey*). In particular, was the operation:

  . . . planned and controlled by the authorities so as to minimise, to the greatest extent possible, recourse to lethal force? (*McCann and others v UK*, para. 194)

- Failure to follow the procedures laid down in domestic law, automatically breaches Article 2 (*X v Belgium*).

18.3   INVESTIGATION AND PROSECUTION

Key ECHR cases

Andronicou and Constantinou v Cyprus (1997) 25 EHRR 491, ECtHR
Assenov v Bulgaria (1998) 28 EHRR 652, ECtHR
Kaya v Turkey (1998) 28 EHRR 1, ECtHR
McCann and others v UK (1995) 21 EHRR 97, ECtHR
Osman v UK (1998) 29 EHRR 245, ECtHR
Salman v Turkey (27 June 2000), ECtHR
Timurtas v Turkey (13 June 2000), ECtHR
Velikova v Bulgaria (27 April 2000), ECtHR

Taylor, Crampton, Gibson and King v UK (1994) 79-A DR 127, ECmHR

ECHR principles

- Article 2(1) should be applied so as to make its safeguards practical and effective (*McCann and others v UK*, paras 146–147; *Osman v UK*, para. 116).

- This requires some form of effective investigation when individuals have been killed or injured as a result of the use of force by agents of the state (*McCann and others v UK*, para. 161; *Kaya v Turkey*, para. 86).

- The nature and degree of scrutiny required will vary from case to case, but the minimum requirements are that the investigation be thorough, effective and impartial (*Velikova v Bulgaria*, para. 80).

- What is required is public and independent scrutiny:

  . . . [the investigation obligation under Article 2] . . . includes the minimum requirement of a mechanism whereby the circumstances of a deprivation of life by the agents of a state may receive public and independent scrutiny. The nature and degree of scrutiny which satisfies this minimum threshold must . . . depend on the circumstances of the particular case. There may be cases where the facts surrounding a deprivation of life are clear and undisputed and the subsequent inquisitorial examination may legitimately be reduced to a minimum formality. But equally, there may be other cases, where a victim dies in circumstances which are unclear, in which event the lack of an effective procedure to investigate the cause of the deprivation of life could by itself raise an issue under Article 2. (*Taylor, Crampton, Gibson and King v UK*, p. 136 – *although inquiry into deaths of children killed by Beverley Allitt not public, families could attend and report was published*)

- The investigation must cover not only the actions of those directly responsible for the death, but also the planning and organisation lying behind those actions (*McCann and others v UK*, paras 200–201; *Andronicou and Constantinou v Cyprus*).

- The duty to carry out an effective investigation has procedural implications; in particular, the relevant authorities are under a duty to disclose material or risk adverse inferences:

A failure on a Government's part to submit such information which is in their hands without a satisfactory explanation may not only reflect negatively on the level of compliance by a respondent state . . . but may also give rise to the drawing of an inference as to the well foundedness of [the state's case]. (*Timurtas v Turkey*, para. 66)

- Lack of an effective investigation is itself a breach of Article 2 (*McCann and others v UK*; *Kaya v Turkey*; *Assenov v Bulgaria*; *Salman v Turkey*).

- The wider duties of investigation and prosecution arising under the ECHR are dealt with in **6.1**.

18.4   ABORTION

Key ECHR cases

Bruggemann and Scheuten v Germany (1977) 10 DR 100, ECmHR
H v Norway (1992) (App. No. 17004/90), ECmHR[CD]
Knudsen v Norway (1985) 42 DR 247, ECmHR
Paton v UK (1980) 19 DR 244, ECmHR[CD]
X v Austria (1976) 7 DR 87, ECmHR

ECHR principles

- Article 2(1), ECHR does not require states to prohibit abortion, because a foetus has no 'absolute right' to life:

  The 'life' of the foetus is intimately connected with, and cannot be regarded in isolation of, the pregnant woman. If Article 2 were held to cover the foetus and its protection under the Article were, in the absence of any express limitation, seen as absolute, an abortion would have to be considered as prohibited even where the continuance of the pregnancy would involve a serious risk to the life of the pregnant woman. This would mean that the 'unborn life' of the foetus would be regarded as being of a higher value than the life of the pregnant woman. The 'right to life' of a person already born would thus be considered as subject not only to the express limitations [set out in Article 2(2)] but also to a further, implied limitation. (*Paton v UK*, para. 19)

- Neither does the ECHR prohibit abortions based on the ability of the mother to cope with a baby (*H v Norway*).

- But (reasonable) rules regulating abortion are not incompatible with the ECHR: pregnancy and abortion are not solely within the private sphere of a mother (*Bruggemann and Scheuten v Germany*).

- A father of an unborn child does not have a right under the ECHR to insist that his child be born against the wishes of the mother (*Paton v UK*).

18.5   EUTHANASIA

Key ECHR cases

Widmer v Switzerland (App. No. 20527/92), ECmHR

ECHR principles

- Article 2, ECHR does not require states to make passive euthanasia a crime (*Widmer v Switzerland*).

- Active euthanasia remains to be considered.

18.6   THE DEATH PENALTY

Key ECHR cases

Öcalan v Turkey (14 December 2000), ECtHR (admissibility)[CD]

ECHR principles

- The death penalty is not prohibited under Article 2, ECHR, but in this respect Article 2 has been supplemented by Optional Protocol 6, which outlaws the death penalty in peacetime.

- Whether an individual is likely to be exposed to the death penalty is an important consideration whenever extradition or expulsion decisions are taken (see **28.3**).

PHYSICAL INTEGRITY

Torture, inhuman and/or degrading treatment/punishment are all prohibited absolutely by Article 3, ECHR and cannot be justified on any grounds, including the need to combat terrorism (*Ireland v UK; Tomasi v France*). However, for Article 3 to be breached the conduct must attain a 'minimum level of severity' (*Ireland v UK*). Whether this threshold is reached will depend on all the circumstances of the case. Relevant factors include duration of the treatment, its physical or mental effects and, in some instances, the sex, age and state of health of the victim.

19.1 THE PROHIBITION ON TORTURE

Key ECHR cases

Aksoy v Turkey (1996) 23 EHRR 553, ECtHR
Ireland v UK (1978) 2 EHRR 25, ECtHR
Mahmut Kaya v Turkey (28 March 2000), ECtHR
Selmouni v France (1999) 29 EHRR 403, ECtHR
T v UK, V v UK (1999) 30 EHRR 121, ECtHR

Greek Case, the (1969) 12 Yearbook 1, ECmHR

ECHR principles

- Torture has been defined as:

    . . . deliberate inhuman treatment causing very serious and cruel suffering. (*Ireland v UK*, para. 167)

- Suffering must be inflicted intentionally; torture is an aggravated form of inhuman treatment:

    . . . which has a purpose, such as the obtaining of information or confession, or the infliction of punishment. (*The Greek Case*, p. 186; see also *Aksoy v Turkey*, para. 64)

- It was the intention of the Convention that a special stigma should be attached to torture as a deliberate inhuman treatment (*Mahmut Kaya v Turkey*), and a high threshold therefore applies: stripping someone naked, tying their arms behind their back and suspending them by their arms has been found to be torture (*Aksoy v Turkey*, para. 64); but not interrogation techniques such as sleep deprivation and denial of adequate food and drink (*Ireland v UK*, para. 167 – *inhuman and degrading, but not torture*).

- However, the classification of ill-treatment as torture, inhuman or degrading treatment/punishment is not fixed and should reflect contemporary standards:

  > The Court has previously examined cases in which it concluded that there had been treatment which could only be described as torture . . . However, having regard to the fact that the Convention is a 'living instrument' which must be interpreted in the light of present-day conditions . . . the Court considers that certain acts which were classified in the past as 'inhuman and degrading treatment' as opposed to 'torture' could be classified differently in future. It takes the view that the increasingly high standard being required in the area of the protection of human rights and fundamental liberties correspondingly and inevitably requires greater firmness in assessing breaches of the fundamental values of democratic societies. (*Selmouni v France*, para. 101; see also *T v UK, V v UK*, para. 72, where reference is made to the relevance of prevailing standards in Europe)

19.2   THE PROHIBITION ON INHUMAN TREATMENT/ PUNISHMENT

Key ECHR cases

Aydin v Turkey (1997) 25 EHRR 251, ECtHR
Campbell and Cosans v UK (1982) 4 EHRR 293, ECtHR
Costello-Roberts v UK (1993) 19 EHRR 112, ECtHR
Ireland v UK (1978) 2 EHRR 25, ECtHR
Tomasi v France (1992) 15 EHRR 1, ECtHR

Cyprus v Turkey (1976) 4 EHRR 482, ECmHR
Greek Case, the (1969) 12 Yearbook 1, ECmHR

ECHR principles

- Treatment/punishment will be inhuman if it 'causes intense physical or mental suffering' (*Ireland v UK*, para. 167).

- It is less severe than torture, but can include threats of torture (*Campbell and Cosans v UK*, para. 26) and the infliction of psychological harm (*Ireland v UK*, paras 167–168).

- Physical assaults can amount to inhuman treatment if sufficiently serious: the use of weapons and/or implements will usually breach Article 3 (*The Greek Case*), as will sexual assaults (*Cyprus v Turkey*, para. 374; *Aydin v Turkey*, para. 86).

- Where an individual is in custody, the threshold for inhuman treatment is lowered:

  > Although the injuries observed might appear to be relatively slight, they nevertheless constituted outward signs of the use of physical force on an individual deprived of his liberty and therefore in a state of inferiority. The treatment had therefore been both inhuman and degrading. (*Tomasi v France*, para. 113)

19.3   THE PROHIBITION ON DEGRADING TREATMENT/ PUNISHMENT

Key ECHR cases

Ireland v UK (1978) 2 EHRR 25, ECtHR
Ribitsch v Austria (1995) 21 EHRR 573, ECtHR
T v UK, V v UK (1999) 30 EHRR 121, ECtHR

East African Asians v UK (1973) 3 EHRR 76, ECmHR
Hilton v UK (1976) 4 DR 177, ECmHR

ECHR principles

- Treatment/punishment will be degrading if it arouses in the victim a feeling of fear, anguish and inferiority capable of debasing him or her and breaking his or her physical or moral resistance (*Ireland v UK*); but only if it reaches a particular level of severity.

- The vulnerability of the victim will be important:

  . . . in respect of a person deprived of his liberty, any recourse to physical force which has not been made strictly necessary by his own conduct diminishes human dignity and is, in principle, an infringement of the rights set forth in Article 3 of the Convention. (*Ribitsch v Austria*, para. 38)

- Unlike the position with torture, where inhuman and degrading treatment/ punishment is in issue, intention is relevant but not determinative:

  The question whether the purpose of the treatment was to humiliate or debase the victim is a . . . factor to be taken into account . . . but the absence of any such purpose cannot conclusively rule out a finding of a violation of Article 3. (*T v UK, V v UK*, para. 71)

- Institutional racism can amount to degrading treatment in breach of Article 3, as can grossly racist remarks (*East African Asians v UK*, paras 207–208) and racial harassment (*Hilton v UK*, p. 187).

- The fact that an individual is serving a sentence of the court is relevant to the threshold of degrading punishment under Article 3:

  In order for a punishment or treatment associated with it to be 'inhuman' or 'degrading', the suffering or humiliation involved must in any event go beyond that inevitable element of suffering or humiliation connected with a given form of legitimate treatment or punishment. (*T v UK, V v UK*, para. 71 – imposition of indeterminate sentence on two 11-year-olds not inhuman or degrading)

19.4   PHYSICAL INTEGRITY UNDER ARTICLE 8

Key ECHR cases

A v UK (1998) 27 EHRR 611, ECtHR
Costello-Roberts v UK (1993) 19 EHRR 112, ECtHR
Osman v UK (1998) 29 EHRR 245, ECtHR

Stubbings and others v *UK* (1996) 23 EHRR 213, ECtHR

X and Y v *Netherlands* (1985) 8 EHRR 235, ECtHR

ECHR principles

- Article 8 also covers physical integrity, and it is capable of protecting individuals against forms of ill-treatment which do not reach the high Article 3 threshold.

- It has been invoked in cases of excessive corporal punishment (*A* v *UK*; *Costello-Roberts* v *UK*), sexual assault (*X and Y* v *Netherlands*, *Stubbings and others* v *UK*) and harassment (*Osman* v *UK*).

- However, Article 8 is a qualified right; unlike Article 3 (see **1.2**).

19.5   THE INVESTIGATION OF CLAIMS OF ILL-TREATMENT

Key ECHR cases

Assenov v *Bulgaria* (1998) 28 EHRR 652, ECtHR

ECHR principles

- Where an individual raises an arguable claim that he has been seriously ill-treated by the police or other such agents of the state unlawfully and in breach of Article 3, that provision, read in conjunction with the state's general duty under Article 1 of the Convention to 'secure to everyone within their jurisdiction the rights and freedoms in [the] Convention', requires by implication that there should be an effective official investigation (*Assenov* v *Bulgaria*, para. 102).

- This obligation, as with that under Article 2, should be capable of leading to the identification and punishment of those responsible:

  > If this were not the case, the general legal prohibition of torture and inhuman and degrading treatment and punishment, despite its fundamental importance . . . would be ineffective in practice and it would be possible in some cases for agents of the state to abuse the rights of those within their control with virtual impunity. (*Assenov* v *Bulgaria*, para. 102)

- The scope of the obligation under Article 13 varies depending on the nature of the appellant's complaint under the Convention:

  > Where an individual has an arguable claim that he has been ill-treated in breach of Article 3, the notion of an effective remedy entails, in addition to a thorough and effective investigation of the kind also required by Article 3 . . . effective access to the investigatory procedure and the payment of compensation where appropriate . . . (*Assenov* v *Bulgaria*, para. 117)

19.6   RESPONSIBILITY FOR ILL-TREATMENT

Key ECHR cases

A v *UK* (1998) 27 EHRR 611, ECtHR

Ireland v *UK* (1978) 2 EHRR 25, ECtHR

Cyprus v *Turkey* (1976) 4 EHRR 482, ECmHR

ECHR principles

- Where ill-treatment occurs in breach of Article 3, it will be incumbent on the relevant authorities to show that they took adequate steps to prevent such treatment if they are to escape liability:

    The evidence shows that rapes were committed by Turkish soldiers and at least in two cases even by Turkish officers . . . it has not been shown that the Turkish authorities took adequate measures to prevent this happening or that they generally took any disciplinary measures following such incidents. The Commission therefore considers that the non-prevention of the said acts is imputable to Turkey under the Convention. (*Cyprus v Turkey*, para. 373)

- Constructive knowledge may also be enough for state liability to arise:

    It is inconceivable that the higher authorities of a state should be, or at least should be entitled to be, unaware of the existence of [the interrogation practices]. Furthermore, under the Convention those authorities are strictly liable for the conduct of their subordinates; they are under a duty to impose their will on subordinates and cannot shelter behind their inability to ensure that it is respected. (*Ireland v UK*, para. 159)

- State responsibility can also arise where ill-treatment is carried out by private individuals (e.g., A v UK – *father's excessive corporal punishment on son*).

SECTION 20

HEALTH CARE

20.1 PROVIDING MEDICAL CARE

Key ECHR cases

Association X v UK (1978) 14 DR 31, ECmHR
Tanko v Finland (App. No. 23634/94), ECmHR[CD]
X v Ireland (1976) 7 DR 78, ECmHR

ECHR principles

- Under Article 2, ECHR, the relevant authorities are under a duty to take appropriate measures to preserve life; and under Article 3, ECHR, they are under a duty to prevent individuals being subjected to inhuman or degrading treatment. In some circumstances, this might require the provision of medical care:

  > . . . a lack of proper medical care in a case where someone is suffering from a serious illness could in certain circumstances amount to treatment contrary to Article 3. (*Tanko v Finland*; see also *Association X v UK* and *X v Ireland*, where this question was left open by the ECmHR)

- There is a general duty on the relevant authorities to safeguard the health and well-being of prisoners, within the confinements of imprisonment (*McFeeley v UK*: see **13.1**).

Relevant domestic cases

R v North and East Devon Health Authority, ex parte Coughlan [2000] 2 WLR 622

- Where a severely disabled person in residential care requires the provision of special accommodation, Article 8 will be engaged whenever a decision is taken to move him or her:

  > The judge was entitled to treat this as a case where the health authority's conduct was in breach of Article 8(1) and was not justified by the provisions of Article 8(2). By the closure of Mardon House, the health authority will interfere with . . . her right to her home . . . The health authority would not be justified in doing so without providing accommodation which meets her needs. (*R v North and East Devon Health Authority, ex parte Coughlan*)

Relevant New Zealand cases

Shortland v Northland Health Ltd [1998] 1 NZLR 433

- The positive duty on health care providers, as agents of the state, to provide patients with the 'necessities of life' is not satisfied unless an appropriate and lawful clinical assessment of need is made (*Shortland v Northland Health Ltd*, p. 445 – *challenge to decision not to proceed with kidney transplant and cease dialysis because patient could not understand, or provide level of cooperation needed*).

Relevant South African cases

Soobramoney v Minister of Health (26 November 1997)

- The consideration of health care rights cannot be constrained within a traditional legal context structured around the idea of human autonomy, but has to be undertaken in a new analytical framework based on the notion of human interdependence:

  > When rights by their very nature are shared and interdependent, striking appropriate balances between the equally valid entitlements or expectations of a multitude of claimants should not be seen as imposing limits on those rights, but as defining the circumstances in which the rights may most fairly and effectively be enjoyed.
  >
  > However, the right to life may come to be defined in South Africa, there is in reality no meaningful way in which it can constitutionally be extended to encompass the right indefinitely to evade death . . . We can, however, influence the manner in which we come to terms with our mortality. It is precisely here, where scarce artificial life-prolonging resources have to be called upon, that tragic medical choices have to be made. (*Soobramoney v Minister of Health*, paras 54 and 57 – *no violation of Constitution where patient with chronic renal failure denied dialysis treatment due to hospital budget constraints*)

Relevant Commonwealth cases

Paschim Banga Khet Mazdoor Samity and others v State of West Bengal and another [1996] AIR SC 2426

- Where a welfare state is set up, an obligation to provide medical care can arise:

  > In a welfare State the primary duty of the Government is to secure the welfare of the people. Providing adequate medical facilities for the people is an essential part of the obligations undertaken by the Government in a welfare State. The Government discharges this obligation by running hospitals and health centres which provide medical care to the person seeking to avail those facilities. Preservation of human life is of paramount importance. The Government hospitals run by the State and the medical officers employed therein are duty bound to extend medical assistance for preserving human life. Failure on the part of a Government hospital to provide timely medical treatment to a person in need of such treatment results in violation of his right to life. (*Paschim Banga Khet Mazdoor Samity and others v State of West Bengal and another* – *victim of serious rail accident forced to receive treatment at private hospital after being turned away by number of state hospitals which could have accommodated him*)

20.2   WITHDRAWING MEDICAL TREATMENT

Key ECHR cases

D v UK (1997) 24 EHRR 423, ECtHR

ECHR principles

- The termination or withdrawal of existing treatment in serious cases might breach Articles 2 and/or 3, ECHR:

    In view of these exceptional circumstances and bearing in mind the critical stage now reached in the applicant's fatal illness, the implementation of the decision to remove him to St Kitt's would amount to inhuman treatment by the respondent State in violation of Article 3. (D v UK, para. 53 – *challenge to deportation decision in relation to man in an advanced stage of a terminal and incurable disease*)

Relevant domestic cases

In re A (Minors) (Conjoined Twins) (22 September 2000), CA

- Lawful for doctors to carry out an operation to separate conjoined twins (*In re A (Minors) (Conjoined Twins)*).

20.3   CONSENT

Key ECHR cases

X v *Germany* (1985) 7 EHRR 152, ECmHR

ECHR principles

- Medical treatment carried out without consent engages Article 8, ECHR (privacy and physical integrity), and may engage Article 3 (inhuman and degrading treatment).

- Force feeding may amount to inhuman or degrading treatment under Article 3, but not where it is carried out pursuant to the state's positive obligation to protect life (*X v Germany*).

Other international human rights standards

- In relation to the banning of medical or scientific experimentation without free consent, special protection is required in the case of persons who are unable to give such valid consent, in particular those under any form of detention or imprisonment. Such persons should not be subjected to any experimentation that may be detrimental to their health (UN Human Rights Committee, General Comment 20, para. 7).

Relevant New Zealand cases

Re G [1997] 2 NZLR 201

- Where life support patients are unable to give consent to medical treatment, it can be given on their behalf by a court, which has assessed what is in the patient's best interests and which has given weight to likely wishes of the patient and his or her family and medical carers (*Re G*, p. 210).

20.4   ADVICE ON HEALTH ISSUES

Key ECHR cases

LCB v UK (1998) 27 EHRR 212, ECtHR
McGinley and Egan v UK (1998) 27 EHRR 1, ECtHR

ECHR principles

- Where individuals are exposed to a specific health risk, a duty to give appropriate health advice can arise (*LCB v UK*, para. 36 (by implication)).

- In similar circumstances, the relevant authorities can come under a duty to provide relevant and appropriate information:

    Where a Government engages in hazardous activities, such as those in issue in the present case, which might have hidden adverse consequences on the health of those involved in such activities, respect for private and family life under Article 8 requires that an effective and accessible procedure be established which enables persons to seek all relevant and appropriate information. (*McGinley and Egan v UK*, para. 101)

20.5   MEDICAL RECORDS

Key ECHR cases

Gaskin v UK (1989) 12 EHRR 36, ECtHR
Z v Finland (1997) 25 EHRR 371, ECtHR

Chave née Jullien v France (1991) 71 DR 141, ECmHR
Martin v Switzerland (1995) 81-A DR 136, ECmHR

ECHR principles

- The collection of medical data and the maintenance of medical records falls within the sphere of private life protected by Article 8 (*Chave née Jullien v France; Z v Finland*).

- Restrictions on patient access to medical records must therefore be justified as necessary and proportionate (*Gaskin v UK; Martin v Switzerland*).

20.6   MEDICAL CONFIDENTIALITY

Key ECHR cases

Z v Finland (1997) 25 EHRR 371, ECtHR

ECHR principles

- Medical confidentiality is a 'vital principle', crucial to privacy and also to preserving confidence in the medical profession and in the health services in general (*Z v Finland*, para. 95).

- Disclosure is therefore very tightly controlled under the ECHR:

  . . . any state measures compelling communication or disclosure of such information without the consent of the patient call for the most careful scrutiny . . . (Z v *Finland*, para. 96)

- The public interest in the investigation and prosecution of crime and the public interest in the publicity of court proceedings can outweigh medical confidentiality, but only in limited circumstances and where safeguards exist to protect the rights and interests of patients (Z v *Finland*, para. 97).

SLAVERY, SERVITUDE AND FORCED LABOUR

21.1 SLAVERY AND SERVITUDE

Key ECHR cases

Van Droogenbroeck v Belgium (1982) 4 EHRR 443, ECtHR

W, X, Y and Z v UK (1968) 11 Yearbook 562, ECmHR

ECHR principles

- Slavery is not defined in the ECHR, but is defined in the 1926 Slavery Convention as:

  . . . the status or condition of a person over whom any or all of the powers attaching to the right of ownership are exercised. (Article 1(1))

- Servitude, by contrast, does not connote ownership and means:

  . . . the obligation to provide another with certain services, [and] the obligation on the part of the 'serf' to live on another's property and the impossibility of changing his condition. (*Van Droogenbroeck v Belgium*)

- Servitude is unlikely to include military service even where enlistment is for a long period and there is no prospect of early discharge (*W, X, Y and Z v UK*).

21.2 FORCED LABOUR

Key ECHR cases

Van der Mussele v Belgium (1983) 6 EHRR 163, ECtHR

Talmon v Netherlands (1997) EHRLR 448, ECmHR[CD]
W, X, Y and Z v Austria (1977) 7 DR 148, ECmHR
X v Germany (1974) 46 Coll Dec 22, ECmHR
X v Germany (1980) 18 DR 216, ECmHR
X v Germany (1982) 26 DR 97, ECmHR
X v Netherlands (1976) 7 DR 161, ECmHR
X and Y v Germany (1978) 10 DR 224, ECmHR

ECHR principles

- Forced or compulsory labour is not defined in the ECHR, but it covers:

  . . . all work or service which is exacted from any person under the menace of any penalty and for which the said person has not offered himself voluntarily. (Article 2, ILO Convention No. 29; see also *Van der Mussele v Belgium*, para. 32)

- Forced labour connotes some form of physical or mental constraint (*Van der Mussele v Belgium*, para. 34).

- Compulsory labour connotes work 'exacted under the menace of any penalty' and performed against the will of the individual in question, and can include paid work (*Van der Mussele v Belgium*, para. 34).

- But too rigid an approach should be avoided: forced labour is a concept intended to evolve over time, because Article 4, ECHR is to be interpreted 'in the light of the notions currently prevailing in democratic States' (*Van der Mussele v Belgium*, para. 32).

- An obligation to provide free legal services as part of a barrister's training does not amount to compulsory labour (*Van der Mussele v Belgium*); neither does legal aid work on limited fees (*X and Y v Germany; X v Germany*).

- Withdrawing unemployment benefit from those who refuse to accept a job offer does not infringe the prohibition on forced or compulsory labour (*X v Netherlands*); neither does a rule making unemployment benefit dependent on the applicant seeking suitable work (*Talmon v Netherlands*).

21.3   WORK IN PRISON OR ON LICENCE

- See 13.9.

21.4   MILITARY SERVICE

Key ECHR cases

Johansen v Norway (1985) 44 DR 155, ECmHR

ECHR principles

- Article 4(3)(b), ECHR excludes from the definition of forced or compulsory labour, 'any service of a military character or, in case of conscientious objectors in countries where they are recognised, service exacted instead of compulsory military service'.

- It does not give conscientious objectors the right to exemption from military service (*Johansen v Norway*).

21.5   EMERGENCY SERVICE

- Article 4(3)(c), ECHR excludes from the definition of forced or compulsory labour, 'any service exacted in case of an emergency or calamity threatening the life or well-being of the community'.

21.6   NORMAL CIVIC OBLIGATIONS

Key ECHR cases

Karlheinz Schmidt v Germany (1994) 18 EHRR 513, ECtHR

Societies W, X, Y and Z v Austria (1977) 7 DR 148, ECmHR

ECHR principles

- Article 4(3)(d), ECHR excludes from the definition of forced or compulsory labour 'any work or service which forms part of civic obligations'.

- Assisting others fill in tax forms might qualify as a civil obligation (*Societies W, X, Y and Z v Austria*); but an obligation to serve in the fire brigade on pain of a financial penalty does not (*Karlheinz Schmidt v Germany*).

THE RIGHT TO LIBERTY

Article 5, ECHR is concerned with the right to liberty and security of person. It provides that a state may legitimately detain someone, but only if the grounds for detention can be found in the list set out in Article 5(1). It also provides associated procedural rights to ensure speedy and effective judicial determination of the justification of detention. It is best treated as a two-limbed provision:

(a) a test for the legality of detention; and
(b) a set of procedural safeguards for detainees.

22.1 THE MEANING OF LIBERTY

Key ECHR cases

Amuur v France (1996) 22 EHRR 533, ECtHR
Blume v Spain (21 September 1999), ECtHR
De Wilde, Ooms and Versyp v Belgium (1971) 1 EHRR 373, ECtHR
Guzzardi v Italy (1980) 3 EHRR 333, ECtHR

Guenat v Switzerland (1995) 81-A DR 130, ECmHR
SM and MT v Austria (1993) 74 DR 179, ECmHR
Walverens v Belgium (5 March 1980), ECmHR
X v Austria (1979) 18 DR 154, ECmHR
X v Germany (1981) 24 DR 158, ECmHR
X and Y v Sweden (1977) 7 DR 123, ECmHR

ECHR principles

- Article 5(1), ECHR provides that everyone has the right to liberty and security of person.

- It is not, in principle, concerned with mere restrictions on freedom of movement; such restrictions are governed by Article 2 of the Fourth Protocol.

- But the distinction between deprivation of liberty and restrictions on freedom of movement can be a fine one:

  . . . the difference between deprivation of and restriction upon liberty is nonetheless merely one of degree or intensity, and not one of nature and substance. (*Guzzardi v Italy*, para. 93)

- The period of detention is important, but not definitive. Article 5 can apply to very short periods of detention, e.g., to allow a blood test to be taken (*X v Austria*).

- Other important factors are the objective of the measure taken, the manner in which it is effected and the reason for it:

  > Deprivation of liberty may take numerous other forms [to detention in prison]. Their variety is being increased by developments in legal standards and in attitudes; and the Convention is to be interpreted in the light of the notions currently prevailing in democratic states. (*Guzzardi v Italy*, para. 95)

- Relevant to the question of whether an individual has been deprived of his or her liberty will be the purpose of any confinement, its duration, effect and manner of implementation (*Guzzardi v Italy*).

- The fact that an individual voluntarily surrenders to custody will not preclude the applicability of Article 5:

  > . . . the right to liberty is too important in a 'democratic society' within the meaning of the Convention for a person to lose the benefit of the protection of the Convention for the single reason that he gives himself up to be taken into detention. Detention might violate Article 5 even although the person concerned might have agreed to it. (*De Wilde, Ooms and Versyp v Belgium*, para. 65)

- In general, individuals are not deprived of their liberty if they are free to leave the area of confinement (e.g., an airport transit area to go to another country) (*SM and MT v Austria*).

- However, if the only option for those seeking asylum is to leave for another country where they cannot be guaranteed safety, their freedom to leave is ineffective (*Amuur v France*).

- In addition, Article 5 can apply even where an individual is technically free to leave detention if he or she is unaware of the legal position and/or feels constrained from leaving (*Walverens v Belgium*).

- Where the authorities 'acquiesce' in detention, they may be liable under Article 5, even where others are primarily responsible for the detention (*Blume v Spain*, para. 35).

22.2   CURFEWS

Key ECHR cases

Guzzardi v Italy (1980) 3 EHRR 333, ECtHR

Cyprus v Turkey (1976) 4 EHRR 482, ECmHR

ECHR principles

- Curfews can amount to a deprivation of liberty, depending on the degree of restriction imposed.

- Confining individuals to their homes is a deprivation of liberty within the meaning of Article 5 (*Cyprus v Turkey*); so too is an order confining an individual to a small area on an island (*Guzzardi v Italy*).

- But a night curfew – preventing individuals being in public places at night – is not a deprivation of liberty (*Cyprus v Turkey*, para. 235).

22.3   THE LEGALITY OF DETENTION

Key ECHR cases

Baranowski v Poland (28 March 2000), ECtHR
Bouamar v Belgium (1988) 11 EHRR 1, ECtHR
Bozano v France (1986) 9 EHRR 297, ECtHR
Litwa v Poland (4 April 2000), ECtHR
Perks and others v UK (1999) 30 EHRR 33, ECtHR
Raninen v Finland (1997) 26 EHRR 563, ECtHR
Steel and others v UK (1998) 28 EHRR 603, ECtHR
Winterwerp v Netherlands (1979) 2 EHRR 387, ECtHR

Caprino v UK (1980) 22 DR 5, ECmHR
Zamir v UK (1985) 40 DR 42, ECmHR

ECHR principles

- Each of the subparagraphs in Article 5(1) expressly provides that detention must be 'lawful'.

- This requirement has three aspects:

  (a)   there must be a basis in domestic law for detention;
  (b)   detention must conform with the general requirements of the ECHR; and
  (c)   detention must not be arbitrary.

- Whether there is a basis in domestic law for detention is usually a straightforward question; but where domestic law requires certain pre-conditions to be fulfilled (e.g., evidence of 'unsound mind') this may involve a factual assessment (*Winterwerp v Netherlands*).

- Where detention is unlawful in domestic law, it is automatically unlawful under the ECHR (*Raninen v Finland*, para. 46).

- The second aspect of legality – the general requirements of the ECHR – imports into Article 5 the rule that any restriction on rights must be prescribed by law (see **1.3**).

- According to this rule, the domestic law upon which detention is based must be accessible and precise:

  . . . where deprivation of liberty is concerned it is particularly important that the general principle of legal certainty be satisfied. It is therefore essential that the conditions for deprivation of liberty under domestic law be clearly defined and that the law itself be foreseeable in its application, so that it meets the standard of 'lawfulness' set out by the Convention, a standard which requires that all law be sufficiently precise to allow the person – if need be, with appropriate advice – to foresee, to a degree that is reasonable in the circumstances, the consequences which a given action may entail . . . (*Baranowski v Poland*, para. 52, citing *Steel and others v UK*; see also *Zamir v UK*)

- The notion of 'lawfulness' in Article 5 implies more than compliance with domestic law, it also prohibits 'arbitrary' deprivation of liberty (*Baranowski v Poland*, para. 51).

- It is primarily concerned with detention that is procured by an abuse of power or through bad faith, e.g., clandestinely transporting an individual from France to Switzerland to circumvent an adverse court order in France:

   . . . depriving [the applicant] of his liberty in this way amounted in fact to a disguised extradition designed to circumvent the negative ruling [of the French Court] and not to 'detention' necessary in the ordinary course of 'action . . . taken with a view to deportation'. (*Bozano v France*, para. 60)

- But it goes beyond this:

   The notion of 'lawfulness' runs through Article 5. As a result it is not enough simply to establish that one of the grounds for detention under Article 5(1)(a) to (f) is made out, detention must also be *necessary*. And detention will not be necessary unless the authorities can show that other measures short of detention were considered but rejected as insufficient. (*Litwa v Poland*, para. 78)

- Repeated orders for detention which are clearly not serving their intended purpose, e.g., educational supervision, are likely to be arbitrary:

   . . . the nine placement orders, taken together, were not compatible with [Article 5(1)(d)]. Their fruitless repetition had the effect of making them less and less 'lawful' . . . especially as Crown Counsel never instituted criminal proceedings in respect of the alleged offences against [the applicant]. (*Bouamar v Belgium*, para. 53)

- Fettering a discretionary power or failing to have proper regard to relevant evidence may render detention arbitrary, even where it is otherwise lawful within the meaning of Article 5 (*Perks v UK*, para. 70).

- Detention may also be arbitrary where, although properly motivated, it is wholly disproportionate to the (legitimate) aim being pursued (*Winterwerp v Netherlands*; *Caprino v UK*, para. 67).

Relevant domestic cases

R v *Governor of Brockhill Prison, ex parte Evans (No. 2)* [2000] 4 All ER 15

- Detention which might otherwise be lawful under domestic law could be 'nevertheless open to criticism on the ground that it is arbitrary because, for example, it was resorted to in bad faith or was not proportionate' (*R v Governor of Brockhill Prison, ex parte Evans (No. 2)*).

22.4   PROCEDURE

Key ECHR cases

Van der Leer v *Netherlands* (1990) 12 EHRR 567, ECtHR
Winterwerp v *Netherlands* (1979) 2 EHRR 387, ECtHR

ECHR principles

- Article 5(1), ECHR expressly provides that detention should be 'in accordance with a procedure prescribed by law'.

- Where there is no procedure in domestic law, or the procedure laid down is not followed, Article 5(1) will be breached.

- As with the requirement that detention be 'lawful', the general principles of the ECHR are imported into the requirement that detention should be 'in accordance with a procedure prescribed by law' (*Winterwerp* v *Netherlands*).

- A breach of natural justice is likely to render an otherwise lawful procedure unlawful, e.g., where the court fails to hear from the detained person (*Van der Leer* v *Netherlands* – *applicant not given an opportunity to be heard before being confined to a psychiatric hospital*).

22.5   THE LIMITED GROUNDS FOR DETENTION

Key ECHR cases

Winterwerp v *Netherlands* (1979) 2 EHRR 387, ECtHR

ECHR principles

- Article 5(1)(a) to (f) provide an exhaustive definition of the circumstances in which individuals may be lawfully deprived of their liberty (*Winterwerp* v *Netherlands*, para. 37).

- They are to be narrowly construed (*Winterwerp* v *Netherlands*, para. 37).

22.6   DETENTION AFTER CONVICTION

Key ECHR cases

De Wilde, Ooms and Versyp v *Belgium* (1971) 1 EHRR 373, ECtHR
Douiyeb v *Netherlands* (4 August 1999), ECtHR
Drozd and Janousek v *France and Spain* (1992) 14 EHRR 745, ECtHR
Perks and others v *UK* (1999) 30 EHRR 33, ECtHR
Thynne, Wilson and Gunnell v *UK* (1990) 13 EHRR 666, ECtHR
Tsirlis and Kouloumpas v *Greece* (1997) 25 EHRR 198, ECtHR
Weeks v *UK* (1987) 10 EHRR 293, ECtHR

Kotalla v Netherlands (1978) 14 DR 238, ECmHR
Krzycki v Germany (1978) 13 DR 57, ECmHR
X v *Austria* (1968) 11 Yearbook 322, ECmHR
X v *Austria* (1969) 12 Yearbook 206, ECmHR
X v *Austria* (1970) 13 Yearbook 798, ECmHR
X v *Germany* (1963) 6 Yearbook 494, ECmHR
X v *UK* (1981) A/46, ECmHR

ECHR principles

- Article 5(1)(a) provides for 'the lawful detention of a person after conviction by a competent court'.

- A competent court is one with jurisdiction to try the case (X v *Austria* (1968), p. 348; X v *Austria* (1970), p. 804).

- The fact that a conviction is overturned on appeal does not necessarily affect the lawfulness of detention pending appeal; Article 5(1)(a) does not require a lawful conviction, only lawful detention:

    A period of detention will in principle be lawful if it is carried out pursuant to a court order. A subsequent finding that the court erred under domestic law in making the order will not necessarily retrospectively affect the validity of the intervening period of detention. For this reason, the Convention organs have consistently refused to uphold applications from persons convicted of criminal offences who complain that their convictions or sentences were found by the appellate courts to have been based on errors of fact or law. (*Douiyeb v Netherlands*, para. 45; see also *Krzycki v Germany*)

- The same applies to acquittals after a retrial (X v *Austria*).

- However, Article 5(1)(a) will be breached where the conviction had no basis in domestic law (*Tsirlis and Kouloumpas v Greece*).

- In the magistrates' court, jurisdictional questions are therefore important.

- In *Perks and others v UK*, the ECtHR accepted as valid the House of Lords distinction between errors within magistrates' courts' jurisdiction and those outwith jurisdiction, namely jurisdiction exceeded where: (a) magistrates act without having jurisdiction over the cause; (b) although magistrates have jurisdiction, there is a gross or obvious irregularity of procedure; or (c) magistrates make an order that has no proper foundation in law because of a failure to observe a statutory condition precedent (*McC v Mullan* [1985] AC 528).

- To satisfy Article 5(1)(a), a conviction must be the cause of detention:

    . . . the word 'after' in sub-paragraph (a) does not simply mean that the detention must follow the 'conviction' in point of time: in addition, the detention must result from, 'follow and depend upon' or occur 'by virtue of' the 'conviction'. In short, there must be a sufficient causal connection between the conviction and the deprivation of liberty at issue. (*Weeks v UK*, para. 42)

- Detention after conviction covers confinement in a mental institution for treatment (X v *UK*) and detention as an alternative to any original sentence (*Kotalla v Netherlands*).

- The fact that a sentence is passed abroad does not, in itself, make detention unlawful under Article 5(1)(a) (*X v Germany; Drozd and Janousek v France and Spain*).

Relevant domestic cases

R v Governor of Brockhill Prison, ex parte Evans (No. 2) [2000] 4 All ER 15; see **22.3**

22.7   DETENTION TO ENFORCE COURT ORDERS

Key ECHR cases

Steel and others v UK (1998) 28 EHRR 603, ECtHR

Airey v Ireland (1977) 8 DR 42, ECmHR
K v Austria (1993) A/255 B, ECmHR
Shobiye v UK (1976), ECmHR
X v Austria (1979) 18 DR 154, ECmHR
X v Germany (1971) 14 Yearbook 692, ECmHR
X v Germany (1975) 3 DR 92, ECmHR

ECHR principles

- Article 5(1)(b) provides for the lawful arrest or detention of a person for non-compliance with the lawful order of a court.

- This authorises detention to effect the execution of an order of the court where there has been hindrance or obstruction.

- Detention may be justified under Article 5(1)(b) to enable a blood test to be taken (*X v Austria*), to enable an affidavit to be prepared (*X v Germany* (1971)), a psychiatric opinion to be obtained (*X v Germany* (1975)), or to secure compliance with an order to deliver up property (*Shobiye v UK*) or pay a fine (*Airey v Ireland*).

- Detention for refusing to be bound over to keep the peace and be of good behaviour can also be justified under this provision (*Steel v UK*).

- But if the court order itself breaches the ECHR, detention pursuant to it will not be lawful under Article 5(1)(b) (*K v Austria*).

22.8   DETENTION TO FULFIL AN OBLIGATION PRESCRIBED BY LAW

Key ECHR cases

Engel and others v Netherlands (1976) 1 EHRR 647, ECtHR
Lawless v Ireland (1961) 1 EHRR 1, ECtHR
Perks and others v UK (1999) 30 EHRR 33, ECtHR

McVeigh, O'Neill and Evans v UK (1981) 5 EHRR 71, ECmHR

ECHR principles

- Article 5(1)(b) further provides for the lawful arrest or detention of a person in order to secure the fulfilment of any obligation prescribed by law.

- It does not authorise detention to secure the performance of a general legal duty: the obligation must be specific and concrete (*Engel and others v Netherlands*). A general obligation not to commit offences against public peace or state security cannot legitimise detention under Article 5(1)(b) (*Lawless v Ireland*).

- The general rule is that detention under Article 5(1)(b) is not permitted unless and until the individual has had the opportunity, but failed, to fulfil the obligation in question:

  > The Court considers that the words 'secure the fulfilment of any obligation prescribed by law' concern only cases where the law permits the detention of a person to compel him to fulfil a specific and concrete obligation which he has until then failed to satisfy. A wide interpretation would entail consequences incompatible with the notion of the rule of law from which the whole Convention draws its inspiration. (*Engel v Netherlands*, para. 69)

- But detention to facilitate questioning at ports and airports under anti-terrorism legislation might fall within Article 5(1)(b) (*McVeigh, O'Neill and Evans v UK*).

- Detention for non-payment of the community charge may come within Article 5(1)(b) (*Perks and others v UK*, para. 70).

22.9   ARREST AND DETENTION

- Article 5(1)(c) provides for 'the lawful arrest or detention of a person effected for the purpose of bringing him before the competent legal authority on reasonable suspicion of having committed an offence or when it is reasonably considered necessary to prevent his committing an offence or fleeing after having done so'.

- See **Section 7**.

22.10   PREVENTATIVE DETENTION

Key ECHR cases

Guzzardi v Italy (1980) 3 EHRR 333, ECtHR
Ireland v UK (1978) 2 EHRR 25, ECtHR

ECHR principles

- Although Article 5(1)(c) authorises detention to prevent the commission of offences, it does not authorise a policy of general preventative detention directed against an individual or group of individuals on the basis that they have a propensity to commit crime; it does no more than afford a means of preventing a 'concrete and specific' offence (*Guzzardi v Italy*; see also *Ireland v UK* – *internment policy unlawful*).

22.11   THE DETENTION OF CHILDREN

- Article 5(1)(d) provides for 'the detention of a minor by lawful order for the purpose of educational supervision or his lawful detention for the purpose of bringing him before the competent legal authority'.

- See **27.5**.

Relevant domestic cases

In Re K (a child) (15 November 2000), CA

- Educational supervision is a wider concept than merely compelling a child to sit in a classroom (*In Re K (a child)*; see further 27.5).

22.12   THE DETENTION OF PERSONS OF UNSOUND MIND

- Article 5(1)(e) provides for 'the lawful detention . . . of persons of unsound mind'.

- See **23.1**.

22.13   THE DETENTION OF ALCOHOLICS, DRUG ADDICTS AND VAGRANTS

Key ECHR cases

De Wilde, Ooms and Versyp v Belgium (1971) 1 EHRR 373, ECtHR
Guzzardi v Italy (1980) 3 EHRR 333, ECtHR
Litwa v Poland (4 April 2000), ECtHR

ECHR principles

- Article 5(1)(e) provides for 'the lawful detention . . . of alcoholics . . . drug addicts or vagrants'.

- Convention rights should be interpreted in light of their objects and purpose. The objects and purposes of Article 5(1)(e) of the Convention include protection of the public and protection of the individual himself or herself. As a result, the word 'alcoholics' in Article 5(1)(e) should not be limited to clinical alcoholics; it also includes those temporarily under the influence of alcohol. However, detention will be justified only where an individual poses a threat to others or to himself or herself (*Litwa v Poland*, para. 61).

- Detention will not be necessary unless the authorities can show that other measures short of detention were considered but rejected as insufficient; and it will be difficult to establish that the detention of an individual under the influence of drink is necessary unless other measures, such as taking him or her home, have been considered (*Litwa v Poland*, para. 79).

- The term 'vagrants' is not defined in Article 5(1)(e), but the ECtHR did not disapprove a Belgian definition of vagrants as 'persons with no fixed abode, no means of subsistence and no trade or profession' (*De Wilde, Ooms and Versyp v Belgium*).

• Antisocial behaviour of suspected mafia members, with no identifiable source of income, is insufficient (*Guzzardi v Italy*).

22.14   DETENTION PENDING DEPORTATION OR EXTRADITION

• Article 5(1)(f) provides for 'the lawful arrest and detention of a person to prevent his effecting an unauthorised entry into the country or of a person against whom action is being taken with a view to deportation or extradition'.

• See **28.4**.

22.15   REASONS FOR DETENTION

• Article 5(2) provides that 'Everyone who is arrested shall be informed promptly, in a language which he understands, of the reasons for his arrest and of any charge against him.'

• See **7.3**.

22.16   PRE-TRIAL DETENTION AND BAIL UNDER ARTICLE 5(3)

• Article 5(3) provides: 'Everyone arrested or detained in accordance with the provisions of paragraph 1(c) of this Article shall be brought promptly before a judge or other officer authorised by law to exercise judicial power and shall be entitled to trial within a reasonable time or to release pending trial. Release may be conditioned by guarantees to appear for trial.'

• See **7.9** to **7.11**.

22.17   REVIEW UNDER ARTICLE 5(4): *HABEAS CORPUS*

22.17.1   *Procedural aspects*

Key ECHR cases

Ashingdane v UK (1985) 7 EHRR 528, ECtHR
Bezicheri v Italy (1989) 12 EHRR 210, ECtHR
Chahal v UK (1996) 23 EHRR 413, ECtHR
Curley v UK (28 March 2000), ECtHR
De Wilde, Ooms and Versyp v Belgium (1971) 1 EHRR 373, ECtHR
Johnson v UK (1997) 27 EHRR 296, ECtHR
Megyeri v Germany (1992) 15 EHRR 584, ECtHR
Sanchez-Reisse v Switzerland (1986) 9 EHRR 71, ECtHR
Singh and Hussain v UK (1996) 22 EHRR 1, ECtHR
Soumare v France (24 August 1998), ECtHR

Thynne, Wilson and Gunnell v *UK* (1990) 13 EHRR 666, ECtHR
Weeks v *UK* (1987) 10 EHRR 293, ECtHR
X v *UK* (1981) 4 EHRR 188, ECtHR

Benjamin and Wilson v *UK* [1998] EHRLR 226, ECmHR[CD]
Dhoest v *Belgium* (1988) 55 DR 5, ECmHR
KM v *UK* [1997] EHRLR 299, ECmHR
Roux v *UK* (1986) 48 DR 263, ECmHR
Tomsett v *UK* [1997] EHRLR 104, ECmHR
Woukam Moudefo v *France* (1988) A 141-B, ECmHR
Zamir v *UK* (1985) 40 DR 42, ECmHR

ECHR principles

- Article 5(4) provides: 'Everyone who is deprived of his liberty by arrest or detention shall be entitled to take proceedings by which the lawfulness of his detention shall be decided speedily by a court and his release ordered if the detention is not lawful.'

- Its purpose is:

  . . . to assure to persons who are arrested or detained the right to a judicial supervision of the lawfulness of the measure to which they are thereby subjected. (*De Wilde, Ooms and Versyp* v *Belgium*, para. 76)

- The scope of the supervision required under Article 5(4) varies with the context. A full review by a 'court' is needed where:

  (a) the initial decision to detain was not taken by a court or tribunal;
  (b) the grounds for detention may change over time, e.g., those detained on mental health grounds or prisoners serving the preventative part of their sentence.

- For prisoners serving fixed-term sentences, the judicial supervision of the lawfulness of detention required by Article 5(4) is incorporated in the decision of the trial court (*De Wilde, Ooms and Versyp* v *Belgium*, para. 76).

- For prisoners serving indeterminate sentences, separate Article 5(4) proceedings are required to determine release once the 'tariff' period has been served (*Thynne, Wilson and Gunnell* v *UK*, paras 73 and 74 – *concerning discretionary life sentences.*

- For preventative sentences generally, see **10.5**.

- Where the grounds for detention may change over time, *periodic* review is required (*Bezicheri* v *Italy*). For mental health cases, see also **23.3**.

- Where a court passes a sentence and imposes forfeiture or a fine with further detention in default, that second period (unlike the first) is subject to review under Article 5(4), depending as it does on solvency (*Soumare* v *France*).

- The degree of scrutiny required under Article 5(4) also varies with the context, but unless the court can review compliance with domestic law and the general requirements of the ECHR, and examine the soundness of the factual basis put forward in support of detention, Article 5(4) will be breached:

  . . . it is clear that Article 5(4) does not guarantee a right to judicial review of such breadth as to empower the court, on all aspects of the case including questions of pure expediency, to substitute its own discretion for that of the decision-making authority. The review should, however, be wide enough to bear on those conditions which are essential for the 'lawful' detention of a person according to Article 5(1). (*Chahal v UK*, para. 127)

- The irrationality test of lawfulness provides insufficiently close scrutiny for Article 5(4) purposes (*Weeks v UK; Thynne, Wilson and Gunnell v UK*).

- Any body tasked with determining the lawfulness of a detention must be independent of both the executive and the parties and follow a procedure which has:

  . . . a judicial character and gives to the individual concerned guarantees, appropriate to the kind of deprivation of liberty in question, of [a] judicial procedure the forms of which may vary from one domain to another. (*De Wilde, Ooms and Versyp v Belgium*, paras 76–78; *X v UK*)

- It must have the power to take a legally binding decision to release the prisoner (*Hussain v UK*, para. 67 – *breach of Article 5(4) because Parole Board (then) was unable to order release; Curley v UK – interim release powers of Parole Board for those detained during Her Majesty's Pleasure not sufficient*).

- However, merely because a body lacks some relevant powers under Article 5(4), this does not necessarily invalidate its status when exercising the powers it has (*Roux v UK – Mental Health Review Tribunal's lack of power to direct temporary release did not result in a violation; Ashingdane v UK; KM v UK*, p. 300 – *inability of Discretionary Life Panel to order transfer of convicted rapist to open conditions*).

- If the assistance of other public authorities is required to provide a suitable release plan then the state must ensure that this occurs, or provide judicial review to ensure there is no unreasonable delay (*Johnson v UK*, para. 67 – *failure to provide a hostel place for a discharged mental health patient;* see also *Tomsett v UK*, p. 105 – *complaint about decision not to refer mental health case to Discretionary Life Panel declared admissible*).

- The principle of 'equality of arms' applies under Article 5(4), and this implies that proceedings will be adversarial (*Sanchez-Reisse v Switzerland*) but the precise requirements will vary from case to case.

- Where a detainee's character or personal attitudes are in issue, he or she should be given an opportunity to participate fully in an oral hearing and be able to examine and cross-examine witnesses. This is an especially important safeguard in cases where prisoner misconduct is alleged and the facts are disputed (*Singh and Hussain v UK*, para. 59).

- In addition, detainees are entitled to full disclosure of any adverse material in Article 5(4) proceedings (*Weeks v UK*, para. 66; *Thynne, Wilson and Gunnell v UK*, para. 80; *Woukam Moudefo v France*, paras 86–91; *Megyeri v Germany*, para. 23).

- In criminal cases, this applies at an early stage and can require pre-bail disclosure (see **7.11**).

- However, there is no general requirement that the hearing be a public one (*Dhoest v Belgium*, p. 26).

- The burden of proving the legality of the detention is on the authority responsible for the detention (*Zamir v UK*, para. 102).

22.17.2   *Right to have lawfulness of detention determined speedily*

Key ECHR cases

E v Norway (1990) 17 EHRR 30, ECtHR
Johnson v UK (1997) 27 EHRR 296, ECtHR
Koendjbiharie v Netherlands (1990) 13 EHRR 820, ECtHR
Luberti v Italy (1984) 6 EHRR 440, ECtHR
Oldham v UK (24 October 2000), ECtHR
Sanchez-Reisse v Switzerland (1986) 9 EHRR 71, ECtHR

Krzycki v Germany (1978) 13 DR 57, ECmHR
Roux v UK (1986) 48 DR 263, ECmHR
X v UK B/41, ECmHR

ECHR principles

- Any review decision – up to and including the enforcement of remedies – must be made speedily.

- This means:
  - (a)   a detainee must have speedy access to a remedy (*X v UK*, para. 138 – *delay of six months before a patient recalled under the Mental Health Act was entitled to apply for release violated Article 5(4)*);
  - (b)   once the remedy has been obtained it must be implemented quickly (*Sanchez-Reisse v Switzerland*, para. 55; see also *Roux v UK*).

- In this context both the diligence of the authorities and the cause of the delay – state or detainee – are relevant (*Koendjbiharie v Netherlands*, para. 29 – *four-month delay before release from extended confinement in psychiatric clinic ordered by Court of Appeal considered unreasonable as it included a month-long adjournment without good reason; E v Norway*, para. 66 – *12 months too long, part of the delay arising from the judge's absence on vacation*).

- But it is for the detaining authority to justify any delay which appears prima facie to violate the need for speedy action (*Koendjbiharie v Netherlands*, paras 28–30).

- Any review period ends with the final determination of the case, whether that involves an appeal or a judicial review, and an assessment of delay must look at all the relevant proceedings (*Luberti v Italy*, para. 33).

- Two years delay between Parole Board reviews may not meet the requirements of Article 5(4) (*Oldham v UK*).

22.18   COMPENSATION FOR WRONGFUL DETENTION

Key ECHR cases

Benham v UK (1996) 22 EHRR 293, ECtHR
Brogan and others v UK (1988) 11 EHRR 117, ECtHR
Caballero v UK (2000) 30 EHRR 643, ECtHR
Fox, Campbell and Hartley v UK (1990) 13 EHRR 157, ECtHR
Santa Cruz Ruiz v UK (19 February 1999), ECtHR
Wassink v Netherlands (1990) A/185-A, ECtHR

Huber v Austria (1976) 6 DR 65, ECmHR
L v Sweden (1988) 61 DR 62, ECmHR

ECHR principles

- Article 5(5) provides: 'Everyone who has been the victim of arrest or detention in contravention of the provisions of this article shall have an enforceable right to compensation.'

- This is distinct from and without prejudice to the power of the ECtHR to award just satisfaction under Article 41, ECHR.

- The fact that detention is lawful in domestic law does not affect the right to compensation under Article 5(5) if it is unlawful under the ECHR (*Brogan and others v UK*; *Fox, Campbell and Hartley v UK*); any detention which is unlawful in domestic law is automatically unlawful under the ECHR (*L v Sweden*).

- Article 5(5) gives a *right* to compensation; an *ex gratia* payment is insufficient.

- A rule that compensation is payable only on proof of damage is not contrary to Article 5(5) (*Wassink v Netherland*); but damage encompasses both pecuniary and non-pecuniary damage, including 'moral' damage such as distress, pain and suffering (*Huber v Austria*, p. 69).

- Damages will be awarded for breach of Article 5(3) of the Convention only where the applicant can establish a link between the breach and any subsequent deprivation of liberty (*Caballero v UK*, para. 30).

- Article 5(5) does not require the detainee to establish bad faith on the part of the authorities (*Santa Cruz Ruiz v UK*).

- However, an error within jurisdiction does not necessarily give rise to a claim under Article 5(5) (*Benham v UK*).

- On jurisdictional issues in the magistrates' court, see **22.6**.

SECTION 23

MENTAL HEALTH

Issues concerning mental health arise under a number of ECHR Articles, including Article 3 (prohibition on inhuman and degrading treatment), Article 6(1) (right to a fair trial), Article 8 (the protection of private life) and Article 13 (the right to marry). In addition, the ECHR is concerned with the circumstances in which those with mental health problems can be lawfully detained under Article 5.

23.1 THE DETENTION OF PERSONS OF UNSOUND MIND UNDER ARTICLE 5

Key ECHR cases

Aerts v *Belgium* (1998) 29 EHRR 50, ECtHR
Ashingdane v *UK* (1985) 7 EHRR 528, ECtHR
De Wilde, Ooms and Versyp v *Belgium* (1971) 1 EHRR 373, ECtHR
Guzzardi v *Italy* (1980) 3 EHRR 333, ECtHR
Van der Leer v *Netherlands* (1990) 12 EHRR 567, ECtHR
Wassink v *Netherlands* (1990) A/185-A, ECtHR
Winterwerp v *Netherlands* (1979) 2 EHRR 387, ECtHR
X v *UK* (1981) 4 EHRR 188, ECtHR

ECHR principles

- Article 5(1)(e), ECHR provides for the 'lawful detention . . . of persons of unsound mind'.

- Detention under this provision is justified not only in the public interest, but also in the interests of the individuals themselves (*Guzzardi* v *Italy*, para. 98).

- As for the general requirements of Article 5, see **Section 22**.

23.1.1 *Meaning of 'unsound mind'*

- Determining whether somebody is of 'unsound mind' to justify detention will require reliable evidence from an objective medical expert: mental disorder must be of a kind or degree warranting compulsory confinement and must persist during the period of detention (*Winterwerp* v *Netherlands*, para. 39).

- However, since the medical profession is still developing the notion of what constitutes an 'unsound mind', it should not be given too definitive an interpretation: relevant domestic law should be applied in the light of current psychiatric knowledge (*Winterwerp v Netherlands*, paras 37 and 38).

- But an 'unsound mind' does not include holding views or exhibiting behaviour that deviates from the prevailing norms of society (*Winterwerp v Netherlands*, para. 37).

23.1.2   *Lawfulness*

- Detention under Article 5(1)(e) must be 'lawful'. For a full analysis of this requirement, see **1.3** and **22.3**.

- Under Article 5(1)(e), there is a relationship between the basis for detention and the place and conditions of detention. In principle, the detention of an individual as a mental health patient will be 'lawful' only if effected in a hospital, clinic or other appropriate institution (*Aerts v Belgium*, para. 46).

- If temporary detention in a prison psychiatric wing, pending placement in an appropriate hospital, does not provide a proper therapeutic environment and is harmful to an individual's mental health, Article 5 will be breached (*Aerts v Belgium*, para. 49; qualifying *Ashingdane v UK*, para. 44).

- Consequently, in cases involving detention under Article 5(1)(e), the ability to test the lawfulness of detention required under Article 5(4) must include an ability to put in issue the appropriateness of the place and conditions of detention (*Aerts v Belgium*, para. 54).

23.1.3   *Procedure prescribed by law*

- Under Article 5(1)(e), the appropriate procedure laid down in domestic law must be strictly followed and that law itself must conform to the general requirements of the ECHR, e.g., it must be accessible, clear and not arbitrary (*Winterwerp v Netherlands*, para. 45).

- Where the procedural requirements of domestic law (e.g., that the court should hear from the individual concerned in person before ordering detention unless an objection is raised and supported by a psychiatric report) are not complied with then the detention will be unlawful under Article 5(1)(e):

   . . . the main issue to be determined in the present case is whether the disputed detention was 'lawful', including whether it complied with 'a procedure prescribed by law.' The Convention here refers back essentially to national law and lays down the obligation to conform to the substantive and procedural rules thereof, but it requires in addition that any deprivation of liberty should be consistent with the purpose of Article 5, namely to protect individuals from arbitrariness. (*Van der Leer v Netherlands*, para. 22)

23.1.4   *Emergency admissions*

- Emergency cases can constitute an exception to the rule that individuals should not be detained unless 'reliably' shown to be of 'unsound mind' (*Winterwerp v Netherlands*, para. 39).

- Where emergency confinement is authorised by domestic law, there is no requirement, as a matter of practicality, that a thorough medical examination be carried out prior to detention: in these circumstances the interests of the community at large outweigh the rights of the individual and the normal guarantees implied by Article 5(1)(e) (*X v UK*, paras 41 and 45).

- As a result, it is sufficient for emergency admissions to consult experts and witnesses by telephone rather than hearing them in person (*Wassink v Netherlands*, paras 33 and 34)

23.1.5   *Voluntary surrender*

- Article 5 does not inhibit voluntary detention whereby those with mental health problems seek appropriate care and attention: however, the mere fact that an individual voluntarily surrenders to detention does not mean that the Article 5(1)(e) safeguards do not apply:

  > The right to liberty is too important in a 'democratic society' within the meaning of the Convention for a person to lose the benefit of the protection of the Convention for the single reason that he gives himself up to be taken into detention. (*De Wilde, Ooms and Versyp v Belgium*, para. 65)

23.1.6   *The meaning of 'detention' under Article 5*

Detention has the same meaning in mental health cases under the ECHR as it does for other types of detention (see **X.X**).

- It covers both detention in special secure establishments and detention in non-secure hospitals (*Ashingdane v UK*, paras 42 and 47).

Relevant Scottish cases

Anderson, Doherty and Reid v The Scottish Ministers and the Scottish AG (16 June 2000)

- Detention on the basis of 'treatability' is not sufficient for initial detention, but the 'serious harm test' is (*Anderson, Doherty and Reid v The Scottish Ministers and the Scottish AG*).

- It is not contrary to the ECHR to change the criteria for admission and/or release during detention because the notion of 'unsound mind' and the requirements of the ECHR are not rigid or fixed (*Anderson, Doherty and Reid v The Scottish Ministers and the Scottish AG – retrospective legislation on mental health provisions*).

- Since psychiatric opinion is subject to change, governments must be free to alter their laws and policies to reflect that change, and as a result to change the conditions for admission and release, and this may involve alteration to the existing statutory framework.

- Detention in a hospital as an alternative to prison for those with mental health problems is not dependent on there being an alleviation of the detainee's mental health condition:

The Court has indicated that although the Convention is not concerned with suitable treatment or conditions, the detention of a person of unsound mind should be effected in a hospital, clinic or other appropriate institution. (*Anderson, Doherty and Reid v The Scottish Ministers and the Scottish AG*, para. 30)

23.2   DETENTION AFTER OR AS A RESULT OF CRIMINAL PROCEEDINGS

Key ECHR cases

Aerts v Belgium (1998) 29 EHRR 50, ECtHR
X v UK (1981) 4 EHRR 188, ECtHR

ECHR principles

- Where those with mental health problems are convicted of criminal offences, their detention is governed by Article 5(1)(a) (see **22.6**).

- However, where conviction results in an order for treatment not punishment, Article 5(1)(e) applies (*X v UK*, para. 39).

- Equally, where a court orders the detention of an individual on the basis that he or she is so mentally disturbed as to be incapable of controlling his or her actions, and therefore not criminally liable, that detention falls to be considered under Article 5(1)(e) and not Article 5(1)(a) of the Convention (*Aerts v Belgium*, para. 45).

- Article 5(1)(e) equally applies where an individual is not convicted but is detained as a result of mental health problems that come to light because of or during criminal proceedings (*X v UK*, para. 39).

- Where Article 5(1)(e) is the governing provision, periodic review of detention under Article 5(4) is required; such review may also be required where preventative sentences are imposed, e.g., discretionary life sentences or detention during Her Majesty's Pleasure (see **10.6** and **22.17**).

Relevant Scottish cases

Michael Wilkinson v Secretary of State for Scotland (16 February 1999), AC

- Sexual deviancy does not always presume mental illness for the purpose of detention under the Mental Health Act:

  [I]t is clear that there may be people disposed to, affected by, and exhibiting sexual deviancy, and even engaging in sexually deviant behaviour, who could in no sense be regarded as suffering from 'mental disorder' within the meaning of the Act. (*Michael Wilkinson v Secretary of State for Scotland*, p. 5)

Relevant Canadian cases

Bese v B.C. (Forensic Psychiatric Institute) [1999] 2 SCR 722
Orlowski v B.C. (Forensic Psychiatric Institute) [1999] 2 SCR 733

- Where an individual is found not guilty in criminal proceedings by reason of mental disorder, an order can be made restricting his or her movements and freedom in the community; but if there is no significant danger to the public, such an order cannot be justified (*Bese v B.C. (Forensic Psychiatric Institute)*, para. 19; *Orlowski v B.C. (Forensic Psychiatric Institute)*, para. 17).

23.3   PERIODIC REVIEW OF DETENTION

Key ECHR cases

De Wilde, Ooms and Versyp v Belgium (1971) 1 EHRR 373, ECtHR
E v Norway (1990) 17 EHRR 30, ECtHR
Johnson v UK (1997) 27 EHRR 296, ECtHR
Keus v Netherlands (1990) 13 EHRR 700, ECtHR
Koendjbiharie v Netherlands (1990) 13 EHRR 820, ECtHR
Luberti v Italy (1984) 6 EHRR 440, ECtHR
Megyeri v Germany (1992) 15 EHRR 584, ECtHR
Van Droogenbroeck v Belgium (1982) 4 EHRR 443, ECtHR
Wassink v Netherlands (1990) A/185-A, ECtHR
Winterwerp v Netherlands (1979) 2 EHRR 387, ECtHR
X v UK (1981) 4 EHRR 188, ECtHR

Benjamin and Wilson v UK [1998] EHRLR 226, ECmHR[CD]
Boucheras v France (1991) 69 DR 236, ECmHR
Kay v UK (1 March 1994), ECmHR

ECHR principles

23.3.1   *The need for review*

- Article 5(4) provides for review of any detention (see **22.17**).

- For those detained on mental health grounds, this must be *periodic* review because detention is lawful only for so long as the condition persists and persists with sufficient intensity:

  > A person of unsound mind who is compulsorily confined in a psychiatric institution for an indefinite or lengthy period is in principle entitled, at any rate where there is no automatic periodic review of a judicial character, to take proceedings 'at reasonable intervals' before a court to put in issue the 'lawfulness' – within the meaning of the Convention – of his detention. (*Megyeri v Germany*, para. 22)

23.3.2   *The reviewing body*

- The body undertaking the review must be a 'court', but this does not necessarily mean a court of law in the classic sense: it is sufficient if the body is judicial in character (i.e. independent of both the executive and parties to the case) and can provide the procedural guarantees appropriate to the type of detention under review (*De Wilde, Ooms and Versyp v Belgium*, paras 76–77).

- A specialised body can suffice, provided it meets the necessary criteria; but it must possess sufficient powers, and in particular the ability to make a legally binding decision concerning the release or continued detention of the individual (*Van Droogenbroeck v Belgium*, para. 49).

- A Mental Health Review Tribunal, unable to order release but able to give an advisory opinion, does not meet these criteria (*X v UK*, para. 61; *Benjamin and Wilson v UK*).

23.3.3   *The nature of the review*

- Since continued detention under Article 5(1)(e) is lawful only for so long as the individual's mental health condition persists and persists with sufficient intensity, the review body under Article 5(4) must have power to investigate and determine the detainee's current mental state.

- Although *habeas corpus* proceedings may suffice in emergency cases, they are insufficiently exacting for general purposes; further or other review is required (*X v UK*).

23.3.4   *Procedural safeguards at review hearings*

- The procedural safeguards needed for periodic review of detention under Article 5(4) will vary (*Wassink v Netherlands*, para. 30).

- Although the full Article 6 fair trial requirements cannot be read into Article 5(4), some have been imported to ensure *effective* review (see **22.17**).

- What is essential is that the person concerned should have proper access to a court and a proper opportunity to be heard either in person, or, where necessary, through a representative; and further procedural safeguards may be required where those with mental health problems are unable to act for themselves (*Megyeri v Germany*, para. 22; *Winterwerp v Netherlands*, para. 60).

- The burden is on the detaining authority to justify continued detention; Article 5(4) does not require detainees to prove grounds of unlawfulness, nor – procedurally – do they have to take the initiative themselves in obtaining legal advice and representation (*Winterwerp v Netherlands*, para. 66).

23.3.5   *The timing of reviews*

- Initial reviews should take place very speedily – it is unlikely that a six-week delay is acceptable, even as an emergency measure (*Winterwerp v Netherlands*, para. 66).

- Periods of five months (*Kay v UK*), four months (*Koendjbiharie v Netherlands*, paras 29–30), eight weeks (*E v Norway*, para. 66) or even three weeks (*Wassink v Netherlands*, para. 34) have been found to be too long.

- However, the applicants' conduct – e.g., absconding (*Keus v Netherlands*, para. 26); requesting additional reports (*Boucheras v France*, p. 250); lodging excessive proceedings (*Luberti v Italy*, para. 34) – and/or that of their legal representative

(*Boucheras v France*, p. 250) will be a relevant factor in determining whether a review has been conducted quickly enough.

- The rules governing subsequent reviews, while not so strict, nonetheless call for expedition. Short intervals are called for where conditional release has been ordered, but then deferred (*Johnson v UK*, para. 62)

23.4   CONDITIONS OF DETENTION

Key ECHR cases

Aerts v Belgium (1998) 29 EHRR 50, ECtHR
Herczegfalvy v Austria (1992) 15 EHRR 437, ECtHR
Ireland v UK (1978) 2 EHRR 25, ECtHR

A v UK (1980) 3 EHRR 131, ECmHR
B v UK (1981) 32 DR 5, ECmHR
Buckley v UK (1997) 23 EHRR CD 129, ECmHR
Dhoest v Belgium (1988) 55 DR 5, ECmHR
Grare v France (1992) 15 EHRR CD 100, ECmHR
Simon-Herold v Austria (1971) 14 Yearbook 352, ECmHR
X v Germany (1980) 20 DR 193, ECmHR

ECHR principles

23.4.1   *Article 5*

- Detention under Article 5(1)(e) must be 'lawful'; and in principle, the detention of an individual as a mental health patient will be 'lawful' only if effected in a hospital, clinic or other appropriate institution (*Aerts v Belgium*, para. 46).

- If temporary detention in a prison psychiatric wing, pending placement in an appropriate hospital, does not provide a proper therapeutic environment and is harmful to an individual's mental health, Article 5 will be breached (*Aerts v Belgium*, para. 49; qualifying *Ashingdane v UK*, para. 44).

23.4.2   *Article 3*

- For Article 3 generally, see **Section 19**.

- For conditions of detention generally, see **13.3**.

- The threshold for Article 3 is high: in the past 'deplorable overcrowding' and 'less than satisfactory' sanitary conditions have been found not to reach the threshold (*B v UK*, pp. 29–30).

- As a general rule, where the conditions of those detained under Article 5(1)(e) of the Convention are so poor that they lead to a deterioration in the detainees' mental health, Article 3 might be engaged, but not otherwise (*Aerts v Belgium*, para. 66).

- It is also difficult to establish that treatment administered is itself inhuman or degrading, e.g., the unpleasant side-effects caused by medication administered as part of psychiatric treatment were considered insufficiently serious to amount to a breach of Article 3 (*Grare v France*, paras 100–101).

- Likewise the forcible administration of food and drugs to a patient on hunger strike, together with the use of handcuffs to fasten him to a security bed, provided that the measures conform to 'psychiatric principles generally accepted at the time' and justified on the grounds of medical necessity (*Herczegfalvy v Austria*, para. 83).

- If forcibly administering drugs is the only method for stabilising and ultimately improving the mental health of a patient then it can be justified even if carried out under constraint (*X v Germany*, p. 194; see also *Buckley v UK*).

- Nonetheless:

  > The position of inferiority and powerlessness which is typical of patients confined in psychiatric hospitals calls for increased vigilance in reviewing whether the Convention has been complied with. While it was for the medical authorities to decide, on the basis of the recognised rules of medical science, on the therapeutic methods to be used, if necessary by force, to preserve the physical and mental health of patients who are entirely incapable of deciding for themselves, such patients nevertheless remain under the protection of Article 3, whose requirements permit no derogation. (*Herczegfalvy v Austria*, para. 82)

- And the cited cases are a guide, not a rule: the ECHR is a living instrument to be interpreted according to contemporary standards and expectations (see **1.13**) and friendly settlements in Strasbourg led to improvements in relation to segregated patients (*A v UK*) and closed wards (*Simon-Herold v Austria*).

23.4.3 *Article 8*

- Among other things, Article 8 protects privacy, moral and physical integrity. It can provide a basis for challenging conditions of detention and its threshold is not as high as that for Article 3 – albeit that, unlike Article 3, Article 8 is not an absolute, but a qualified, right.

- Article 8 can be breached where the authorities enjoy too much discretionary power in relation to interfering with correspondence, particularly since this is often the detainee's only contact with the outside world (*Herczegfalvy v Austria*, para. 91).

23.4.4 *Remedies for conditions of detention*

- Just satisfaction is available where conditions of detention fall below the standard required by the ECHR.

- In addition, where the conditions render otherwise lawful detention unlawful, an enforceable right to damages is required under Article 5(5) (see **22.18**).

- As a matter of procedure, where an individual seeks an order that he or she be transferred to an appropriate place as required by Article 5(1)(e), and seeks, in addition, compensation in default, his or her 'civil rights and obligations' are being determined within the meaning of Article 6(1) (*Aerts v Belgium*).

23.5   RELEASE

Key ECHR cases

Johnson v UK (1997) 27 EHRR 296, ECtHR
Luberti v Italy (1984) 6 EHRR 440, ECtHR

Gordon v UK (1986) 47 DR 36, EcmHR
L v Sweden (1988) 61 DR 62, ECmHR
W v Sweden (1988) 59 DR 158, ECmHR[CD]

ECHR principles

- A cautious approach to release has been adopted under the ECHR:

  . . . the termination of the confinement of an individual who has previously been found by a court to be of unsound mind and to present a danger to society is a matter that concerns, as well as that individual, the community in which he will live if released. (*Luberti v Italy*, para. 29)

- Where a case concerns homicide, the release assessment will be particularly difficult (*Luberti v Italy*, para. 29; *Gordon v UK*).

- Even where expert opinion is that the detainee's mental condition no longer persists, this does not automatically justify release because the assessment of mental illness is not an exact science (*Johnson v UK*, para. 61).

- Making release subject to conditions – including taking appropriate medication – can be justified (*W v Sweden*, p. 160; see also *L v Sweden*, p. 73).

23.6   MEDICAL TREATMENT

Key ECHR cases

Matter v Slovakia (5 July 1999), ECtHR

ECHR principles

- Compulsory sterilisation was intended to be contrary to the ECHR when it was drafted (1 *Travaux Preparatoires* 116–7).

- Compulsory psychiatric examination to ascertain whether an individual should be afforded legal status can be justified under Article 8 of the Convention (*Matter v Slovakia*).

Relevant Canadian cases

Re K (1985) 63 BCLR 145, CA

- Compulsory sterilisation is not absolutely prohibited, but requires a very delicate balancing exercise (*Re K*).

SECTION 24

PRIVACY

24.1 THE MEANING OF PRIVATE LIFE

Key ECHR cases

Botta v Italy (1998) 26 EHRR 241, ECtHR
Costello-Roberts v UK (1993) 19 EHRR 112, ECtHR
Niemietz v Germany (1992) 16 EHRR 97, ECtHR

Bruggemann and Scheuten v Germany (1981) 3 EHRR 244, ECmHR

ECHR principles

- Article 8(1), ECHR provides that 'Everyone has the right to respect for his private and family life, his home and his correspondence.'

- The notion of private life is a broad one and is not susceptible to exhaustive definition (*Niemietz v Germany*; *Costello-Roberts v UK*).

- It involves the idea of an 'inner circle' in which individuals may live their personal lives as they choose without interference from the state:

  . . . private life . . . includes a person's physical and psychological integrity; the guarantee afforded by Article 8 is primarily intended to ensure development, without outside interference, of the personality of each individual in his relations with other human beings. (*Botta v Italy*, para. 32)

- It extends to the development of relationships with others, and includes activities of a business or professional nature:

  . . . it is, after all, in the course of their working lives that the majority of people have a significant, if not the greatest, opportunity of developing relationships with the outside world. (*Niemietz v Germany*)

- It can also cover physical and moral integrity.

- The limits are unclear, but where individuals put aspects of their private lives in the public domain, this will be relevant:

  . . . there are limits to the personal sphere. While a large proportion of the law existing in a given state has some immediate or remote effect on the individual's possibility of developing his personality by doing what he wants to do, not all of these can be considered to constitute an interference with private life in the sense of Article 8 . . . the claim to respect for private life is automatically reduced to the extent that the individual himself brings his private life into contact with public life or into close connection with other protected interests. (*Bruggemann and Scheuten v Germany*, para. 56)

- So, for example, where individuals attend a public demonstration, they cannot expect the same degree of privacy as they enjoy in their own homes (see **6.7** and **24.9**).

24.2   PHYSICAL AND MORAL INTEGRITY

Key ECHR cases

A v UK (1998) 27 EHRR 611, ECtHR
Costello-Roberts v UK (1993) 19 EHRR 112, ECtHR
Osman v UK (1998) 29 EHRR 245, ECtHR
Stubbings and others v UK (1996) 23 EHRR 213, ECtHR
X and Y v Netherlands (1985) 8 EHRR 235, ECtHR

Whiteside v UK (1994) 76-A DR 80, ECmHR[CD]

ECHR principles

- Article 8, ECHR protects an individual's moral and physical integrity and has been invoked in the context of sex abuse (*X and Y v Netherlands; Stubbings and others v UK*), corporal punishment (*Costello-Roberts v UK; A v UK*) and harassment (*Osman v UK; Whiteside v UK*).

- But not every act or measure which may be said to have an adverse effect on the physical or moral integrity of a person necessarily gives rise to an interference with that person's private life (*Costello-Roberts v UK*, para. 36).

24.3   PERSONAL IDENTITY

Key ECHR cases

Burghartz v Switzerland (1994) 18 EHRR 101, ECtHR
Stjerna v Finland (1994) 24 EHRR 195, ECtHR

Guillot v France (24 October 1996), ECmHR

ECHR principles

- An individual's name does concern his or her private and family life on the basis that it constitutes a means of personal identification and a link to a family (*Burghartz v Switzerland*, para. 24 – *sex discrimination concerning the ability to choose family name; husband unable to put his own surname before the family name, even though married women were able to; Stjerna v Finland*, para. 37).

- However, where individuals are free to use their chosen name without any real hindrance, the administrative inconvenience of changing all official records to reflect that name can justify not doing so (*Guillot v France*).

24.4   RELATIONS WITH OTHERS

Key ECHR cases

Niemietz v Germany (1992) 16 EHRR 97, ECtHR
Rotaru v Romania (4 May 2000), ECtHR

ECHR principles

- Private life extends beyond traditional notions of privacy and includes establishing and developing relationships with others:

    . . . it would be too restrictive to limit the notion of [private life] to an 'inner circle' in which the individual may live his own personal life as he chooses and to exclude therefrom entirely the outside world not encompassed within that circle. Respect for private life must also comprise to a certain degree the right to establish and develop relationships with other human beings. (*Niemietz v Germany*, para. 29)

- This applies both in the private sphere and in the work environment (*Rotaru v Romania*, para. 43).

24.5   SEXUAL ORIENTATION

Key ECHR cases

ADT v UK (31 July 2000), ECtHR
Dudgeon v UK (1981) 4 EHRR 149, ECtHR
Laskey, Jaggard & Brown v UK (1997) 24 EHRR 39, ECtHR
Lustig-Prean and Beckett v UK (1999) 29 EHRR 548, ECtHR
Norris v Ireland (1988) 13 EHRR 186, ECtHR
Sutherland v UK (1 July 1997), [1998] EHRLR 117, ECtHR

MK v Austria (1997) 24 EHRR CD 59, ECmHR[CD]

ECHR principles

- An individual's sex life and sexuality are protected under Article 8, ECHR (*Dudgeon v UK; Norris v Ireland; Lustig-Prean and Beckett v UK; Sutherland v UK*).

- However, not every sexual activity carried out in private falls within the scope of Article 8(1):

    The Court observes that not every sexual activity carried out behind closed doors necessarily falls within the scope of Article 8. In the present case, the applicants were involved in consensual sadomasochistic activities for purposes of sexual gratification. There can be no doubt that sexual orientation and activity concern an intimate aspect of private life. However, a considerable number of people were involved in the activities in question which included, *inter alia*, the recruitment of new 'members', the provision of several specially-equipped 'chambers', and the shooting of many videotapes which were distributed among the 'members'. It may thus be open to question whether the sexual activities of the applicants fell entirely within the notion of 'private life' . . . (*Laskey, Jaggard & Brown v UK*, para. 36)

- Restrictions on sexual activity must be shown to be authorised by law, legitimate, necessary and proportionate: easy to justify in relation to child abuse (*MK v Austria*); difficult to justify in relation to consenting adults in private (*Dudgeon v UK; Norris v Ireland; Lustig-Prean and Beckett v UK; Sutherland v UK*); and finely balanced in relation to group sado-masochistic sex (*Laskey, Jaggard & Brown v UK*).

- The prosecution and conviction of a man for engaging in non-violent homosexual acts with up to four other men breached Article 8 (*ADT v UK*).

24.6   SEXUAL IDENTITY: TRANSSEXUALS

Key ECHR cases

B v France (1992) 16 EHRR 1, ECtHR
Cossey v UK (1990) 13 EHRR 622, ECtHR
Rees v UK (1986) 9 EHRR 56, ECtHR
Sheffield and Horsham v UK (1998) 27 EHRR 163, ECtHR

ECHR principles

- The issue of the sexual identity is most acute in relation to transsexuals. So far the ECtHR has maintained that since there remains a lack of consensus on the position of transsexualism, the authorities cannot be expected to change the existing legal system to facilitate the alteration of birth certificates (*Rees v UK*, para. 42).

- However, this is an issue the ECtHR has returned to several times (*Cossey v UK; B v France; Sheffield and Horsham v UK*), and it has given the clearest indication that (since the ECHR is a living instrument) this position may soon change:

    . . . it must for the time being be left to the respondent State to determine to what extent it can meet the remaining demands of transsexuals. However, the Court is conscious of the seriousness of the problems affecting these persons and the distress they suffer. The Convention has always to be interpreted and applied in the light of current circumstances. The need for appropriate legal measures should therefore be kept under review having regard particularly to scientific and societal developments. (*Rees v UK*, para. 47)

    . . . it is nevertheless the case that there is an increased social acceptance of transsexualism and an increased recognition of the problems which post-operative transsexuals encounter. Even if it finds no breach of Article 8 in this case, the Court reiterates that this area needs to be kept under review by contracting States. (*Sheffield and Horsham v UK*, para. 60)

- And some judges have clearly indicated that they are likely to vote differently in future:

    My vote in favour of the finding that there had been no violation of Article 8 was cast after much hesitation and even with some reluctance. The cases disclosed a wider range of situations in which difficulty and embarrassment may be caused to post-operative transsexuals than had been demonstrated . . . in the Rees and Cossey cases continued inaction on the part of the respondent State, taken together with further developments elsewhere, could well tilt the balance in the other direction. (*Sheffield and Horsham v UK*, concurring opinion of Judge Sir John Freeland, pp. 199–200)

24.7   REPUTATION

Key ECHR cases

Stewart-Brady v UK (1997) 24 EHRR CD 38, ECmHR[CD]
T.E.E. v UK (1996) 21 EHRR CD 108, ECmHR
Winer v UK (1986) 48 DR 154, ECmHR[CD]
Young v Ireland (1996) 21 EHRR CD 91, ECmHR

ECHR principles

- Respect for private life may require protection of an individual's reputation (*Winer v UK*; *Stewart-Brady v UK*).

- This includes professional reputation (*T.E.E. v UK*; *Young v Ireland*).

- For the balance between freedom of expression and privacy in relation to reputation, see **32.5**.

24.8   INTERCEPTION OF COMMUNICATIONS

Key ECHR cases

Amann v Switzerland (16 February 2000), ECtHR
Foxley v UK (20 June 2000), ECtHR
Halford v UK (1997) 24 EHRR 523, ECtHR

ECHR principles

- Interception of communications constitutes an interference with the right to respect for both private life and correspondence, both at home and at work (*Halford v UK*; *Amann v Switzerland*).

- The extent to which an individual must have a 'reasonable expectation of privacy' before Article 8 can be invoked in relation to the interception of communications is unclear, but may be relevant when an individual leaves his or her private space/home and enters communal or public space, including the workplace (*Halford v UK*).

- Enforcing bankruptcy proceedings is a legitimate basis for intercepting communications, subject to strict limits:

    . . . in the field under consideration – the concealment of a bankrupt's assets to the detriment of his creditors – the authorities may consider it necessary to have recourse to the interception of a bankrupt's correspondence in order to identify and trace the sources of his income. Nevertheless, the implementation of the measures must be accompanied by adequate and effective safeguards which ensure minimum impairment of the right to respect for his correspondence. This is particularly so where . . . correspondence with the bankrupt's legal advisers may be intercepted. (*Foxley v UK*, para. 43)

- The lawyer/client relationship is, in principle, privileged and correspondence in that context, whatever its purpose, concerns matters of a private and confidential nature:

    Admittedly, as the government have pointed out, it may be difficult to identify from the envelope whether its contents attract legal professional privilege. However, the government have not challenged the accuracy of the applicant's allegations that letters from his legal advisers, once opened, were read, photocopied and a copy committed to file before being forwarded to him. The Court can see no justification for this procedure and considers that the action taken was not in keeping with the principles of confidentiality and professional privilege attaching to relations between a lawyer and his client. It notes in this respect that the government have not sought to argue that the privileged channel of communication was being abused; nor have they invoked any other exceptional circumstances which would serve to justify the interference with reference to the margin of appreciation. (*Foxley v UK*, para. 44)

- Most interception of communications takes place in the course of investigating crime, and this is dealt with at **6.2**.

24.9   PHOTOGRAPHS, CLOSED-CIRCUIT TV AND VIDEO RECORDINGS

Key ECHR cases

Murray v UK (1994) 19 EHRR 193, ECtHR

Friedl v Austria (1995) A/305-B, ECmHR
McVeigh, O'Neill and Evans v UK (1981) 5 EHRR 71, ECmHR
X v FRG 9 Coll Dec 53, ECmHR

ECHR principles

- The privacy individuals enjoy within their own space is better protected than the privacy they enjoy in public spaces:

    . . . there was no intrusion into the 'inner circle' of the applicant's private life in the sense that the authorities entered his home and took the photographs there; . . . the photographs related to a public incident . . . in which the applicant was voluntarily taking part and . . . were solely taken for the purposes of recording the character of the [incident] . . . the Commission attaches weight to the assurances given [that] . . . the individual persons on the photographs taken remained anonymous . . . the personal data recorded and photographs taken were not entered into a data processing system, and no action was taken to identify the persons photographed. (*Friedl v Austria*, paras 49–50 – *photographs taken by police at demonstration, not for identification, but for collation into general file*)

- The same principle (probably) applies to CCTV and video recordings.

- Photographing detainees in police custody without their knowledge or consent will interfere with privacy rights, but can be justified in certain circumstances (*Murray v UK*, para. 86).

Relevant domestic cases

R v Broadcasting Standards Commission, ex parte British Broadcasting Corporation (6 April 2000), CA

- Companies have a right to privacy that can be protected, and which will be infringed by filming without consent:

  > While the intrusions into privacy of an individual which are possible are no doubt more extensive than the infringements of privacy which are possible in the case of a company, a company does have activities which need protection from unwarranted intrusion. I consider that the BSC has jurisdiction to determine the application of Article 8 of the ECHR to companies. (*per* Lord Woolf MR)

  > The infringement consists in depriving the person filmed of the possibility of refusing consent. If this is so for an individual, I cannot see why it should not also be capable of being so for a company. The company will have its own reasons (good or bad) for wanting or not wanting to object and the secrecy of the filming has deprived it of the opportunity to do so . . .
  >   If there is a good reason for the infringement then it will not be unwarranted. (*R v Broadcasting Standards Commission, ex parte British Broadcasting Corporation, per* Lord Hale)

Relevant Canadian cases

Aubry v Vice-Versa [1998] 1 SCR 591

- Reproduction of an individual's image without his or her consent is a clear violation of his or her privacy rights which will be difficult to justify in the public interest unless the image is purely incidental to a significant event (*Aubry v Vice-Versa*, p. 607 – *picture of 17-year-old girl in arts magazine without her consent*).

Relevant New Zealand cases

TV3 Network Services Ltd v Broadcasting Standards Authority [1995] 2 NZLR 720

- Privacy guidelines – issued by the New Zealand Broadcasting Standards Authority – have now been incorporated into case law:

  1. The protection of privacy includes legal protection against the public disclosure of private facts where the facts disclosed are highly offensive and objectionable to a reasonable person of ordinary sensibilities.
  2. It also protects against the public disclosure of some kinds of public facts. The 'public' facts contemplated concern events such as criminal behaviour which have in effect become private again, for example, through the passage of time. Nevertheless, the public disclosure of facts will have to be highly offensive to the reasonable person.

3.   In addition to a complaint for the public disclosure of private and public facts, an intentional interference (in the nature of prying) with an individual's interest in solitude or seclusion will also form ground for complaint. The intrusion must be offensive to the ordinary person but an individual's interest in solitude or seclusion does not provide the basis for a privacy action for an individual to complain about being observed or followed or photographed in a public place.

4.   Discussing the matter in the 'public interest', defined as a legitimate concern to the public, is a defence to an individual's claim to privacy.

5.   An individual who consents to the invasion of his or her privacy cannot later succeed in a claim for breach of privacy.

6.   The protection of privacy also protects against the disclosure of private acts to abuse, denigrate or ridicule personally an identifiable person. This principle is of particular relevance should a broadcaster use the airwaves to deal with a private dispute. However, the existence of a prior relationship between a broadcaster and the named individual is not an essential criterion.

7.   It also includes the protection against the disclosure by the broadcaster without consent of the name and/or address and/or telephone number of an identifiable person. This principle does not apply to details which are public information or to news and current affairs reporting and is subject to the public interest.

(*TV3 Network Services Ltd v Broadcasting Standards Authority – guidelines upheld where woman had been secretly filmed while being interviewed at her door*)

•   In this context a distinction must be drawn between matters properly within the public interest, in the sense of being a legitimate concern to the public, and those that are merely interesting to the public on a human level (*TV3 Network Services Ltd v Broadcasting Standards Authority*).

24.10   PERSONAL DATA

Key ECHR cases

Gaskin v UK (1989) 12 EHRR 36, ECtHR
Leander v Sweden (1987) 9 EHRR 433, ECtHR
Rotaru v Romania (4 May 2000), ECtHR

Adamson v UK (26 January 1999), ECmHR
Hewitt and Harman v UK (1992) 14 EHRR 657, ECmHR
Ibbotson v UK [1999] EHRLR 218, ECmHR
McVeigh, O'Neill and Evans v UK (1981) 5 EHRR 71, ECmHR

ECHR principles

•   The collection, storage and use of personal data concerning an individual's private life amounts to an interference with Article 8 rights (*Leander v Sweden; Hewitt and Harman v UK; Gaskin v UK*).

•   The processing of any information about an identifiable individual also interferes with Article 8 rights when interpreted consistently with the European Convention for the Protection of Individuals with Regard to Automatic Processing of Personal Data (*Rotaru v Romania*, para. 43).

- Article 8 is also engaged where a public authority refuses an opportunity to refute information it is storing (*Rotaru v Romania*, para. 46).

- In this respect, both public and private information can qualify for Article 8 protection where it is systematically collated and retained in files; this is particularly so in respect of information concerning an individual's distant past (*Rotaru v Romania*, para. 43).

- Whether such collection can be justified will depend on the circumstances; but in all cases it will have to be shown to be authorised by law, legitimate, necessary and proportionate.

- The taking of personal data to combat terrorist crime can be justified as long as 'the means ... adopted merely [seek] to identify the persons concerned and to ascertain whether or not they [are] concerned in terrorist activities', and then retention of personal data can be justified as long as there remains a serious threat to public safety posed by organised terrorism (*McVeigh, O'Neill and Evans v UK*, paras 224 and 230).

- A requirement that an individual register on a list, e.g., a sex offenders' list, also interferes with Article 8 rights; but it is capable of justification to protect the rights of others (*Ibbotson v UK; Adamson v UK*).

- Establishing that an individual is a victim for Article 8 purposes in cases involving personal data is subject to a special (wide) test:

  > ... an individual may, under certain conditions, claim to be the victim of a violation occasioned by the mere existence of secret measures or of legislation permitting secret measures, without having to allege that such measures were in fact applied to him ... Furthermore, a 'decision or measure favourable to the applicant is not in principle sufficient to deprive him of his status as a victim unless the national authorities have acknowledged, either expressly or in substance, and then afforded redress for, the breach of the Convention'. (*Rotaru v Romania*, para. 35)

- Medical records are clearly protected by Article 8 and should be disclosed – even in the context of legal proceedings – only in very strictly controlled circumstances (see **14.7**).

Relevant domestic cases

R v Local Authority and Police Authority in the Midlands, ex parte LM [2000] 1 FLR 612

- Disclosure of unsubstantiated allegations of sex abuse by the police to an employer will breach Article 8 if not subjected to the strictest control:

  > The facts of this case show how disclosure can lead to loss of employment and social ostracism, if not worse. Disclosure should, therefore, only be made if there is a pressing need for it. (*R v Local Authority and Police Authority in the Midlands, ex parte LM*, p. 622)

24.11 POSITIVE OBLIGATIONS UNDER ARTICLE 8

Key ECHR cases

Marckx v Belgium (1979) 2 EHRR 330, ECtHR
Rees v UK (1986) 9 EHRR 56, ECtHR

ECHR principles

- The primary duty of the state and public authorities under Article 8 is to refrain from interfering with an individual's right to respect for his or her private life.

- However, the ECtHR has interpreted the words 'right to respect' in Article 8(1) as requiring the state to take positive steps to secure or protect the enjoyment of rights under Article 8(1):

  . . . the object of the Article is 'essentially' that of protecting the individual against arbitrary interference by public authorities. Nevertheless, it does not merely compel the state to abstain from such interference: in addition to this primary negative undertaking, there may be positive obligations inherent in an effective 'respect' for family life. (*Marckx* v *Belgium*, para. 31)

- The scope of such positive obligations should reflect the balance that needs to be maintained between the rights of the individual and the interest of the community at large:

  . . . in determining whether or not a positive obligation exists, regard must be had to the fair balance that has to be struck between the general interest of the community and the interests of individuals . . . In striking this balance the aims mentioned in [Article 8(2)] may be of a certain relevance, although this provision refers in terms only to 'interferences' with the right protected by [Article 8(1)] . . . (*Rees* v *UK*, para. 56)

- For the extensive Strasbourg jurisprudence on positive obligations, see **1.8**.

FAMILY LIFE

25.1   THE MEANING OF FAMILY LIFE UNDER ARTICLE 8

Key ECHR cases

Abdulaziz, Cabales and Balkandali v UK (1985) 7 EHRR 471, ECtHR
Berrehab v Netherlands (1988) 11 EHRR 322, ECtHR
Keegan v Ireland (1994) 18 EHRR 342, ECtHR
Kroon v Netherlands (1994) 19 EHRR 263, ECtHR
X, Y and Z v UK (1997) 24 EHRR 143, ECtHR

K v UK (1986) 50 DR 199, ECmHR[CD]
Soderback v Sweden [1998] EHRLR 342, ECmHR
X and Y v UK (1983) 32 DR 220, ECmHR

ECHR principles

- The existence or non-existence of 'family life' is essentially a question of fact dependent upon real evidence of close personal ties (*K v UK*, p. 207 – *parent given restricted access to child in foster care*).

- Family includes the relationship that arises from a lawful and genuine marriage, even if 'family life' has not yet been fully established (*Abdulaziz, Cabales and Balkandali v UK*, para. 62 – *husbands of applicants refused permission to remain with or join them in UK*).

- But 'family life' is not confined solely to marriage-based relationships; it may arise where parties are living together outside marriage and sufficient family ties exist in reality.

- Where partners do not live together, other factors may also exceptionally serve to demonstrate that the relationship between them has sufficient constancy, e.g., having children together (*Kroon v Netherlands*, para. 30 – *non-recognition of paternity due to mother being married to another man at time of child's birth – couple in long-term relationship with three other children*).

- The length of the relationship will also be a relevant factor:

  When deciding whether a relationship can be said to amount to 'family life', a number of factors may be relevant, including whether the couple live together, the length of their relationship and whether they have demonstrated their commitment to each other by having children together or by any other means. (*X, Y and Z v UK*, para. 36– *refusal to register post-operative transsexual as father of a child born to his partner by artificial insemination by donor*)

- A child born to a cohabiting couple will be part of the family unit, and the ties will remain even if the couple subsequently split up (*Keegan v Ireland*, para. 44 – *father applied to be guardian of his child after latter was put up for adoption by his former co-habitee without his knowledge or consent*).

- Family life will even cover a potential relationship that might develop between a father and an illegitimate child:

  > Article 8 not only protected family life which had already been established, but could also extend to the potential relationship which might develop between a natural father and a child born out of wedlock. (*Soderback v Sweden*, p. 343 – *father of child had been friends with mother, but had never lived with or had steady relationship with her – mother subsequently married someone else who applied to adopt child – father, who, against his wishes, had enjoyed very limited contact with child during intervening period, objected*)

- Children born out of a genuine and lawful marriage will have a bond between themselves and their parents amounting to 'family life', even if the parents do not then live together. Subsequent events may break that tie, but not if frequent and regular contact is maintained (*Berrehab v Netherlands*, para. 21 – *Moroccan refused residence permit after divorce from Dutch wife – access to his daughter threatened by deportation*).

- A stable relationship between lesbian and/or gay couples is protected under Article 8 as 'private' life, but not as 'family life' (*X and Y v UK*, p. 221 – *gay partner threatened with deportation*; *S v UK*, pp. 277–8 – *claim for tenancy to be vested in partner of deceased lesbian*).

Relevant domestic cases

Fitzpatrick v Sterling House Association Ltd [1999] 3 WLR 1113

- Regarding same-sex couples who live together as 'husband and wife':

  > The courts have already decided that family includes relationships other than those based on consanguinity or affinity. To include same sex partners is to do not more than apply to them the same rationale as that underlying the inclusion of different sex partners. (*Fitzpatrick v Sterling House Association Ltd, per* Lord Nicolls, p. 1130 – *tenancy succession*)

25.2   ADOPTION AND FOSTERING

Key ECHR cases

Bronda v Italy (9 June 1998), ECtHR
Eriksson v Sweden (1989) 12 EHRR 183, ECtHR
Gaskin v UK (1989) 12 EHRR 36, ECtHR
Keegan v Ireland (1994) 18 EHRR 342, ECtHR

Soderback v Sweden [1998] EHRLR 342, ECmHR
X v Belgium (1975) 7 DR 75, ECmHR
X v France (1982) 31 DR 241, ECmHR
X v Switzerland (1978) 13 DR 248, ECmHR

ECHR principles

25.2.1   *Adoption as 'family life'*

- The existence of a couple is fundamental to the right to *found* a family within the meaning of Article 12, ECHR.

- However, this does not mean that the relationship between an adoptive parent and a child is unprotected by Article 8:

  > . . . although the right to adopt is not one of the rights specifically guaranteed under the Convention, the relations between an adoptive parent and an adopted child are as a rule the same family relations protected by Article 8.
  >
  > A judicial decision separating two persons united by the bond of adoption may amount to an interference with the right to respect for the adopting parent's and/or the adopted child's family life within the meaning of Article 8(1). (*X v France*, p. 244 – *parental authority withdrawn from adoptive parent*; see also *X v Belgium*, p. 77 – *single Dutch man living in Belgium refused permission under Dutch law to adopt an abandoned child he had been looking after for five years*)

- Taking children into care (e.g., for adoption) does not terminate their relationship with their natural family:

  > The mutual enjoyment by parent and child of each other's company constitutes a fundamental element of family life; furthermore, the natural family relationship is not terminated by reason of the fact that the child has been taken into public care. (*Eriksson v Sweden*, para. 58)

- But equally the private life of an adoptive parent who has cared for a child is affected by a court order about his or her custody:

  > Bearing in mind that the applicant has cared for the child for many years and is deeply attached to him, the separation ordered by the Court undoubtedly affects her 'private life', the respect for which is also guaranteed by Article 8. In this connection . . . the concept of private life also includes 'to a certain extent the right to establish and develop relationships with other human beings.' (*X v Switzerland*, p. 253 – *foster-parent ordered to give up child to real parents after caring for him for many years*)

25.2.2   *Adoption proceedings*

- The interests of both parents must be respected in adoption proceedings. Legislation permitting one to place a child for adoption without the other's knowledge or consent will not be justified (*Keegan v Ireland*, para. 55).

- Adoption which denies any contact between the natural parent and child will be permitted only in exceptional circumstances when the child's best interests clearly demand it:

  > In the present case, there was no evidence to suggest that the applicant had the intention of disrupting his daughter's family situation. It appeared that he only wished to have access to her. It had not been shown that the measure corresponded to any overriding requirement in the child's best interest and accordingly the courts overstepped their margin of appreciation. (*Soderback v Sweden*, p. 343)

- However, when determining whether a measure such as adoption is necessary and proportionate, consideration of what is in the best interests of the child will always be of critical importance: while a fair balance has to be struck between the interests of the parents/grandparents and the child, the ECtHR attaches special weight to the overriding interests of the child (*Bronda* v *Italy*, para. 62).

25.3   EMBRYOLOGY AND SURROGACY

Key ECHR cases

X, Y and Z v UK (1997) 24 EHRR 143, ECtHR

G v Netherlands (1990) 16 EHRR CD 38, ECmHR

ECHR principles

- The case law of the ECtHR on embryology and surrogacy has yet to be developed. As a result, a degree of latitude is permitted under Article 8:

  . . . there is no consensus amongst the Member States and the Council of Europe on the question whether the interests of a child conceived in such a way are best served by the preserving the anonymity of the donor of the sperm or whether the child should have the right to know the donor's identity.
    Since the issues . . . therefore touch on areas where there is little common ground amongst the Member States of the Council of Europe and generally speaking, the law appears to be in a transitional stage, the respondent State must be afforded a wide margin of appreciation. (X, Y and Z v UK, para. 36)

- Nonetheless, it is clear that a long, stable relationship will establish family ties between a couple and a child conceived artificially (X, Y and Z v UK, para. 44).

- But where an individual donates sperm only to enable a woman to become pregnant through artificial insemination, this does not on its own establish a family link between the donor and the child (G v Netherlands, p. 39 – *man denied access to child conceived by lesbian through donation of his sperm*).

25.4   LESBIAN AND GAY COUPLES

Key ECHR cases

S v UK (1986) 47 DR 274, ECmHR
W v UK (1989) 63 DR 34, ECmHR
X and Y v UK (1983) 32 DR 220, ECmHR

ECHR principles

- Stable relationships between lesbian and/or gay couples are protected under Article 8 as 'private' life.

- But not – at least by the ECmHR – as 'family life' (*X and Y v UK*, p. 221 – *gay partner threatened with deportation*; *S v UK*, pp. 277–8 – *claim for tenancy to be vested in partner of deceased lesbian*).

- There is no consensus that this is the right approach (dissenting opinion of Mr Schermers in *W v UK*, pp. 48–49; see **26.5**).

25.5 TRANSSEXUALS

Key ECHR cases

B v France (1992) 16 EHRR 1, ECtHR
X, Y and Z v UK (1997) 24 EHRR 143, ECtHR

ECHR principles

- Family life can include a relationship between a transsexual and an opposite-sex partner (*X, Y and Z v UK*, para. 37).

- For the issue of the sexual identity of transsexuals, see **24.6**.

25.6 WIDER FAMILY RELATIONSHIPS

Key ECHR cases

Boughanemi v France (1996) 22 EHRR 228, ECtHR
Boyle v UK (1994) 19 EHRR 179, ECtHR
Bronda v Italy (9 June 1998), ECtHR
Marckx v Belgium (1979) 2 EHRR 330, ECtHR
Moustaquim v Belgium (1991) 13 EHRR 802, ECtHR

Price v UK (1988) 55 DR 224, ECmHR[CD]

ECHR principles

- Ties with siblings can qualify as a 'family life' relationship (*Boughanemi v France*, para. 35; *Moustaquim v Belgium*, para. 36).

- Family life can also include ties between near relatives, such as grandparents and grandchildren, 'since such relatives may play a considerable part in family life' (*Marckx v Belgium*, para. 45; see also *Bronda v Italy*, para. 51 – *child living with grandparents*).

- But the nature of the relationship between grandparents and grandchildren – and as a result the protection it attracts – is different:

  . . . in normal circumstances the relationship between grandparents and grandchildren is different in nature and degree from the relationship between parent and child . . . When a parent is denied access to a child taken into public care this would constitute in most cases an interference with the parent's right to respect for family life as protected by Article 8(1), but this would not necessarily be the case where grandparents are concerned . . . there may be interference by the local authority if it diminishes contacts by refusing to grandparents what is in all the circumstances the reasonable access necessary to preserve a normal grandparent–grandchild relationship. (*Price v UK*, pp. 234–5 – *adoptive paternal grandparents denied access to child in care after initial substantial contact since birth*)

- Where a wider relative establishes a very close relationship with a child, e.g., acting as a 'father figure', family life capable of protection may exist:

   . . . the applicant had frequent contact with [his nephew] from the time of [his] birth and spent considerable time with him. While it appears the two families did not share the same household, they lived in close proximity and [the nephew] often made 'weekend stays' at the applicant's home. The guardian ad litem in the care proceedings described the applicant as a 'good father figure' to [the nephew].

   In the circumstances, and having regard to the absence of [the child's] father . . . there was a significant bond between the applicant and [the child] and this relationship fell within the scope of the concept of 'family life'. (*Boyle v UK*, paras 44 and 45 – *uncle denied access to nephew in care*)

25.7   THE SCOPE OF PROTECTION UNDER ARTICLE 8

Key ECHR cases

Airey v Ireland (1979) 2 EHRR 305, ECtHR
Gaskin v UK (1989) 12 EHRR 36, ECtHR
Hokkanen v Finland (1994) 19 EHRR 139, ECtHR
Marckx v Belgium (1979) 2 EHRR 330, ECtHR
Olsson v Sweden (No. 1) (1988) 11 EHRR 259, ECtHR

Z and E v Austria (1986) 49 DR 67, ECmHR

ECHR principles

- The right to family life is multifaceted. The essential ingredient is the right to develop normal family relationships, e.g., living together and enjoying each other's company (*Olsson v Sweden (No. 1)*).

- Where this is not possible – or desired – the right to family life safeguards contact between family members by subjecting any limitations on contact to close scrutiny for compliance with Article 8(2).

- And the state has a positive duty to respect this broad notion of family life:

   . . . although the object of Article 8 is essentially that of protecting the individual against arbitrary interference by the public authorities, it does not merely compel the State to abstain from such interference: in addition to this primarily negative undertaking, there may be positive obligations inherent in an effective respect for family life . . .

   Effective respect for private or family life obliges [the state] to make this means of protection effectively accessible, where appropriate, to anyone who may wish to have recourse thereto. (*Airey v Ireland*, paras 32 and 33)

- One aspect of this duty is to put in place a legal framework within which parents and children can lead a normal family life (*Marckx v Belgium*, para. 31), including the use of family property (*Z and E v Austria*, p. 76).

- Another aspect can be to make information available about an individual's childhood and early development, where he or she has been in care or adopted:

    . . . persons in the situation of the applicant have a vital interest, protected by the Convention, in receiving the information necessary to know and to understand their childhood and early development . . . (*Gaskin v UK*, para. 49)

25.8 CUSTODY AND ACCESS

Key ECHR cases

Hendriks v Netherlands (1983) 5 EHRR 233, ECtHR
Hoffmann v Austria (1993) 17 EHRR 293, ECtHR
Hokkanen v Finland (1994) 19 EHRR 139, ECtHR
Nuutinen v Finland (27 June 2000), ECtHR

Whitear v UK [1997] EHRLR 291, ECmHR[CD]

ECHR principles

25.8.1 *The right of access*

- The right to respect for family life includes the right of a divorced parent, who is deprived of custody following the breakup of marriage, to have access to or contact with his or her child:

    . . . the natural link between a parent and a child is of fundamental importance and that, where the actual 'family life' in the sense of 'living together' has come to an end, continued contact between them is desirable and should in principle remain possible. Respect for family life within the meaning of Article 8 thus implies that this contact should not be denied unless there are strong reasons which justify such an interference. (*Hendriks v Netherlands*, para. 95 – *divorced father denied access to his child because the mother's refusal to cooperate might harm the child*)

25.8.2 *The best interests of the child*

- Where there is a serious conflict between the interests of the child and one of its parents that can only be resolved to the disadvantage of one of them, the interests of the child prevail:

    . . . feelings of distress and frustration because of the absence of one's child may cause considerable suffering to the non-custodial parent. However, where there is a serious conflict between the interests of the child and one of its parents which can only be resolved to the disadvantage of one of them, the interests of the child must, under Article 8(2), prevail. (*Hendriks v Netherlands*, para. 124; *Whitear v UK*)

- On this basis, restrictions on access to children in care by parents and grandparents – even to the point of no contact – can be justified where sexual abuse is suspected and backed up by medical evidence, even though there have been no court proceedings to determine whether, in fact, abuse occurred (*L v Finland*, para. 127).

- But the relevant authorities should not discriminate against one parent in a custody case purely on religious grounds (*Hoffmann v Austria*, para. 36 – *Jehovah's witness denied custody of her children due to her religious beliefs*).

25.8.3   *The duty to facilitate contact*

- The duty on the relevant authorities to 'respect' family life means that they bear a responsibility for facilitating contact between parent(s) and child.

- This can include making and enforcing court orders, where necessary (*Hokkanen v Finland*, para. 58).

- However, this duty is not absolute – coercive steps should not be taken lightly and the best interest of the child must prevail:

  The obligation on the national authorities to take measures to facilitate meetings between a parent and his or her child is not absolute, especially where the two are still strangers to one another . . . Whilst national authorities must do their utmost to facilitate . . . cooperation [between all the interested parties], any obligation to apply coercion in this area must be limited since the interests as well as the rights and freedoms of all concerned must be taken into account, and more particularly the best interests of the child and his or her rights under Article 8 of the Convention. Where contact with the parent might appear to threaten those interests or interfere with those rights, it is for the national authorities to strike a fair balance between them. What is decisive is whether the national authorities have taken all necessary steps to facilitate access as can reasonably be demanded in the special circumstances of each case. . . . (*Nuutinen v Finland*, para. 128)

Relevant New Zealand cases

G v N (9 June 1999), FC Wanganui FP083/363/97
M v Y [1994] 1 NZLR 527
N v A (25 June 1999), DC Auckland FP004/975/95

- In cases concerning custody and guardianship of children the UN Convention on the Rights of the Child, in particular the principle of acting in the 'best interests of the child' (Article 12) by taking their views into account, is increasingly relevant (*G v N – father's application for custody of 11-year-old daughter granted on the basis that it accorded with child's views*).

- To this end, it would be an error of law not to ascertain the wishes of the child in such cases and to fail to indicate in a judgment the extent to which those wishes have been given weight (M v Y).

- With the result that in some cases no judgment can be made until the court is furnished with such information:

  Of considerable significance in my view is the fact that the wishes of the child are conspicuously absent from the matter at this stage. They cannot be presumed; nor can either parent be safely relied upon to dispassionately convey the wishes of the child to the Court uncoloured by their perception of what is in the child's best interests. (*N v A – custody case adjourned for representation of a child and ascertainment of her wishes*)

25.9 MAINTENANCE PAYMENTS

Key ECHR cases

Karakuzey v Germany (1996) 23 EHRR CD 92, ECmHR[CD]
Logan v UK (1996) 22 EHRR CD 178, ECmHR[CD]

ECHR principles

- Family life is not infringed merely because one parent has to make maintenance payments; but very high payments may need detailed justification (*Logan v UK*, p. 181 – *challenge to level of maintenance payments assessed by Child Support Agency on basis that detrimental to ability to visit children*).

- The legitimacy of refusing to pay maintenance payments on religious grounds under Article 9, ECHR is very difficult to establish:

    Article 9 primarily protects the sphere of personal beliefs and religious creeds, but does not cover every act which is motivated by religion or belief. In protecting the said personal sphere, Article 9 does not always guarantee the right to behave in the public sphere in a way which is dictated by such a belief, e.g. by refusing to pay certain taxes because part of the revenue so raised may be applied for military expenditure, the obligation of a parent to pay maintenance to his child who is living with the other parent applies generally and has no specific conscientious implications in itself. Article 9 does not confer on the applicant a right to refuse, on the basis of religious beliefs, to abide by the court decisions at issue. (*Karakuzey v Germany*, p. 94 – *refusal of divorced Muslim father to make maintenance payments to daughter who had changed religion from Islam to Catholicism*)

25.10 PLACING CHILDREN IN CARE

Key ECHR cases

B v UK (1987) 10 EHRR 87, ECtHR
Eriksson v Sweden (1989) 12 EHRR 183, ECtHR
H v UK (1987) 10 EHRR 95, ECtHR
Johansen v Norway (1996) 23 EHRR 33, ECtHR
K and T v Finland (27 April 2000), ECtHR
L v Finland (27 April 2000), ECtHR

ECHR principles

25.10.1 *The decision to take a child into care*

- Decisions to place children in care clearly engage Article 8, ECHR and have to be justified as legitimate, necessary and proportionate.

- The reasons for taking a child into care must be established under Article 8(2); but in most cases the protection of the rights of others – the child – will be enough.

- Where there is a tension between the parent(s) and the child, consideration of what is in the best interest of the child is crucial and should prevail:

> The Court recalls that taking a child into care should normally be regarded as a temporary measure to be discontinued as soon as circumstances permit, and that any measures of implementation of temporary care should be consistent with the ultimate aim of reuniting the natural parent and child . . . In this regard a fair balance has to be struck between the interests of the child in remaining in public care and those of the parent in being reunited with the child . . . In carrying out this balancing exercise, the Court will attach particular importance to the best interests of the child, which, depending on their nature and seriousness, may override those of the parent. In particular, the parent cannot be entitled under Article 8 of the Convention to have such measures taken as would harm the child's health and development. (L v Finland, para. 122; see also Johansen v Norway)

- A decision to take a newly born child into care is particularly severe and demands strong justification and the involvement of the parents in the decision-making process (K and T v Finland, paras 144–146).

- Nonetheless, Article 8 does not rule out care proceedings where the parents are incapable of stimulating the proper growth and development of their children, and this will not necessarily breach Article 8 (L v Finland).

- But where there is evidence that a parent with mental health problems will not be permanently incapable of looking after his or her child, the authorities should be slow to make final and irreversible decisions because there is the prospect that the family could, at some stage, be reunited (K and T v Finland, para. 158).

25.10.2   *The procedural requirements of Article 8 in care cases*

- Under Article 8, the parents of a child whom the relevant authorities propose to take into care should be involved in the decision-making process.

- This does not rule out speedy action, where such is required; save in exceptional circumstances, the parent(s) should be consulted (see **25.11**).

25.10.3   *The position after a child is taken into care*

- After a care order is made, parents retain a right of access to their child.

- Restricting this access must be justified as legitimate, necessary and proportionate (Eriksson v Sweden, para. 71).

- Care proceedings obviously have a profound impact on parent and child; as a result, an adult who was in care as a child is entitled to have access to his or her personal files to better understand his or her development (Gaskin v UK, para. 37 – *access to personal files kept whilst in foster care*).

25.11 PROCEDURAL FAIRNESS IN PROCEEDINGS CONCERNING FAMILY LIFE

Key ECHR cases

B v UK (1987) 10 EHRR 87, ECtHR
H v UK (1987) 10 EHRR 95, ECtHR
Hokkanen v Finland (1994) 19 EHRR 139, ECtHR
McMichael v UK (1995) 20 EHRR 205, ECtHR
W v UK (1987) 10 EHRR 29, ECtHR

ECHR principles

- There is a strict requirement of procedural fairness in proceedings concerning family life; this is derived from Articles 6(1) and 8.

- The Article 6(1) requirements of fairness are dealt with at **Section 17**.

- The Article 8 requirements are more complicated because they arise at an earlier stage – e.g., when the relevant authority is taking or proposing to take a decision affecting the family lives of others – and because they are less clear. Nonetheless:

  . . . what . . . has to be determined is whether, having regard to the particular circumstances of the case and notably the serious nature of the decisions to be taken, the parents have been involved in the decision-making process, seen as a whole, to a degree sufficient to provide them with the requisite protection of their interests. If they have not, there will have been a failure to respect their family life and the interference resulting from the decision will not be capable of being regarded as 'necessary' within the meaning of Article 8. (*B v UK*, para. 64)

- This may entail disclosure of material, particularly where it is adverse, and an effective opportunity to make representations:

  In the context of the present case, the lack of disclosure of such vital documents as social reports is capable of affecting the ability of participating parents not only to influence the outcome of the children's hearing in question but also to assess their prospects of success. (*McMichael v UK*, para. 80)

- Moreover, the proceedings as a whole should be speedy; not least because they involve decisions which may have a quality of irreversibility if delayed (*H v UK; Hokkanen v Finland*).

Relevant Scottish cases

Appeal for LJ in petition of Aberdeen City Council (11 February 1999), AC

- The court should hear from an individual (genuinely) claiming to be the father of a child before making adoption decisions, even if his name is not on the birth certificate (*Appeal for LJ in petition of Aberdeen City Council*, p. 5).

MARRIAGE AND THE RIGHT TO FOUND A FAMILY

26.1 MARRIAGE

Key ECHR cases

Cossey v UK (1990) 13 EHRR 622, ECtHR
F v Switzerland (1987) 10 EHRR 411, ECtHR
Rees v UK (1986) 9 EHRR 56, ECtHR

A and A v Netherlands (1992) 72 DR 118, ECmHR[CD]
Adam and Khan v UK (1967) 10 Yearbook 478, ECmHR
Benes v Austria (1992) 72 DR 271, ECmHR
Draper v UK (1981) 24 DR 72, ECmHR
Hamer v UK (1979) 24 DR 5, ECmHR
Lindsay v UK (1986) 49 DR 181, ECmHR[CD]
Staarman v Netherlands (1985) 42 DR 162, ECmHR

ECHR principles

- The right to marry is provided for in Article 12, ECHR.
- It protects 'the formation of a legally binding association between a man and a woman' (*Hamer v UK*).
- The only permitted restrictions are:

  (a) that the individuals in question be of marriageable age; and
  (b) that they comply with the rules of domestic law.

- The limits permitted by domestic law are not clear, save that they should not destroy the very essence of the right to marriage (*Cossey v UK*).
- Impediments – or disincentives – such as loss of welfare benefits and increased tax burdens, within reason, do not have that effect and are acceptable (*Staarman v Netherlands*).
- Cohabitation is not a pre-condition for marriage:

  It is for [the parties to a marriage] to decide whether or not they wish to enter an association in circumstances where they cannot cohabit. (*Hamer v UK*, p. 16)

- Neither is procreation (*Hamer v UK*, p. 16).

- Prisoners should be free to marry:

  > . . . the right to marry . . . is . . . essentially, a right to form a legal relationship, to acquire a status. Its exercise by prisoners involves no general threat to prison security or good order. A person deprived of his liberty under Article 5 remains in principle entitled to the right to marry and any restriction or regulation of the exercise of that right must not be such as to injure its substance. (*Hamer v UK*, pp. 13–14 – *prisoner refused temporary release to marry outside – no facilities available within prison to marry; Draper v UK*, p. 80 – *life sentence prisoner denied permission to leave prison in order to marry*)

- In this context, it is not up to the authorities to decide to delay a marriage because a prisoner and his partner are unable to consummate it. That is a decision for the couple themselves (*Hamer v UK*, p. 16).

- Nonetheless, there may be some occasions where delaying a prisoner's marriage for reasons of public interest may be justified; but a *carte blanche* restriction on life sentence prisoners is not consistent with Article 12 (*Draper v UK*, p. 81).

- Polygamous marriages can establish family life, but there is no obligation to give them effect in domestic law (*Adam and Khan v UK*).

- And a marriage entered into for the sole purpose of obtaining nationality is not protected under the ECHR (*Benes v Austria*, p. 274).

Other international human rights standards

- The right of men and women of marriageable age to marry and to found a family shall be recognised (International Covenant on Civil and Political Rights, Article 23).

- No marriage shall be entered into without the free and full consent of the intending spouses (International Covenant on Civil and Political Rights, Article 23).

- Marriageable age should be set at a level as to enable each of the intending spouses to give his or her free and full personal consent (UN Human Rights Committee, General Comment 19, para. 4).

- Any legal provisions relating to marriage must be compatible with the full exercise of other Covenant rights, e.g., the right to freedom of thought, conscience and religion implies that legislation should provide for the possibility of both religious and civil marriages. However, it is not incompatible for a state to require that a religious marriage should also be conducted, affirmed or registered under civil law (UN Human Rights Committee, General Comment 19, para. 4).

26.2   FOUNDING A FAMILY

Key ECHR cases

Abdulaziz, Cabales and Balkandali v UK (1985) 7 EHRR 471, ECrHR

X and Y v Switzerland (1978) 13 DR 241, ECmHR

ECHR principles

- A fairly restrictive notion has been taken of founding a family so far: in *X and Y v Switzerland*, the family was said to be founded upon marriage.

- However, it at least extends to living together:

  . . . it is scarcely conceivable that the right to found a family . . . should not encompass the right to live together. (*Abdulaziz, Cabales and Balkandali v UK*)

- Except in the prison environment, where, as presently interpreted, the right to found a family in Article 12 cannot provide a basis for conjugal visits (*X and Y v Switzerland*).

Other international human rights standards

- The right of men and women of marriageable age to marry and to found a family shall be recognised (International Covenant on Civil and Political Rights, Article 23).

- The right to found a family implies, in principle, the possibility to procreate and live together. Therefore, when states adopt family planning policies, they should be compatible with the International Covenant on Civil and Political Rights. In particular, they should not be discriminatory or compulsory (UN Human Rights Committee, General Comment 19, para. 5).

- Similarly, the possibility to live together implies the adoption of appropriate measures, both at the domestic level and in cooperation with other states, to ensure the unity or reunification of families when they are separated for political, economic or similar reasons (UN Human Rights Committee, General Comment 19, para. 5).

26.3   CHILDREN BORN OUT OF WEDLOCK

Key ECHR cases

Inze v Austria (1987) 10 EHRR 394, ECtHR
Johnston and others v Ireland (1986) 9 EHRR 203, ECtHR
Marckx v Belgium (1979) 2 EHRR 330, ECtHR
Rasmussen v Denmark (1984) 7 EHRR 371, ECtHR
Vermeire v Belgium (1991) 15 EHRR 488, ECtHR

B, R and J v Germany (1984) 36 DR 130, ECmHR

ECHR principles

- Children born out of wedlock should not suffer on account of their birth:

  By guaranteeing the right to respect for family life, Article 8 presupposes the existence of a family. The Court concurs that Article 8 makes no distinction between the 'legitimate' and 'illegitimate' family. Such a distinction would not be consonant with the word 'everyone', and this is confirmed by Article 14 with its prohibition . . . of discrimination grounded on 'birth'. In addition, . . . the Committee of Ministers of the Council of Europe regards the single woman and her child as one form of family no less than others.

Article 8 thus applies to the 'family life' of the 'illegitimate' family. [The applicant] assumed responsibility for her daughter . . . from the moment of her birth and has continuously cared for her, with the result that a real family life existed and still exists between them. (*Marckx v Belgium*, para. 31; see also *Johnston and others v Ireland*, para. 56 – *parents of illegitimate child prevented from remarrying due to prohibition on divorce*)

- Very weighty reasons would therefore have to be advanced for a distinction in treatment between legitimate and illegitimate children (*Inze v Austria*, para. 41).

26.4   DIVORCE AND SEPARATION

Key ECHR cases

Airey v Ireland (1979) 2 EHRR 305, ECtHR
F v Switzerland (1987) 10 EHRR 411, ECtHR
Johnston and others v Ireland (1986) 9 EHRR 203, ECtHR

ECHR principles

- The right to marry under Article 12, ECHR does not imply a right to divorce (*Johnston v Ireland*).

- Nonetheless, the protection of family life requires the law to recognise a right of married couples physically to separate and to be free from any obligation to live together (*Airey v Ireland*).

- And where domestic law does permit divorce, Article 12 secures for divorced persons the right to remarry without unreasonable restrictions (*F v Switzerland*).

26.5   LESBIAN AND GAY COUPLES

Key ECHR cases

Cossey v UK (1990) 13 EHRR 622, ECtHR
Rees v UK (1986) 9 EHRR 56, ECtHR

S v UK (1986) 47 DR 274, ECmHR
W v UK (1989) 63 DR 34, ECmHR
X and Y v UK (1983) 32 DR 220, ECmHR

ECHR principles

- A stable relationship between lesbian and/or gay couples is protected under Article 8 as 'private' life, but not as 'family life' (*X and Y v UK*, p. 221 – *gay partner threatened with deportation*; *S v UK*, pp. 277–8 – *claim for tenancy to be vested in partner of deceased lesbian*).

- So far, Article 12 has not been interpreted as conferring a right to marry on same-sex couples:

> . . . the right to marry guaranteed by Article 12 refers to the traditional marriage between persons of opposite biological sex. This appears also from the wording of the Article which makes it clear that Article 12 is mainly concerned to protect marriage as the basis of the family . . . (*Rees v UK*, para. 63; see also *Cossey v UK*)

- However, the matter has not yet been addressed directly by the ECtHR and there is no consensus that this approach of the ECmHR is right:

> Article 12 contains two (interconnected) rights: the right to marry and the right to found a family. Unlike Articles 8–11, Article 12 has no second paragraph providing for interference with these rights in exceptional circumstances. This underlines the fundamental character of the right to marry and to found a family. In principle, these rights cannot be set aside in the public interest. In my opinion the fundamental human right underlying Article 12 should also be granted to homosexual and lesbian couples. They should not be denied the right to found a family without good reasons. (*Dissenting opinion of Mr Schermers in W v UK* pp. 48–49 – transsexual prevented from changing the indication of his sex in the birth register)

Relevant domestic cases

Fitzpatrick v Sterling House Association Ltd [1999] 3 WLR 1113

- Regarding same-sex-couples who live together as 'husband and wife':

> The courts have already decided that family includes relationships other than those based on consanguinity or affinity. To include same sex partners is to do no more than apply to them the same rationale as that underlying the inclusion of different sex partners. (*Fitzpatrick v Sterling House Association Ltd*, per Lord Nicolls, p. 1130; *tenancy succession*)

Relevant Canadian cases

Layland v Ontario Minister Consumer & Commercial Relations (1993) 14 OR (3d)
M v H [1999] 2 SCR 3

- There is a strong argument to suggest that the traditional concept of marriage can be discriminatory (*Layland v Ontario Minister Consumer & Commercial Relations*, p. 568).

- Since the characteristics of a same-sex relationship are the same as those of a heterosexual relationship in many ways, same-sex relationships should enjoy the same protection when the parties separate:

> Same-sex relationships are capable of meeting [the requirements for spousal support for unmarried couples]. Certainly same-sex couples will often form long, lasting, loving and intimate relationships. The choices they make in the context of those relationships may give rise to the financial dependence of one partner on the other . . .
> While it is true that there may not be any consensus as to the societal perception of same-sex couples, there is agreement that [they] share many other 'conjugal' characteristics.
> Being in a same-sex relationship does not mean that it is an impermanent or a non-conjugal relationship. (M v H, paras 58, 59 and 70)

- This has implications for the children of same-sex relationships:

> An increasing percentage of children are being conceived and raised by lesbian and gay couples as a result of adoption, surrogacy and donor insemination. Although their

numbers are still fairly small . . . the goal of protecting children cannot be but incompletely achieved by denying some children the benefits that flow from a spousal support award merely because their parents were in a same-sex relationship. (M v H, para. 114)

Relevant New Zealand cases

Quilter v Attorney-General [1998] 1 NZLR 523, CA

- It remains open to question whether the traditional concept of marriage amounts to discrimination against same-sex couples (*Quilter v Attorney-General – refusal to grant marriage licences to three lesbian couples – no agreement on whether amounted to discrimination contrary to Bill of Rights*).

SECTION 27

CHILDREN

27.1 THE STATUS OF CHILDREN UNDER THE ECHR

Key ECHR cases

A v UK (1998) 27 EHRR 611, ECtHR
Costello-Roberts v UK (1993) 19 EHRR 112, ECtHR
Olsson v Sweden (No. 2) (1992) 17 EHRR 134, ECtHR
T v UK, V v UK (1999) 30 EHRR 121, ECtHR

ECHR principles

- The ECHR makes no express reference to the rights of children.

- However, all the Convention rights apply to all individuals irrespective of age.

- And there has been increasing reference and weight attached to the UN Convention on the Rights of the Child (*Olsson v Sweden (No. 2)*, p. 192; *Costello-Roberts v UK*, paras 27 and 35; *A v UK*, para. 22; *T v UK, V v UK*).

- One of the fundamental guiding principles of the UN Convention on the Rights of the Child is that '[i]n all actions concerning children . . . the best interests of the child shall be a primary consideration' (Article 3(1)); and this principle is increasingly applied under the ECHR (*Olsson v Sweden*, para. 90).

Other international human rights standards

- All children benefit from all the civil rights listed in the International Covenant on Civil and Political Rights, together with greater protection in areas such as juvenile justice (UN Human Rights Committee, General Comment 17, para. 2).

27.2 PARENTAL CONTROL OVER CHILDREN

Key ECHR cases

Nielsen v Denmark (1988) 11 EHRR 175, ECmHR
X v Netherlands (1974) 2 DR 118, ECmHR

ECHR principles

- Although ECHR rights apply to all individuals irrespective of age, the right of parents to restrict the rights of their children in a manner that would be unacceptable in relation to adults is well established:

As a general proposition, and in the absence of any special circumstances, the obligation of children to reside with their parents and to be otherwise subjected to particular control is necessary for the protection of children's health and morals, although it might constitute, from a particular child's point of view, an interference with his or her own private life. (*X v Netherlands*, p. 119)

- This parental role is seen as a core component of the right to family life:

  ... family life in the contracting States encompasses a broad range of parental rights and responsibilities in regard to care and custody of minor children. The care and upbringing of children normally and necessarily require that the parents or an only parent decide where the child must reside and also impose, or authorise others to impose, various restrictions on the child's liberty. . . . Family life in this sense, and especially the rights of parents to exercise parental authority over their children, having due regard to their corresponding parental responsibilities, is recognised and protected by the Convention in particular by Article 8. Indeed the exercise of parental rights constitutes a fundamental element of family life. (*Nielsen v Denmark*, para. 61)

- This concept of parental rights has been used to justify the unnecessary detention of a 12-year-old boy in a psychiatric institution on the basis that the aim was legitimate – based on medical advice – and genuine (*Nielsen v Denmark*, paras 70 and 73).

- However, there are clear limits to parental control:

  ... the rights of the holder of parental authority cannot be unlimited and . . . it is incumbent on the State to provide safeguards against abuse. (*Nielsen v Denmark*, para. 72)

27.3   CORPORAL PUNISHMENT

Key ECHR cases

A v UK (1998) 27 EHRR 611, ECtHR
Campbell and Cosans v UK (1982) 4 EHRR 293, ECtHR
Costello-Roberts v UK (1993) 19 EHRR 112, ECtHR
Tyrer v UK (1978) 2 EHRR 1, ECtHR

Seven Individuals v Sweden (1982) 29 DR 104, ECmHR
Warwick v UK (1986) 60 DR 5, ECmHR
Y v UK (1992) A-247 A, ECmHR

ECHR principles

- Standards and expectations in relation to the punishment of children have altered since the ECHR was drafted and a more sophisticated notion of the limits of corporal punishment now prevails.

- Birching as punishment for a criminal offence was found to be degrading in *Tyrer v UK*, but not torture or inhuman treatment.

- Numerous factors are relevant to the question of whether the particular application of corporal punishment breaches Article 3, Article 8, or both.

- Relevant are: the degree and intensity of the beating; whether there is any delay; the sex and status of the person inflicting the punishment; whether the punishment takes place in public or private; and the degree of any injury (*Tyrer v UK*; *Campbell and Cosans v UK*; *Costello-Roberts v UK*; *A v UK*).

- As a general rule, in the absence of any real and immediate threat, mere exposure to the possibility of corporal punishment at school will not engage Article 3 (*Campbell and Cosans* v *UK*, para. 27).

- However, the right to education (protected by Protocol 1, Article 2) may be breached if a school refuses to admit children because of their parents' objection to corporal punishment (*Campbell and Cosans* v *UK*, para. 41).

- And state liability is engaged whether the school is state-funded or private (*Costello-Roberts* v *UK*, paras 26–28).

- It is also engaged where a father severely beats his son in his own home (*A* v *UK*, para. 24).

27.4   PROTECTION FROM ABUSE

- See **1.8**, **14.1** and **Section 19**.

27.5   DETENTION FOR EDUCATIONAL SUPERVISION

Key ECHR cases

Bouamar v *Belgium* (1988) 11 EHRR 1, ECtHR

ECHR principles

- Article 5(1)(d) specifically provides for the detention of a minor by lawful order for the purpose of educational supervision.

- For the meaning of the word 'lawful' in this context, see **22.3**.

- The word 'order' refers to an order of a court or administrative authority.

- The provision in general is intended to underpin a basic obligation to attend school.

- Short periods of detention in furtherance of that aim can be justified; prolonged periods without any real education cannot (*Bouamar* v *Belgium*).

Relevant domestic cases

In Re K (a child) (15 November 2000), CA

- Secure accommodation orders must comply with Article 5(1)(d) if they are to be compatible with the ECHR (*In Re K (a child)*).

27.6   DETAINING CHILDREN TO BRING THEM BEFORE A COURT

ECHR principles

- Article 5(1)(d) specifically provides for the detention of a minor for the purpose of bringing him before the competent legal authority.

- This is intended to provide a mechanism for securing a child's removal from harmful surroundings, e.g., as an urgent measure prior to full care proceedings.

IMMIGRATION, ASYLUM, EXTRADITION AND DEPORTATION

28.1 THE ECHR FRAMEWORK FOR ADMISSION AND EXPULSION

Key ECHR cases

Chahal v UK (1996) 23 EHRR 413, ECtHR
Soering v UK (1989) 11 EHRR 439, ECtHR

ECHR principles

- There is no right under the ECHR to enter, reside or remain in a particular country (*Soering v UK*, para. 85), recognising that states are entitled to control who leaves and enters their borders (*Chahal v UK*, para. 73).

- However, decisions about admission or expulsion from a state party must not violate any of the Convention rights, including the right to life (Article 2), the right not to be tortured or suffer inhuman or degrading treatment (Article 3) or the right to a family life (Article 8).

- In addition, a person can be lawfully detained to 'prevent his effecting an unauthorised entry into the country or of a person against whom action is being taken with a view to deportation or extradition' (Article 5(1)(f)); but detention on this basis should not be discriminatory (Article 14).

- Additional protection against arbitrary expulsion and the guarantee of freedom of movement are provided for in Protocol 4, Articles 2–4 but this has not yet been ratified by the UK.

28.2 CONTROL OF ADMISSIONS

Key ECHR cases

Abdulaziz, Cabales and Balkandali v UK (1985) 7 EHRR 471, ECtHR
Amuur v France (1996) 22 EHRR 533, ECtHR

Adegbie v Austria (1997), ECmHR[CD]
Akhtar v UK (12 February 1992), ECmHR
East African Asians v UK (1973) 3 EHRR 76, ECmHR
Lalljee v UK (1986) 8 EHRR 84, ECmHR
SM and MT v Austria (1993) 74 DR 179, ECmHR
X v UK (28 February 1996), ECmHR

ECHR principles

28.2.1   *Article 3*

- Once an individual is physically within the jurisdiction of a state, he or she is entitled to the full protection of the ECHR, even if (technically) he or she has not 'entered' the country (*SM and MT v Austria* – *applicants confined to Vienna Airport*; *Amuur v France* – *applicants confined to transit area in Paris*).

- However, the application of Article 3 to admission cases is rare, and the main focus has been on discrimination in relation to admission policy and practice.

- Although the threshold for degrading treatment under Article 3 is high, in certain circumstances institutional discrimination is *capable* of reaching that threshold:

  . . . a special importance should be attached to discrimination based on race; that publicly to single out a group of persons for differential treatment on the basis of race might, in certain circumstances, constitute a special form of affront to human dignity; and that differential treatment of a group of persons on the basis of race might therefore be capable of constituting degrading treatment when differential treatment on some other ground would raise no such question. (*East African Asians v UK*, para. 207)

- The 'certain circumstances' referred to include (but are not limited to): reneging on specific pledges; the destitution faced by returning immigrants; and the manner in which immigration is operated.

- Absent the same, or similar, circumstances, Article 3 is unlikely to be engaged, e.g., so long as there are no aggravating features, operating a quota system is not necessarily degrading (*Lalljee v UK*, p. 85), the focus being dignity and respect:

  . . . the difference in treatment . . . did not denote any contempt or lack of respect for the personality of the applicants . . . it was not designed to, and did not, humiliate or debase them. (*Abdulaziz, Cabales and Balkandali v UK*, para. 91)

28.2.2   *Article 8*

- Although Article 8 applies in immigration cases, the exclusion of family members is not necessarily a breach of its provisions (*East African Asians v UK*, para. 232; *Abdulaziz, Cabales and Balkandali v UK*, para. 60).

- The general presumption is that the state is under no obligation to admit family members of those within its jurisdiction, save where it can be established that:

  (a)   there are real obstacles to the establishment of family life elsewhere; or

(b)   there are special reasons why the individuals in question should not be expected to establish family life elsewhere.

(*East African Asians v UK*, para. 232; *Abdulaziz, Cabales and Balkandali v UK*, para. 60)

- Real obstacles might include the ability of the parties to adapt to living overseas, language difficulties, cultural, religious and social practices and compelling health, employment or family issues (*Adegbie v Austria*); but not the fact that one party may have to give up a job or business (*X v UK*) or might be ill (*Akhtar v UK*).

- Knowledge of the problems of admission and settlement before family life was established will also be a relevant factor (*Abdulaziz, Cabales and Balkandali v UK*, para. 68).

28.3   RESTRICTIONS ON EXPULSION

Key ECHR cases

Ahmed v Austria (1996) 24 EHRR 278, ECtHR
Beldjoudi v France (1992) 14 EHRR 801, ECtHR
Berrehab v Netherlands (1988) 11 EHRR 322, ECtHR
Boughanemi v France (1996) 22 EHRR 228, ECtHR
Chahal v UK (1996) 23 EHRR 413, ECtHR
Cruz Varas v Sweden (1991) 14 EHRR 1, ECtHR
D v UK (1997) 24 EHRR 423, ECtHR
Drozd and Janousek v France and Spain (1992) 14 EHRR 745, ECtHR
HLR v France (1997) 26 EHRR 29, ECtHR
Ireland v UK (1978) 2 EHRR 25, ECtHR
Jabari v Turkey (11 July 2000), ECtHR
Lamguindaz v UK (1993) 17 EHRR 213, ECtHR
Moustaquim v Belgium (1991) 13 EHRR 802, ECtHR
Nasri v France (1995) 21 EHRR 458, ECtHR
Soering v UK (1989) 11 EHRR 439, ECtHR
Vilvarajah v UK (1991) 14 EHRR 248, ECtHR

A v Switzerland (1986) 46 DR 257, ECmHR
A and FBK v Turkey (1991) 68 DR 188, ECmHR
Altun v Germany (1983) 36 DR 209, ECmHR
Aylor-Davis v France (1994) 76A DR 164, ECmHR
Bahaddar v Netherlands (1995), ECmHR[CD]
Bulus v Sweden (1984) 35 DR 57 and 39 DR 75, ECmHR
C v Germany (1986) 46 DR 176, ECmHR
Giama v Belgium (1980) 21 DR 73, ECmHR
Harabi v Netherlands (1986) 46 DR 112, ECmHR
Jaramillo v UK (23 October 1995), ECmHR
Popescu and Cucu v France (11 September 1995), ECmHR
Sorabjee v UK (23 October 1995), ECmHR
Taspinar v Netherlands (1985) 44 DR 262, ECmHR
X v Germany (1969) 32 CD 96, ECmHR

ECHR principles

28.3.1 *Article 3*

- There is no right under the ECHR to protection from expulsion or extradition:

  [States are free] to control the entry, residence and expulsion of aliens. (*Chahal v UK*, para. 73; *Altun v Germany*, p. 231)

- Nonetheless, expulsion and extradition powers must be operated within clear ECHR limits:

  . . . the decision by a Contracting State to extradite a fugitive may give rise to an issue under Article 3, and hence engage the responsibility of that State under the Convention, where substantial grounds have been shown for believing that the person concerned, if extradited, faces a real risk of being subjected to torture or to inhuman or degrading treatment or punishment in the requesting country. (*Soering v UK*, para. 91)

- Responsibility lies with the state not to expel or extradite individuals in circumstances which might place them at real risk of torture on inhuman or degrading treatment/punishment contrary to Article 3 (*Soering v UK*, paras 85–86).

- The ill-treatment feared as a consequence of expulsion must be severe (see **19.2**).

- Being forced to do military service (*X v Germany*, p. 97; *A and FBK v Turkey*, p. 193), facing criminal proceedings with a potentially long prison sentence (*C v Germany*, p. 181) and facing desertion proceedings (*Popescu and Cucu v France*) are not enough; prosecution for a political offence with a substantial sentence (*A v Switzerland*, p. 271; *Altun v Germany*, pp. 232–2) and exposure to the 'death row' phenomenon (*Soering v UK*) are enough.

- A risk of exposure to stoning for adultery under Islamic law is sufficient to engage the Article 3 obligation on the state not to expel an individual exposed to such a risk (*Jabari v Turkey*, para. 41).

- The mere possibility of ill-treatment is not enough; but the risk must be taken seriously and carefully assessed (*Soering v UK*).

- Assurances by the receiving state – particularly in extradition cases – about how individuals will be treated if sent to their jurisdiction are important (*Aylor-Davis v France*); but should be treated with caution where they are untested and might be ineffective (*Soering v UK*).

- Beyond extradition, risk assessment becomes more difficult. In expulsion cases the unpredictability of what might happen when an individual is sent to another state is sometimes very hard to gauge, particularly where there is a fear that ill-treatment might be clandestine – either by the state or by others (*Ahmed v Austria*, paras 39 and 47).

- The approach under the ECHR is to assess any information about the likely risks when the decision to expel was taken, and then to supplement it by anything further that comes to light before that decision is implemented (*Vilvarajah v UK*;

Cruz Varas v Sweden – political developments in Chile between decision and expulsion taken into account).

- What is called for is a rigorous examination focused on the foreseeable consequences of removal (*Vilvarajah v UK*, para. 108; *Cruz Varas v Sweden; Hatami v Sweden*).

- Where short time limits, e.g., for making asylum claims, preclude the court from making an assessment of risk, Article 3 might be breached:

  The Court is not persuaded that the authorities . . . conducted any meaningful assessment of the applicant's claim, including its arguability. It would appear that her failure to comply with the five-day registration requirement under the Asylum Regulations 1994 denied her any scrutiny of the factual basis of her fears about being removed to Iran . . . In the Court's opinion, the automatic and mechanical application of such a short time-limit for submitting an asylum application must be considered at variance with the protection of the fundamental value embodied in Article 3 of the Convention. (*Jabari v Turkey*, para. 40)

- Provided that a threat is both specific and significant, its source is not a decisive factor:

  . . . owing to the absolute character of the right guaranteed, the Court does not rule out the possibility that Article 3 of the Convention may also apply where the danger emanates from persons or groups of persons who are not public officials. However, it must be shown that the risk is real and that the authorities in the receiving state are not able to obviate the risk by providing appropriate protection. (*HLR v France*, para. 40 – *risk of reprisals from drug traffickers in Colombia*)

- But the concept of a 'threat' is a very broad one, and can include a threat of ill-treatment because inadequate medical facilities may well lead to an accelerated and painful death:

  It is true that [the principle of non-expulsion] has so far been applied . . . in contexts of which the risk to the individual of being subjected to any of the proscribed forms of treatment emanates from intentionally inflicted acts of the public authorities in the receiving country or from those of non-State bodies in that country when the authorities there are unable to afford him protection.

  Aside from these situations and given the fundamental importance of Article 3 in the convention system, the Court must reserve to itself sufficient flexibility to address the application of that Article in other contexts which might arise. It is therefore not prevented from scrutinising an applicant's claim under Article 3 where the source of the risk of proscribed treatment in the receiving country stems from factors which cannot engage either directly or indirectly the responsibility of the public authorities in that country, or which taken alone, do not in themselves infringe the standards of that Article. To limit the application of Article 3 in this manner would undermine the absolute character of its protection. (*D v UK*, para. 49)

- For health care generally, see **Section 20**.

- The feared ill-treatment is not to be balanced against other interests, e.g., national security:

  . . . even in these circumstances [where it has been established that expulsion is in the public interest], the Convention prohibits in absolute terms torture or inhuman or degrading treatment or punishment, irrespective of the victim's conduct . . . (*Chahal v UK*, para. 79)

- Removal to a safe third country is permitted, provided that there is no chance that the third country will remove the individual to another country where there is a real risk of ill-treatment (*Giama v Belgium*).

28.3.2 *Article 6*

- The fact that an individual might be exposed to criminal proceedings falling short of Article 6, ECHR standards if extradited or expelled, is not, in itself, sufficient to breach the ECHR:

  > Article 1 cannot be read as justifying a general principle to the effect that, notwithstanding its extradition obligations, a Contracting State may not surrender an individual unless satisfied that the conditions awaiting him in the country of destination are in full accord with each of the safeguards of the Convention. (*Soering v UK*, para. 86)

- Unless there is a risk of a flagrant denial of justice:

  > The right to a fair trial in criminal proceedings, as embodied in Article 6, holds a prominent place in a democratic society. The Court does not exclude that an issue might exceptionally be raised under Article 6 by an extradition decision in circumstances where the fugitive has suffered or risks suffering a flagrant denial of a fair trial in the requesting country. (*Soering v UK*, para. 113; *Drozd and Janousek v France*, para. 110)

28.3.3 *Article 8*

- Article 8, ECHR is relevant where a family member is threatened with expulsion; particularly where he or she has been lawfully resident in the state for a significant period of time.

- However, as with admission cases, this does not mean that expulsion is always prohibited merely because it disrupts family life.

- Provided the expulsion is in accordance with domestic law and pursues a legitimate aim under Article 8(2), the crucial test is one of proportionality: is the extreme act of expulsion a proportionate response in all the circumstances?

- In assessing proportionality relevant factors will be the reason for expulsion, the applicant's ties with the expelling state, the extent of the disruption to family life and whether there are any real obstacles to establishing family life elsewhere (*Moustaquim v Belgium*, para. 45; *Beldjoudi v France*; *Lamguidaz v UK*; *Nasri v France*; *Boughanemi v France*).

- The situation of children is particularly difficult; it is likely that expulsion to a country where there is nobody to care for them on arrival will amount to inhuman treatment (*Taspinar v Netherlands*, p. 264; *Bulus v Sweden*, p. 65).

- Similarly, the disruption to family life by the expulsion of one parent might outweigh otherwise good reasons for deportation. (*Berrehab v Netherlands*, para. 29).

- However, there is case law from the ECmHR that there is no breach of the ECHR where a custodial parent is expelled if the children are young enough to adapt to a new country, even where the children themselves are citizens of the expelling state (*Jaramillo v UK; Sorabjee v UK*).

Relevant domestic cases

B v Secretary of State for the Home Department (18 May 2000)
R v Secretary of State for the Home Department, ex parte Ali (28 October 1999)

- Article 8 is relevant to admission and expulsion cases; any Article 8(2) justification for refusing admission has to be carefully examined:

  It is clear that the applicant and his wife and children are a family and that a bar to the family living together as such in the UK is capable of amounting to a failure to show respect for family life and so of breaching Article 8(1). Whether or not it does in any particular case will depend upon the circumstances of that case. While it may be easier to demonstrate such a breach in the case of a deportation, there is no reason to limit the protection of Article 8 to such cases. It is in my judgment of fundamental importance that in the *Abdulaziz* case the applicants had not shown that there were obstacles to establishing family life in their own or their husband's own countries or that there were special reasons why that could not be expected of them (para. 68). If such obstacles or special reasons had been shown, it seems to me that the court would (and in my judgment, should) have decided that Article 8(1) was breached since refusal of leave to enter would have prevented any family life.
  . . . it is, as it seems to me, justifiable to avoid any recourse to public funds. But the barrier must not be greater than necessary. Accordingly, the Rules would not in my view be in accordance with Article 8 if they were construed so as to exclude a spouse when his or her admission would not affect the economic well-being of the country because there would be no recourse to public funds or any other detriment caused by it. (*R v Secretary of State for the Home Department, ex parte Ali*)

- And the test of proportionality properly applied:

  In essence [the test of proportionality] amounts to this: a measure which interferes with a [European] Community or human right must not only be authorized by law but must correspond to a pressing social need and go no further than is strictly necessary in a pluralistic society to achieve its permitted purpose; or more shortly, must be appropriate and necessary to its legitimate aim . . .
  What in my judgment renders deportation a disproportionate response to this appellant's offending, serious as it is, and to his propensity to offend such as it may now be, is the fact that it will take him from the country in which he has grown up, has lived his whole adult life and has such social relationships as he possesses. It would negate both his freedom of movement and respect for his private life in the one place, the United Kingdom, where these have real meaning for him . . . In relation to Article 8 of the ECHR, it is because the jurisprudence of the Strasbourg court has carried the notion of private life beyond simple autonomy and 'to a certain degree' into 'the right to establish and develop relationships with other human beings' (*Niemietz v Germany* (1993) 16 EHRR 97, para. 29). What is proposed in the present case, although in law deportation, is in substance more akin to exile. As such it is in my judgment so severe as to be disproportionate to this man's particular offending, serious as it was, and to his propensities. (*B v Secretary of State for the Home Department*, per Sedley LJ)

  The deportation of an EC national can be justified only by the existence of 'a genuine and sufficiently serious threat to the requirements of public policy affecting one of the fundamental interests in society' – see *R v Bouchereau* [1978] QB 732, 760. And even if such a threat exists, deportation, because it interferes with the fundamental right of free movement of workers (Article 48, now 39, of the Treaty of Rome) and the right to respect for private life (Article 8 of the ECHR) must be proportionate. The requirement for proportionality in this context means that deportation must be both appropriate and necessary for the attainment of the public policy objective sought – here the containment of the threat – and also must not impose an excessive burden on the individual, the deportee. (B v *Secretary of State for the Home Department*, per Simon Brown LJ)

Relevant Scottish cases

Harinder Singh (11 November 1999), CS
Kulwinder Singh Saini (12 March 1999), HC
Malkiat Singh (24 March 1999), HC
Mohammed Akhtar (23 March 2000), CS
Mohammed Irfan Ul-Haq (3 December 1998), HC
Nisar Ahmed (14 March 2000), CS
Saleem Ahmed (28 March 2000), CS

- Where family life begins after an individual has entered and remained in the receiving country illegally, and enforcement action has been commenced, it is highly unlikely that Article 8 rights can defeat expulsion (*Saleem Ahmed*, para. 11; *Mohammed Akhtar*, para. 18; *Nisar Ahmed*, para. 22; *Mohammed Irfan Ul-Haq*, p. 3).

- Generally, the need to respect family life must be balanced against the need to maintain a 'firm but fair' immigration policy, with the result that any deportation decision must take into account the impact on the spouse and children (*Malkiat Singh*, p. 4; *Harinder Singh*, p. 7).

- But a decision which is likely to result in a permanent separation of the family is likely to be disproportionate:

  I accept that, if [permanent separation of the family] was indeed the likelihood, the decision would be so disproportionate as to be unreasonable. (*Kulwinder Singh Saini*, p. 8 – *no breach on the facts*)

Relevant Canadian cases

Baker v Minister of Citizenship and Immigration [1999] 2 SCR 817
Re Ng Extradition [1991] 2 SCR 858

- Where an individual faces the death penalty if extradited, a state which has abolished the death penalty is under a duty either to obtain an undertaking that the death penalty will not be imposed, or to refuse extradition (*Re Ng Extradition*, p. 865).

- Where immigration decisions have an impact on children of deportees then their interests must be given sufficient weight in accordance with the require-ments of Article 3(1) of the UN Convention on the Rights of the Child:

  For the exercise of [statutory discretion] to fall within the standard of reasonableness, the decision-maker should consider children's best interests as an important factor, give them substantial weight, and be alert, alive and sensitive to them. That is not to say that children's best interests must always outweigh other considerations, or that there will not be other reasons for denying a claim even when children's interests are given this consideration. However, where the interests of children are minimized, in a manner inconsistent with Canada's humanitarian and compassionate tradition the decision will be unreasonable. (*Baker* v *Minister of Citizenship and Immigration*, para. 75)

28.4   DETENTION TO PREVENT ENTRY OR PENDING EXPULSION

Key ECHR cases

Bozano v *France* (1986) 9 EHRR 297, ECtHR
Chahal v *UK* (1996) 23 EHRR 413, ECtHR
Kolompar v *Belgium* (1992) 16 EHRR 197, ECtHR
Winterwerp v *Netherlands* (1979) 2 EHRR 387, ECtHR

Ali v *Switzerland* (App. No. 24881/94), ECmHR
Caprino v *UK* (1980) 22 DR 5, ECmHR
Zamir v *UK* (1985) 40 DR 42, ECmHR

ECHR principles

- Article 5(1)(f), ECHR provides for 'the lawful arrest and detention of a person to prevent his effecting an unauthorised entry into the country or of a person against whom action is being taken with a view to deportation or extradition'.

- For the general principles on the lawfulness of detention under Article 5, see **22.3**.

- Detention under Article 5(1)(f) will be justified only for as long as deportation or extradition proceedings are in progress.

- And where deportation or extradition is impossible, Article 5(1)(f) cannot be relied upon as a basis for detention (*Ali* v *Switzerland*).

- Delay can render Article 5(1)(f) detention unlawful; and, under Article 5(4), everyone deprived of their liberty has the right (with procedural safeguards: *Zamir* v *UK*, legal aid) to have the legality of their detention reviewed by a court.

- Nonetheless, the terms of Article 5(1)(f) are wide:

  Article 5(1)(f) does not demand that the detention of a person against whom action is being taken with a view to deportation be reasonably considered necessary, for example to prevent his committing an offence or fleeing; in this respect Article 5(1)(f) provides a different level of protection from Article 5(1)(c).
  Indeed, all that is required under this provision is that 'action is being taken with a view to deportation.' It is therefore immaterial, for the purposes of Article 5(1)(f), whether the underlying decision to expel can be justified under national or Convention law. (*Chahal* v *UK*, para. 112)

28.5   PROCEDURAL SAFEGUARDS IN ADMISSION AND EXPULSION CASES

Key ECHR cases

Agee v UK (1976) 7 DR 164, ECmHR
Kirkwood v UK (1984) 37 DR 158, ECmHR
Omkarananda and the Divine Light Zentrum v Switzerland (1981) 25 DR 105, ECmHR
S v Switzerland (1988) 59 DR 256, ECmHR[CD]
Saleem v UK (App. No. 38294/97, 4 March 1998), ECmHR

ECHR principles

- So far, the ECmHR has adopted the view that decisions on admission to and expulsion from a country do not determine civil rights and obligations:

  > The Commission notes that its case-law has held that the right of an alien to reside in a particular country is a matter governed by public law and that proceedings relating to deportation, expulsion or asylum fall outside the scope of [Article 6(1)] as not concerning any determination of civil rights and obligations. Accordingly, it has been previously held that the state is not required to grant a hearing conforming to the requirements of [Article 6(1)]. (*Saleem v UK*)

- This applies even where deportation leads to the loss of employment as a 'secondary and indirect result' (*Saleem v UK*).

- Extradition proceedings probably do not attract the fair trial rights of Article 6 because they do not 'determine' a criminal charge; but possibly this only applies where the receiving state determines guilt according to Article 6 standards (*Kirkwood v UK*, p. 191).

Relevant Canadian cases

Baker v Minister of Citizenship and Immigration [1999] 2 SCR 817

- Immigration decisions are subject to the requirements of procedural fairness:

  > . . . the circumstances require a full and fair consideration of the issues, and the claimant and others whose important interests are affected by the decision in a fundamental way must have a meaningful opportunity to present the various types of evidence relevant to their case and have it fully and fairly considered. (*Baker v Minister of Citizenship and Immigration*, para. 32)

- And a reasoned decision is one aspect of procedural fairness:

  > [I]t is now appropriate to recognise that, in certain circumstances, the duty of procedural fairness will require the provision of a written explanation for a decision. The strong arguments demonstrating the advantages of written reasons suggest that, in cases such as this where the decision has important significance for the individual, when there is a statutory right of appeal, or in other circumstances, some form of reasons should be required. (*Baker v Minister of Citizenship and Immigration*, para. 43)

HOUSING

29.1 THE RIGHT TO A HOME

Key ECHR cases

D v UK (1997) 24 EHRR 423, ECtHR

Burton v UK (1996) 22 EHRR CD 135, ECmHR[CD]
X v Germany (1956) 1 Yearbook 202, ECmHR

ECHR principles

- Article 8(1), ECHR provides that 'Everyone has a right to respect for his . . . home.'

- This should not be restricted unless domestic law clearly permits restrictions which are legitimate, necessary and proportionate.

- Primarily Article 8(1) protects an already existing home, not the right to a home (*X v Germany*).

- But there may be exceptional circumstances in which an obligation arises in relation to the relevant authorities to provide a home:

  > In so far as the applicant complains that she has not been able to return to living in a caravan due to a failure of the local authority to provide a site or an alternative mobile home, the Commission recalls that although the essential object of Article 8 is to protect against arbitrary interference by public authorities, there may in addition be positive obligations inherent in an effective 'respect' for family life . . . (*Burton v UK*, p. 35 – *Romany cancer sufferer not provided with a caravan place where she could live the rest of her life according to her traditions – no breach on the facts*)

- But not a home of choice:

  > However, the Commission does not consider that Article 8 can be interpreted in such a way as to extend a positive obligation to provide alternative accommodation of an applicant's choosing . . . [neither can it] be construed as conferring a right to take up residence on land belonging to others nor as imposing a positive obligation to ensure vacancies on official sites for persons wishing to return after a number of years to the traditional way of life of a gypsy. (*Burton v UK*, p. 35)

- A stronger obligation to provide a home may arise under Article 2 or Article 3 where there is a real risk that failure to provide accommodation will result in death or serious ill-treatment (*D v UK*; *Burton v UK*).

Relevant domestic authorities

R v North and East Devon Health Authority, ex parte Coughlan [2000] 2 WLR 622

- Where a severely disabled person is living in special accommodation, moving him or her will breach Article 8(1) unless suitable alternative accommodation is provided:

  > The judge was entitled to treat this as a case where the health authority's conduct was in breach of Article 8(1) and was not justified by Article 8(2). By the closure of Mardon House, the health authority will interfere with . . . her right to her home . . . [T]he health authority would not be justified in doing so without providing accommodation which meets her needs. (*R v North and East Devon Health Authority, ex parte Coughlan*)

29.2   PROTECTION OF THE HOME

29.2.1   *Article 8*

Key ECHR cases

Buckley v UK (1996) 23 EHRR 101, ECtHR
Gillow v UK (1986) 11 EHRR 335, ECtHR
Niemietz v Germany (1992) 16 EHRR 97, ECtHR

G and E v Norway (1983) 35 DR 30, ECmHR
Kanthak v Germany (1988) 58 DR 94, ECmHR[CD]
Mabey v UK (1996) 22 EHRR CD 123, ECmHR[CD]
S v UK (1986) 47 DR 274, ECmHR
Smith v UK (1998) EHRLR 499, ECmHR[CD]
Turner v UK (1997) 23 EHRR CD 181, ECmHR[CD]
Wiggins v UK (1978) 13 DR 40, ECmHR

ECHR principles

- Where a 'home' already exists, it will be protected by Article 8(1).

- 'Home', for these purposes, includes any premises or shelter used by an individual as a home, provided a sufficient link can be established and provided the individual has a sufficient interest in the premises.

- The mere fact that an individual is occupying premises unlawfully does not automatically preclude Article 8(1) protection (*Wiggins v UK*, p. 44 – *applicant lived in a 'home' she owned for a number of years, but had no legal permission to occupy*; *Buckley v UK*, para. 54 – *caravan without planning permission was a home since applicant had bought land and been living in it for five years*; *Gillow v UK*, para. 46 – *permission refused to live in home and applicant prosecuted for unlawful occupancy*).

- However, when all rights of occupation are extinguished, Article 8(1) may cease to apply (*S v UK*, p. 278 – *no right to succeed for lesbian partner of tenant*).

- Nevertheless, the test is a broad one:

  . . . whether or not a particular habitation constitutes a 'home' for the purposes of Article 8(1) will depend on the factual circumstances of the particular case, namely the existence of sufficient and continuous links. It is not limited necessarily to those homes which have been lawfully occupied or lawfully established. (*Mabey v UK*, p. 124 – *residence in a caravan for 20 years sufficient to constitute a home; Turner v UK*, p. 184 – *enforcement notice issued against caravan dweller amounted to interference with right to 'home'; Smith v UK*, p. 500 – *planning restrictions on use of land for gypsy site amounted to an interference on basis that had lived there for 20 years*; but see *Kanthak v Germany*, p. 98 – *left open whether protection extended to a camper van parked on a public road*)

- Lifestyle is also capable of protection under Article 8(1):

  [Even though] the Convention does not guarantee specific rights to minorities . . . a minority group is, in principle, entitled to claim the right to respect for the particular lifestyle it may lead as being private life, family life or home. (*G and E v Norway*, p. 35 – *construction of hydroelectric plant in a very small area of land populated by Lapps – no breach on the facts*)

- Likewise, business premises are protected:

  . . . activities which are related to a profession or business may well be conducted from a person's private residence and activities which are not so related may well be carried on in an office or commercial premises . . . it may not always be possible to draw precise distinctions. (*Niemietz v Germany*, para. 30)

29.2.2   *Protocol 1, Article 1*

Key ECHR cases

Gasus Dosier- und Fördertechnik GmbH v Netherlands (1995) 20 EHRR 403, ECtHR
James v UK (1986) 8 EHRR 123, ECtHR

Antoniades v UK (1990) 64 DR 232, ECmHR[CD]
Durini v Italy (1994) 76-A DR 76, ECmHR
Association of General Practitioners v Denmark (1989) 62 DR 226, ECmHR[CD]
DP v UK (1986) 51 DR 195, ECmHR
Howard v UK (1985) 52 DR 198, ECmHR[CD]
Panikian v Bulgaria (1997) 24 EHRR CD 63, ECmHR[CD]
S v UK (1984) 41 DR 226, ECmHR

ECHR principles

- Protocol 1, Article 1, ECHR entitles everyone to the peaceful enjoyment of their possessions.

- Interference with peaceful enjoyment of possessions is permitted, but only where it can be shown to be in the public interest, lawful and proportionate.

- 'Possessions' (for the purposes of Protocol 1, Article 1) covers not just property and chattels, but also acquired rights with economic interest; including the reversionary rights of landlords (*James v UK*, para. 38), tenants' interests under a lease (*DP v UK*, p. 209) and licensees' interests under a contract (*Association of General Practitioners v Denmark*, p. 234; *Gasus Dosier- und Fördertechnik GmbH v Netherlands*, para. 53 – *contractual rights amount to acquired rights with economic interest*).

- In some circumstances, the notion of possessions under Protocol 1, Article 1 even extends to the benefit of covenants under a lease (*S v UK*, p. 232).

- Retrospective legislation extinguishing title – albeit title seized as part of a compulsory state nationalisation scheme – may not defeat Protocol 1, Article 1 rights:

    . . . the applicants had a 'possession' within the meaning of Article 1 of Protocol No. 1 even if their title was null and *void ab initio*. Thus, for about 35 years they possessed the apartment in question and were considered owners for all legal purposes. Moreover, it would be unreasonable to accept that a state may enact legislation which allows nullification *ab initio* of contracts or other titles to property and thus escape the responsibility for an interference with property rights under the Convention. (*Panikian v Bulgaria*, p. 67)

29.3   ACCESS AND OCCUPATION

Key ECHR cases

Buckley v UK (1996) 23 EHRR 101, ECtHR
Gillow v UK (1986) 11 EHRR 335, ECtHR

Howard v UK (1985) 52 DR 198, ECmHR[CD]
S v UK (1986) 47 DR 274, ECmHR
Wiggins v UK (1978) 13 DR 40, ECmHR
X v UK (1982) 28 DR 177, ECmHR

ECHR principles

- Implicit in the right to respect for a home under Article 8(1), is a right to access and occupation.

- This means that Article 8(1) can be engaged even before occupancy is taken up (*Gillow v UK*, para. 47).

- However, the right to access and occupation is not absolute; it can be restricted so long as any restrictions are lawful, necessary and proportionate (*Wiggins v UK*, p. 44 – *refusal of licence to Guernsey resident after divorce not subject to disproportionate interference since offered alternatives*; *Gillow v UK*, paras 47 and 58 – *Channel Islands strict residential housing control pursued legitimate aim of regulating population to prevent overdevelopment but was disproportionate when prevented occupancy*; *Buckley v UK*, paras 60 and 84 – *not disproportionate to refuse planning permission to enable gypsies to live in caravans on their own land*; *X v UK*, p. 183 – *compulsory purchase not disproportionate given that housing was no longer habitable*; *Howard v UK* – *compulsory purchase not disproportionate since land was in need of improvement*; *S v UK* p. 278).

Relevant Canadian cases

Godbout v Longueuil City [1997] 3 SCR 844

- For a public employer to stipulate where employees should live will be very hard to justify unless they perform essential functions which require proximity (*Godbout v Longueuil City*, para. 91 – *requirement that municipal workers live within city borders unacceptable under the Charter*).

29.4   PEACEFUL ENJOYMENT

Key ECHR cases

Fredin v Sweden (1991) 13 EHRR 784, ECtHR
Guerra and others v Italy (1998) 26 EHRR 357, ECtHR
López Ostra v Spain (1994) 20 EHRR 277, ECtHR
Osman v UK (1998) 29 EHRR 245, ECtHR

Whiteside v UK (1994) 76-A DR 80, ECmHR[CD]

ECHR principles

- Article 8, ECHR guarantees individuals the right to peaceful enjoyment of their homes.

- Severe pollution is likely to breach this right (*Fredin v Sweden; López Ostra v Spain; Guerra and others v Italy*).

- As are harassment and vandalism (*Whiteside v UK; Osman v UK*).

- In relation to the environment, see **Section 30**.

29.5   EVICTION

Key ECHR cases

Larkos v Cyprus (18 February 1999), ECtHR
Saffi v Italy (28 July 1999), ECtHR
Spadea and Scalabrino v Italy (1995) 21 EHRR 482, ECtHR
Velosa Bareto v Portugal (1996) A/334, ECtHR

S v UK (1986) 47 DR 274, ECmHR
Wood v UK (1997) 24 EHRR CD 69, ECmHR[CD]

ECHR principles

- Eviction interferes with Article 8(1) rights and has to be justified as lawful, necessary and proportionate. (But see *S v UK – no Article 8(1) right to succession where no legal interest in premises*.)

- The protection of the rights of others is a legitimate basis for eviction (*Wood v UK*, pp. 70–71 – *moneylenders had a right to secure their loan in repossession proceedings*).

- So long as there is no discrimination in policy or practice, Article 14 can be relied upon in eviction proceedings even where there is no suggestion that the eviction itself breaches Article 8, because the complaint is within the ambit of Article 8 (*Larkos v Cyprus*, para. 28 – *tenants of government agency treated differently from those renting from private landlords*).

- But the suspension of eviction orders will not necessarily breach Protocol 1, Article 1 property rights (*Spadea and Scalabrino v Italy*, paras 31 and 40 – *reasonable and proportionate aim of preventing a large number of people potentially all becoming homeless; Velosa Bareto v Portugal*, p. 215 – *right of repossession could be limited in the public interest to protect the well-being of tenants where landlord had no urgent need of property*).

- Even court extensions of leases can be justified as emergency measures to deal with chronic housing shortages (*Saffi v Italy*).

- Failure to implement eviction orders does not amount to a deprivation of property, but may amount to 'control' (*Saffi v Italy*, para. 46).

29.6   INTERFERENCE WITH PROPERTY RIGHTS

Key ECHR cases

James v UK (1986) 8 EHRR 123, ECtHR
Mellacher v Austria (1989) 12 EHRR 391, ECtHR
Scollo v Italy (1995) 22 EHRR 514, ECtHR
Spadea and Scalabrino v Italy (1995) 21 EHRR 482, ECtHR

Antoniades v UK (1990) 64 DR 232, ECmHR[CD]
App. No. 15434/89 v UK (1990), ECmHR
Katte Klitsche de la Grange v Italy (1994) A293B, ECmHR
Kilbourn v UK (16 May 1985), ECmHR
Wasa Liv Omsesidigt Forsakringbolaget valands Pensionsstiftelse v Sweden (1988) 58 DR 163, ECmHR[CD]
X v Austria (1979) 3 EHRR 285, ECmHR

ECHR principles

- Interference with peaceful enjoyment of possessions is permitted under Protocol 1, Article 1, but only where it can be shown to be in the public interest, lawful and proportionate.

- The public interest in this context is a broad concept:

  The taking of property in pursuance of a policy calculated to enhance social justice within the community can properly be described as being 'in the public interest' . . . (*James v UK*, para. 49 – *statute conferred a right to long leaseholders to acquire the freehold of Duke of Westminster's property in London*)

- The community at large need not directly benefit from the measure in question provided legitimate 'social, economic or other policies' are being pursued (*James v UK*, paras 46–47 – *elimination of social injustice through leasehold reform was a legitimate aim*). Examples include preventing widespread homelessness (*Spadea and Scalabrino v Italy*, paras 31–32 – *eviction orders suspended against old and infirm tenants and rents frozen to prevent housing crisis*); protecting the interests of tenants where there is a shortage of cheap housing (*X v Austria*, p. 293; *Antoniades v UK*, p. 236 – *rent control legislation*; *Kilbourn v UK*); and significant rent reductions to make accommodation available for the less affluent (*Mellacher v Austria*, para. 47 – *reductions of up to 79% did not violate freedom of contract*; *App. No. 15434/89 v UK* – *not disproportionate to reduce rents by up to £45 to ensure compliance with Rent Acts*).

- However, a distinction has to be drawn between interference with property and deprivation of property; the latter will usually breach Protocol 1, Article 1 where no compensation is paid (*Katte Klitsche de la Grange v Italy*), although this need not necessarily be at full value (*James v UK*, para. 54 – *where state pursuing economic reform or social justice less than full market value acceptable as compensation*).

THE ENVIRONMENT

Key ECHR cases

Fredin v Sweden (1991) 13 EHRR 784, ECtHR
Guerra and others v Italy (1998) 26 EHRR 357, ECtHR
López Ostra v Spain (1994) 20 EHRR 277, ECtHR
McGinley and Egan v UK (1998) 27 EHRR 1, ECtHR
Pine Valley Developments and others v Ireland (1991) 14 EHRR 319, ECtHR

ECHR principles

- Article 8, ECHR guarantees individuals the right to peaceful enjoyment of their homes.

- Excessive noise, harassment and/or pollution can interfere with this right and, as a result, the relevant authorities may come under a duty to protect individuals from such interference (*López Ostra v Spain*; *Guerra and others v Italy*). For positive obligations generally, see **1.8**.

- There is no need to show actual damage to health:

    . . . severe environmental pollution may affect individuals' well-being and prevent them from enjoying their homes in such a way as to affect their private and family life adversely, without, however, seriously endangering their health. (*Lopez-Ostra v Spain*)

- One means of protecting individuals from pollution is to exercise control of property rights by effective licensing policies; protection of the environment is a legitimate basis for refusing, revoking or attaching conditions to a planning or operating licence (*Fredin v Sweden*; *Pine Valley Developments and others v Ireland*, para. 57).

- This has to be balanced with the rights of property owners; but an important element in the balancing exercise is the risk they take in purchasing land for potential development (*Pine Valley Developments and others v Ireland*).

- The duty on the relevant authorities to take action to protect individuals from severe pollution and serious health risks is most acute when the authorities, themselves, have created the threat:

    Where a Government engages in hazardous activities such as those in issue in the present case, which might have hidden adverse consequences on the health of those involved in such activities, respect for private and family life under Article 8 requires that an effective and accessible procedure be established which enables persons to seek all relevant and appropriate information. (*McGinley and Egan v UK*, para. 101)

- But it also extends to situations where others are responsible for pollution:

  > Whether the question is analysed in terms of the positive duty on the state to take reasonable and appropriate measures to secure the applicant's rights under paragraph 1 of Article 8 or in terms of an interference by a public authority to be justified in accordance with paragraph 2, the applicable principles are broadly similar. (*López-Ostra v Spain*; *Guerra and others v Italy*, para. 51)

- So where the relevant authorities are aware that environmental harm may be caused from pollution from a particular location or plant, they may come under a duty to inform those living in the neighbourhood so that they can make an informed decision about their course of action, even if the authorities are not primarily responsible:

  > [The state] cannot be said to have 'interfered' with the applicants' private or family life; they complained not of an act by the state but its failure to act. However, although the object of Article 8 is essentially that of protecting the individual against arbitrary interference by the public authorities, it does not merely compel the state to abstain from such interference: in addition to this primarily negative undertaking, there may be positive obligations inherent in effective respect for private or family life. (*Guerra and others v Italy*, para. 58 – *delay in passing information to residents who lived near 'high risk' chemical factory*)

- Equally, the relevant authorities may be under a duty to assist those in the neighbourhood seeking to prevent pollution, rather than hindering them (*López-Ostra v Spain* – *local authority took no steps to limit pollution from a waste plant and prolonged exposure to the effects by opposing residents' court proceedings to close it down*).

FREEDOM OF THOUGHT, CONSCIENCE AND RELIGION

31.1 THE RIGHT TO THOUGHT, CONSCIENCE AND RELIGION

Key ECHR cases

Buscarini v San Marino (18 February 1999), ECtHR
Darby v Sweden (1990) 13 EHRR 774, ECtHR
Dudgeon v UK (1981) 4 EHRR 149, ECtHR
Hoffmann v Austria (1993) 17 EHRR 293, ECtHR
Johnston and others v Ireland (1986) 9 EHRR 203, ECtHR
Kokkinakis v Greece (1993) 17 EHRR 397, ECtHR
Norris v Ireland (1988) 13 EHRR 186, ECtHR
Valsamis v Greece (1996) 24 EHRR 294, ECtHR

Ahmad v UK (1982) 4 EHRR 126, ECmHR
Angelini v Sweden (1986) 51 DR 41, ECmHR
Arrowsmith v UK (1978) 19 DR 5, ECmHR
Chappell v UK (1987) 53 DR 241, ECmHR[CD]
Iskcon v UK (1994) 76A DR 90, ECmHR[CD]
McFeeley v UK (1980) 20 DR 44, ECmHR
Omkarananda and the Divine Light Zentrum v Switzerland (1981) 25 DR 105, ECmHR
Vereniging Rechtswinkels Utrecht v Netherlands (1986) 46 DR 200, ECmHR
X v UK (App. No. 18187/91, 10 February 1993), ECmHR
X and Church of Scientology v Sweden (1979) 16 DR 68, ECmHR

ECHR principles

- Article 9(1), ECHR provides: 'Everyone has the right to freedom of thought, conscience and religion; this right includes freedom to change his religion or belief and freedom, either alone or in community with others and in public or private, to manifest his religion or belief, in worship, teaching, practice and observance.'

- Freedom of thought, conscience and religion is absolute; it cannot be restricted.

- Freedom to manifest religion or belief is qualified; it can be restricted so long as any restriction is lawful, legitimate, necessary and proportionate.

- The scope of protection offered by Article 9 is wide and includes:

  (a) Islam (*Ahmad v UK*, para. 4);
  (b) the Krishna consciousness movement (*Iskcon v UK*, p. 106);
  (c) Jehovah's Witnesses (*Kokkinakis v Greece*, para. 32; *Hoffmann v Austria*, para. 33);
  (d) the Divine Light Zentrum (*Omkarananda and the Divine Light Zentrum v Switzerland*, p. 117; equated to an association with religious and philosophical objects capable of exercising Article 9 rights);
  (e) the Church of Scientology (*X and Church of Scientology v Sweden*);
  (f) Druidism (*Chappell v UK*, p. 246).

- It also covers non-religious beliefs such as pacifism (*Arrowsmith v UK*, p. 19) and veganism (*X v UK*):

  > [Article 9] is, in its religious dimension, one of the most vital elements that go to make up the identity of believers and of their conception of life, but it is also a precious asset for atheists, agnostics, sceptics and the unconcerned. (*Kokkinakis v Greece*, para. 31)

- However, purely idealistic or altruistic beliefs are not covered (*Vereniging Rechtswinkels Utrecht v Netherlands*, p. 202); nor are political beliefs (*McFeeley v UK*, p. 77 – IRA *prisoners claiming 'special category status' (including the right to wear their own clothes) on the basis of their beliefs could not rely on Article 9, but may be protected under Article 10 as free expression*).

- Indoctrination is not permissible under Article 9; but so long as membership is not compulsory, the maintaining of an established church does not offend this provision (*Darby v Sweden*, para. 45).

- Neither does the promulgation of policies based on religious beliefs (*Johnston and others v Ireland*, para. 63).

- However, a requirement to take an oath that includes swearing allegiance to a particular religion is not compatible with Article 9 (*Buscarini v San Marino*, para. 39).

Other international human rights standards

- Article 18 of the International Covenant on Civil and Political Rights (freedom of religion) distinguishes the freedom of thought, conscience, religion or belief from the freedom to manifest . . . [no] limitations whatsoever on the freedom of thought and conscience or on the freedom to have or adopt a religion or belief of one's choice no one can be compelled to reveal his thoughts or adherence to a religion or belief (UN Human Rights Committee, General Comment 22, para. 3).

- Article 18 protects theistic, non-theistic and atheistic beliefs, as well as the right not to profess any religion or belief. The terms 'religion' and 'belief' are to be broadly construed. [It] is not limited in its application to traditional religions or to religions and beliefs with institutional characteristics or practices analogous to those of traditional religions . . . [matter of] concern any tendency to discriminate against any religion or belief for any reason, including the fact that they are newly established, or represent religious minorities that may be the subject of hostility on the part of the a predominant religious community (UN Human Rights Committee, General Comment 22, para. 2).

- Article 18(4) permits instruction in state schools in subjects such as the general history of religions and ethics if it is given in a neutral and objective way [however] state education that includes instruction in a particular religion or belief is inconsistent with Article 18(4) unless provision is made for non-discriminatory exemptions or alternatives that would accommodate the wishes of parents and guardians (UN Human Rights Committee, General Comment 22, para. 6).

Relevant Canadian cases

Peel (Regional Municipality) v *Great Atlantic and Pacific Co. of Canada Ltd* [1992] 3 SCR 762
Prior v *The Queen* [1988] 2 FC 371, FCTD
R v *Big M Drug Mart* [1985] 1 SCR 295
R v *Edwards Books and Art Ltd* [1986] 2 SCR 713
Roach v *Canada* [1994] 2 FC 406, CA
Schachtschneider v *Canada* [1994] 1 FC 40, FCA

- Freedom of religion is a broad concept, to be protected from direct and indirect infringement:

    The essence of the concept of freedom of religion is the right to entertain such religious beliefs as a person chooses, the right to declare religious beliefs openly and without fear of hindrance or reprisal, and the right to manifest religious belief by worship and practice or by teaching and dissemination provided such manifestations do not injure his or her neighbours or their parallel rights to hold and manifest beliefs and opinions of their own. (*R* v *Big M Drug Mart*, pp. 336 and 346)

- There is prima facie infringement if a law or policy coerces or restrains the exercise of religious or conscientious beliefs (*Prior* v *the Queen*; *Schachtschneider* v *Canada*; *Roach* v *Canada*).

- But inquiring about religious faith will not necessarily infringe the rights to freedom of religion, so long as there is a good reason for doing so (*R* v *Edwards Books and Art Ltd*; *Peel (Regional Municipality)* v *Great Atlantic and Pacific Co. of Canada Ltd*).

31.2   MANIFESTING RELIGION AND BELIEFS

Key ECHR cases

Jewish Liturgical Association Cha'Are Shalom Ve Tsedek v *France* (27 June 2000), ECtHR
Kokkinakis v *Greece* (1993) 17 EHRR 397, ECtHR

A v Switzerland (1984) 38 DR 219, ECmHR
Arrowsmith v UK (1978) 19 DR 5, ECmHR
Autio v Finland (1991) 72 DR 245, ECmHR
Chappell v UK (1987) 53 DR 241, ECmHR[CD]
C v UK (1983) 37 DR 142, ECmHR
D.S. and E.S. v UK (1990) 65 DR 245, ECmHR
Iskcon v UK (1994) 76A DR 90, ECmHR[CD]
Johansen v Norway (1985) 44 DR 155, ECmHR
Khan v UK (1986) 48 DR 253, ECmHR
N v Sweden (1984) 40 DR 203, ECmHR
Seven Individuals v Sweden (1982) 29 DR 104, ECmHR
Stedman v UK (1997) 89-A DR 104, ECmHR[CD]
X v Austria (App. No. 5591/72), 43 Coll 161, ECmHR
X v Germany (1981) 24 DR 137, ECmHR
X v UK (1981) 22 DR 27, ECmHR

ECHR principles

- Article 9(1), ECHR provides that 'Everyone has the right to freedom . . ., either alone or in community with others and in public or private, to manifest his religion or belief, in worship, teaching, practice and observance.'

- It is a qualified right and can be restricted so long as any restriction is lawful, legitimate, necessary and proportionate.

- In this context, 'practice' does not cover every act 'which is motivated or influenced by a religion or belief':

  Article 9 primarily protects the sphere of personal beliefs and religious creeds, i.e., the area which is sometimes called the forum internum. In addition it protects acts which are intimately linked to these attitudes, such as acts of worship or devotion which are aspects of the practice of a religion or belief in a generally recognised form.
  However, in protecting this personal sphere, Article 9 of the Convention does not always guarantee the right to behave in the public sphere in a way which is dictated by belief:– for instance by refusing to pay certain taxes because part of the revenue so raised may be applied for military expenditure. (*C v UK*, p. 147)

- Manifestation does include the right to try to convince one's neighbour (*Kokkinakis v Greece*) and to undertake a particular diet (*D.S. and E.S. v UK*, p. 247 – *kosher diet for prisoners*).

- But not necessarily the distribution of leaflets urging soldiers in Northern Ireland to disaffect, protection only extending to:

  . . . public declarations proclaiming generally the idea of pacifism and urging the acceptance of a commitment to non-violence . . . (*Arrowsmith v UK*, p. 20)

- Conscientious objectors cannot derive the right to alternative military service from the ECHR:

  [The Commission] has also taken into consideration the terms of Article 4(3)(b) of the Convention which states that forced or compulsory labour shall not include 'any service of a military character or, in case of conscientious objectors in countries where they are recognised, service exacted instead of compulsory military service'. This provision clearly shows that, by including the words 'in countries where they are recognised' in Article 4(3)(b), a choice is left to the High Contracting Parties to the Convention whether or not to recognise conscientious objectors and, if so required, to provide some substitute service for them. (*X v Austria*; see also *N v Sweden*; *A v Switzerland*; *Johansen v Norway*; *Autio v Finland*)

- Ritual slaughter is capable of constituting a rite and thus can come within the ambit of Article 9; but:

  . . . the fact that the exceptional rules designed to regulate the practice of ritual slaughter permit only ritual slaughterers authorised by approved religious bodies to engage in it does not in itself lead to the conclusion that there has been an interference with freedom to manifest one's religion. The Court considers . . . that it is in the general interest to avoid unregulated slaughter, carried out in conditions of doubtful hygiene, and that it is therefore preferable, if there is to be ritual slaughter, for it to be performed in slaughter-houses supervised by the public authorities.
  In the Court's opinion, there would only be interference with the freedom to manifest one's religion if the illegality of performing ritual slaughter made it impossible for ultra-orthodox Jews to eat meat from animals slaughtered in accordance with the religious prescriptions they considered applicable. (*Jewish Liturgical Association Cha'Are Shalom Ve Tsedek v France*, paras 73, 77 and 80)

Relevant Canadian cases

Beena B v Children's Aid Society of Metropolitan Toronto [1995] 1 SCR 315
R v Big M Drug Mart [1985] 1 SCR 295
R v Edwards Books and Art Ltd [1986] 2 SCR 713
R v Grant [1993] 3 SCR 223
R v Gruenke [1991] 3 SCR 263
R v Hothi et al. (1985) 33 Man R (3d)
R v Morgentaler et al. [1988] 1 SCR 30
Roach v Canada (1994) 2 FC 406, CA
Ross v New Brunswick School District No. 15 [1996] 1 SCR 825

- Religious conduct covers entertaining religious beliefs, declaring them, manifesting them by worship and practice (*R v Big M Drug Mart*); and teaching and dissemination even where the beliefs are intolerant of others (*Ross v New Brunswick School District No. 15*).

- Certain conduct is clearly religious in nature, such as religious expression and observing the Sabbath (*R v Big M Drug Mart*).

- But the right to manifest religion includes the right of parents to bring up their children according to their religious beliefs, e.g., the choice of medical treatment (*Beena B v Children's Aid Society of Metropolitan Toronto* – decision of parents to prohibit doctors from giving a blood transfusion to their baby daughter was protected by freedom of religion but interference justified).

- In addition, symbolic conduct, e.g., diet or dress codes, is also protected (*R v Grant*; *R v Hothi et al.*).

- Furthermore, conduct which takes place in a secular context, e.g., refusal to fight, abortion, may be covered if motivated by religious or conscientious beliefs (*R v Morgentaler et al.*).

- In this context, the decision to terminate a pregnancy is a 'matter of conscience' (R v Morgentaler et al., pp. 175–6).

Relevant New Zealand cases

Re J (An Infant) [1996] 2 NZLR 134

- A child's right to life is paramount and takes priority over the exercise of other fundamental freedoms, such as parental rights to freedom of religion:

  > The parents' right to practise their religion cannot extend to imperil the life or health of the child . . . We define the scope of the parental right under s. 15 of the Bill of the Rights to manifest their religion in practice so as to exclude doing or omitting anything likely to place at risk the life, health or welfare of their children. We conclude there was no breach of the parents' rights. (*Re J (An Infant)* – *refusal of Jehovah's Witnesses parents to agree to blood transfusion for child*)

31.3 PROTECTING RELIGIOUS AND OTHER BELIEFS

Key ECHR cases

Hoffmann v Austria (1993) 17 EHRR 293, ECtHR
Kokkinakis v Greece (1993) 17 EHRR 397, ECtHR
Manoussakis v Greece (1996) 23 EHRR 387, ECtHR
Otto Preminger Institute v Austria (1994) 19 EHRR 34, ECtHR
Serif v Greece (14 December 1999), ECtHR

Choudhury v UK (App. No. 17439/90, 5 March 1991), ECmHR[CD]
Dubowska and Skup v Poland (1997) 24 EHRR CD 75, ECmHR[CD]
Lemon v UK (1982) 28 DR 77, ECmHR
M v Bulgaria (1996) 22 EHRR CD 101, ECmHR[CD]

ECHR principles

- The relevant authorities have a duty to ensure that people who hold religious or other beliefs are able to enjoy them peacefully:

  > . . . there may be certain positive obligations on the part of a State inherent in an effective respect for rights guaranteed under Article 9 of the Convention, which may involve the adoption of measures designed to secure respect for freedom of religion even in the sphere of the relations of individuals between themselves. Such measures may, in certain circumstances, constitute a legal means of ensuring that an individual will not be disturbed in his worship by the activities of others. (*Dubowska and Skup v Poland*, p. 78; see also *Otto Preminger Institute v Austria*, para. 47)

- Pluralism demands that there be balance between different religions and beliefs (*Lemon v UK*, pp. 82–83 – *law of blasphemy acceptable to protect the Article 9 rights of Christians*; *Choudhury v UK* – *but not necessary for Muslims*).

- But restrictions on freedom of religion may be necessary to reconcile the interests of various religious groups; but they can only be justified in so far as they correspond to a 'pressing social need' and are 'proportionate':

. . . the Court does not consider that, in democratic societies, the State needs to take measures to ensure that religious communities remain or are brought under a unified leadership.

Although the Court recognises that tension is created in situations where a religious or any other community becomes divided, it considers that this is one of the unavoidable consequences of pluralism. The role of the authorities in such circumstances is not to remove the cause of tension by eliminating pluralism, but to ensure that the competing groups tolerate each other. (*Serif* v *Greece*, paras 49, 52 and 53)

Relevant Canadian cases

Adler v *Ontario* [1996] 3 SCR 609

- The duty of the state not to interfere with religious freedom does not include a corresponding obligation to provide positive assistance to individuals in furtherance of their religion (*Adler* v *Ontario*).

Relevant New Zealand cases

Mendelssohn v *Attorney-General* [1999] 2 NZLR 268

- While the state is under a duty not to interfere unduly in the exercise of freedom of religion, it is not under a positive duty to protect it (*Mendelssohn* v *Attorney-General*, p. 273 – *failure of A-G to restore a charitable trust to its original religious purposes*).

31.4   OBEYING THE LAW

Key ECHR cases

Bouessel du Bourg v *France* (1993) 16 EHRR CD 49, ECmHR
C v *UK* (1983) 37 DR 142, ECmHR
Iskcon v *UK* (1994) 76A DR 90, ECmHR[CD]
Karakuzey v *Germany* (1996) 23 EHRR CD 92, ECmHR[CD]
V v *Netherlands* (1984) 39 DR 267, ECmHR
X v *UK* (1976) 5 DR 100, ECmHR
X v *UK* (1978) 14 DR 234, ECmHR
X v *UK* (1982) 28 DR 5, ECmHR

ECHR principles

- The manifestation of religious or other beliefs rarely justifies breaking a law of general application:

   The obligation to pay taxes is a general one which has no specific conscientious implications in itself. Its neutrality in this sense is also illustrated by the fact that no taxpayer can influence or determine the purpose for which his or her contributions are applied, once they are collected. Furthermore, the power of taxation is expressly recognised by the Convention system and is ascribed to the State by Article 1, First Protocol.

It follows that Article 9 does not confer on the applicant the right to refuse, on the basis of his convictions to abide by legislation, the operation of which is provided for by the Convention, and which applies neutrally and generally in the public sphere, without impinging on the freedoms guaranteed by Article 9. (*C v UK*, p. 147 – *Quaker's objection on religious grounds to paying taxes for defence rejected*; *Bouessel du Bourg v France*, p. 49 – *denial of request to withhold part of social security contributions on grounds that applicant objected to payments being used to fund abortions*)

- Similarly attempts to avoid paying pension contributions (*V v Netherlands*, p. 268), maintenance orders (*Karakuzey v Germany*, p. 94) and to circumvent planning restrictions (*Iskcon v UK*, p. 107) – and to be allowed to marry a 14-year-old (*Khan v UK*) or have ashes scattered in a particular location (*X v Germany*) – have all failed.

- Generally speaking, the same is true where contractual obligations in the employment sphere clash with religious beliefs (*Stedman v UK*, p. 108; *X v UK*, pp. 37–8: see **37.4**).

- However, where legislation does interfere with the private sphere, it has to be justified under Article 9(2) as being legitimate, lawful, necessary and proportionate (*X v UK*, p. 235 – *requirement that Sikhs wear crash-helmets could be justified on the grounds of public health*; *X v UK*, p. 101 – *prisoner's access to a religious book denied on basis that contained chapter on martial arts – allowed to protect rights of others*; *X v UK* (1982), p. 38 – *making Sikh prisoner clean floors could transgress his beliefs but was necessary for the protection of public health*; *Chappell v UK*, p. 247 – *closing Stonehenge to Druids during the solstice might be justified on public safety grounds*; *Seven Individuals v Sweden*, pp. 114–15 – *Swedish law which criminalised parental chastisement of children did not violate Article 9*; *Kokkinakis v Greece*, para. 49 – *prohibition on all proselytism could not be justified as fulfilling a pressing social need*).

31.5 PROSELYTISM

Key ECHR cases

Kokkinakis v Greece (1993) 17 EHRR 397, ECtHR
Larissis v Greece (1998) 27 EHRR 329, ECtHR

X and Church of Scientology v Sweden (1979) 16 DR 68, ECmHR

ECHR principles

- In cases of proselytism, a careful balance should be struck between the rights of those who want to convert others and the rights of those who do not want to be converted.

- It is legitimate to prohibit improper proselytism:

  [Improper proselytism is the] corruption or deformation of [true evangelism]. It may take the form of activities offering material or social advantages with a view to gaining new members for a Church or exerting improper pressure on people in distress or in need; it may even entail the use of violence or brainwashing; more generally, it is not compatible with respect for the freedom of thought, conscience and religion of others. (*Kokkinakis v Greece*, para. 48; *Larissis v Greece*, p. 506; see also *X and Church of Scientology v Sweden*, p. 72 in relation to advertising and marketing)

- But there should not be a blanket ban on all proselytism (*Kokkinakis v Greece*, para. 49).

31.6   BLASPHEMY

Key ECHR cases

Kokkinakis v Greece (1993) 17 EHRR 397, ECtHR
Otto Preminger Institute v Austria (1994) 19 EHRR 34, ECtHR
Wingrove v UK (1996) 24 EHRR 1, ECtHR

Lemon v UK (1982) 28 DR 77, ECmHR

ECHR principles

- Pluralism demands tolerance of views critical of religion(s):

  Those who choose to exercise the freedom to manifest their religion, irrespective of whether they do as members of a religious majority or a minority, cannot reasonably expect to be exempt from all criticism. They must tolerate and accept the denial by others of . . . their faith. (*Otto Preminger Institute v Austria*, para. 47)

- But if the protection afforded to religious beliefs in Article 9 is to have any meaning, a balance must be struck:

  The respect for the religious feelings of believers as guaranteed in Article 9 can legitimately be thought to have been violated by provocative portrayals of objects of religious veneration; and such portrayals can be regarded as malicious violation of the spirit of tolerance, which must also be a feature of democratic society. The Convention is to be read as a whole and therefore the interpretation and application of Article 10 in the present case must be in harmony with the logic of the Convention. (*Otto Preminger Institute v Austria*, para. 47; see also *Kokkinakis v Greece*, para. 48)

- Therefore, maintaining an offence of blasphemy is not automatically a breach of Article 9 (*Wingrove v UK*; *Lemon v UK*).

FREEDOM OF EXPRESSION

32.1   THE STATUS OF FREEDOM OF EXPRESSION

Key ECHR cases

Castells v Spain (1992) 14 EHRR 445, ECtHR
Ezelin v France (1991) 14 EHRR 362, ECtHR
Handyside v UK (1976) 1 EHRR 737, ECtHR
Jersild v Denmark (1994) 19 EHRR 1, ECtHR
Lingens v Austria (1986) 8 EHRR 103, ECtHR
Otto Preminger Institute v Austria (1994) 19 EHRR 34, ECtHR
Sunday Times v UK (No. 2) (1991) 14 EHRR 229, ECtHR

ECHR principles

- Freedom of expression has frequently been referred to as 'one of the essential foundations of a democratic society' (*Handyside v UK*, para. 49; *Jersild v Denmark*, para. 31) in recognition that it is often a prerequisite for the enjoyment of many other rights.

- The media, in particular, attract special protection because of their role as a public watchdog:

    Freedom of the press affords the public one of the best means of discovering and forming an opinion of the ideas and attitudes of their political leaders. In particular, it gives politicians the opportunity to reflect and comment on the preoccupations of public opinion; it thus enables everyone to participate in the free political debate which is at the very core of the concept of a democratic society. (*Castells v Spain*, para. 43)

- Therefore any restrictions on freedom of expression are subjected to very close scrutiny, since as a matter of general principle:

    . . . the necessity for any restriction of freedom of expression must be convincingly established. (*Sunday Times v UK (No. 2)*, para. 50)

32.2   THE SCOPE OF ARTICLE 10

Key ECHR cases

Autronic AG v Switzerland (1990) 12 EHRR 485, ECtHR
Barthold v Germany (1985) 7 EHRR 383, ECtHR

Handyside v UK (1976) 1 EHRR 737, ECtHR
Hashman and Harrup v UK (1999) 30 EHRR 241, ECtHR
Janowski v Poland (1999) 29 EHRR 705, ECtHR
Lehideux and Isorni v France (23 September 1998), ECtHR
Müller v Switzerland (1988) 13 EHRR 212, ECtHR
Otto Preminger Institute v Austria (1994) 19 EHRR 34, ECtHR

K v Austria (1993) A 255-B, ECmHR
Stevens v UK (1986) 46 DR 245, ECmHR

ECHR principles

32.2.1 *The broad nature of Article 10*

- Freedom of expression is a very broad concept under Article 10.

- It covers political speech, commercial speech and artistic expression.

- It also covers valueless or offensive speech:

  > [Freedom of expression] is applicable not only to 'information' or 'ideas' that are favourably received or regarded as inoffensive or as a matter of indifference, but also to those that offend, shock or disturb the State or any sector of the population. Such are the demands of . . . pluralism, tolerance and broadmindedness, without which there is no democratic society. (*Handyside v UK*, para. 49)

- However, public officials are entitled to be protected from offensive and abusive verbal attacks in the public performance of their duties, except (by implication) where the remarks form part of an open discussion on matters of public concern or involve freedom of the press (*Janowski v Poland*, paras 32–34).

- A publication which is part of an ongoing debate amongst historians about the events in question and their interpretation, and not the negation or revision of clearly established facts such as the Holocaust, attracts Article 10 protection, despite the fact that it is deeply offensive to some (*Lehideux and Isorni v France*, para. 47).

- And as time passes, the appropriate response to certain types of publication changes. The lapse of time makes it in appropriate to deal with some remarks 40 years on with the same severity as 10 or 20 years previously. This forms part of the efforts that every country must make to debate its own history openly and dispassionately (*Lehideux and Isorni v France*, para. 54).

- But 'like any other remark directed against the Convention's underlying values . . . the justification of a pro-Nazi policy could not be allowed to enjoy the protection afforded by Article 10' (*Lehideux and Isorni v France*, para. 53).

32.2.2 *The medium of expression*

- The medium as well as the content of expression is protected under Article 10 (*Autronic AG v Switzerland*, para. 47).

- Article 10 therefore covers words (including adverts) (*Barthold v Germany*, para. 42), pictures (*Müller v Switzerland*, para. 27), video and cinema (*Otto Preminger*

Institute v Austria, para. 43), electronic transmission, and even conduct intended to convey ideas or information, such as wearing particular clothes (*Stevens v UK*, p. 247).

- Protest which takes the form of impeding the activities of others (such as fox-hunting) is nonetheless an expression of an opinion and is therefore protected by Article 10 (*Hashman and Harrup v UK*, para. 28).

Relevant Canadian cases

Irwin Toy v Quebec [1989] 1 SCR 927
Prostitution Reference [1990] 1 SCR 1123
R v Keegstra [1990] 3 SCR 697
R v Zundel [1992] 2 SCR 731
RJR Macdonald v Canada [1995] 3 SCR 199
Rocket v Royal College of Dental Surgeons [1990] 2 SCR 232

- In line with the general principle that Charter rights would be given a generous interpretation, expression is defined in broad terms:

    Activity is expressive if it attempts to convey meaning. (*Irwin Toy v Quebec*, p. 968)

- Only activity that is 'purely physical and does not convey or attempt to convey meaning' is excluded (*Irwin Toy v Quebec*, p. 968).

- The mere fact that the means of communication chosen are criminal does not automatically exclude the possibility of Charter protection, e.g., preventing advertising by dentists (*Rocket v Royal College of Dental Surgeons*) and tobacco companies (*RJR Macdonald v Canada*).

- But there are exceptions:

    . . . a murderer or a rapist cannot invoke freedom of expression in justification of the form of expression he has chosen. (*Prostitution Reference*, p. 1185)

32.3   LICENSING

Key ECHR cases

Groppera Radio AG v Switzerland (1990) 12 EHRR 321, ECtHR
Informationsverein Lentia v Austria (1993) 17 EHRR 93, ECtHR
Radio ABC v Austria (1997) 25 EHRR 185, ECtHR

Bellis v UK (1997) 24 EHRR CD 71, ECmHR[CD]
Brind v UK (1994) 77-A DR 42, ECmHR[CD]
Purcell v Ireland (1989) 70 DR 262, ECmHR
Radio X, S, W and A v Switzerland (1984) 37 DR 236, ECmHR
X v UK (1978) 16 DR 190, ECmHR

ECHR principles

- Article 10 specifically provides that 'This Article shall not prevent States from requiring the licensing of broadcasting, television or cinema enterprises.'

- Taking action against unlicensed broadcasters is therefore legitimate (*X v UK*, p. 192; *Radio X, S, W and A v Switzerland*, p. 240; *Bellis v UK*, p. 72).

- However, this provision cannot be used to regulate the *content* of broadcasts, only the technical means of broadcasting (*Groppera Radio AG v Switzerland*, para. 61): regulation of the contents has to be justified under Article 10(2) in the usual way.

- Since it is legitimate to attach conditions to licences intended to assure objectivity and balance, state monopolies in broadcasting are very difficult to justify:

  > Of all the means of ensuring that these values are respected, a public monopoly is one which imposes the greatest restrictions on freedom of expression . . . (*Informationsverein Lentia v Austria*, para. 39; see also *Radio ABC v Austria*, paras 31 and 33 – *only two frequencies reserved for non-state radio transmissions*)

32.4   PRIOR RESTRAINT

Key ECHR cases

Markt Intern Verlag GmbH and Klaus Beermann v Germany (1989) 12 EHRR 161, ECtHR
Observer and Guardian v UK (1991) 14 EHRR 153, ECtHR

ECHR principles

- Although not prohibited under Article 10, prior restraint should be a restriction of last resort:

  > . . . the dangers inherent in prior restraint are such that they call for the most careful scrutiny. (*Observer and Guardian v UK*, para. 60)

- Particularly in relation to news items:

  > . . . news is a perishable commodity and to delay its publication, even for a short period, may well deprive it of all its value and interest. (*Observer and Guardian v UK*, para. 60)

- And once information is in the public domain, restrictions on further publication will rarely, if ever, be justified (*Observer and Guardian v UK*, para. 60).

Relevant Canadian cases

BCGEU v BC (Vancouver Courthouse) [1988] 2 SCR 214
Canadian Newspapers Co. v Canada [1988] 1 SCR 122
Luscher v Revenue Canada (1985) 1 FC 85, CA
Re Ontario Film and Video Appreciation Society (1983) 41 OR (2d) 583, CA
Re Southam and the Queen (No. 1) (1983) 41 OR (2d) 113, CA
Re Southam and the Queen (No. 2) (1986) 53 OR (2d) 663, CA
Thomson Newspapers Co. v Canada [1998] 1 SCR 877

- Prior restraint can take many forms: film censorship (*Re Ontario Film and Video Appreciation Society*); import controls on books and magazines (*Luscher v Revenue Canada*); restricting access to the courts (*Re Southam and the Queen (No. 1)*); reporting restrictions (*Canadian Newspapers Co. v Canada*); prohibiting opinion polls three days before elections (*Thomson Newspapers Co. v Canada*); injunctions against picketing (*BCGEU v BC*).

- Unless strictly proportionate, it is likely to be struck down.

32.5 DEFAMATION PROCEEDINGS

Key ECHR cases

Lingens v Austria (1986) 8 EHRR 103, ECtHR
Nilsen and Johnsen v Norway (29 November 1999), ECtHR
Thorgeirson v Iceland (1992) 14 EHRR 843, ECtHR
Tolstoy Miloslavsky v UK (1995) 20 EHRR 442, ECtHR
Wabl v Austria (21 March 2000), ECtHR

Ediciones Tiempo SA v Spain (1989) 62 DR 247, ECmHR

ECHR principles

- Reputation is protected as an aspect of private life under Article 8 and under Article 10(2).

- Defamation proceedings are not, therefore, contrary to the ECHR in principle, so long as they are necessary and proportionate.

- The words actually used and the context will be important when assessing whether speech exceeds the limits of permissible criticism. In particular, oral statements made to the press require some latitude because the makers of such statements are unlikely to have had any real opportunity to reformulate, perfect or retract their words before publication (*Nilsen and Johnsen v Norway*, para. 48).

- When considering whether a restriction on free speech is necessary to protect an individual's reputation, the role played by that individual in the debate will be important; individuals who publish damning comments should expect harsh criticism in reply:

  . . . a degree of exaggeration should be tolerated in the context of such a heated and continuing public debate of affairs of general concern, whereon both sides professional reputations were at stake. (*Nilsen and Johnsen v Norway*, para. 52 – *reply to serious allegations of police brutality*)

- But an accusation that someone has deliberately lied exceeds the limits of permissible criticism if no factual basis for it can be established (*Nilsen and Johnsen v Norway*, para. 49).

- When considering whether the publication of a reply by a public figure to an attack on him or her breaches Article 10, the terms of the attack are important (*Wabl v Austria*, para. 40).

- Excessively high awards of damages in defamation proceedings are unlikely to satisfy the requirements of necessity and proportionality under Article 10 (*Tolstoy Miloslavsky v UK* – *£1.5 million awarded*).

- For truth defences, see **32.6**.

- A rule requiring publications to permit a right of reply, however, is not a breach of Article 10:

  > ... the purpose of the regulations governing the right of reply is to safeguard the interest of the public in receiving information from a variety of sources and thereby to guarantee the fullest possible access to information. (*Ediciones Tiempo SA v Spain*, p. 254)

32.6   TRUTH DEFENCES

Key ECHR cases

Bergens Tidende v Norway (2 May 2000), ECtHR
Hertel v Switzerland (25 August 1998), ECtHR
Lingens v Austria (1986) 8 EHRR 103, ECtHR
Thorgeirson v Iceland (1992) 14 EHRR 843, ECtHR

Bladet Tromso and Stensaas v Norway (1997) 23 EHRR CD 40, ECmHR[CD]
Ediciones Tiempo SA v Spain (1989) 62 DR 247, ECmHR

ECHR principles

- Any rule requiring authors/publishers to prove the truth of their assertions in criminal proceedings is likely to violate Article 10 (*Lingens v Austria*, para. 46; *Thorgeirson v Iceland*, para. 65).

- More generally, where a journalist makes factual statements derived from another source, the courts should consider whether there are any special grounds for dispensing with an obligation imposed on the journalist to verify the truth of the statements in question (*Bladet Tromso and Stensaas v Norway*).

- Any requirement to establish the truth of factual statements derived from other sources will depend on the nature and degree of the defamation in question and the extent to which the publisher could reasonably be expected to regard the source as reliable, judged at the time of publication and not with the benefit of hindsight:

  > In the view of the Court, the press should normally be entitled, when contributing to public debate on matters of legitimate concern, to rely on the contents of official reports without having to undertake independent research. (*Bladet Tromso and Stensaas v Norway*, paras 66 and 68)

- Where a newspaper carries articles with quotes and extracts from others which were credible and essentially accurate, defamation proceedings can amount to an unjustifiable interference with Article 10 rights:

  > By reason of the 'duties and responsibilities' inherent in the exercise of freedom of expression, the safeguard afforded by Article 10 to journalists in relation to reporting

on issues of general interest is subject to the proviso that they are acting in good faith in order to provide accurate and reliable information in accordance with the ethics of journalism . . .

The methods of objective and balanced reporting may vary considerably, depending among other things on the medium in question; it is not for the Court, any more than it is for the national courts, to substitute its own views for those of the press as to what techniques of reporting should be adopted by journalists . . . (*Bergens Tidende v Norway*, paras 53 and 57 – *women patients of a doctor complaining about the effects of his cosmetic surgery*)

- And proving the truth of stories and rumours in cases concerning allegations of police brutality is an unreasonable if not impossible task (*Thorgeirson v Iceland*, para. 65).

- A measure which restricts free speech in an area where there is little certainty about the truth of fears about health is likely to be disproportionate:

    It matters little that the opinion in question is a minority one and may appear to be devoid of merit since, in a sphere in which it is unlikely that any certainty exists, it would be particularly unreasonable to restrict freedom of expression only to generally accepted ideas. (*Hertel v Switzerland*, para. 50 – *health risks associated with microwave ovens*)

32.7   PUBLIC INTEREST DEFENCES

Key ECHR cases

Castells v Spain (1992) 14 EHRR 445, ECtHR
Fressoz and Roire v France (21 January 1999), ECtHR
Lingens v Austria (1986) 8 EHRR 103, ECtHR
Prager and Oberschlick v Austria (1995) 21 EHRR 1, ECtHR
Sürek v Turkey (No. 2) (8 July 1999), ECtHR
Thorgeirson v Iceland (1992) 14 EHRR 843, ECtHR

Bladet Tromso and Stensaas v Norway (1997) 23 EHRR CD 40, ECmHR[CD]

ECHR principles

- Whenever a publication concerns a public official or a matter of public interest, there are very strict limits on permissible restrictions:

    Whilst the press must not overstep the bounds set, *inter alia*, for the protection of the reputation of the others, it is nevertheless incumbent on it to impart information and ideas on political issues just as on those in other areas of public interest.
    . . . The limits of acceptable criticism are accordingly wider as regards a politician as such than as regards a private individual. Unlike the latter, the former inevitably and knowingly lays himself open to close scrutiny of every word and deed by both journalists and the public at large, and he must consequently display a greater degree of tolerance. No doubt Article 10(2) enables the reputation of others – that is to say, of all individuals – to be protected, and this protection extends to politicians too, even when they are not acting in their private capacity, but in such cases the requirements of such protection have to be weighed in relation to the interest of open discussion of

political issues. (*Lingens v Austria*, paras 41 and 42; see also *Prager and Oberschlick v Austria*, paras 57–59)

- A similar approach prevails where publication is in the public interest: although journalists are not released from the general duty to obey the criminal law, Article 10 protects their right to divulge information on issues of general interest provided that they are acting in good faith and on an accurate factual basis and provide 'reliable and precise' information in accordance with the ethics of journalism (*Fressoz and Roire v France*, para. 54).

- Restrictions on publications that are in the public interest can only be justified by a 'competing and *overriding* public interest' (*Fressoz and Roire v France*, para. 51).

- And where information is already available to the public, an overriding interest in preserving confidentiality is unlikely to be made out (*Fressoz and Roire v France*, para. 53).

- This is particularly the case where a publication concerns criticism of the government:

  > In a democratic system the actions or omissions of the government must be subject to the close scrutiny not only of the legislative and judicial authorities but also of the press and public opinion. (*Castells v Spain*, para. 46)

- And the public interest is fairly wide: reports about the income of the chairman of a major car manufacturing company during a period of industrial unrest in which the employees were seeking a pay increase were in the public interest (*Fressoz v France*, para. 51).

- And even where the subjects of an article are not public figures but private individuals, publication may be in the public interest if it covers matters of concern to the local, national and international public (*Bladet Tromso and Stensaas v Norway*, para. 63).

- Protecting the identities of those who might be targeted for terrorist attacks is legitimate under Article 10; but where the identities have already been put into the public domain, there can be no proper basis for prosecuting those who repeat those identities (*Sürek v Turkey (No. 2)*, para. 40).

Relevant domestic cases

Turkington and others v The Times (2 November 2000), HL

- The media enjoy qualified privilege in reporting public meetings and press conferences (*Turkington and others v The Times*).

32.8   PROTECTION OF THE JUDICIARY

Key ECHR cases

Barfod v Denmark (1989) 13 EHRR 493, ECtHR
De Haes and Gijsels v Belgium (1997) 25 EHRR 1, ECtHR
Prager and Oberschlick v Austria (1995) 21 EHRR 1, ECtHR

ECHR principles

- In contrast to other public officials, the judiciary enjoy special protection from criticism.

- This reflects 'the special role of the judiciary' in a democracy and the need to maintain their authority:

    The courts – the guarantors of justice, whose role is fundamental in a State based on the rule of law – must enjoy public confidence. They must accordingly be protected from destructive attacks that are unfounded, especially in view of the fact that judges are subject to a duty of discretion that precludes them from replying to criticism. (*De Haes and Gijsels v Belgium*, para. 37; see also *Prager and Oberschlick v Austria*, para. 35; *Barfod v Denmark*, para. 31)

- But judges are not completely sheltered from legitimate comment (*De Haes and Gijsels v Belgium*, para. 48 – *comments about judges, although strongly expressed, were proportionate to the public interest created in the case itself and did not justify contempt proceedings*).

Relevant Canadian cases

BCGEU v BC (Vancouver Courthouse) [1988] 2 SCR 214
R v Kopyto (1987) 62 OR (2d) 449, CA

- The imposition of an injunction as a basis for holding someone in criminal contempt is an interference with freedom of expression, but may be justified under the Charter provided it guarantees unimpeded access to justice and is reasonable in the circumstances (*BCGEU v BC (Vancouver Courthouse)*).

- However, criticism of the judicial process, even where it amounts to criminal contempt, may be protected as free speech if it does not prejudice an ongoing or pending trial (*R v Kopyto*).

32.9   COURT REPORTING AND CONTEMPT OF COURT

Key ECHR cases

Sunday Times v UK (1979) 2 EHRR 245, ECtHR
Worm v Austria (1997) 25 EHRR 454, ECtHR

C Ltd v UK (1989) 61 DR 285, ECmHR
Hodgson and others v UK (1987) 51 DR 136, ECmHR

ECHR principles

- Court reporting is an important aspect of fair trial under Article 6, ECHR and is protected as 'free speech' under Article 10.

- However, it is not absolute and can be restricted:

    . . . in so far as the law of contempt may serve to protect the rights of litigants, this purpose is already included in the phrase 'maintaining the authority and impartiality of the judiciary': the rights so protected are the rights of individuals in their capacity as litigants, that is as persons involved in the machinery of justice, and the authority of that machinery will not be maintained unless protection is afforded to all those involved in or having recourse to it. (*Sunday Times v UK*, para. 56)

- Restrictions must be lawful, legitimate, necessary and proportionate.

- And a careful balance has to be struck:

  There is a general recognition . . . that courts cannot operate in a vacuum. Whilst the courts are the forum for the determination of a person's guilt or innocence on a criminal charge, this does not mean that there can be no prior or contemporaneous discussion of the subject-matter of criminal trials elsewhere, be it in specialised journals, in the general press or amongst the public at large.
    Provided it does not overlap the bounds imposed in the interests of the proper administration of justice, reporting, including comment, on court proceedings contributes to their publicity and is thus perfectly consonant with the requirement under Article 6(1) of the Convention that hearings be in public. (*Worm v Austria*, para. 50)

- Prejudice to the administration of justice is usually the touchstone:

  . . . comment may not extend to statements which are likely to prejudice, whether intentionally or not, the chances of a person receiving a fair trial or to undermine the confidence of the public in the role of the courts in the administration of justice. (*Worm v Austria*, para. 50)

- On pre-trial publicity, see **8.12**.

Relevant Canadian cases

Canadian Newspapers Co. v Canada [1988] 1 SCR 122
CBC v New Brunswick [1996] 3 SCR 480
Dagenais v CBC [1994] 3 SCR 835
Edmonton Journal v Alberta [1989] 2 SCR 1326
Re Southam and the Queen (No. 1) (1983) 41 OR (2d) 113, CA
Southam v Coulter (1990) 75 OR (2d) 1, CA

- Press freedom includes the freedom to publish reports of court proceedings since the 'courts must be open to public scrutiny and to public criticism of their operation by the public' (*Edmonton Journal v Alberta*, p. 1337).

- But the right to privacy would justify limitations in some circumstances (e.g., in matrimonial cases); and a mandatory prohibition on identifying victims in sexual offences cases can be justified (*Canadian Newspapers Co. v Canada*).

32.10   DISCLOSURE OF JOURNALISTS' SOURCES AND MATERIALS

Key ECHR cases

Fressoz and Roire v France (21 January 1999), ECtHR
Goodwin v UK (1996) 22 EHRR 123, ECtHR

BBC v UK (1996) 84-A DR 129, ECmHR[CD]

ECHR principles

- The protection of journalistic sources is 'one of the basic conditions for press freedom' (*Goodwin v UK*, para. 39) and hence very well protected:

  . . . reflected by the laws and professional codes of conduct in a number of Contracting States [the protection of sources] is affirmed in several international instruments on journalistic freedoms. Without such protection, sources may be deterred from assisting the press in informing the public on matters of public interest. As a result the vital public watchdog role of the press may be undermined and the ability of the press to provide accurate and reliable information may be adversely affected. Having regard to the importance of the protection of journalistic sources and press freedom in a democratic society and the potentially chilling effect an order of source disclosure has on the exercise of that freedom, such a measure cannot be compatible with Article 10 of the Convention unless it is justified by an overriding requirement in the public interest. (*Goodwin v UK*, para. 39)

- However, where disclosure is ordered in the course of criminal proceedings, the protection afforded to journalists may be less extensive (*BBC v UK*, p.132).

Relevant Canadian cases

CBC v Lessard [1991] 3 SCR 421
CBC v NB [1991] 3 SCR 459

- The police may justifiably search and seize material from the media which assists with the prosecution of crime (e.g., film footage), but caution must be exercised (*CBC v Lessard*; *CBC v NB*).

Relevant New Zealand cases

Broadcasting Corporation of New Zealand v Alex Harvey Industries Ltd [1980] 1 NZLR 163

- Disclosure of journalists' sources should be ordered only in the exceptional circumstances:

  The reasons for the rule [protecting sources] are not found simply in the needs of particular litigants. The broader purpose is to encourage the flow of information to the public and thereby facilitate free trade in ideas. That flow is dependent on the reporting of matters of public interest to the news media. The rule promotes this end by holding out to news gatherers and contributors of information to the news media the assurance that unless and until a matter goes to trial, and in the setting of the trial itself, identification of the source of the news media's information will not ordinarily be compelled. (*Broadcasting Corporation of New Zealand v Alex Harvey Industries Ltd*, p. 172)

32.11   COMMERCIAL SPEECH

Key ECHR cases

Casado Coca v Spain (1994) 18 EHRR 1, ECtHR
Hertel v Switzerland (25 August 1998), ECtHR

Jacubowski v Germany (1994) 19 EHRR 64, ECtHR
Markt Intern Verlag GmbH and Klaus Beerman v Germany (1989) 12 EHRR 161, ECtHR

ECHR principles

- Commercial speech is protected under Article 10 (*Markt Intern Verlag GmbH and Klaus Beerman v Germany*).

- And fairly wide restrictions are permitted in relation to commercial speech because there is a recognised need to protect commercial and confidential information (*Markt Intern Verlag GmbH and Klaus Beerman v Germany; Jacubowski v Germany*).

- However, while a fairly wide margin of appreciation may be appropriate in areas such as the regulation of competition, that does not hold where an individual's statements or publications relate to a matter of general interest, e.g., public health (*Hertel v Switzerland*, para. 47 – *criticism of safety of microwave ovens*).

Relevant Canadian cases

Ford v Quebec [1988] 2 SCR 712

- Commercial speech is important to the speaker and to the public:

  > Over and above its intrinsic value as expression, commercial expression which . . . protects listeners as well as speakers plays a significant role in enabling individuals to make informed economic choices, an important aspect of individual self-fulfilment and personal autonomy. (*Ford v Quebec*, p. 767)

32.12   ARTISTIC EXPRESSION

Key ECHR cases

Müller v Switzerland (1988) 13 EHRR 212, ECtHR

Hoare v UK [1997] EHRLR 678, ECmHR[CD]
Scherer v Switzerland (1994) 18 EHRR 276, ECmHR

ECHR principles

- Artistic expression is protected by Article 10 (*Muller v Switzerland*).
- However, artists and those who promote their work are not immune from the general constraints of Article 10(2) (*Muller v Switzerland*, para. 34).
- Hence pornography can be controlled (*Hoare v UK*, p. 679), but not prohibited (*Scherer v Switzerland*, para. 65).

Relevant Canadian cases

R v Butler [1992] 1 SCR 452

- A general prohibition on pornography is contrary to the Charter (*R v Butler*, p. 489).

32.13   RACE HATRED

Key ECHR cases

Jersild v Denmark (1994) 19 EHRR 1, ECtHR
Sürek v Turkey (No. 1) (8 July 1999), ECtHR

Glimmerveen and Hagenbeek v Netherlands (1979) 18 DR 187, ECmHR
Kuhnen v Germany (1988) 56 DR 205, ECmHR^{CD}

ECHR principles

- Restrictions on the expression of racist ideas are legitimate under Article 10(2), ECHR and Article 17 (the prohibition on abuse of rights: see **1.11**).

- These provisions can justify the seizure of racist material, and the criminal prosecution of those espousing racist views (*Glimmerveen and Hagenbeek v Netherlands*; *Kuhnen v Germany*).

- Generally, the criminal prosecution of a journalist who merely broadcast an interview with known racists as part of an ongoing debate about racism will be disproportionate (*Jersild v Denmark*).

- But where a publication does incite violence or amounts to hate speech, prosecution of those who provide an outlet for such publication does not necessarily breach Article 10, even where the individual in question does not personally associate himself or herself with the publication (*Sürek v Turkey (No. 1)*, para. 63).

Relevant Canadian cases

R v Keegstra [1990] 3 SCR 697
R v Zundel [1992] 2 SCR 731

- Laws that are specifically directed at prohibiting the wilful promotion of hatred against identifiable religious or racial groups are likely to be upheld as serving the important objective of preventing harm and protecting the rights of others (*R v Keegstra*).

- But not if they are too vague and overbroad (*R v Zundel*).

32.14   INCITEMENT TO VIOLENCE

Key ECHR cases

Arslan v Turkey (8 July 1999), ECtHR
Ceylan v Turkey (8 July 1999), ECtHR
Gerger v Turkey (8 July 1999), ECtHR
Karatas v Turkey (8 July 1999), ECtHR
Öztürk v Turkey (8 July 1999), ECtHR

Polat v *Turkey* (8 July 1999), ECtHR
Sürek and Özdemir v *Turkey* (8 July 1999), ECtHR
Sürek v *Turkey (No. 4)* (8 July 1999), ECtHR

Brind v *UK* (1994) 77-A DR 42, ECmHR[CD]
Purcell v *Ireland* (1989) 70 DR 262, ECmHR

ECHR principles

- So long as a publication does not incite violence, restrictions imposed to protect national integrity will be hard to justify; the public has a right to be informed of different perspectives – e.g., the PKK's perspective in South East Turkey – no matter how unpalatable that perspective may be for the authorities (*Sürek* v *Turkey (No. 4)*, para. 58).

- However, caution should be exercised by those publishing the views of others who promote violence:

  > The Court stresses that the 'duties and responsibilities' which accompany the exercise of the right to freedom of expression by media professionals assume special significance in situations of conflict and tension. Particular caution is called for when consideration is being given to the publication of views of representatives of organisations which resort to violence against the state lest the media become a vehicle for the dissemination of hate speech and the promotion of violence. At the same time, where such views cannot be categorised as such, contracting states cannot with reference to the protection of territorial integrity or national security or the prevention of crime or disorder restrict the right of the public to be informed of them by bringing the weight of the criminal law to bear on the media. (*Sürek* v *Turkey (No. 4)*, para. 60)

- So long as it does not incite violence, publication of an interview with the leader of a proscribed organisation cannot in itself justify an interference with freedom of expression, even where the interview contains hard-hitting criticism of official policy and presents a one-sided view (*Sürek and Özdemir* v *Turkey*).

- Publication of views that are intransigent and convey an unwillingness to compromise with the authorities is to be distinguished from publication of views that incite violence, or might incite violence (*Sürek and Özdemir* v *Turkey*, para. 61; but see the ECmHR's approach in *Purcell* v *Ireland*; *Brind* v *UK*).

- With artistic expression, the medium should be considered before concluding that publication incites violence:

  > . . . Article 10 includes freedom of artistic expression – notably within freedom to receive and impart information and ideas – which affords the opportunity to take part in the public exchange of cultural, political and social information and ideas of all kinds . . . Those who create, perform, distribute or exhibit works of art contribute to the exchange of ideas and opinions which is essential for a democratic society. . . .
  >   . . . As to the tone of the poems in the present case . . . it must be remembered that Article 10 protects not only the substance of the ideas and information expressed but also the form in which they are conveyed . . . (*Karatas* v *Turkey*, para. 49)

- The size of the target audience will be important in assessing the legitimacy of restrictions on free speech:

The Court observes . . . that the applicant is a private individual who expressed his views through poetry – which by definition is addressed to a very small audience – rather than through the mass media, a fact which limited their potential impact on 'national security', 'public order' and 'territorial integrity' to a substantial degree. Thus, even though some of the passages from the poems seems very aggressive in tone and to call for the use of violence, the Court considers that the fact that they were artistic in nature and of limited impact made them less a call to an uprising than an expression of deep distress in the face of a difficult political situation. (*Karatas v Turkey*, para. 52; *Polat v Turkey*, *Arslan v Turkey* and *Öztürk v Turkey* – *publication of books*; *Gerger v Turkey*, – *address at a political memorial ceremony*; *Ceylan v Turkey*, – *publication by a trade union leader*)

FREEDOM OF INFORMATION

33.1 FREEDOM OF INFORMATION UNDER ARTICLE 10

Key ECHR cases

Autronic AG v Switzerland (1990) 12 EHRR 485, ECtHR
Gaskin v UK (1989) 12 EHRR 36, ECtHR
Leander v Sweden (1987) 9 EHRR 433, ECtHR
Open Door and Dublin Well Woman v Ireland (1992) 15 EHRR 244, ECtHR
Sunday Times v UK (1979) 2 EHRR 245, ECtHR

Bader v Austria (1996) EHRR CD 213, ECmHR[CD]
Z v Austria (1988) 56 DR 13, ECmHR[CD]

ECHR principles

- Freedom of expression under Article 10 specifically includes freedom to 'receive and impart information and ideas' without interference and regardless of frontiers.

- However, this does not confer a right of access to information as such: it prohibits restrictions on the receipt of information, but does not oblige public authorities to disclose information against their will (*Gaskin v UK*; *Leander v Sweden*; *Z v Austria*; *Bader v Austria*).

- Nonetheless, freedom to receive and impart information and ideas will protect those who are prevented from receiving information that others are willing to impart:

  > [The Court is] struck by the absolute nature of the . . . injunctions which imposed a 'perpetual' restraint on the provision of information to pregnant women concerning abortion facilities abroad, regardless of age, state of health or their reasons for seeking counselling on the termination of pregnancy. (*Open Door and Dublin Well Woman v Ireland*, para. 74 – *injunction preventing clinic from imparting abortion advice*; see also *Autronic AG v Switzerland*)

- In this sense there is a real overlap between freedom of expression and freedom to receive and impart information under Article 10, particularly where the press is involved:

Whilst the mass media must not overstep the bounds imposed in the interests of the proper administration of justice, it is incumbent on them to impart information and ideas concerning matters that come before the courts just as in other areas of public interest. Not only do the media have the task of imparting such information and ideas: the public also has a right to receive them. (*Sunday Times v UK*, para. 65)

33.2   FREEDOM OF INFORMATION UNDER ARTICLE 8

Key ECHR cases

Gaskin v UK (1989) 12 EHRR 36, ECtHR
Guerra and others v Italy (1998) 26 EHRR 357, ECtHR
LCB v UK (1998) 27 EHRR 212, ECtHR
McGinley and Egan v UK (1998) 27 EHRR 1, ECtHR

ECHR principles

- A duty to provide information arises in three ways under Article 8.

- First, where the provision of information is a vital aspect of private or family life (*Gaskin v UK – restrictions on access to confidential records concerning the period when the applicant was in local authority care as a child were disproportionate*).

- Secondly, as one aspect of the positive obligations imposed on the relevant authorities to respect privacy and family life:

  . . . although the object of Article 8 is essentially that of protecting the individual against arbitrary interference by the public authorities, it does not merely compel the State to abstain from such interference: in addition to this primary negative undertaking, there may be positive obligations inherent in effective respect for private or family life. (*Guerra v Italy*, para. 58 – *positive duty on authorities to provide information to families at risk from environmental pollution*)

- This obligation is particularly acute where the relevant authorities have themselves created a risk to health:

  Where a Government engages in hazardous activities . . . which might have hidden adverse consequences on the health involved . . . respect for private and family life under Article 8 requires that an effective and accessible procedure be established which enables persons to seek all relevant and appropriate information. (*McGinley and Egan v UK*, para. 101 – *radiation level records should have been made available to RAF personnel*)

- For positive obligations in general, see **1.8**.

- The third way in which a right of access to information arises under Article 8 is as an aspect of procedural fairness when Article 8 issues are determined:

  In the context of the present case, the lack of disclosure of such vital documents as social reports is capable of affecting the ability of participating parents not only to influence the outcome of the children's hearing in question but also to assess their prospects of making an appeal . . . (*McMichael v UK*, para. 80)

FREEDOM OF ASSEMBLY

34.1 THE RIGHT TO PEACEFUL ASSEMBLY

Key ECHR cases

Hashman and Harrup v UK (1999) 30 EHRR 241, ECtHR
Piermont v France (1995) 20 EHRR 301, ECtHR
Plattform "Ärzte für das Leben" v Austria (1988) 13 EHRR 204, ECtHR
Steel and others v UK (1998) 28 EHRR 603, ECtHR

Anderson and others v UK [1998] EHRLR 218, ECmHR[CD]
Christians Against Racism and Fascism v UK (1980) 21 DR 138, ECmHR
G v Germany (1989) 60 DR 256, ECmHR[CD]
Rassemblement Jurassien and Unité Jurassienne v Switzerland (1979) 17 DR 93, ECmHR

ECHR principles

- Article 11, ECHR provides that 'Everyone has the right to freedom of peaceful assembly.'

- This right overlaps with freedom of expression under Article 10.

- It is a qualified right; it can be restricted, but only where such restrictions are lawful, legitimate, necessary and proportionate.

- The right to peaceful assembly is not confined to static meetings; it also covers marches and processions (*Christians Against Racism and Fascism v UK*, p. 148), sit-ins, and both public and private events (*Rassemblement Jurassien and Unité Jurassienne v Switzerland*, p. 119).

- The purpose of the assembly is irrelevant, so long as it is peaceful; but where there is no real purpose at all (e.g., youths hanging out in a shopping centre) Article 11 probably does not apply (*Anderson and others v UK*, p. 219).

- The mere fact that an assembly may not be peaceful does not automatically preclude Article 11 protection – peaceful intent is sufficient, even if disorder results:

  > Under Article 11(1) of the Convention, the right to freedom of peaceful assembly is secured to everyone who has the intention of organising a peaceful demonstration. . . . the possibility of violent counter-demonstrations, or the possibility of extremists with violent intentions, not members of the organising association, joining the demonstration cannot as such take away that right. Even if there is a real risk of a public

procession resulting in disorder by developments outside the control of those organising it, such procession does not for this reason alone fall outside the scope of Article 11(1) . . . (*Christians Against Racism and Fascism v UK*, para. 4)

- Article 11 may even apply where an assembly is illegal (*G v Germany*, p. 263 – *non-violent but illegal sit-down demonstration at entrance of military barracks*).

- Moreover, as with free speech under Article 10, an assembly may annoy or give offence, but it is nonetheless protected under Article 11 (*Plattform "Ärzte für das Leben" v Austria*, para. 32).

- In particular, those opposed to official views must find a place for the expression of their views (*Piermont v France*, para. 56).

- Protest which takes the form of impeding the activities of others (such as fox-hunting) is nonetheless an expression of an opinion and is therefore protected by Article 10 (*Hashman and Harrup v UK*, para. 28).

- Where there is a threat of disruption or disorder from others, the relevant authorities are under a duty to take appropriate steps to protect those who want to exercise their right of peaceful assembly:

  > . . . a demonstration may annoy or give offence to persons opposed to the ideas or claims that it is seeking to promote. The participants must however be able to hold the demonstration without having to fear that they will be subjected to physical violence by their opponents; such a fear would be liable to deter associations or other groups supporting common ideas or interests from openly expressing their opinions on highly controversial issues affecting the community. In a democracy the right to counter-demonstrate cannot extend to inhibiting the exercise of the right to demonstrate.
  >
  > Genuine, effective freedom of peaceful assembly cannot, therefore, be reduced to a mere duty on the part of the state not to interfere; a purely negative conception would not be compatible with the object and purpose of Article 11. Like Article 8, Article 11 sometimes requires positive measures to be taken, even in the sphere of relations between individuals, if need be. (*Plattform "Ärzte für das Leben" v Austria*, para. 32 – *counter-demonstrators repeatedly broke up applicants' peaceful assembly*)

- There is no absolute duty to protect those who want to exercise their right of peaceful assembly: the obligation is to take 'reasonable and appropriate measures', and a wide discretion is left to the authorities responsible for regulating the assembly (*Plattform "Ärzte für das Leben" v Austria*, para. 34).

34.2 LOCATION

Key ECHR cases

Chorherr v Austria (1993) 17 EHRR 358, ECtHR
Ezelin v France (1991) 14 EHRR 362, ECtHR
Plattform "Ärzte für das Leben" v Austria (1988) 13 EHRR 204, ECtHR

Anderson and others v UK [1998] EHRLR 218, ECmHR[CD]
Friedl v Austria (App. No. 15225/89), ECmHR
MG v Germany (App. No. 13079/87), ECmHR[CD]
Rassemblement Jurassien and Unite Jurassienne v Switzerland (1979) 17 DR 93, ECmHR

ECHR principles

- Article 11, ECHR confers a right to hold meetings, marches and demonstrations in public places, including on the public highway:

  . . . the right of peaceful assembly stated in this Article is a fundamental right in a democratic society and, like the right to freedom of expression, is one of the foundations of such society . . . as such this right covers both private meetings and meetings in public thoroughfares . . . (*Rassemblement Jurassien and Unité Jurassienne v Switzerland*, p. 119)

- But not the right to hang-out in a shopping mall (*Anderson and others v UK*, p. 219).

- The right to hold meetings, marches and demonstrations in public places is not absolute and has to be balanced with the rights of others who want to use the same space, particularly on the highway.

- Some obstruction is acceptable, so long as it is reasonable in size and duration (*MG v Germany*, p. 7).

Relevant domestic cases

Jones & Lloyd v DPP [1999] 2 AC 40, HL

- Peaceful assembly on the highway is lawful:

  Unless the common law recognizes that assembly on the public highway may be lawful, the right contained in Article 11(1) of the Convention is denied. Of course the right may be subject to restrictions (e.g. the requirements that user of the highway for the purposes of assembly must be reasonable and non-obstructive, and must not contravene the criminal law of wilful obstruction of the highway). But, in my judgment our law will not comply with the Convention unless its starting point is that assembly on the highway will not necessarily be unlawful. I reject an approach which entails that such an assembly will always be tortious and therefore unlawful. The fact that the letter of the law may not always in practice be invoked is irrelevant: mere toleration does not secure a fundamental right. (*Jones & Lloyd v DPP*, *per* Lord Irvine)

Relevant Canadian cases

Dieleman v Ontario (AG) (1994) 20 OR (3d) 229, Ont Ct (Gen Div)

- Freedom to assemble includes, in principle, a right to choose where to demonstrate (*Dieleman v Ontario*).

34.3   THE PREVENTION OF DISORDER

Key ECHR cases

Chorherr v Austria (1993) 17 EHRR 358, ECtHR
Ezelin v France (1992) 14 EHRR 362, ECtHR
Steel and others v UK (1998) 28 EHRR 603, ECtHR

Arrowsmith v UK (1978) 19 DR 5, ECmHR

ECHR principles

- The prevention of disorder is a legitimate ground for restricting the right to peaceful assembly under Article 11, so long as any restrictions are also lawful, necessary and proportionate (*Choherr v Austria*, para. 33).

- But the balance struck between freedom of assembly and the prevention of disorder should not result in individuals being discouraged from making clear their beliefs (*Ezelin v France*, paras 52–53).

- Removing those who are peacefully handing out leaflets because others might react is likely to be disproportionate (*Steel and others v UK*, paras 105, 109 and 110).

- Where there is disorder, proceedings – whether criminal or disciplinary – should not be taken against those who did not participate in, or encourage, any such disorder (*Ezelin v France*, paras 52–53).

Relevant New Zealand cases

Minto v Police (1991) 7 CRNZ 38)

- Before police officers require protesters to move because of anticipated breaches of the peace, they should ensure that no alternative course of action is available (*Minto v Police*).

34.4 BANNING ORDERS

Key ECHR cases

Christians Against Racism and Fascism v UK (1980) 21 DR 138, ECmHR
Pendragon v UK [1999] EHRLR 223, ECmHR
Rai and others v UK (1995) 82-A DR 134, ECmHR[CD]
Rassemblement Jurassien and Unite Jurassienne v Switzerland (1979) 17 DR 93, ECmHR

ECHR principles

- A requirement of prior notice or authorisation for a march or meeting is not necessarily a breach of Article 11, ECHR, so long as the purpose behind the procedure is not to frustrate peaceful assemblies (*Rassemblement Jurassien and Unite Jurassienne v Switzerland*, p. 119).

- But orders banning meetings and marches can only be justified in extreme circumstances:

  A general ban on demonstrations can only be justified if there is a real danger of their resulting in disorder which cannot be prevented by other less stringent measures. In this connection, the authority must also take into account the effect of a ban on processions which do not by themselves constitute a danger for public order. Only if the disadvantage of such processions being caught by the ban is clearly outweighed by the security considerations justifying the issue of the ban, and if there is no possibility of avoiding such undesirable side effects of the ban by a narrow circumspection of its scope in terms of its territorial application and duration, can the ban be regarded as being necessary within the meaning of Article 11(2). (*Christians Against Racism and Fascism v UK*, para. 5 – *ban justified in the prevailing atmosphere of violence*)

- The length of any ban and the question of what alternatives, if any, are available will always be relevant:

  Having regard to the fact that the refusal of permission did not amount to a blanket prohibition on the holding of the applicant's rally but only prevented the use of a high profile location (other venues being available in Central London) the Commission concludes that that restriction in the present case may be regarded as proportionate and justified as necessary in a democratic society. (*Rai and others v UK*; also *Pendragon v UK* – *not unreasonable to prohibit assemblies at Stonehenge for a given period since there had been considerable disorder in recent years and still possible to participate in a gathering of less than 20 people within exclusion zone*)

34.5   THE ARMED FORCES, THE POLICE AND CIVIL SERVANTS

Key ECHR cases

Rekvényi v Hungary (20 May 1999), ECtHR

CCSU v UK (1987) 50 DR 228, ECmHR[CD]

ECHR principles

- Article 11(2) makes special reference to the army, police and civil servants.

- The effect is to exclude these groups from the general protection of Article 11.

- As a result there is no requirement that any restrictions on their right of peaceful assembly be necessary and proportionate: they need only be lawful and non-arbitrary.

- Restrictions on the political activities of police officers can be justified under Article 10 of the Convention on the basis that a politically neutral police force is in the public interest (*Rékvenyi v Hungary*, para. 41). The same principle presumably applies in relation to Article 11.

SECTION 35

FREEDOM OF ASSOCIATION

35.1 THE SCOPE OF FREEDOM OF ASSOCIATION

Key ECHR cases

Le Compte, Van Leuven and De Meyere v Belgium (1981) 4 EHRR 1, ECtHR
Sidiropoulos v Greece (1998) 27 EHRR 633, ECtHR
Sigurjónsson v Iceland (1993) 16 EHRR 462, ECtHR
United Communist Party of Turkey v Turkey (1998) 26 EHRR 121, ECtHR
Young, James and Webster v UK (1981) 4 EHRR 38, ECtHR

A and others v Spain (1990) 66 DR 309, ECmHR
McFeeley v UK (1980) 20 DR 44, ECmHR
Revert v France (1989) 62 DR 309, ECmHR

ECHR principles

- Article 11, ECHR provides that 'Everyone has the right to . . . freedom of association with others, including the right to form and to join trade unions for the protection of his interests.'

- It is a qualified right; it can be restricted, but only where such restrictions are lawful, legitimate, necessary and proportionate.

- It implies the right of individuals to come together on a voluntary basis to further a common interest:

    That citizens should be able to form a legal entity in order to act collectively in a field of mutual interest is one of the most important aspects of the right to freedom of association, without which that right would be deprived of any meaning. (*Sidiropoulos v Greece*, para. 40; see also *Young, James and Webster v UK*)

- Political parties are protected by Article 11:

    . . . political parties are a form of association essential to the proper functioning of democracy. In view of the importance of democracy in the Convention system, there can be no doubt that political parties come within the scope of Article 11. (*United Communist Party of Turkey v Turkey*, para. 24)

- It does not include the right to share the company of others (*McFeeley v UK* – *no right of association for prisoner*).

- Neither does it include the right to belong to a particular association.

- The non-voluntary and public nature of most professional regulatory bodies usually excludes them from Article 11 protection (*Le Compte, Van Leuven and De Meyere v Belgium; Revert v France; A and others v Spain;* but see *Sigurjónsson v Iceland*).

Relevant New Zealand cases

Lewis v Real Estate Institute of New Zealand Inc. [1995] NZLR 385

- Restrictions on professional or business activities whereby associations cannot be set up without approval, do not come within the scope of freedom of association (*Lewis v Real Estate Institute of New Zealand Inc.*, p. 393).

35.2 RESTRICTIONS ON FREEDOM OF ASSOCIATION

Key ECHR cases

Özdep v Turkey (8 December 1999), ECtHR
Sidiropoulos v Greece (1998) 27 EHRR 633, ECtHR

ECHR principles

- Freedom of association can be restricted, but only where restrictions are lawful, legitimate, necessary and proportionate.

- Exceptions to freedom of association must be narrowly interpreted; their enumeration in Article 11(2) is strictly exhaustive and the definition necessarily restrictive:

  . . . only convincing and compelling reasons can justify restrictions on freedom of association. (*Sidiropoulos v Greece*, para. 40)

- Where an organisation does not call for the use of violence or otherwise reject democratic principles, it should not be restricted:

  It is of the essence of democracy to allow diverse political projects to be proposed and debated, even those that call into question the way a state is currently organised, provided that they do not harm democracy itself. (*Özdep v Turkey*, para. 41)

- Upholding national cultural traditions and historic and cultural symbols is not a legitimate basis for restricting freedom of association under Article 11 (*Sidiropoulos v Greece*).

- Registration or licensing schemes are not prohibited, so long as they do not impair the activities of the association.

- But a refusal to register a particular association has to be justified under Article 11(2) (*Sidiropoulos v Greece*).

- Associations are free to regulate their own membership and activities.

35.3 TRADE UNIONS

- Article 11, ECHR specifically provides for the right to form and to join trade unions.

- See **37.3**.

35.4 THE RIGHT NOT TO ASSOCIATE

Key ECHR cases

Chassagnou and others v *France* (1999) 29 EHRR 615, ECtHR
Gustafsson v *Sweden* (1996) 22 EHRR 409, ECtHR
Sigurjónsson v *Iceland* (1993) 16 EHRR 462, ECtHR
Young, James and Webster v *UK* (1981) 4 EHRR 38, ECtHR

ECHR principles

- The right to freedom of association can include a right not to belong to a particular association:

    Article 11 must be viewed as encompassing a negative right of association. It is not for the Court to determine . . . whether this right is to be considered on an equal footing with the positive right. (*Sigurjonsson* v *Iceland*, para. 35; see also *Young, James and Webster* v *UK* and *Chassagnou and others* v *France*, para. 117)

- The relevant authorities may be obliged to protect this negative freedom even in relations between private individuals:

    It follows that national authorities may, in certain circumstances, be obliged to intervene in the relationships between private individuals by reasonable and appropriate measures to secure the effective enjoyment of the negative right to freedom of association. (*Gustafsson* v *Sweden*, para. 45)

Relevant New Zealand cases

Air NZ Ltd v *Trustees of the NZALP Mutual Benefit Fund* [2000] 1 NZLR 418

- While the provision of benefits by an organisation may offer an incentive for people to join it, this does not mean that they are obliged to do so or to remain members, thereby preserving their freedom of association (*Air NZ Ltd* v *Trustees of the NZALP Mutual Benefit Fund*, p. 429 – *benefits for members of union provided by mutual benefit fund*).

35.5 THE ARMED FORCES, THE POLICE AND CIVIL SERVANTS

- Article 11(2) makes special reference to the army, police and civil servants.

- The effect is to exclude these groups from the general protection of Article 11.

- See **34.5**.

SECTION 36

PROPERTY RIGHTS

36.1 THE PROTECTION OF POSSESSIONS

Key ECHR cases

Chassagnou and others v France (1999) 29 EHRR 615, ECtHR
Greek Refineries Stran and Stratis Andreadis v Greece (1994) 19 EHRR 293, ECtHR
Holy Monasteries v Greece (1994) 20 EHRR 1, ECtHR
Inze v Austria (1987) 10 EHRR 394, ECtHR
Marckx v Belgium (1979) 2 EHRR 330, ECtHR
Matos e Silva, Lda and others v Portugal (1996) 24 EHRR 573, ECtHR
Mellacher v Austria (1989) 12 EHRR 391, ECtHR
National and Provincial Building Society and others v UK (1997) 25 EHRR 127, ECtHR
Pine Valley Developments Ltd and others v Ireland (1991) 14 EHRR 319, ECtHR
Pressos Compania Naviera SA v Belgium (1995) 21 EHRR 301, ECtHR
Pudas v Sweden (1987) 10 EHRR 380, ECtHR
Tre Traktörer AB v Sweden (1989) 13 EHRR 309, ECtHR
Van Marle v Netherlands (1986) 8 EHRR 483, ECtHR

Agneessens v Belgium (1988) 58 DR 63, ECmHR
Baner v Sweden (1989) 60 DR 128, ECmHR[CD]
Batelaan and Huiges v Netherlands (1984) 41 DR 170, ECmHR
Bramelid and Malmstrom v Sweden (1982) 29 DR 64, ECmHR
Greek Federation of Customs Officers et al. v Greece 81-B DR 123, ECmHR
Gudmunsson v Iceland (1996) 21 EHRR CD 89, ECmHR
JS v Netherlands (1995) 20 EHRR CD 42, ECmHR
Karni v Sweden (1988) 55 DR 157, ECmHR
S v UK (1984) 41 DR 226, ECmHR
S v UK (1986) 47 DR 274, ECmHR
Smith Kline and French Laboratories Ltd v Netherlands (1990) 66 DR 70, ECmHR[CD]
X v Germany (1980) 18 DR 216, ECmHR
X v Germany (1981) 26 DR 255, ECmHR

ECHR principles

- Protocol 1, Article 1, ECHR protects peaceful enjoyment of possessions, and in effect amounts to a right of property (*Marckx v Belgium*).

- It comprises three rules:

    (a) individuals are entitled to the peaceful enjoyment of their property/ possessions;

(b)   the state can deprive them of their property/possessions, but only in defined circumstances;

(c)   the state can control (or impose restrictions on) property/possessions, but again only in defined circumstances.

- The term 'possessions' in Protocol 1, Article 1 has a very wide meaning, including all property and chattels and also acquired rights with economic interest such as:

(a)   shares (*Bramelid and Malmstrom v Sweden*, p. 81);

(b)   patents (*Smith Kline and French Laboratories Ltd v Netherlands*, p. 79);

(c)   fishing rights (*Baner v Sweden*, p. 138);

(d)   licences, so long as they give rise to a reasonable and legitimate expectation of a lasting nature (*Tre Traktörer AB v Sweden*, para. 53; *JS v Netherlands*; *Pudas v Sweden*; *Gudmunsson v Iceland*);

(e)   restrictive covenants and receipt of rent on a property (*S v UK* (1984), p. 232);

(f)   leases (*Mellacher v Austria*, para. 43);

(g)   planning consents (*Pine Valley Developments Ltd and others v Ireland*);

(h)   the ownership of a debt or claim, provided it is sufficiently established (*Greek Refineries Stran and Stratis Andreadis v Greece*, paras 61–62);

(i)   an arbitration award in favour of a company pursuing damages against the state for breach of contract to build an oil refinery (*Agneessens v Belgium*, p. 83);

(j)   the vested interests of a doctor in private practice (*Karni v Sweden*, p. 165; but see *Batelaan and Huiges v Netherlands*, pp. 172–3);

(k)   goodwill (*Van Marle v Netherlands*, para. 41 – *the ability to retain clientele which had built up over number of years*; *Tre Traktörer AB v Sweden*, para. 53 – *goodwill of restaurant customers*).

- There is no right to acquire property or possessions (*Marckx v Belgium*, para. 50; *X v Sweden*).

- But the right to exclude others from land is protected (*Chassagnou and others v France*, para. 73).

- Hence, there is no guarantee to obtain possessions by way of intestacy or involuntary dispositions, although differences in treatment in matters of inheritance could raise issues under the non-discrimination provision of Article 14 in conjunction with Article 1 (*Marckx v Belgium*).

- Income can only be a possession where it has already been earned or there is an enforceable claim to it (*Greek Federation of Customs Officers et al. v Greece*, pp. 127–8; *Matos e Silva, Lda and others v Portugal*; *Batelaan and Huiges v Netherlands*, p. 173).

- Mere expectations are not protected (*X v Germany*, p. 219).

- But an arbitration award that is enforceable is a possession (*Greek Refineries Stran and Stratis Andreadis v Greece*); and so is a pending claim in civil proceedings, so long as it is sufficiently established (*Pressos Compania Naviera SA v Belgium*, para. 31; but see *National and Provincial Building Society and others v UK*).

36.2   DEPRIVATION OF POSSESSIONS/PROPERTY

Key ECHR cases

Air Canada v UK (1995) 20 EHRR 150, ECtHR
Aka v Turkey (23 September 1998), ECtHR
Hakansson and Sturesson v Sweden (1990) 13 EHRR 1, ECtHR
Handyside v UK (1976) 1 EHRR 737, ECtHR
Hentrich v France (1994) 18 EHRR 440, ECtHR
Holy Monasteries v Greece (1994) 20 EHRR 1, ECtHR
James v UK (1986) 8 EHRR 123, ECtHR
Papachelas v Greece (25 March 1999), ECtHR
Pine Valley Developments Ltd and others v Ireland (1991) 14 EHRR 319, ECtHR
Raimondo v Italy (1994) 18 EHRR 237, ECtHR
Saffi v Italy (28 July 1999), ECtHR
Sporrong and Lönnroth v Sweden (1982) 5 EHRR 35, ECtHR
Venditelli v Italy (1994) 19 EHRR 464, ECtHR

ECHR principles

36.2.1   *Meaning of deprivation*

- Deprivation of property occurs only where deprivation is permanent.

- However, no formal act of expropriation is necessary:

  > Since the Convention is intended to guarantee rights that are 'practical and effective', it has to be ascertained whether [the] situations amounted to a *de facto* expropriation. (*Sporrong and Lönnroth v Sweden*, para. 63)

- Temporary interference is not deprivation (*Handyside v UK* para. 62 – *seizure of obscene publications; Raimondo v Italy; Venditelli v Italy – interim seizure of assets where drug charges pending; Air Canada v UK – temporary seizure of aircraft to enforce special provisions in drugs legislation*).

- Failure to implement an eviction order is not deprivation of property, but might be control (*Saffi v Italy*, para. 46).

36.2.2   *Justifying deprivation*

- The right to peaceful enjoyment of possessions, or property, is not absolute; but deprivation can be justified only where it is:

  (a)   lawful;
  (b)   in the public interest; and
  (c)   reasonably proportionate.

- Where the property of non-nationals is concerned, any deprivation of property must also be in accordance with the conditions provided by the general principles of international law.

36.2.3   *Lawfulness*

- The requirement that any deprivation of property be 'provided for by law' imports into Protocol 1, Article 1, the requirement of lawfulness or legality found elsewhere in the ECHR (*James v UK*).

- For a detailed examination of this requirement, see **1.3**.

- In some cases, the requirement of lawfulness guards against arbitrariness by introducing a measure of procedural fairness into the decision-making process (*Hentrich v France*).

36.2.4   *Public interest*

- The public interest is a very broad concept, and the ECtHR has been most reluctant to interfere with its assessment by the relevant domestic authorities.

- It can include the pursuit of social justice (*James v UK*, para. 41).

36.2.5   *Fair balance*

- The fair balance test under Protocol 1, Article 1 is less exacting than the test for interfering with qualified rights such as those set out in Articles 8 to 11 of the ECHR.

- What has to be shown is that a fair balance has been struck between the demands of the general/public interest and the protection of the individual right to peaceful enjoyment of possessions/property.

- This balance will not be established if the individual who has been deprived of his or her possessions/property has had to bear an excessive burden:

  > There must . . . be a reasonable relationship of proportionality between the means employed and the aim sought to be realised. (*James v UK*, para. 51; *Hakansson and Sturesson v Sweden*)

- The fact that there is an alternative means of achieving the same result does not, *of itself*, mean that there is no relationship of reasonable proportionality (*James v UK*, para. 51; *Hentrich v France*, para. 47).

- And the degree of risk taken on by an individual deprived of his or her property is relevant (*Pine Valley Developments Ltd and others v Ireland – speculative acquisition of land with only outline planning permission*).

- But a measure which is truly arbitrary may mean that no relationship of reasonable proportionality can be established; and this can be another basis for introducing a degree of procedural fairness into the decision-making process in some cases (*Papachelas v Greece*).

36.2.6   *Compensation*

- Compensation is nearly always relevant to the question of whether a fair balance has been struck between the demands of the general/public interest and the protection of the individual right to peaceful enjoyment of possessions/property.

- Although full compensation is not required:

  . . . the taking of property without payment of an amount reasonably related to its value will normally constitute a disproportionate interference and total lack of compensation can be considered justifiable under Article 1 only in exceptional circumstances. (*Holy Monasteries v Greece*, para. 70)

- An irrefutable statutory presumption that all landowners have derived benefit from a road building scheme and which influences the compensation paid to them breaches Article 1 of Protocol 1 because it does not allow individuals to argue the particular circumstances of their individual cases (*Papachelas v Greece*, para. 53).

- Long delays in the payment of compensation for expropriated land can infringe Article 1 of Protocol 1 (*Aka v Turkey*, para. 49).

Relevant Scottish cases

Booker Aquaculture Ltd v Secretary of State for Scotland (12 August 1999), CS
Her Majesty's Advocate v Harry McSalley (10 April 2000), HC

- Confiscation orders requiring defendants to pay substantial sums of money can be justified under Protocol 1, Article 1, ECHR:

  I do not consider that the making of a confiscation order such as is sought in this case contravenes the reasonable relationship of proportionality between the means employed and the aim pursued . . . It is necessary to keep in mind the important underlying purposes which are the combating of drug trafficking. . . . It is of vital significance in this connection to ensure that those involved in the network of drug dealing in which substantial profits can be made are prevented, so far as is possible, from benefiting from their crimes even after their release . . . notwithstanding the apparent harsh effect of any order. (*Her Majesty's Advocate v Harry McSalley*, p. 8)

- The compulsory slaughter and destruction of farmed animals can deprive the owner of property in them. Similarly, subjecting the slaughter of the animals for human consumption to certain conditions restricts the owner's exercise of his right to property in them (*Booker Aquaculture Ltd v Secretary of State for Scotland*, p. 10 – *salmon farm subject to MAFF regulations following outbreak of fish disease*).

- Therefore, although such measures may be in the public interest, compensation should be paid (*Booker Aquaculture Ltd v Secretary of State for Scotland*, pp. 11–12).

36.3   CONTROL OF POSSESSIONS/PROPERTY

Key ECHR cases

Air Canada v UK (1995) 20 EHRR 150, ECtHR
Fredin v Sweden (1991) 13 EHRR 784, ECtHR
Handyside v UK (1976) 1 EHRR 737, ECtHR
Holy Monasteries v Greece (1994) 20 EHRR 1, ECtHR
Mellacher v Austria (1989) 12 EHRR 391, ECtHR

Marckx v Belgium (1979) 2 EHRR 330, ECtHR
Matos e Silva, Lda and others v Portugal (1996) 24 EHRR 573, ECtHR
National and Provincial Building Society and others v UK (1997) 25 EHRR 127, ECtHR
Pine Valley Developments Ltd and others v Ireland (1991) 14 EHRR 319, ECtHR
Raimondo v Italy (1994) 18 EHRR 237, ECtHR
Spadea and Scalabrino v Italy (1995) 21 EHRR 482, ECtHR
Tre Traktörer AB v Sweden (1989) 13 EHRR 309, ECtHR
Van Marle v Netherlands (1986) 8 EHRR 483, ECtHR
Venditelli v Italy (1994) 19 EHRR 464, ECtHR

ECHR principles

36.3.1 *Meaning of control*

- Measures short of deprivation but which substantially interfere with an individual's peaceful enjoyment of his or her possessions/property are capable of constituting control within the meaning of Protocol 1, Article 1.

- Such measures can include positive requirements to use possessions/property in a particular way and negative restrictions on the use of possessions/property, e.g., rent restrictions (*Mallacher v Austria*), planning controls (*Pine Valley Developments Ltd and others v Ireland*), temporary seizure of assets in criminal proceedings (*Raimondo v Italy; Venditelli v Italy*), seizure of obscene publications (*Handyside v UK*), the temporary seizure of aircraft to enforce special provisions in drugs legislation (*Air Canada v UK*), the withdrawal of a licence (*Tre Traktörer AB v Sweden; Fredin v Sweden*), retroactive tax measures (*National and Provincial Building Society and others v UK*) and a refusal to register the applicants as certified accountants (*Van Marle v Netherlands*).

36.3.2 *Justifying control*

- The right to peaceful enjoyment of possessions, or property, is not absolute; but control can be justified only where it is:
  - (a) lawful;
  - (b) in the public interest *or* aimed at securing the payment of taxes or other contributions or penalties; *and*
  - (c) deemed 'necessary' by the state.

36.3.3 *Lawful control*

- This has the same meaning in relation to the control of possessions/property as it has for deprivation (see **36.2.3**).

36.3.4 *Public interest*

- The public interest is a very broad concept, including protecting tenants from homelessness (*Spadea and Scalabrino v Italy*), protection of the environment (*Pine*

Valley Developments Ltd and others v Ireland; Fredin v Sweden; Matos e Silva, Lda and others v Portugal), and the preservation of evidence and assets (*Venditelli v Italy*).

36.3.5   *Taxes, contributions and penalties*

- See **36.4**.

36.3.6   *Necessity*

- At one stage, the ECtHR afforded a wide discretion to the relevant authorities to assess necessity (e.g., *Handyside v UK*, para. 62; *Marckx v Belgium*, para. 64).

- However, a stricter approach is now required:

  According to the Court's well-established case law, an interference, including one resulting from a measure to secure the payment of taxes, must strike a 'fair balance' between the demands of the general interest of the community and the requirements of the protection of the individual's rights. The concern to achieve this balance is reflected in the structure of Article 1 as a whole, including the second paragraph: there must therefore be a reasonable relationship of proportionality between the means employed and the aims pursued. (*National and Provincial Building Society v UK*, para. 80)

- This is effectively the same as the 'fair balance' test where an individual is deprived of his or her possessions/property; but less exacting than the test for interfering with qualified rights such as those set out in Articles 8 to 11 of the ECHR:

  The possible existence of alternative solutions does not in itself render the contested legislation unjustified. Provided that the legislature remains within the bounds of its margin of appreciation, it is not for the Court to say whether the legislation represented the best solution for dealing with the problem or whether the legislative discretion should have been exercised in another way. (*Mellacher v Austria*, para. 53)

36.4   TAXES, CONTRIBUTIONS AND PENALTIES

Key ECHR cases

Bendenoun v France (1994) 18 EHRR 54, ECtHR
Darby v Sweden (1990) 13 EHRR 774, ECtHR
Editions Périscope v France (1992) 14 EHRR 597, ECtHR
Gasus Dosier- und Fördertechnik GmbH v Netherlands (1995) 20 EHRR 403, ECtHR
National and Provincial Building Society and others v UK (1997) 25 EHRR 127, ECtHR
Sporrong and Lönnroth v Sweden (1982) 5 EHRR 35, ECtHR

Abas v Netherlands (App. No. 27943/95), ECmHR[CD]
A.B.C. and D. v UK (1981) 23 DR 203, ECmHR
Lindsay v UK (1986) 49 DR 181, ECmHR[CD]
Perin v France (App. No. 18565/91, 1 December 1992), ECmHR
Smith v UK (1996) 21 EHRR CD 74, ECmHR[CD]
X v Austria (1980) 21 DR 247, ECmHR
X v France 32 DR 266, ECmHR

ECHR principles

36.4.1 *Protocol 1, Article 1 possessions/property*

- Protocol 1, Article 1, ECHR specifically provides that the right to peaceful enjoyment of possessions/property it enshrines 'shall not . . . in any way impair the right of a State to enforce such laws as it deems necessary . . . to secure the payment of taxes or other contributions or penalties.'

- No definition of the term 'tax' has been formulated, but a distinction has to be drawn between tax and state appropriation.

- At one stage, the term 'secure' was interpreted as distinguishing between the collection and the levying of tax (*Gasus Dosier- und Fördertechnik GmbH v Netherlands*); but it is now clear that the provision in Protocol 1, Article 1 applies to both (*National and Provincial Building Society and others v UK*).

- The collection of taxes inevitably interferes with the right to peaceful enjoyment of possessions/property (*Lindsay v UK*, p. 189).

- It must therefore be shown to be 'lawful'; and it must be 'deemed necessary'.

- The term 'lawful' is considered at **1.3** and **36.2.3**.

- Whether tax collection is 'deemed necessary' involves an assessment of whether 'a reasonable relationship of proportionality between the means employed and the aims pursued' can be shown (*National and Provincial Building Society v UK*, para. 80).

- In this tax context, a wide discretion is left with the relevant authorities on this question: the ECtHR recognises that the ECHR was intended to allow states to pass whatever fiscal laws they felt necessary as long as the measures implemented did not amount to arbitrary confiscation (*Gasus Dosier- und Fördertechnik GmbH v Netherlands*, para. 59).

- As a result, only tax measures that are wholly disproportionate, wholly arbitrary, or discriminatory are likely to breach Protocol 1, Article 1 (*Gasus Dosier- und Fördertechnik GmbH v Netherlands*; *Sporrong and Lönnroth v Sweden*).

- Tax collection measures which are retrospective in nature are not prohibited, but must be treated with considerable caution. They are (probably) legitimate only in so far as they are genuinely introduced to counter a tax-avoidance scheme (*A.B.C. and D. v UK*; *National and Provincial Building Society v UK*).

36.4.2 *Article 14 discrimination*

- The prohibition on discrimination set out in Article 14, ECHR applies to tax levying and collection (*Darby v Sweden*).

- For Article 14, see **Section 40**.

36.4.3 *Article 6 fair trial*

- Ordinary measures to enforce tax payments do not involve the determination of a criminal charge within the meaning of Article 6, ECHR (*X v Austria*; *Abas v Netherlands*).

- However, where penalties are imposed in tax cases, closer scrutiny is required (*Perin v France – tax penalties of 30%–50% attract criminal safeguards; Bendenoun v France – as do surcharges of half a million francs; but see Smith v UK – 10% surcharge, which could not be converted into imprisonment, not criminal*).

- Similarly, as a general rule, disputes about tax do not determine 'civil rights and obligations' under Article 6(1) (*X v France; Editions Périscope v France*, pp. 612–13).

- However, there may be exceptions, e.g., proceedings for damages for losses sustained as a result of the unlawful deprivation of certain tax concessions:

  > . . . the subject-matter of the applicant's action was 'pecuniary' in nature and . . . the action was founded on an alleged infringement of rights which were likewise pecuniary rights. (*Editions Périscope v France*, para. 40)

  or restitution proceedings for taxes paid under regulations later declared invalid (*National & Provincial Building Society v UK*).

36.5   WELFARE PAYMENTS AND PENSIONS

Key ECHR cases

Cornwell v UK (25 April 2000), ECtHR
Deumeland v Germany (1986) 8 EHRR 448, ECtHR
Feldbrugge v Netherlands (1986) 8 EHRR 425, ECtHR
Gaygusuz v Austria (1996) 23 EHRR 365, ECtHR
Leary v UK (25 April 2000), ECtHR
Salesi v Italy (1993) 26 EHRR 187, ECtHR
Schouten and Meldrum v Netherlands (1994) 19 EHRR 432, ECtHR
Schuler-Zgraggen v Switzerland (1993) 16 EHRR 405, ECtHR

Mann v Germany (1996) EHRR CD 157, ECmHR
Muller v Austria (1975) 3 DR 25, ECmHR
Szrabjer and Clark v UK [1998] EHRLR 230, ECmHR
X v Sweden (1986) 8 EHRR 252, ECmHR

ECHR principles

36.5.1   *Protocol 1, Article 1 possessions/property*

- While there is no right to welfare payments and/or a pension as such under the ECHR, property interests can arise in certain circumstances:

  > . . . the payment of contributions to a pension fund may in certain circumstances create a property right in a portion of such a fund and a modification of the pension rights under such a system could therefore in principle raise an issue under [Protocol 1, Article 1]. (*X v Sweden; Muller v Austria;* see also *Mann v Germany*)

- This general rule applies to compulsory pension schemes and pension schemes based on employment:

> . . . the right to a pension which is based on employment can in certain circumstances be assimilated to a property right, and this can be the case, whether special contributions have been paid or the employer has given a more general undertaking to pay a pension on conditions which can be considered to be part of the employment contract. (X v Sweden, p. 270)

- However, the right is a right to 'derive benefit' from the scheme, not a right to a pension of a particular amount:

> The operation of a social security system is essentially different from the management of a private life insurance company. Because of its public importance, the social security system must take account of political considerations, in particular those of financial policy. It is conceivable, for instance, that a deflationary trend may oblige a State to reduce the nominal amount of pensions. Fluctuations of this kind have nothing to do with the guarantee of ownership as a human right. (X v Sweden; Muller v Austria)

- Nonetheless, a substantial reduction in the amount of a pension might be regarded as destroying its 'very essence' (X v Sweden; Muller v Austria – a 3% reduction is unlikely to have that effect).

- The right to emergency assistance under a pension scheme can be a protected property right under Protocol 1, Article 1, where payment was linked to contributions to an unemployment insurance fund (Gaygusuz v Austria; see also Szrabjer and Clark v UK – pension dependent on contribution).

36.5.2 *Article 6 fair trial*

- As a general rule, Article 6(1) will apply to disputes about welfare payments and pensions:

> . . . the development in the law that was initiated by [the] judgments [in Feldbrugge and Deumeland] and the principle of equality of treatment warrant taking the view that today the general rule is that Article 6(1) does apply in the field of social insurance.
> . . . In the present case . . . the question arises in connection with welfare assistance and not . . . social insurance. Certainly there are differences between the two, but they cannot be regarded as fundamental at the present stage of development in social security law . . . State intervention is not sufficient to establish that Article 6(1) is inapplicable. (Salesi v Italy, para. 19; drawing on Feldbrugge v Netherlands and Deumeland v Germany; see also Schuler-Zgraggen v Switzerland)

- However, this general rule may not extend to the *payment* rather than the *receipt* of contributions (Schouten and Meldrum v Netherlands).

- For the substantive fair trial guarantees of Article 6, see **Section 17**.

36.5.3 *Article 14 discrimination*

- Failure to pay male applicants social security benefits on the same basis as bereaved widows may violate Article 14 (Cornwall v UK; Leary v UK – friendly settlement).

EMPLOYMENT

37.1 PRIVACY AT WORK

Key ECHR cases

Amann v Switzerland (16 February 2000), ECtHR
Halford v UK (1997) 24 EHRR 523, ECtHR
Niemietz v Germany (1992) 16 EHRR 97, ECtHR
Rotaru v Romania (4 May 2000), ECtHR

ECHR principles

- The right to respect for private life under Article 8, ECHR extends into the workplace (*Halford v UK*, para. 44; see also *Niemietz v Germany*).

- Therefore measures which interfere with privacy must be lawful, legitimate, necessary and proportionate (see **1.3** to **1.6**).

- The unregulated interception of employees' communications is likely to breach this requirement, but only where there is a 'reasonable expectation of privacy' (*Halford v UK; Amann v Switzerland*).

- The notion of private life is a broad one and can include the right to develop relations with others:

  . . . it would be too restrictive to limit the notion of [private life] to an 'inner circle' in which the individual may live his own personal life as he chooses and to exclude therefrom entirely the outside world not encompassed within that circle. Respect for private life must also comprise to a certain degree the right to establish and develop relationships with other human beings. (*Niemietz v Germany*, para. 29)

- And this notion of private life applies in the workplace (*Rotaru v Romania*, para. 43).

37.2 SECURITY VETTING

Key ECHR cases

Leander v Sweden (1987) 9 EHRR 433, ECtHR

Hilton v UK (1988) 57 DR 108, ECmHR[CD]
Kara v UK [1999] EHRLR 232, ECmHR

ECHR principles

- Security vetting inevitably engages Article 8, ECHR.

- Therefore it must be lawful, legitimate, necessary and proportionate (see **1.3** to **1.6**).

- These requirements are likely to be fulfilled where important issues of national security are at stake:

    There can be no doubt as to the necessity, for the purposes of protecting national security, for the Contracting States to have laws granting the competent domestic authorities power, firstly, to collect and store in registers not accessible to the public, information on persons and, secondly, to use this information when assessing the suitability of candidates for employment in posts of importance for national security. (*Leander v Sweden*, para. 59 – *storage of information in a secret police register for release to prospective employers*)

- But safeguards need to be in place to control the collection, use and retention of private information used for security vetting purposes (*Hilton v UK*).

- For the meaning of 'victim' in security vetting cases, see **4.2**.

Relevant Canadian cases

Godbout v Longueil [1997] 3 SCR 844

- Requiring employees to live in a particular area is an unjustifiable interference with their privacy, unless there is a very good reason for it (*Godbout v Longueil*).

37.3   TRADE UNIONS

37.3.1   *Forming and joining trade unions*

Key ECHR cases

Schmidt and Dahlström v Sweden (1976) 1 EHRR 632, ECtHR
Sibson v UK (1993) 17 EHRR 193, ECtHR
Sigurjónsson v Iceland (1993) 16 EHRR 462, ECtHR
Swedish Engine Drivers' Union v Sweden (1976) 1 EHRR 617, ECtHR
Young, James and Webster v UK (1981) 4 EHRR 38, ECtHR

Cheall v UK (1985) 42 DR 178, ECmHR
Englund v Sweden (1994) 77-A DR 10, ECmHR[CD]
Johansson v Sweden (1990) 65 DR 202, ECmHR

ECHR principles

- Article 11, ECHR provides: 'Everyone has . . . the right to form and join trade unions for the protection of his interests.'

- Any restriction on this right must be lawful, legitimate, necessary and proportionate (see **1.3** to **1.6**).

- But that does not mean that trade unions cannot regulate their own activities, including membership rules:

  > The right to join a union 'for the protection of his interests' cannot be interpreted as conferring a general right to join the union of one's choice irrespective of the rules of the union. In the exercise of their rights under Article 11 para. 1, unions must remain free to decide, in accordance with union rules, questions concerning admission to and expulsion from the union. (*Cheall v UK*, p. 185 – *expulsion from trade union pursuant to decision of TUC disputes committee*)

- Nonetheless, the individual is entitled to protection from any abuse of dominant power, such as expulsion in breach of the rules; arbitrary or unreasonable treatment; and expulsion resulting in exceptional hardship, e.g., where a closed shop arrangement is in force (*Young, James and Webster v UK*).

- A negative right not to join a trade union can be derived from Article 11 (see **35.4**).

37.3.2   *Trade union activities*

Key ECHR cases

Gustafsson v Sweden (1996) 22 EHRR 409, ECtHR
National Union of Belgian Police v Belgium (1975) 1 EHRR 578, ECtHR
Schmidt and Dahlström v Sweden (1976) 1 EHRR 632, ECtHR
Swedish Engine Drivers' Union v Sweden (1976) 1 EHRR 617, ECtHR

CCSU v UK (1987) 50 DR 228, ECmHR[CD]
NATFHE v UK (1998) 25 EHRR CD 122, ECmHR[CD]
S v Germany (1984) 39 DR 237, ECmHR

ECHR principles

- The right to form and join trade unions for the protection of collective interests must be effective; and that means that trade unions have a right to be heard:

  > . . . the Convention safeguards freedom to protect the occupational interests of trade union members by trade union action, the conduct and development of which the Contracting States must both permit and make possible . . .
  > . . . the members of a trade union have a right, in order to protect their interests, that the trade union should be heard. (*National Union of Belgian Police v Belgium*, para. 39)

- But no one form of trade union activity is absolutely protected:

  > . . . while Article 11(1) presents trade union freedom as one form or a special aspect of freedom of association, the Article does not secure any particular treatment of trade unions, or their members, by the State, such as the right that the State should conclude any given collective agreement with them. Not only is this latter right not mentioned in Article 11(1), but neither can it be said that all the Contracting States incorporate it in their national law or practice, or that it is indispensable for the effective enjoyment of trade union freedom. (*Swedish Engine Drivers' Union v Sweden*, para. 39)

- Hence, no general right to consultation can be read into Article 11, the relevant authorities having a discretion how to give effect to trade union rights (*National Union of Belgian Police v Belgium*, para. 39).

- However, a right to take industrial action is inherent in Article 11; but not absolute:

  The grant of a right to strike represents without any doubt one of the most important means [by which a trade union can protect its members' interests], but there are others. Such a right, which is not expressly enshrined in Article 11, may be subject under national law to regulation . . . that limits its exercise in certain instances. (*Schmidt and Dahlström v Sweden* para. 36)

- A duty to disclose names of trade union members before strike action is taken does not significantly affect the right to take industrial action (*NATFHE v UK*).

37.3.3 *The army, police and public officials*

Key ECHR cases

Rekvényi v Hungary (20 May 1999), ECtHR

CCSU v UK (1987) 50 DR 228, ECmHR[CD]

ECHR principles

- Article 11(2) makes special reference to the army, police and civil servants.

- The effect is to exclude these groups from the general protection of Article 11.

- As a result, there is no requirement that any restrictions on their right of peaceful assembly be necessary and proportionate; they need only be lawful and non-arbitrary.

- Restrictions on the political activities of police officers can be justified under Article 10 of the Convention on the basis that a politically neutral police force is in the public interest (*Rekvényi v Hungary*, para. 41).

37.4 FREEDOM OF THOUGHT, CONSCIENCE AND RELIGION

Key ECHR cases

Ahmad v UK (1982) 4 EHRR 126, ECmHR
Knudsen v Norway (1985) 42 DR 247, ECmHR
Stedman v UK (1997) 23 EHRR CD 168, ECmHR[CD]
X v Denmark (1976) 5 DR 157, ECmHR
X v Finland (App. No. 24949/94, 3 December 1996), ECmHR

ECHR principles

- Freedom of thought, conscience and religion under Article 9, ECHR extends into the workplace; but the ECmHR has given it extremely narrow meaning in this context.

- Where there is a tension between the ability of an individual to manifest his or her religion or beliefs and the working timetable or regime, the knowledge of the tension when the job was accepted or the ability to leave will be significant.

- Broadly speaking, if the individual knew when he or she accepted a job that there would be a tension between his or her beliefs and the job, a binding choice is said to have been exercised at that stage:

    . . . in a State church system its servants are employed for the purpose of applying and teaching a specific religion. Their individual freedom of thought, conscience or religion is exercised at the moment they accept or refuse employment as clergymen, and their right to leave the church guarantees their freedom of religion in case they oppose its teaching. (*X v Denmark*, p. 158; see also *Ahmad v UK*, pp. 134–5 – *schoolteacher's resignation after refusal of permission to attend mosque during working hours did not give rise to violation since issue not raised at interview*)

- Equally if an employee is free to leave, no Article 9 issue arises, even if he or she is actually dismissed (*Stedman v UK* – *dismissal for refusal to work Sundays*).

- The position may be different, however, where an individual is faced with the threat of dismissal unless his or her beliefs are changed (*Knudsen v Norway*, p. 258).

37.5   FREEDOM OF EXPRESSION

Key ECHR cases

Ahmed and others v *UK* (1998) 29 EHRR 1, ECtHR
Glasenapp v *Germany* (1986) 9 EHRR 25, ECtHR
Kosiek v *Germany* (1986) 9 EHRR 328, ECtHR
Vogt v *Germany* (1995) 21 EHRR 205, ECtHR

Grigoriades v *Greece* [1998] EHRLR 222, ECmHR
Haseldine v *UK* (1992) 73 DR 225, ECmHR
Morissens v *Belgium* (1988) 56 DR 127, ECmHR
Tucht v *Germany* (1982) ECmHR
Van der Heijden v *Netherlands* (1985) 41 DR 264, ECmHR

ECHR principles

- The right to freedom of expression under Article 10, ECHR extends into the workplace.

- Therefore restrictions on free expression must be lawful, legitimate, necessary and proportionate (see **1.3** to **1.6**).

- Some employment by its very nature involves a degree of restriction:

  By entering the civil service [as a teacher], the applicant accepted certain restrictions on the exercise of her freedom of expression, as being inherent in her duties. (*Morissens v Belgium*, p. 136 – *declaration by teacher on television of homosexuality and criticism of employers*)

- The manner and mode of expression is relevant to the legitimacy of restrictions (*Morissens v Belgium*; *Tucht v Germany*).

- Those in public duty may owe a duty of moderation during their employment (*Morissens v Belgium*; *Kosiek v Germany*).

- And this may even limit their ability to engage in some types of political activity (*Ahmed and others v UK*).

Relevant Canadian cases

UFWC v Kmart Canada [1999] 2 SCR 1083

- Restrictions on free speech relating to working conditions can rarely, if ever, be justified (*UFWC v Kmart Canada*).

37.6   EMPLOYMENT DISPUTES

Key ECHR cases

Abenavoli v Italy (2 September 1997), ECtHR
Albert and Le Compte v Belgium (1983) 5 EHRR 533, ECtHR
Benkessiour v France (24 August 1998), ECtHR
Cazenave de la Roche v France (9 June 1998), ECtHR
Frydlender v France (27 June 2000), ECtHR
Lapalorcia v Italy (2 September 1997), ECtHR
Le Calvez v France (29 July 1998), ECtHR
Lombardo v Italy (1992) 21 EHRR 188, ECtHR
Massa v Italy (1993) 18 EHRR 266, ECtHR
Nicodemo v Italy (2 September 1997), ECtHR
Obermeier v Austria (1990) 13 EHRR 290, ECtHR

X v UK (1984) 6 EHRR 583, ECmHR

ECHR principles

37.6.1   *Article 6(1) fair trial*

- Disputes relating to private law relations between private employers and employees are governed by the fair trial guarantees of Article 6(1), ECHR.

- However, professional disciplinary proceedings are subject to special rules (see **15.4**).

37.6.2   *Article 6(1) public officials*

- Disputes relating to the recruitment, careers and termination of service of public servants are as a general rule outside the scope of Article 6(1), except where the claim in issue relates to:

  (a)   a 'purely economic' right, such as the payment of salary (*Lapalorcia v Italy* and *Abenavoli v Italy*) or pension (*Lombardo v Italy*; *Massa v Italy*); or

  (b)   an 'essentially economic one' (see *Nicodemo v Italy*).

  (*Benkessiour v France*, para. 29 – *decision to refuse sick pay and reduce salary essentially economic*; see also *Le Calvez v France*; *Cazenave de la Roche v France*)

- But the test for public servants is now a functional test; there should be no discrimination under Article 6(1) of the Convention between public officials who are employed under a contract and those who are classified as 'civil servants':

  . . . the only disputes excluded from the scope of Article 6(1) are those raised by public officials whose duties typify activities of the public service in so far as they are acting as the depositary of public authority responsible for protecting the general interests of the state or other public authorities. A manifest example of such activities is provided by the armed forces and the police. (*Frylander v France*, para. 33)

EDUCATION

38.1   THE RIGHT TO EDUCATION

Key ECHR cases

Belgian Linguistic Case (1968) 1 EHRR 252, ECtHR
Belilos v Switzerland (1988) 10 EHRR 466, ECtHR
Campbell and Cosans v UK (1982) 4 EHRR 293, ECtHR
Kjeldsen, Busk Madsen and Pedersen v Denmark (1976) 1 EHRR 711, ECtHR

SP v UK (1997) 23 EHRR CD 139, ECmHR[CD]
X v UK (1979) 16 DR 101, ECmHR

ECHR principles

* Article 2 of Protocol 1 of the Convention provides: 'No person shall be denied the right to education. In the exercise of any functions which it assumes in relation to education and to teaching, the state shall respect the right of parents to ensure such education and teaching in conformity with their own religious and philosophical aims.'

* The UK has entered a reservation in respect of this right:

  . . . in view of certain provisions of the Education Acts in the United Kingdom, the principle affirmed in the second sentence of Article 2 is accepted by the United Kingdom only in so far as it is compatible with the provision of efficient instructions and training, and the avoidance of unreasonable public expenditure.

* Under the HRA 1998, this reservation has effect in domestic law (see **5.5**).

* The validity of this reservation is open to question (*SP v UK*; *Belilos v Switzerland*, paras 52–59).

* And even if valid, it may not apply to provisions which entered into force after it was made.

38.2   SCOPE OF THE RIGHT TO EDUCATION

Key ECHR cases

Belgian Linguistic Case (1968) 1 EHRR 252, ECtHR
Campbell and Cosans v UK (1982) 4 EHRR 293, ECtHR

Glazewska v *Sweden* (1985) 45 DR 300, ECmHR
X v *Belgium* (1979) 16 DR 82, ECmHR
X v *UK* (1 December 1986), ECmHR

ECHR principles

- Despite its negative formulation, there is no doubt that Protocol 1, Article 2 enshrines a right.

- But the right to education does not bestow on individuals a right to require state authorities to set up a particular type or level of education.

- Rather it bestows on them a 'right of access' to education facilities that already exist (*Belgian Linguistic Case*).

- The right to education is to be construed so that it is 'practical and effective'; a simple 'right' of access to education facilities is not, in itself, enough.

- Individuals must have the opportunity to draw benefit from the education they receive (*Belgian Linguistic Case*, para. 4).

- This means at the very least that:

  (a) there is a right to be taught in the national language, or one of the national languages, as the case may be; and
  (b) there should be official recognition of any qualifications obtained on the completion of studies.

  (*Belgian Linguistic Case*, para. 4)

- However, there is no right for individuals to be taught in the language of their, or their parents', choice (*Belgian Linguistic Case*, para. 6).

- Neither is there a right of access to a particular school of choice (*X* v *UK*).

- Education is widely defined:

  . . . the education of children is the whole process whereby, in any society, adults endeavour to transmit their beliefs, culture and other values to the young, whereas teaching or instruction refers in particular to the transmission of knowledge and to intellectual development. (*Campbell and Cosans* v *UK*, para. 33)

- Consequently, where private bodies or individuals undertake education in this broad sense, the state should refrain from interfering save to the extent that it can legitimately regulate education in accordance with Article 2 of Protocol 1.

38.3   REGULATION OF THE RIGHT TO EDUCATION

Key ECHR cases

Belgian Linguistic Case (1968) 1 EHRR 252, ECtHR

App. No. 17678/91 v *Sweden* (30 June 1993), ECmHR
Family H v *UK* (1984) 37 DR 105, ECmHR
Jordebo v *Sweden* (1987) 51 DR 125, ECmHR[CD]

ECHR principles

- Regulation is an integral aspect of the right to education:

    . . . the right to education guaranteed by the first sentence of Article 2 of the [First] Protocol by its very nature calls for regulation by the State. (*Belgian Linguistic Case*, para. 5)

- Such restriction 'may vary in time and place according to the needs and resources of the community and of individuals' but 'must never injure the substance of the right to education nor conflict with other rights enshrined in the Convention' (*Belgian Linguistic Case*, para. 5).

- States can therefore regulate both public schools and private schools, often taking the form of quality control (*Jordebo v Sweden*, p. 129).

- Regulation can include compulsory schooling for all persons below a certain age, coupled with the power to punish parents who refuse to comply with the requirement (*Family H v UK*, p. 108 – *parents' conviction for failing to comply with attendance order by teaching dyslexic children at home held not to be a violation of Article 2 of Protocol 1; App. No. 17678/91 v Sweden – permission for missionary parents to educate their own children under a certain age withdrawn on basis that education required increasing specialisation and social contact*).

38.4 THE RIGHT TO RESPECT FOR RELIGIOUS AND PHILOSOPHICAL CONVICTIONS

Key ECHR cases

Belgian Linguistic Case (1968) 1 EHRR 252, ECtHR
Campbell and Cosans v UK (1982) 4 EHRR 293, ECtHR
Kjeldsen, Busk Madsen and Pedersen v Denmark (1976) 1 EHRR 711, ECtHR
Valsamis v Greece (1996) 24 EHRR 294, ECtHR

Aminoff v Sweden (1985) 43 DR 120, ECmHR
B and D v UK (1986) 49 DR 44, ECmHR
Family H v UK (1984) 37 DR 105, ECmHR
W and KL v Sweden (1985) 45 DR 143, ECmHR
W and others v UK (1984) 37 DR 96, ECmHR
Warwick v UK (1986) 60 DR 5, ECmHR
X v Sweden (1977) 12 DR 192, ECmHR
X v UK (1977) 11 DR 160, ECmHR
X v UK (1978) 14 DR 179, ECmHR

ECHR principles

- The second sentence of Article 2 of Protocol 1 enjoins the state to respect parents' religious and philosophical convictions.

- This duty applies not only to the content of education and the manner of its provision, but also to the performance of all the 'functions' assumed by the state, e.g., the internal administration of a school, including discipline (*Campbell and Cosans v UK*).

- Where education at home is permitted, the state does not breach the requirement to respect parents' convictions by requiring them to cooperate in the assessment of their children's educational attainments (*Family H v UK*).

- The adjective 'philosophical' in this context is not capable of exhaustive definition, but it will be relevant for education purposes only where:

  (a) such convictions are worthy of respect in a 'democratic society';
  (b) they are not incompatible with human dignity; and
  (c) they do not conflict with the fundamental right of the child to education.

  (*Campbell and Cosans v UK*, para. 36)

- Strongly held views about corporal punishment satisfy these criteria (*Campbell and Cosans v UK*, para. 36).

- The word 'respect' means more than 'acknowledge' or 'take into account'; in addition to a primarily negative undertaking, it implies some positive obligations on the part of the state (*Campbell and Cosans v UK*, para. 37; *Valsamis v Greece*, para. 27).

- But the duty is to respect parents' convictions, not to comply with them (*Family H v UK*; see also *W and others v UK – parents' requirement was for same-sex grammar school not mixed-sex comprehensive*).

- Moreover, 'respect' is to be interpreted objectively (*Valsamis v Greece – applicants' daughter required, on pain of suspension, to take part in a school parade contrary to their convictions as Jehovah's Witnesses – no breach of ECHR because (objectively) nothing in the purpose of the parade or in the arrangements for it could offend pacifist convictions*).

- Although Protocol 1, Article 2 refers to the convictions of the 'parents', where a child is in the custody of another, the convictions of that person are relevant (*X v Sweden*; *X v UK – adoptive parents*; *Aminoff v Sweden – where a child is simply taken into care, the convictions of the natural parents are still relevant*).

38.5 THE LEVEL OF EDUCATION PROVIDED FOR

Key ECHR cases

Belgian Linguistic Case (1968) 1 EHRR 252, ECtHR

App. No. 5492/72 (16 July 1973) 44 Coll 63, ECmHR
Foreign Students v UK (1977) 9 DR 185, ECmHR
Glazewska v Sweden (1985) 45 DR 300, ECmHR
Sulak v Turkey (1996) 84-A DR 98, ECmHR[CD]
X v UK (1975) 2 DR 50, ECmHR
X v UK (1980) 23 DR 228, ECmHR
Yanasik v Turkey (1993) 74 DR 14, ECmHR

ECHR principles

- The right to education envisaged in Article 2 of Protocol 1 is concerned primarily with elementary education and not necessarily advanced studies (*Belgian Linguistic Case*).

- Universal access to elementary education is required; but selective access to higher education is permitted:

    . . . where certain, limited, higher education facilities are provided by a State, in principle it is not incompatible with Article 2 of Protocol 1, to restrict access thereto to those students who have attained the academic level required to most benefit from the courses offered. (*X v UK*, p. 229)

38.6   PRIVATE SCHOOLS

Key ECHR cases

Campbell and Cosans v UK (1982) 4 EHRR 293, ECtHR
Kjeldsen, Busk Madsen and Pedersen v Denmark (1976) 1 EHRR 711, ECtHR

Jordebo v Sweden (1987) 51 DR 125, ECmHR[CD]
Verein Gemeinsam Lernen v Austria (1995) 82-A DR 41, ECmHR[CD]

ECHR principles

- Private schools are permitted on the basis that the right to education includes a 'right' to establish and run such institutions (*Jordebo v Sweden*, p. 128; *Verein Gemeinsam Lernen v Austria*, p. 45; see also *Kjeldsen, Busk Madsen and Pedersen v Denmark*, para. 50 – *ECHR intended to guarantee the 'freedom' to set up and maintain private schools*).

- However, this freedom is subject to legitimate state interference with the aim of maintaining standards across both the public and private sectors:

    It must be subject to regulation by the State in order to ensure a proper educational system as a whole. (*Jordebo v Sweden*, p. 128 – *private school refused permission to teach children above 16 years old because it lacked teachers with the necessary qualifications to maintain quality standards*)

- And it is subject to the aim of ensuring that ECHR rights are respected within private schools (*Campbell and Cosans v UK*, para. 41).

38.7   FUNDING

Key ECHR cases

Belgian Linguistic Case (1968) 1 EHRR 252, ECtHR

Simpson v UK (1989) 64 DR 188, ECmHR[CD]
Verein Gemeinsam Lernen v Austria (1995) 82-A DR 41, ECmHR

W and KL v Sweden (1985) 45 DR 143, ECmHR
W and others v UK (1984) 37 DR 96, ECmHR
X v Sweden (7 May 1984), ECmHR
X v UK (1978) 14 DR 179, ECmHR
Y v Sweden (7 May 1984), ECmHR

ECHR principles

- Funding obligations are very limited:

  [There is no obligation on states to] require them to establish at their own expense, or to subsidise, education of any particular type or at any particular level. (*Belgian Linguistic Case*, para. 3)

- This includes non-denominational schools (*X v UK*, p. 180 – *legitimate and not unreasonable for the state to require the private body to pay for 15% of capital costs as opposed to public ones*; single-sex grammar schools (*W and others v UK*, p. 100); private schools (*X v Sweden*; *Y v Sweden*; *W and KL v Sweden*, p. 149; *Verein Gemeinsam Lernen v Austria*, p. 46); and special needs schools (*Simpson v UK*, pp. 194–5).

- Nevertheless, failure to fund some schools while funding others may give rise to discrimination issues (*Verein Gemeinsam Lernen, v Austria* p. 45 – *on the facts non-religious private schools not discriminated against since there was a need for state funding of Church schools*).

38.8   SPECIAL NEEDS

Key ECHR cases

Kjeldsen, Busk Madsen and Pedersen v Denmark (1976) 1 EHRR 711, ECtHR

Graeme v UK (1990) 64 DR 158, ECmHR[CD]
Karnell and Hardt v Sweden (1971) 14 Yearbook 664, ECmHR
PD and LD v UK (1989) 62 DR 292, ECmHR[CD]
Simpson v UK (1989) 64 DR 188, ECmHR[CD]

ECHR principles

- Parents of children with special needs have a right to advance the view that the needs of their children require special facilities, and to have that view respected by the education authorities when determining the nature of provision to be made available.

- However, since the right to education is not absolute, and states must allocate their limited resources to benefit as many as possible, there is no obligation to acquiesce to these views:

  . . . there must be a wide measure of discretion left to the appropriate authorities as to how to make the best use possible of the resources available to them in the interests of disabled children generally. (*Simpson v UK*, p. 195 – *dyslexic child required to take up place in ordinary school with appropriate facilities rather than a special school*)

- Conversely, authorities are not under a duty to integrate children with special needs into ordinary, mainstream schools, even if this is what their parents want in accordance with their own convictions (*PD and LD v UK*; *Graeme v UK*).

38.9 SETTING THE CURRICULUM

Key ECHR cases

Kjeldsen, Busk Madsen and Pedersen v Denmark (1976) 1 EHRR 711, ECtHR

ECHR principles

- Parental rights under Article 2 of Protocol 1 do not extend to demands on the school curriculum, so long as there is no issue of indoctrination (*Kjeldsen, Busk Madsen and Pedersen v Denmark*, para. 53).

- Provided an objective standard is met, both state and private schools can teach a curriculum which includes material which, because of its nature, conflicts with the religious or philosophical beliefs of the parents (*Kjeldsen, Busk Madsen and Pedersen v Denmark*, para. 53 – *parents' objections to compulsory sex education dismissed since did not amount to indoctrination, but merely the provision of information*).

38.10 DISCIPLINARY MATTERS AND CORPORAL PUNISHMENT

Key ECHR cases

Campbell and Cosans v UK (1982) 4 EHRR 293, ECtHR
Costello-Roberts v UK (1993) 19 EHRR 112, ECtHR
Valsamis v Greece (1996) 24 EHRR 294, ECtHR

Warwick v UK (1986) 60 DR 5, ECmHR

ECHR principles

- A disciplinary regime in schools and colleges is permitted under the ECHR:

  The imposition of disciplinary penalties is an integral part of the process whereby a school seeks to achieve the object for which it was established, including the development and moulding of the character and mental powers of its pupils. (*Valsamis v Greece*, para. 29)

- However, it must be operated within certain limits and not conflict with any other fundamental rights such as the prohibition on inhuman and degrading treatment or punishment, the protection of physical integrity and the principle of non-discrimination (see **19.2** to **19.4**).

38.11   SUSPENSION/EXPULSION

Key ECHR cases

Campbell and Cosans v UK (1982) 4 EHRR 293, ECtHR

Sulak v Turkey (1996) 84-A DR 98, ECmHR[CD]
X v UK (App. No. 13477/87, 4 October 1989), ECmHR
Yanasik v Turkey (1993) 74 DR 14, ECmHR

ECHR principles

- Neither suspension nor expulsion gives rise to a 'criminal charge' (*Yanasik v Turkey*, p. 25).

- Nor does it in principle breach a pupil's right to access education (*X v UK* – *suspension not a denial of the right to education where return conditional upon good behaviour*).

- However, where disciplinary action prevents enrolment elsewhere, issues under Protocol 1, Article 2 will be raised:

  It would not be contrary to Article 2 of Protocol 1 for pupils to be suspended or expelled, provided that the national regulations did not prevent them from enrolling in another establishment to pursue their studies. (*Yanasik v Turkey*, p. 27 – *expulsion from military college after participation in Muslim fundamentalist movement*)

38.12   CHALLENGING DISCIPLINARY MEASURES

Key ECHR cases

Valsamis v Greece (1996) 24 EHRR 294, ECtHR

Warwick v UK (1986) 60 DR 5, ECmHR

ECHR principles

- Article 13 of the ECHR guarantees that both children and their parents have the right to challenge a disciplinary measure which they consider to be in violation of one or more of their Convention rights (*Valsamis v Greece*, para. 47).

- This does not necessarily mean that the remedy must be judicial, merely that it must be capable of reversing the measure in dispute (*Warwick v UK*, pp. 17–19 – *violation of Articles 3 and 13 where neither the civil nor the criminal law prohibited degrading treatment which did not constitute an assault, i.e. caning the hand*).

38.13   SCHOOL UNIFORMS

Key ECHR cases

Stevens v UK (1986) 46 DR 245, ECmHR

ECHR principles

- Requiring pupils to wear school uniform does not breach either Article 8 (privacy and family life) or Protocol 1, Article 2 (right to education) (*Stevens* v *UK*).

ELECTION RIGHTS

39.1 THE STATUS OF ELECTION RIGHTS

Key ECHR cases

Mathieu-Mohin and Clerfayt v Belgium (1987) 10 EHRR 1, ECtHR

Gitonas v Greece (1997) RJD 1997-IV No. 42, ECmHR
Greek Case, the (1969) 12 Yearbook 1, ECmHR

ECHR principles

- Protocol 1, Article 3 provides: 'The High Contracting Parties undertake to hold free elections at reasonable intervals by secret ballot, under conditions which will ensure the free expression of the opinion of the people in the choice of the legislature.'

- The impersonal phrasing of this provision is intended to reflect:

  . . . the desire to give great solemnity to the commitment undertaken . . . [to adopt] positive measures to 'hold' democratic elections (*Mathieu-Mohin and Clerfayt v Belgium*, para. 50)

- It presupposes:

  . . . the existence of a representative legislature, elected at reasonable intervals, as the basis of a democratic society. (*The Greek Case*, p. 179)

- Accordingly, any restrictions placed on the exercise of electoral rights must not deprive them of their effectiveness and must be legitimate and strictly proportionate (*The Greek Case*, para. 52; *Gitonas v Greece*, para. 39).

39.2 PERIODIC ELECTIONS FOR THE LEGISLATURE

Key ECHR cases

Booth-Clibborn v UK (1985) 43 DR 236, ECmHR
Matthews v UK (1997), ECmHR
Tete v France (1987) 54 DR 52, ECmHR
Timke v Germany (1995) 82-A DR 158, ECmHR
W, X, Y and Z v Belgium (1975) 2 DR 110, ECmHR
X v Germany (1975) 3 DR 98, ECmHR
X v UK (1976) 3 DR 165, ECmHR

ECHR principles

- The right to take part in free elections for the legislature is not limited; it is capable of reflecting different constitutional arrangements (*Timke v Germany*, p. 159 – *diets of the German länder were legislatures for the purpose of Protocol 1, Article 3*).

- However, Protocol 1, Article 3 does not extend to local government elections, which only concern delegated powers, (*W, X, Y and Z v Belgium*, p. 116 – *regional Belgian councils had no legislative powers*; *Booth-Clibborn v UK*, p. 248 – *metropolitan county councils*).

- Neither does it encompass referenda, which are consultative in nature (*X v UK*, p. 166 – *prisoner unable to vote in EEC referendum*; *X v Germany*, p. 103 – *no right to be consulted about conclusion of international treaties*).

- It is not clear whether the European Parliament now qualifies as a legislature (*Tete v France*, p. 68; *Matthews v UK*).

- The requirement that elections be held at reasonable intervals does not prevent a short extension of the period between voting where this facilitates good government (*Timke v Germany*, p. 160 – *increase from four- to five-year interval for elections*).

39.3   THE RIGHT TO VOTE

Key ECHR cases

Alliance of Belgians within the European Community v Belgium (1979) 15 DR 259, ECmHR
H v Netherlands (1979) 33 DR 242, ECmHR
X v Belgium (1979) 18 DR 250, ECmHR
X v Germany (1966) Coll Dec 25, p. 38, ECmHR
X v Netherlands (1974) 1 DR 87, ECmHR
X v UK (1976) 9 DR 121, ECmHR
X v UK (1979) 15 DR 137, ECmHR
X v UK (1982) 28 DR 99, ECmHR

ECHR principles

- Although Protocol 1, Article 3 does not expressly guarantee the right to vote, it has long been accepted that universal suffrage is implicit in it (*X v Germany*, p. 38).

- However, restrictions are permitted, so long as they are legitimate and not arbitrary (*X v Netherlands*, pp. 89–90 – *legitimate and reasonable both on basis of public safety and in the interests of democracy to prevent persons who had grossly misused their right to participate in public life during wartime from future participation*); *X v Belgium*, pp. 253–4 (*justified to deprive convicted wartime collaborator permanently of their right to vote*).

- Restricting the voting rights of prisoners can be justified in some circumstances:

  Such restrictions can be explained by the notion of dishonour that certain convictions carry with them for a specific period which may be taken into consideration by legislation in respect of the exercise of political rights. Although at first glance, it may seem inflexible that a prison sentence of more than one year should always result in a suspension of the exercise of the right to vote for three years, the Commission does not feel that such a measure goes beyond the restrictions justifiable in the context of Article 3. (H v Netherlands, p. 246 – *prisoners convicted of refusal to undertake military service could legitimately be disenfranchised*)

- Neither is the restriction of voting rights on the basis of residency prohibited, because of:

  . . . firstly, the assumption that a non-resident citizen is less directly or continuously interested in, and has less day-to-day knowledge of [a country's] problems; secondly, the impracticability for Parliamentary candidates of presenting the different electoral issues to citizens abroad so as to secure a free expression of opinion; thirdly, the need to prevent electoral fraud, the danger of which is increased in uncontrolled postal votes; and finally the link between the right of representation in the Parliamentary vote and the obligation to pay taxes . . . (X v UK (1976), p. 122; see also X v UK (1979), p. 139 – *citizens living abroad legitimately prevented from voting for Parliamentary elections, particularly given the absence of a uniform electoral procedure across the EC; Alliance of Belgians within the European Community v Belgium, p. 264 – Belgian resident in France unable to vote in European Parliament elections*)

- The historic exclusion of certain geographical areas can also be justified if based on the particular constitutional arrangements in force (X v UK (1982), p. 105 – *exclusion of Jersey citizen from voting for UK Parliament justified on basis that Channel Islanders were not resident in UK and had own elected legislature*).

- As can the exclusion of non-nationals: see Article 16, ECHR.

39.4 THE RIGHT TO STAND FOR ELECTION

Key ECHR cases

Ahmed and others v UK (1998) 29 EHRR 1, ECtHR

Association X, Y and Z v Germany (1976) 5 DR 90, ECmHR
Desmeules v France (1990) 67 DR 166, ECmHR
Fryske Nasjonale Partij v Netherlands (1985) 45 DR 240, ECmHR
Gitonas v Greece (1997) RJD 1997-IV No. 42, ECmHR
M v UK (1984) 37 DR 129, ECmHR
W, X, Y and Z v Belgium (1975) 2 DR 110, ECmHR
X v Austria (1976) 6 DR 120, ECmHR
X v Germany (2 March 1987), ECmHR

ECHR principles

- A right to stand as a candidate in elections is also implied in Protocol 1, Article 1; but again this is not absolute.

- Qualifying requirements can be laid down (*Gitonas v Greece*, para. 39; *Fryske Nasjonale Partij v Netherlands*, p. 242), provided they are not arbitrary.

- Setting minimum age-limits is acceptable (*W, X, Y and Z v Belgium*, p. 117); so is state funding based on the number of votes gained (*Association X, Y and Z v Germany*, p. 94) and a requirement that political parties obtain a certain number of supporting signatures before being permitted to participate in elections (*Association X, Y and Z v Germany*, p. 94; see also *X v Austria*, p. 121 and *Desmeules v France*, p. 173).

- But the state is under no positive obligation to assist candidates, even where such assistance may be crucial (*X v Germany*).

- Disqualification of candidates who are members of other legislatures is permitted (*M v UK*, p. 134 – *permissible to disqualify a member elected for Northern Ireland Assembly when already a Republic of Ireland MP*).

- And limited restrictions can be applied to public officials if the purpose is to preserve neutrality (*Gitonas v Greece* – *legitimate to disqualify those who had held public office in constituency during the past three years*; *Ahmed and others v UK* – *local authority officers were required to resign if they wanted to stand in elections*).

39.5 ENSURING THE FREE EXPRESSION OF THE PEOPLE

Key ECHR cases

Mathieu-Mohin and Clerfayt v Belgium (1987) 10 EHRR 1, ECtHR

Habsburg-Lothringen v Austria (1989) 64 DR 210, ECmHR[CD]
Huggett v UK (1995) 82-A DR 98, ECmHR
Liberal Party, R and P v UK (1980) 21 DR 211, ECmHR
Lindsay v UK (1979) 15 DR 247, ECmHR
Moureaux v Belgium (1983) 33 DR 97, ECmHR
Tete v France (1987) 54 DR 52, ECmHR
X v Iceland (1981) 27 DR 145, ECmHR
X v UK (1975) 7 DR 95, ECmHR

ECHR principles

- The free expression of the people can only be ensured if there is an unrestrained choice of candidates and voters are not coerced in any way (*Moureaux v Belgium*, p. 131).

- This is especially important to ensure the equal treatment of minorities (*Mathieu-Mohin and Clerfayt v Belgium*, para. 57).

- However, this does not mean that any particular type of electoral system should be adopted (*X v UK*, p. 96 – *complaint that Liberal Party voters were not being properly represented by voting system rejected*).

- Each system must be assessed in the light of political evolution and effectiveness (*Mathieu-Mohin and Clerfayt v Belgium*, para. 54)

- Citizens must enjoy equal treatment (*Mathieu-Mohin and Clerfayt v Belgium*, para. 54).

- But this does not necessarily mean that all votes must be of equal weight, nor that every candidate must enjoy an equal chance of success (*Liberal Party, R and P v UK*, pp. 224–5 – *Liberal Party's complaint about majority vote system in UK rejected since it was overall acceptable and did not become unfair by reason of the results obtained under it*; see also *X v Iceland*, p. 150).

- A system which positively favours minority groups is not necessarily incompatible with Protocol 1, Article 3 if it enables individuals to express their opinion freely (*Lindsay v UK*, p. 251 – *PR system in Northern Ireland justified as protecting the republican minority*).

- Protocol 1, Article 3 does not require a particular status or style for the head of state (*Habsburg-Lothringen v Austria*, p. 219).

39.6   FREE EXPRESSION IN ELECTIONS

Key ECHR cases

Bowman v UK (1998) 26 EHRR 1, ECHR

X v UK (1976) 3 DR 165, ECmHR

ECHR principles

- The right to free expression is guaranteed by Article 10, ECHR. While this does not expressly protect the right to vote (*X v UK*, p. 166), it is highly relevant where restrictions are placed on candidates or others in the election process or in public debate.

- In *Bowman v UK*, the ECtHR found that a statutory limitation on election expenditure operated, for all practical purposes, as a total barrier to the applicant's ability to publish information with a view to influencing voters. Although the aim was legitimate – securing equality between candidates – the restriction was disproportionate.

39.7   ELECTORAL RIGHTS AS CIVIL RIGHTS

Key ECHR cases

Pierre-Bloch v France (1 July 1996), ECtHR

Priorello v Italy (1985) 43 DR 195, ECmHR
X v France (1995) 82-B DR 56, ECmHR

ECHR principles

- As a general rule, electoral and political rights are not 'civil rights' for the purposes of Article 6(1) (*Priorello v Italy*, p. 197).

- As a result, fair trial guarantees do not apply to review proceedings concerning either the legality of an election, or the removal from office of an elected candidate for expenses irregularities (*X* v *France*, p. 74; *Pierre-Bloch* v *France*).

SECTION 40

DISCRIMINATION

40.1 THE MEANING OF DISCRIMINATION UNDER ARTICLE 14

Key ECHR cases

Belgian Linguistic Case (1968) 1 EHRR 252, ECtHR
Thlimmenos v Greece (6 April 2000), ECtHR

ECHR principles

- The prohibition of discrimination in Article 14, ECHR is framed in wide terms:

  The enjoyment of the rights and freedoms set forth in this Convention shall be secured without discrimination on any ground such as sex, race, colour, language, religion, political or other opinion, national or social origin, association with a national minority, property, birth or other status.

- The use of the words 'such as' and 'other status' indicate that the categories of prohibited discrimination under the Convention are not closed.

- Article 14 does not prohibit all kinds of distinction or differential treatment.

- The meaning of 'discrimination' under Article 14 is a difference in treatment which has no reasonable and objective justification.

- And such justification depends upon:

  (a) whether a legitimate aim for the measure can be made out; and
  (b) whether there is a reasonable relationship of proportionality between the means employed and that aim.

  See generally **1.3** to **1.6**.

- Failing to treat different individuals or groups differently may also breach Article 14:

  The Court has so far considered that the right under Article 14 not to be discriminated against in the enjoyment of the rights guaranteed under the Convention is violated when states treat differently persons in analogous situations without providing an objective and reasonable justification . . . However, the Court considers that the right not to be discriminated against in the enjoyment of the rights guaranteed under the Convention is also violated when states without an objective and reasonable justification fail to treat differently persons whose situations are significantly different. (*Thlimmenos v Greece*, para. **44** – *those with convictions for conscientious objection should not be treated the same as those with ordinary criminal convictions*)

- The burden is on the applicant to establish a difference in treatment; it then shifts to the state authority in question to justify that difference.

40.2   DIFFERENTIAL TREATMENT OF ANALOGOUS GROUPS

Key ECHR cases

Chassagnou and others v France (1999) 29 EHRR 615, ECtHR
Marckx v Belgium (1979) 2 EHRR 330, ECtHR
Van der Mussele v Belgium (1983) 6 EHRR 163, ECtHR

Lindsay v UK (1986) 49 DR 181, ECmHR[CD]
Malone v UK [1996] EHRLR 440, ECmHR
Nelson v UK (1986) 49 DR 170, ECmHR[CD]
X v UK (9 December 1992), ECmHR

ECHR principles

- To establish differential treatment, an applicant must show that he or she has been treated less favourably than others who are in a similar or analogous situation (*Marckx v Belgium*; *Van der Mussele v Belgium*).

- The list of characteristics which might render differential treatment discriminatory under Article 14 – sex, race, colour, language, religion, political or other opinion, national or social origin, association with a national minority, property, birth or other status – is the starting point.

- And 'other status' has been interpreted so as to include sexual orientation, marital status, illegitimacy, status as a trade union, military status, conscientious objection, professional status and imprisonment.

- It also includes disability (*Malone v UK*) and a difference between large and small landowners, whereby the former but not the latter may object to hunting on their land, which constitutes discrimination on the ground of property (*Chassagnou and others v France* – *hunting regulations*).

- But it is important to show that any difference in treatment is based on the characteristic identified (*Van der Mussele v Belgium* – *trainee barrister not to be compared with apprentices in other professions*; see also *Lindsay v UK* – *married couples are not in an analogous position to unmarried couples*; *Nelson v UK* – *juvenile prisoner not in an analogous position to prisoner*; *X v UK* – *IRA category A prisoner not in an analogous position to prisoners of no security risk*).

40.3   INDIRECT DISCRIMINATION

Key ECHR cases

Abdulaziz, Cabales and Balkandali v UK (1985) 7 EHRR 471, ECtHR
Belgian Linguistic Case (1968) 1 EHRR 252, ECtHR

ECHR principles

- Indirect discrimination can fall within Article 14: the existence of 'reasonable and objective justification' has to be assessed in relation to the 'aim and *effects*' (emphasis added) of the measure in question (*Belgian Linguistic Case*).

- However, the burden of proving indirect discrimination is heavy (see *Abdulaziz, Cabales and Balkandali v UK*).

40.4   JUSTIFYING DIFFERENTIAL TREATMENT

Key ECHR cases

Darby v Sweden (1990) 13 EHRR 774, ECtHR
Larkos v Cyprus (18 February 1999), ECtHR
National Union of Belgian Police v Belgium (1975) 1 EHRR 578, ECtHR
Rasmussen v Denmark (1984) 7 EHRR 371, ECtHR

ECHR principles

40.4.1   *Justification*

- The meaning of 'discrimination' under Article 14 is a difference in treatment which has 'no reasonable and objective justification'.

- And such justification depends upon:

    (a)   whether a legitimate aim for the measure can be made out; and
    (b)   whether there is a reasonable relationship of proportionality between the means employed and that aim.

40.4.2   *Legitimate aim*

- Once a difference in treatment is established it requires rational justification.

- A measure that has the effect of treating individuals differently can be justified under Article 14 on the basis of the 'public interest', but only where there is convincing evidence as to why the public interest will be served (*Larkos v Greece*, para. 31).

- Where no real justification is advanced, a breach of Article 14 will be found (*Darby v Sweden – Swedish government did not seek to justify a discriminatory tax policy because, in reality, it was based on administrative convenience*).

40.4.3   *Proportionality*

- For a detailed examination of proportionality, see **1.6**.

- An assessment of proportionality inevitably involves a detailed analysis of a number of factors, including:

(a)   whether 'relevant and sufficient' reasons have been advanced in support of the measure in question;

(b)   whether there was a less restrictive alternative; and

(c)   the actual effects on the individuals in question.

- Where the disadvantage suffered by an individual in relation to an otherwise legitimate aim is excessive, Article 14 is likely to be breached (*National Union of Belgian Police v Belgium*).

- Where there is a common standard concerning the prohibition of discrimination in Europe, it will be difficult to justify a measure that falls short of that standard (*Rasmussen v Denmark*).

- And the European Court has, in effect, now developed a number of 'suspect groups' where very weighty reasons will have to be advanced by a state seeking to establish that a discriminatory measure is proportionate (see **40.5**).

40.5   SUSPECT GROUPS

Key ECHR cases

Abdulaziz, Cabales and Balkandali v UK (1985) 7 EHRR 471, ECtHR
Gaygusuz v Austria (1996) 23 EHRR 365, ECtHR
Hoffmann v Austria (1993) 17 EHRR 293, ECtHR
Inze v Austria (1987) 10 EHRR 394, ECtHR
Karlheinz Schmidt v Germany (1994) 18 EHRR 513, ECtHR
Van Raalte v Netherlands (1997) 24 EHRR 503, ECtHR

East African Asians v UK (1973) 3 EHRR 76, ECmHR

ECHR principles

- The ECtHR recognises a number of 'suspect groups' where very weighty reasons will have to be advanced by a state seeking to establish that a discriminatory measure is proportionate:

    . . . the advancement of the equality of the sexes is today a major goal in the Member States of the Council of Europe . . . very weighty reasons would have to be advanced before a difference in treatment on the grounds of sex could be considered compatible with the Convention. (*Abdulaziz, Cabales and Balkandali v UK* para. 78; see also *Karlheinz Schmidt v Germany* and *Van Raalte v Netherlands*)

- Other groups include race (*East African Asians v UK*), nationality (*Gaygusuz v Austria*), illegitimacy (*Inze v Austria*) and religion (*Hoffmann v Austria*).

40.6   POSITIVE DISCRIMINATION

Key ECHR cases

Belgian Linguistic Case (1968) 1 EHRR 252, ECtHR

Lindsay v UK (1986) 49 DR 181, ECmHR[CD]

ECHR principles

- The aim of redressing a pre-existing situation of inequality has been accepted as a legitimate objective of differential treatment (*Belgian Linguistic Case* – *not all instances of differential treatment breached Article 14 and that 'certain legal inequalities tend only to correct factual inequalities'*; see also *Lindsay v UK* – *tax legislation favourable to women justified because designed to encourage more married women to work and thereby overcome male prejudice toward them and advance the equality of the sexes*).

Relevant Canadian cases

Law v *Canada* (*Minister of Employment and Immigration*) [1999] 1 SCR 497
Vriend v *Alberta* [1998] 1 SCR 493

- The right not to be discriminated against (as guaranteed by s. 15(1) of the Canadian Charter) must be interpreted and applied in a purposive and contextual instead of formalistic or mechanical manner:

  > In general terms the purpose of s. 15(1) is to prevent the violation of essential human dignity and freedom through the imposition of disadvantage, stereotyping, or political or social prejudice, and to promote a society in which all persons enjoy equal recognition at law as human beings . . . equally capable and equally deserving of concern, respect and consideration. (*Law* v *Canada* (*Minister of Employment and Immigration*), para. 88)

- Evidence of pre-existing disadvantage will be highly significant in determining whether differential treatment amounts to discrimination:

  > [P]robably the most compelling factor favouring a conclusion that differential treatment imposed by legislation is truly discriminatory will be, where it exists, pre-existing disadvantage, vulnerability, stereotyping, or prejudice experienced by the individual or group. These factors are relevant because, to the extent that the claimant is already subject to unfair circumstances or treatment in society by virtue of personal characteristics or circumstances, persons like him or her have often not been given equal concern, respect and consideration. It is logical to conclude that, in most cases, further differential treatment will contribute to the perpetuation of promotion of their unfair social characterization, and will have a more severe impact upon them, since they are already vulnerable. (*Law* v *Canada* (*Minister of Employment and Immigration*), para. 63)

- Discrimination may not result where the law has an ameliorative purpose or effect for another historically disadvantaged group:

  > An ameliorative purpose or effect which accords with the purpose of s. 15(1) . . . will likely not violate the human dignity of more advantaged individuals where the exclusion of these more advantaged individuals largely corresponds to the greater need or the different circumstances experienced by the disadvantaged group being targeted by the legislation. I emphasise that this factor will likely only be relevant where the person or group that is excluded from the scope of ameliorative legislation or other state action is more advantaged in a relative sense. Underinclusive ameliorative legislation that excludes from its scope the members of an historically disadvantaged group will rarely escape the charge of discrimination. (*Law* v *Canada* (*Minister of Employment and Immigration*), para. 72)

40.7   THE SPECIAL OPERATION OF ARTICLE 14

Key ECHR cases

Abdulaziz, Cabales and Balkandali v UK (1985) 7 EHRR 471, ECtHR
Belgian Linguistic Case (1968) 1 EHRR 252, ECtHR
Rasmussen v Denmark (1984) 7 EHRR 371, ECtHR

X v Germany (1975) 19 Yearbook 276, ECmHR
X v Netherlands (1971) 38 Coll Dec 9, ECmHR
X v Netherlands (1973) 16 Yearbook 274, ECmHR

ECHR principles

40.7.1   *The dependent nature of Article 14*

- The reach of the prohibition of discrimination under Article 14, ECHR is limited to those rights embodied in the Convention and its Protocols.

- It can only be invoked in conjunction with one of the other ECHR rights.

- And in this sense it is dependent upon those other rights.

- However, a breach of Article 14, can be found even where there is no violation of a substantive right:

    While it is true that this guarantee has no independent existence in the sense that under the terms of Article 14 it relates solely to 'rights and freedoms set forth in the Convention', a measure which in itself is in conformity with the requirements of the Article enshrining the right or freedom in question may however infringe this Article when read in conjunction with Article 14 for the reason that it is of a discriminatory nature. (*Belgian Linguistic Case*, para. 9)

- While there can never be a breach of Article 14 considered in isolation, there may be a breach of Article 14 considered in conjunction with another Article of the Convention in cases where there would be no violation of that other Article taken alone (*Abdulaziz, Cabales and Balkandali v UK*).

- Furthermore, issues of discrimination may arise even in areas where states are not obliged to provide specific protection: where a state chooses to do more than is strictly required to 'secure' a Convention right in its domestic law, Article 14 applies to all aspects of the right provided:

    . . . Article 6 of the Convention does not compel States to institute a system of appeal courts. A State which does set up such courts consequently goes beyond its obligations under Article 6. However, it would violate that Article, read in conjunction with Article 14, were it to debar certain persons from these remedies without legitimate reason while making them available to others in respect of the same type of actions. (*Belgian Linguistic Case*)

- The result is that a claim may fail on the basis that the state had no duty to provide the right sought by the applicant, but succeed under Article 14 if the right has, in fact been provided but on a discriminatory basis.

40.7.2 *The ambit test*

- The test for the application of Article 14 is whether the facts in issue 'fall within the ambit' of one or more of the other Convention provisions (*Rasmussen v Denmark*).

- This is fulfilled if the 'subject matter' falls within the scope of the article in question (*X v Germany*); so, for example, Article 14 issues can be examined in relation to possessions/property even where, on analysis, Protocol 1, Article 1 protection does not apply (*X v Netherlands* (1971); *X v Netherlands* (1973)).

40.8 DISCRIMINATION AS DEGRADING TREATMENT

Key ECHR cases

Abdulaziz, Cabales and Balkandali v UK (1985) 7 EHRR 471, ECtHR

East African Asians v UK (1973) 3 EHRR 76, ECmHR
Hilton v UK (1976) 4 DR 177, ECmHR
Lalljee v UK (1986) 8 EHRR 84, ECmHR

ECHR principles

- Although the threshold for degrading treatment under Article 3 is high, in certain circumstances institutional discrimination is *capable* of reaching that threshold:

  > . . . a special importance should be attached to discrimination based on race; that publicly to single out a group of persons for differential treatment on the basis of race might, in certain circumstances, constitute a special form of affront to human dignity; and that differential treatment of a group of persons on the basis of race might therefore be capable of constituting degrading treatment when differential treatment on some other ground would raise no such question. (*East African Asians v UK*, para. 207)

- The certain circumstances referred to include (but are not limited to): reneging on specific pledges; the destitution faced by returning immigrants; and the manner in which immigration is operated.

- Absent the same, or similar, circumstances, Article 3 is unlikely to be engaged; e.g., so long as there are no aggravating features, operating a quota system is not necessarily degrading (*Lalljee v UK*, p. 85), the focus being dignity and respect:

  > . . . the difference in treatment . . . did not denote any contempt or lack of respect for the personality of the applicants . . . it was not designed to, and did not, humiliate or debase them. (*Abdulaziz, Cabales and Balkandali v UK*, para. 91)

- Grossly racist remarks (*East African Asians v UK*, paras 207–208) and racial harassment (*Hilton v UK* p. 187) are also capable of amounting to degrading treatment contrary to Article 3.

APPENDIX 1

THE HUMAN RIGHTS ACT 1998

CHAPTER 42

ARRANGEMENT OF SECTIONS

Parliamentary procedure

19.   Statements of compatibility.

Supplemental

20.   Orders etc. under this Act.
21.   Interpretation, etc.
22.   Short title, commencement, application and extent.

SCHEDULES:

Schedule 1—The Articles.
   Part I—The Convention.
   Part II—The First Protocol.
   Part III—The Sixth Protocol.
Schedule 2—Remedial Orders.
Schedule 3—Derogation and Reservation.
   Part I—Derogation.
   Part II—Reservation.
Schedule 4—Judicial Pensions.

Human Rights Act 1998

1998 CHAPTER 42

An Act to give further effect to rights and freedoms guaranteed under the European Convention on Human Rights; to make provision with respect to holders of certain judicial offices who become judges of the European Court of Human Rights; and for connected purposes.   [9th November 1998]

BE IT ENACTED by the Queen's most Excellent Majesty, by and with the advice and consent of the Lords Spiritual and Temporal, and Commons, in this present Parliament assembled, and by the authority of the same, as follows:—

Introduction

1. The Convention Rights

(1)   In this Act 'the Convention rights' means the rights and fundamental freedoms set out in—

(a)   Articles 2 to 12 and 14 of the Convention,

(b)   Articles 1 to 3 of the First Protocol, and

(c)   Articles 1 and 2 of the Sixth Protocol,

as read with Articles 16 to 18 of the Convention.

(2)   Those Articles are to have effect for the purposes of this Act subject to any designated derogation or reservation (as to which see sections 14 and 15).

(3)   The Articles are set out in Schedule 1.

(4)   The Secretary of State may by order make such amendments to this Act as he considers appropriate to reflect the effect, in relation to the United Kingdom, of a protocol.

(5)   In subsection (4) 'protocol' means a protocol to the Convention—

(a)   which the United Kingdom has ratified; or

(b)   which the United Kingdom has signed with a view to ratification.

(6)   No amendment may be made by an order under subsection (4) so as to come into force before the protocol concerned is in force in relation to the United Kingdom.

2. Interpretation of Convention rights

(1)   A court or tribunal determining a question which has arisen in connection with a Convention right must take into account any—

(a)   judgment, decision, declaration or advisory opinion of the European Court of Human Rights,

(b)   opinion of the Commission given in a report adopted under Article 31 of the Convention,

(c)   decision of the Commission in connection with Article 26 or 27(2) of the Convention, or

(d)   decision of the Committee of Ministers taken under Article 46 of the Convention,

whenever made or given, so far as, in the opinion of the court or tribunal, it is relevant to the proceedings in which that question has arisen.

(2)   Evidence of any judgment, decision, declaration or opinion of which account may have to be taken under this section is to be given in proceedings before any court or tribunal in such manner as may be provided by rules.

(3)   In this section 'rules' means rules of court or, in the case of proceedings before a tribunal, rules made for the purposes of this section—

(a)   by the Lord Chancellor or the Secretary of State, in relation to any proceedings outside Scotland;

(b)   by the Secretary of State, in relation to proceedings in Scotland; or

(c)   by a Northern Ireland department, in relation to proceedings before a tribunal in Northern Ireland—

(i)   which deals with transferred matters; and

(ii)   for which no rules made under paragraph (a) are in force.

Legislation

3.   Interpretation of legislation

(1)   So far as it is possible to do so, primary legislation and subordinate legislation must be read and given effect in a way which is compatible with the Convention rights.

(2)   This section—

(a)   applies to primary legislation and subordinate legislation whenever enacted;

(b)   does not affect the validity, continuing operation or enforcement of any incompatible primary legislation; and

(c)   does not affect the validity, continuing operation or enforcement of any incompatible subordinate legislation if (disregarding any possibility of revocation) primary legislation prevents removal of the incompatibility.

4.   Declaration of incompatibility

(1)   Subsection (2) applies in any proceedings in which a court determines whether a provision of primary legislation is compatible with a Convention right.

(2)   If the court is satisfied that the provision is incompatible with a Convention right, it may make a declaration of that incompatibility.

(3)   Subsection (4) applies in any proceedings in which a court determines whether a provision of subordinate legislation, made in the exercise of a power conferred by primary legislation, is compatible with a Convention right.

(4)   If the court is satisfied—

(a)   that the provision is incompatible with a Convention right, and

(b)   that (disregarding any possibility of revocation) the primary legislation concerned prevents removal of the incompatibility,

it may make a declaration of that incompatibility.

(5)   In this section 'court' means—

(a)   the House of Lords;

    (b)   the Judicial Committee of the Privy Council;

    (c)   the Courts-Martial Appeal Court;

    (d)   in Scotland, the High Court of Justiciary sitting otherwise than as a trial court or the Court of Session;

    (e)   in England and Wales or Northern Ireland, the High Court or the Court of Appeal.

    (6)   A declaration under this section ('a declaration of incompatibility')—

    (a)   does not affect the validity, continuing operation or enforcement of the provision in respect of which it is given; and

    (b)   is not binding on the parties to the proceedings in which it is made.

5. Right of Crown to intervene

    (1)   Where a court is considering whether to make a declaration of incompatibility, the Crown is entitled to notice in accordance with rules of court.

    (2)   In any case to which subsection (1) applies—

    (a)   a Minister of the Crown (or a person nominated by him),

    (b)   a member of the Scottish Executive,

    (c)   a Northern Ireland Minister,

    (d)   a Northern Ireland department,

is entitled, on giving notice in accordance with rules of court, to be joined as a party to the proceedings.

    (3)   Notice under subsection (2) may be given at any time during the proceedings.

    (4)   A person who has been made a party to criminal proceedings (other than in Scotland) as the result of a notice under subsection (2) may, with leave, appeal to the House of Lords against any declaration of incompatibility made in the proceedings.

    (5)   In subsection (4)—

'criminal proceedings' includes all proceedings before the Courts-Martial Appeal Court; and

'leave' means leave granted by the court making the declaration of incompatibility or by the House of Lords.

Public authorities

6. Acts of public authorities

    (1)   It is unlawful for a public authority to act in a way which is incompatible with a Convention right.

    (2)   Subsection (1) does not apply to an act if—

    (a)   as the result of one or more provisions of primary legislation, the authority could not have acted differently; or

    (b)   in the case of one or more provisions of, or made under, primary legislation which cannot be read or given effect in a way which is compatible with the Convention rights, the authority was acting so as to give effect to or enforce those provisions.

    (3)   In this section 'public authority' includes—

    (a)   a court or tribunal, and

    (b)   any person certain of whose functions are functions of a public nature,

but does not include either House of Parliament or a person exercising functions in connection with proceedings in Parliament.

(4)   In subsection (3) 'Parliament' does not include the House of Lords in its judicial capacity.

(5)   In relation to a particular act, a person is not a public authority by virtue only of subsection (3)(b) if the nature of the act is private.

(6)   'An act' includes a failure to act but does not include a failure to—

(a)   introduce in, or lay before, Parliament a proposal for legislation; or

(b)   make any primary legislation or remedial order.

7.   Proceedings

(1)   A person who claims that a public authority has acted (or proposes to act) in a way which is made unlawful by section 6(1) may—

(a)   bring proceedings against the authority under this Act in the appropriate court or tribunal, or

(b)   rely on the Convention right or rights concerned in any legal proceedings,

but only if he is (or would be) a victim of the unlawful act.

(2)   In subsection (1)(a) 'appropriate court or tribunal' means such court or tribunal as may be determined in accordance with rules; and proceedings against an authority include a counterclaim or similar proceeding.

(3)   If the proceedings are brought on an application for judicial review, the applicant is to be taken to have a sufficient interest in relation to the unlawful act only if he is, or would be, a victim of that act.

(4)   If the proceedings are made by way of a petition for judicial review in Scotland, the applicant shall be taken to have title and interest to sue in relation to the unlawful act only if he is, or would be, a victim of that act.

(5)   Proceedings under subsection (1)(a) must be brought before the end of—

(a)   the period of one year beginning with the date on which the act complained of took place; or

(b)   such longer period as the court or tribunal considers equitable having regard to all the circumstances,

but that is subject to any rule imposing a stricter time limit in relation to the procedure in question.

(6)   In subsection (1)(b) 'legal proceedings' includes—

(a)   proceedings brought by or at the instigation of a public authority; and

(b)   an appeal against the decision of a court or tribunal.

(7)   For the purposes of this section, a person is a victim of an unlawful act only if he would be a victim for the purposes of Article 34 of the Convention if proceedings were brought in the European Court of Human Rights in respect of that act.

(8)   Nothing in this Act creates a criminal offence.

(9)   In this section 'rules' means—

(a)   in relation to proceedings before a court or tribunal outside Scotland, rules made by the Lord Chancellor or the Secretary of State for the purposes of this section or rules of court,

(b)   in relation to proceedings before a court or tribunal in Scotland, rules made by the Secretary of State for those purposes,

(c)   in relation to proceedings before a tribunal in Northern Ireland—

(i)   which deals with transferred matters; and

(ii)   for which no rules made under paragraph (a) are in force,

rules made by a Northern Ireland department for those purposes,
and includes provision made by order under section 1 of the Courts and Legal Services Act 1990.

(10) In making rules, regard must be had to section 9.

(11) The Minister who has power to make rules in relation to a particular tribunal may, to the extent he considers it necessary to ensure that the tribunal can provide an appropriate remedy in relation to an act (or proposed act) of a public authority which is (or would be) unlawful as a result of section 6(1), by order add to—

(a) the relief or remedies which the tribunal may grant; or

(b) the grounds on which it may grant any of them.

(12) An order made under subsection (11) may contain such incidental, supplemental, consequential or transitional provision as the Minister making it considers appropriate.

(13) 'The Minister' includes the Northern Ireland department concerned.

8. Judicial remedies

(1) In relation to any act (or proposed act) of a public authority which the court finds is (or would be) unlawful, it may grant such relief or remedy, or make such order, within its powers as it considers just and appropriate.

(2) But damages may be awarded only by a court which has power to award damages, or to order the payment of compensation, in civil proceedings.

(3) No award of damages is to be made unless, taking account of all the circumstances of the case, including—

(a) any other relief or remedy granted, or order made, in relation to the act in question (by that or any other court), and

(b) the consequences of any decision (of that or any other court) in respect of that act,

the court is satisfied that the award is necessary to afford just satisfaction to the person in whose favour it is made.

(4) In determining—

(a) whether to award damages, or

(b) the amount of an award,

the court must take into account the principles applied by the European Court of Human Rights in relation to the award of compensation under Article 41 of the Convention.

(5) A public authority against which damages are awarded is to be treated—

(a) in Scotland, for the purposes of section 3 of the Law Reform (Miscellaneous Provisions) (Scotland) Act 1940 as if the award were made in an action of damages in which the authority has been found liable in respect of loss or damage to the person to whom the award is made;

(b) for the purposes of the Civil Liability (Contribution) Act 1978 as liable in respect of damage suffered by the person to whom the award is made.

(6) In this section—

'court' includes a tribunal;

'damages' means damages for an unlawful act of a public authority; and

'unlawful' means unlawful under section 6(1).

9. Judicial acts

(1) Proceedings under section 7(1)(a) in respect of a judicial act may be brought only—

     (a)   by exercising a right of appeal;

     (b)   on an application (in Scotland a petition) for judicial review; or

     (c)   in such other forum as may be prescribed by rules.

   (2)   That does not affect any rule of law which prevents a court from being the subject of judicial review.

   (3)   In proceedings under this Act in respect of a judicial act done in good faith, damages may not be awarded otherwise than to compensate a person to the extent required by Article 5(5) of the Convention.

   (4)   An award of damages permitted by subsection (3) is to be made against the Crown; but no award may be made unless the appropriate person, if not a party to the proceedings, is joined.

   (5)   In this section—

'appropriate person' means the Minister responsible for the court concerned, or a person or government department nominated by him;

'court' includes a tribunal;

'judge' includes a member of a tribunal, a justice of the peace and a clerk or other officer entitled to exercise the jurisdiction of a court;

'judicial act' means a judicial act of a court and includes an act done on the instructions, or on behalf, of a judge; and

'rules' has the same meaning as in section 7(9).

Remedial action

10.   Power to take remedial action

   (1)   This section applies if—

     (a)   a provision of legislation has been declared under section 4 to be incompatible with a Convention right and, if an appeal lies—

       (i)   all persons who may appeal have stated in writing that they do not intend to do so;

       (ii)   the time for bringing an appeal has expired and no appeal has been brought within that time; or

       (iii)   an appeal brought within that time has been determined or abandoned; or

     (b)   it appears to a Minister of the Crown or Her Majesty in Council that, having regard to a finding of the European Court of Human Rights made after the coming into force of this section in proceedings against the United Kingdom, a provision of legislation is incompatible with an obligation of the United Kingdom arising from the Convention.

   (2)   If a Minister of the Crown considers that there are compelling reasons for proceeding under this section, he may by order make such amendments to the legislation as he considers necessary to remove the incompatibility.

   (3)   If, in the case of subordinate legislation, a Minister of the Crown considers—

     (a)   that it is necessary to amend the primary legislation under which the subordinate legislation in question was made, in order to enable the incompatibility to be removed, and

     (b)   that there are compelling reasons for proceeding under this section,

he may by order make such amendments to the primary legislation as he considers necessary.

   (4)   This section also applies where the provision in question is in subordinate legislation and has been quashed, or declared invalid, by reason of incompatibility

with a Convention right and the Minister proposes to proceed under paragraph 2(b) of Schedule 2.

(5)   If the legislation is an Order in Council, the power conferred by subsection (2) or (3) is exercisable by Her Majesty in Council.

(6)   In this section 'legislation' does not include a Measure of the Church Assembly or of the General Synod of the Church of England.

(7)   Schedule 2 makes further provision about remedial orders.

Other rights and proceedings

11.   Safeguard for existing human rights
A person's reliance on a Convention right does not restrict—

(a)   any other right or freedom conferred on him by or under any law having effect in any part of the United Kingdom; or

(b)   his right to make any claim or bring any proceedings which he could make or bring apart from sections 7 to 9.

12.   Freedom of expression
(1)   This section applies if a court is considering whether to grant any relief which, if granted, might affect the exercise of the Convention right to freedom of expression.

(2)   If the person against whom the application for relief is made ('the respondent') is neither present nor represented, no such relief is to be granted unless the court is satisfied—

(a)   that the applicant has taken all practicable steps to notify the respondent; or

(b)   that there are compelling reasons why the respondent should not be notified.

(3)   No such relief is to be granted so as to restrain publication before trial unless the court is satisfied that the applicant is likely to establish that publication should not be allowed.

(4)   The court must have particular regard to the importance of the Convention right to freedom of expression and, where the proceedings relate to material which the respondent claims, or which appears to the court, to be journalistic, literary or artistic material (or to conduct connected with such material), to—

(a)   the extent to which—

(i)   the material has, or is about to, become available to the public; or

(ii)   it is, or would be, in the public interest for the material to be published;

(b)   any relevant privacy code.

(5)   In this section—
'court' includes a tribunal; and
'relief' includes any remedy or order (other than in criminal proceedings).

13.   Freedom of thought, conscience and religion
(1)   If a court's determination of any question arising under this Act might affect the exercise by a religious organisation (itself or its members collectively) of the Convention right to freedom of thought, conscience and religion, it must have particular regard to the importance of that right.

(2)   In this section 'court' includes a tribunal.

Derogations and reservations

14. Derogations
(1) In this Act 'designated derogation' means—

(a) the United Kingdom's derogation from Article 5(3) of the Convention; and

(b) any derogation by the United Kingdom from an Article of the Convention, or of any protocol to the Convention, which is designated for the purposes of this Act in an order made by the Secretary of State.

(2) The derogation referred to in subsection (1)(a) is set out in Part I of Schedule 3.

(3) If a designated derogation is amended or replaced it ceases to be a designated derogation.

(4) But subsection (3) does not prevent the Secretary of State from exercising his power under subsection (1)(b) to make a fresh designation order in respect of the Article concerned.

(5) The Secretary of State must by order make such amendments to Schedule 3 as he considers appropriate to reflect—

(a) any designation order; or

(b) the effect of subsection (3).

(6) A designation order may be made in anticipation of the making by the United Kingdom of a proposed derogation.

15. Reservations
(1) In this Act 'designated reservation' means—

(a) the United Kingdom's reservation to Article 2 of the First Protocol to the Convention; and

(b) any other reservation by the United Kingdom to an Article of the Convention, or of any protocol to the Convention, which is designated for the purposes of this Act in an order made by the Secretary of State.

(2) The text of the reservation referred to in subsection (1)(a) is set out in Part 11 of Schedule 3.

(3) If a designated reservation is withdrawn wholly or in part it ceases to be a designated reservation.

(4) But subsection (3) does not prevent the Secretary of State from exercising his power under subsection (1)(b) to make a fresh designation order in respect of the Article concerned.

(5) The Secretary of State must by order make such amendments to this Act as he considers appropriate to reflect—

(a) any designation order; or

(b) the effect of subsection (3).

16. Period for which designated derogations have effect
(1) If it has not already been withdrawn by the United Kingdom, a designated derogation ceases to have effect for the purposes of this Act—

(a) in the case of the derogation referred to in section 14(1)(a), at the end of the period of five years beginning with the date on which section 1(2) came into force;

(b) in the case of any other derogation, at the end of the period of five years beginning with the date on which the order designating it was made.

(2)   At any time before the period—
   (a)   fixed by subsection (1)(a) or (b), or
   (b)   extended by an order under this subsection,
comes to an end, the Secretary of State may by order extend it by a further period
of five years.

(3)   An order under section 14(1)(b) ceases to have effect at the end of the
period for consideration, unless a resolution has been passed by each House
approving the order.

(4)   Subsection (3) does not affect—
   (a)   anything done in reliance on the order; or
   (b)   the power to make a fresh order under section 14(1)(b).

(5)   In subsection (3) 'period for consideration' means the period of forty days
beginning with the day on which the order was made.

(6)   In calculating the period for consideration, no account is to be taken of any
time during which—
   (a)   Parliament is dissolved or prorogued; or
   (b)   both Houses are adjourned for more than four days.

(7)   If a designated derogation is withdrawn by the United Kingdom, the
Secretary of State must by order make such amendments to this Act as he considers
are required to reflect that withdrawal.

17.   Periodic review of designated reservations

(1)   The appropriate Minister must review the designated reservation referred to
in section 15(1)(a)—
   (a)   before the end of the period of five years beginning with the date on
which section 1(2) came into force; and
   (b)   if that designation is still in force, before the end of the period of five
years beginning with the date on which the last report relating to it was laid under
subsection (3).

(2)   The appropriate Minister must review each of the other designated reservations (if any)—
   (a)   before the end of the period of five years beginning with the date on
which the order designating the reservation first came into force; and
   (b)   if the designation is still in force, before the end of the period of five years
beginning with the date on which the last report relating to it was laid under
subsection (3).

(3)   The Minister conducting a review under this section must prepare a report
on the result of the review and lay a copy of it before each House of Parliament.

Judges of the European Court of Human Rights

18.   Appointment to European Court of Human Rights

(1)   In this section 'judicial office' means the office of—
   (a)   Lord Justice of Appeal, Justice of the High Court or Circuit judge, in
England and Wales;
   (b)   judge of the Court of Session or sheriff, in Scotland;
   (c)   Lord Justice of Appeal, judge of the High Court or county court judge,
in Northern Ireland.

(2)   The holder of a judicial office may become a judge of the European Court
of Human Rights ('the Court') without being required to relinquish his office.

(3)   But he is not required to perform the duties of his judicial office while he is a judge of the Court.

(4)   In respect of any period during which he is a judge of the Court—

(a)   a Lord Justice of Appeal or Justice of the High Court is not to count as a judge of the relevant court for the purposes of section 2(1) or 4(1) of the Supreme Court Act 1981 (maximum number of judges) nor as a judge of the Supreme Court for the purposes of section 12(1) to (6) of that Act (salaries etc.);

(b)   a judge of the Court of Session is not to count as a judge of that court for the purposes of section 1(1) of the Court of Session Act 1988 (maximum number of judges) or of section 9(1)(c) of the Administration of Justice Act 1973 ('the 1973 Act') (salaries etc.);

(c)   a Lord Justice of Appeal or judge of the High Court in Northern Ireland is not to count as a judge of the relevant court for the purposes of section 2(1) or 3(1) of the Judicature (Northern Ireland) Act 1978 (maximum number of judges) nor as a judge of the Supreme Court of Northern Ireland for the purposes of section 9(1)(d) of the 1973 Act (salaries etc.);

(d)   a Circuit judge is not to count as such for the purposes of section 18 of the Courts Act 1971 (salaries etc.);

(e)   a sheriff is not to count as such for the purposes of section 14 of the Sheriff Courts (Scotland) Act 1907 (salaries etc.);

(f)   a county court judge of Northern Ireland is not to count as such for the purposes of section 106 of the County Courts Act (Northern Ireland) 1959 (salaries etc.).

(5)   If a sheriff principal is appointed a judge of the Court, section 11(1) of the Sheriff Courts (Scotland) Act 1971 (temporary appointment of sheriff principal) applies, while he holds that appointment, as if his office is vacant.

(6)   Schedule 4 makes provision about judicial pensions in relation to the holder of a judicial office who serves as a judge of the Court.

(7)   The Lord Chancellor or the Secretary of State may by order make such transitional provision (including, in particular, provision for a temporary increase in the maximum number of judges) as he considers appropriate in relation to any holder of a judicial office who has completed his service as a judge of the Court.

Parliamentary procedure

19.   Statements of compatibility

(1)   A Minister of the Crown in charge of a Bill in either House of Parliament must, before Second Reading of the Bill—

(a)   make a statement to the effect that in his view the provisions of the Bill are compatible with the Convention rights ('a statement of compatibility'); or

(b)   make a statement to the effect that although he is unable to make a statement of compatibility the government nevertheless wishes the House to proceed with the Bill.

(2)   The statement must be in writing and be published in such manner as the Minister making it considers appropriate.

Supplemental

20.   Orders etc. under this Act

(1)   Any power of a Minister of the Crown to make an order under this Act is exercisable by statutory instrument.

(2)   The power of the Lord Chancellor or the Secretary of State to make rules (other than rules of court) under section 2(3) or 7(9) is exercisable by statutory instrument.

(3)   Any statutory instrument made under section 14, 15 or 16(7) must be laid before Parliament.

(4)   No order may be made by the Lord Chancellor or the Secretary of State under section 1(4), 7(11) or 16(2) unless a draft of the order has been laid before, and approved by, each House of Parliament.

(5)   Any statutory instrument made under section 18(7) or Schedule 4, or to which subsection (2) applies, shall be subject to annulment in pursuance of a resolution of either House of Parliament.

(6)   The power of a Northern Ireland department to make—
  (a)   rules under section 2(3)(c) or 7(9)(c), or
  (b)   an order under section 7(11),
is exercisable by statutory rule for the purposes of the Statutory Rules (Northern Ireland) Order 1979.

(7)   Any rules made under section 2(3)(c) or 7(9)(c) shall be subject to negative resolution; and section 41(6) of the Interpretation Act (Northern Ireland) 1954 (meaning of 'subject to negative resolution') shall apply as if the power to make the rules were conferred by an Act of the Northern Ireland Assembly.

(8)   No order may be made by a Northern Ireland department under section 7(11) unless a draft of the order has been laid before, and approved by, the Northern Ireland Assembly.

21.   Interpretation etc.

(1)   In this Act—
'amend' includes repeal and apply (with or without modifications);
'the appropriate Minister' means the Minister of the Crown having charge of the appropriate authorised government department (within the meaning of the Crown Proceedings Act 1947);
'the Commission' means the European Commission of Human Rights;
'the Convention' means the Convention for the Protection of Human Rights and Fundamental Freedoms, agreed by the Council of Europe at Rome on 4th November 1950 as it has effect for the time being in relation to the United Kingdom;
'declaration of incompatibility' means a declaration under section 4;
'Minister of the Crown' has the same meaning as in the Ministers of the Crown Act 1975;
'Northern Ireland Minister' includes the First Minister and the deputy First Minister in Northern Ireland;
'primary legislation' means any—
  (a)   public general Act;
  (b)   local and personal Act;
  (c)   private Act;
  (d)   Measure of the Church Assembly;
  (e)   Measure of the General Synod of the Church of England;
  (f)   Order in Council—
    (i)   made in exercise of Her Majesty's Royal Prerogative;
    (ii)   made under section 38(1)(a) of the Northern Ireland Constitution
Act 1973 or the corresponding provision of the Northern Ireland Act 1998; or

(iii)   amending an Act of a kind mentioned in paragraph (a), (b) or (c); and includes an order or other instrument made under primary legislation (otherwise than by the National Assembly for Wales, a member of the Scottish Executive, a Northern Ireland Minister or a Northern Ireland department) to the extent to which it operates to bring one or more provisions of that legislation into force or amends any primary legislation;

'the First Protocol' means the protocol to the Convention agreed at Paris on 20th March 1952;

'the Sixth Protocol' means the protocol to the Convention agreed at Strasbourg on 28th April 1983;

'the Eleventh Protocol' means the protocol to the Convention (restructuring the control machinery established by the Convention) agreed at Strasbourg on 11th May 1994;

'remedial order' means an order under section 10;

'subordinate legislation' means any—

(a)   Order in Council other than one—

(i)   made in exercise of Her Majesty's Royal Prerogative;

(ii)   made under section 38(1)(a) of the Northern Ireland Constitution Act 1973 or the corresponding provision of the Northern Ireland Act 1998; or

(iii)   amending an Act of a kind mentioned in the definition of primary legislation;

(b)   Act of the Scottish Parliament;

(c)   Act of the Parliament of Northern Ireland;

(d)   Measure of the Assembly established under section 1 of the Northern Ireland Assembly Act 1973;

(e)   Act of the Northern Ireland Assembly;

(f)   order, rules, regulations, scheme, warrant, byelaw or other instrument made under primary legislation (except to the extent to which it operates to bring one or more provisions of that legislation into force or amends any primary legislation);

(g)   order, rules, regulations, scheme, warrant, byelaw or other instrument made under legislation mentioned in paragraph (b), (c), (d) or (e) or made under an Order in Council applying only to Northern Ireland;

(h)   order, rules, regulations, scheme, warrant, byelaw or other instrument made by a member of the Scottish Executive, a Northern Ireland Minister or a Northern Ireland department in exercise of prerogative or other executive functions of Her Majesty which are exercisable by such a person on behalf of Her Majesty;

'transferred matters' has the same meaning as in the Northern Ireland Act 1998; and

'tribunal' means any tribunal in which legal proceedings may be brought.

(2)   The references in paragraphs (b) and (c) of section 2(1) to Articles are to Articles of the Convention as they had effect immediately before the coming into force of the Eleventh Protocol.

(3)   The reference in paragraph (d) of section 2(1) to Article 46 includes a reference to Articles 32 and 54 of the Convention as they had effect immediately before the coming into force of the Eleventh Protocol.

(4)   The references in section 2(1) to a report or decision of the Commission or a decision of the Committee of Ministers include references to a report or decision

made as provided by paragraphs 3, 4 and 6 of Article 5 of the Eleventh Protocol (transitional provisions).

(5)   Any liability under the Army Act 1955, the Air Force Act 1955 or the Naval Discipline Act 1957 to suffer death for an offence is replaced by a liability to imprisonment for life or any less punishment authorised by those Acts; and those Acts shall accordingly have effect with the necessary modifications.

22.   Short title, commencement, application and extent

(1)   This Act may be cited as the Human Rights Act 1998.

(2)   Sections 18, 20 and 21(5) and this section come into force on the passing of this Act.

(3)   The other provisions of this Act come into force on such day as the Secretary of State may by order appoint; and different days may be appointed for different purposes.

(4)   Paragraph (b) of subsection (1) of section 7 applies to proceedings brought by or at the instigation of a public authority whenever the act in question took place; but otherwise that subsection does not apply to an act taking place before the coming into force of that section.

(5)   This Act binds the Crown.

(6)   This Act extends to Northern Ireland.

(7)   Section 21(5), so far as it relates to any provision contained in the Army Act 1955, the Air Force Act 1955 or the Naval Discipline Act 1957, extends to any place to which that provision extends.

SCHEDULES

Section 1(3)

SCHEDULE 1
THE ARTICLES

PART I
THE CONVENTION

RIGHTS AND FREEDOMS

Article 2
Right to life

1.   Everyone's right to life shall be protected by law. No one shall be deprived of his life intentionally save in the execution of a sentence of a court following his conviction of a crime for which this penalty is provided by law.

2.   Deprivation of life shall not be regarded as inflicted in contravention of this Article when it results from the use of force which is no more than absolutely necessary:

(a)   in defence of any person from unlawful violence;

(b)   in order to effect a lawful arrest or to prevent the escape of a person lawfully detained;

(c)   in action lawfully taken for the purpose of quelling a riot or insurrection.

Article 3
Prohibition of torture

No one shall be subjected to torture or to inhuman or degrading treatment or punishment.

Article 4
Prohibition of slavery and forced labour

1.   No one shall be held in slavery or servitude.

2.   No one shall be required to perform forced or compulsory labour.

3.   For the purpose of this Article the term 'forced or compulsory labour' shall not include:

(a)   any work required to be done in the ordinary course of detention imposed according to the provisions of Article 5 of this Convention or during conditional release from such detention;

(b)   any service of a military character or, in case of conscientious objectors in countries where they are recognised, service exacted instead of compulsory military service;

(c)   any service exacted in case of an emergency or calamity threatening the life or well-being of the community;

(d)   any work or service which forms part of normal civic obligations.

Article 5
Right to liberty and security

1.   Everyone has the right to liberty and security of person. No one shall be deprived of his liberty save in the following cases and in accordance with a procedure prescribed by law:

(a)   the lawful detention of a person after conviction by a competent court;

(b)   the lawful arrest or detention of a person for non-compliance with the lawful order of a court or in order to secure the fulfilment of any obligation prescribed by law;

(c)   the lawful arrest or detention of a person effected for the purpose of bringing him before the competent legal authority on reasonable suspicion of having committed an offence or when it is reasonably considered necessary to prevent his committing an offence or fleeing after having done so;

(d)   the detention of a minor by lawful order for the purpose of educational supervision or his lawful detention for the purpose of bringing him before the competent legal authority;

(e)   the lawful detention of persons for the prevention of the spreading of infectious diseases, of persons of unsound mind, alcoholics or drug addicts or vagrants;

(f)   the lawful arrest or detention of a person to prevent his effecting an unauthorised entry into the country or of a person against whom action is being taken with a view to deportation or extradition.

2.   Everyone who is arrested shall be informed promptly, in a language which he understands, of the reasons for his arrest and of any charge against him.

3.   Everyone arrested or detained in accordance with the provisions of paragraph 1(c) of this Article shall be brought promptly before a judge or other officer authorised by law to exercise judicial power and shall be entitled to trial within a reasonable time or to release pending trial. Release may be conditioned by guarantees to appear for trial.

4.   Everyone who is deprived of his liberty by arrest or detention shall be entitled to take proceedings by which the lawfulness of his detention shall be decided speedily by a court and his release ordered if the detention is not lawful.

5.   Everyone who has been the victim of arrest or detention in contravention of the provisions of this Article shall have an enforceable right to compensation.

Article 6
Right to a fair trial

1.   In the determination of his civil rights and obligations or of any criminal charge against him, everyone is entitled to a fair and public hearing within a reasonable time by an independent and impartial tribunal established by law. Judgment shall be pronounced publicly but the press and public may be excluded from all or part of the trial in the interest of morals, public order or national security in a democratic society, where the interests of juveniles or the protection of the private life of the parties so require, or to the extent strictly necessary in the opinion of the court in special circumstances where publicity would prejudice the interests of justice.

2.   Everyone charged with a criminal offence shall be presumed innocent until proved guilty according to law.

3.   Everyone charged with a criminal offence has the following minimum rights:

(a)   to be informed promptly, in a language which he understands and in detail, of the nature and cause of the accusation against him;

(b)   to have adequate time and facilities for the preparation of his defence;

(c)   to defend himself in person or through legal assistance of his own choosing or, if he has not sufficient means to pay for legal assistance, to be given it free when the interests of justice so require;

(d)   to examine or have examined witnesses against him and to obtain the attendance and examination of witnesses on his behalf under the same conditions as witnesses against him;

(e)   to have the free assistance of an interpreter if he cannot understand or speak the language used in court.

Article 7
No punishment without law

1.   No one shall be held guilty of any criminal offence on account of any act or omission which did not constitute a criminal offence under national or international law at the time when it was committed. Nor shall a heavier penalty be imposed than the one that was applicable at the time the criminal offence was committed.

2.   This Article shall not prejudice the trial and punishment of any person for any act or omission which, at the time when it was committed, was criminal according to the general principles of law recognised by civilised nations.

Article 8
Right to respect for private and family life

1.   Everyone has the right to respect for his private and family life, his home and his correspondence.

2.   There shall be no interference by a public authority with the exercise of this right except such as is in accordance with the law and is necessary in a democratic society in the interests of national security, public safety or the economic well being of the country, for the prevention of disorder or crime, for the protection of health or morals, or for the protection of the rights and freedoms of others.

Article 9
Freedom of thought, conscience and religion

1.   Everyone has the right to freedom of thought, conscience and religion; this right includes freedom to change his religion or belief and freedom, either alone or in community with others and in public or private, to manifest his religion or belief, in worship, teaching, practice and observance.

2.   Freedom to manifest one's religion or beliefs shall be subject only to such limitations as are prescribed by law and are necessary in a democratic society in the interests of public safety, for the protection of public order, health or morals, or for the protection of the rights and freedoms of others.

Article 10
Freedom of expression

1.   Everyone has the right to freedom of expression. This right shall include freedom to hold opinions and to receive and impart information and ideas without interference by public authority and regardless of frontiers. This Article shall not prevent States from requiring the licensing of broadcasting, television or cinema enterprises.

2.   The exercise of these freedoms, since it carries with it duties and responsibilities, may be subject to such formalities, conditions, restrictions or penalties as are prescribed by law and are necessary in a democratic society, in the interests of national security, territorial integrity or public safety, for the prevention of disorder or crime, for the protection of health or morals, for the protection of the reputation or rights of others, for preventing the disclosure of information received in confidence, or for maintaining the authority and impartiality of the judiciary.

Article 11
Freedom of assembly and association

1.   Everyone has the right to freedom of peaceful assembly and to freedom of association with others, including the right to form and to join trade unions for the protection of his interests.

2.   No restrictions shall be placed on the exercise of these rights other than such as are prescribed by law and are necessary in a democratic society in the interests of national security or public safety, for the prevention of disorder or crime, for the protection of health or morals or for the protection of the rights and freedoms of others. This Article shall not prevent the imposition of lawful restrictions on the exercise of these rights by members of the armed forces, of the police or of the administration of the State.

Article 12
Right to marry

Men and women of marriageable age have the right to marry and to found a family, according to the national laws governing the exercise of this right.

Article 14
Prohibition of discrimination

The enjoyment of the rights and freedoms set forth in this Convention shall be secured without discrimination on any ground such as sex, race, colour, language, religion, political or other opinion, national or social origin, association with a national minority, property, birth or other status.

Article 16
Restrictions on political activity of aliens

Nothing in Articles 10, 11 and 14 shall be regarded as preventing the High Contracting Parties from imposing restrictions on the political activity of aliens.

Article 17
Prohibition of abuse of rights

Nothing in this Convention may be interpreted as implying for any State, group or person any right to engage in any activity or perform any act aimed at the destruction of any of the rights and freedoms set forth herein or at their limitation to a greater extent than is provided for in the Convention.

Article 18
Limitation on use of restrictions on rights

The restrictions permitted under this Convention to the said rights and freedoms shall not be applied for any purpose other than those for which they have been prescribed.

PART II
THE FIRST PROTOCOL

Article 1
Protection of property

Every natural or legal person is entitled to the peaceful enjoyment of his possessions. No one shall be deprived of his possessions except in the public interest and subject to the conditions provided for by law and by the general principles of international law.

The preceding provisions shall not, however, in any way impair the right of a State to enforce such laws as it deems necessary to control the use of property in accordance with the general interest or to secure the payment of taxes or other contributions or penalties.

Article 2
Right to education

No person shall be denied the right to education. In the exercise of any functions which it assumes in relation to education and to teaching, the State shall respect the right of parents to ensure such education and teaching in conformity with their own religious and philosophical convictions.

Article 3
Right to free elections

The High Contracting Parties undertake to hold free elections at reasonable intervals by secret ballot, under conditions which will ensure the free expression of the opinion of the people in the choice of the legislature.

PART III
THE SIXTH PROTOCOL

Article 1
Abolition of the death penalty

The death penalty shall be abolished. No one shall be condemned to such penalty or executed.

Article 2
Death penalty in time of war

A State may make provision in its law for the death penalty in respect of acts committed in time of war or of imminent threat of war; such penalty shall be applied only in the instances laid down in the law and in accordance with its provisions. The State shall communicate to the Secretary General of the Council of Europe the relevant provisions of that law.

SCHEDULE 2
REMEDIAL ORDERS

Orders

1.—(1)   A remedial order may—

(a)   contain such incidental, supplemental, consequential or transitional provision as the person making it considers appropriate;

(b)   be made so as to have effect from a date earlier than that on which it is made;

(c)   make provision for the delegation of specific functions;

(d)   make different provision for different cases.

(2)   The power conferred by sub-paragraph (1)(a) includes—

(a)   power to amend primary legislation (including primary legislation other than that which contains the incompatible provision); and

(b)   power to amend or revoke subordinate legislation (including subordinate legislation other than that which contains the incompatible provision).

(3)   A remedial order may be made so as to have the same extent as the legislation which it affects.

(4)   No person is to be guilty of an offence solely as a result of the retrospective effect of a remedial order.

Procedure

2.   No remedial order may be made unless—

(a)   a draft of the order has been approved by a resolution of each House of Parliament made after the end of the period of 60 days beginning with the day on which the draft was laid; or

(b)   it is declared in the order that it appears to the person making it that, because of the urgency of the matter, it is necessary to make the order without a draft being so approved.

Orders laid in draft

3.—(1)   No draft may be laid under paragraph 2(a) unless—

(a)   the person proposing to make the order has laid before Parliament a document which contains a draft of the proposed order and the required information; and

(b)   the period of 60 days, beginning with the day on which the document required by this sub-paragraph was laid, has ended.

(2)   If representations have been made during that period, the draft laid under paragraph 2(a) must be accompanied by a statement containing—

(a)   a summary of the representations; and

(b)   if, as a result of the representations, the proposed order has been changed, details of the changes.

Urgent cases

4.—(1)   If a remedial order ('the original order') is made without being approved in draft, the person making it must lay it before Parliament, accompanied by the required information, after it is made.

(2)   If representations have been made during the period of 60 days beginning with the day on which the original order was made, the person making it must (after the end of that period) lay before Parliament a statement containing—

(a)   a summary of the representations; and

(b)   if, as a result of the representations, he considers it appropriate to make changes to the original order, details of the changes.

(3)   If sub-paragraph (2)(b) applies, the person making the statement must—

(a)   make a further remedial order replacing the original order; and

(b)   lay the replacement order before Parliament.

(4)   If, at the end of the period of 120 days beginning with the day on which the original order was made, a resolution has not been passed by each House approving the original or replacement order, the order ceases to have effect (but without that affecting anything previously done under either order or the power to make a fresh remedial order).

Definitions

5.   In this Schedule—

'representations' means representations about a remedial order (or proposed remedial order) made to the person making (or proposing to make) it and includes any relevant Parliamentary report or resolution; and

'required information' means—

(a)   an explanation of the incompatibility which the order (or proposed order) seeks to remove, including particulars of the relevant declaration, finding or order; and

(b)   a statement of the reasons for proceeding under section 10 and for making an order in those terms.

Calculating periods

6.   In calculating any period for the purposes of this Schedule, no account is to be taken of any time during which—

(a)   Parliament is dissolved or prorogued; or

(b)   both Houses are adjourned for more than four days.

SCHEDULE 3
DEROGATION AND RESERVATION

PART I
DEROGATION

The 1988 notification

The United Kingdom Permanent Representative to the Council of Europe presents his compliments to the Secretary General of the Council, and has the honour to convey the following information in order to ensure compliance with the obligations of Her Majesty's Government in the United Kingdom under Article 15(3) of the Convention for the Protection of Human Rights and Fundamental Freedoms signed at Rome on 4 November 1950.

There have been in the United Kingdom in recent years campaigns of organised terrorism connected with the affairs of Northern Ireland which have manifested themselves in activities which have included repeated murder, attempted murder, maiming, intimidation and violent civil disturbance and in bombing and fire raising which have resulted in death, injury and widespread destruction of property. As a result, a public emergency within the meaning of Article 15(1) of the Convention exists in the United Kingdom.

The Government found it necessary in 1974 to introduce and since then, in cases concerning persons reasonably suspected of involvement in terrorism connected with the affairs of Northern Ireland, or of certain offences under the legislation, who have been detained for 48 hours, to exercise powers enabling further detention without charge, for periods of up to five days, on the authority of the Secretary of State. These powers are at present to be found in Section 12 of the Prevention of Terrorism (Temporary Provisions) Act 1984, Article 9 of the Prevention of Terrorism (Supplemental Temporary Provisions) Order 1984 and Article 10 of the Prevention of Terrorism (Supplemental Temporary Provisions) (Northern Ireland) Order 1984.

Section 12 of the Prevention of Terrorism (Temporary Provisions) Act 1984 provides for a person whom a constable has arrested on reasonable grounds of suspecting him to be guilty of an offence under Section 1, 9 or 10 of the Act, or to be or to have been involved in terrorism connected with the affairs of Northern Ireland, to be detained in right of the arrest for up to 48 hours and thereafter, where the Secretary of State extends the detention period, for up to a further five days. Section 12 substantially re-enacted Section 12 of the Prevention of Terrorism (Temporary Provisions) Act 1976 which, in turn, substantially re-enacted Section 7 of the Prevention of Terrorism (Temporary Provisions) Act 1974.

Article 10 of the Prevention of Terrorism (Supplemental Temporary Provisions) (Northern Ireland) Order 1984 (SI 1984/417) and Article 9 of the Prevention of Terrorism (Supplemental Temporary Provisions) Order 1984 (SI 1984/418) were both made under Sections 13 and 14 of and Schedule 3 to the 1984 Act and substantially re-enacted powers of detention in Orders made under the 1974 and 1976 Acts. A person who is being examined under Article 4 of either Order on his arrival in, or on seeking to leave, Northern Ireland or Great Britain for the purpose of determining whether he is or has been involved in terrorism connected with the affairs of Northern Ireland, or whether there are grounds for suspecting that he has committed an offence under Section 9 of the 1984 Act, may be detained under Article 9 or 10, as appropriate, pending the conclusion of his examination. The period of this examination may exceed 12 hours if an examining officer has reasonable grounds for suspecting him to be or to have been involved in acts of terrorism connected with the affairs of Northern Ireland.

Where such a person is detained under the said Article 9 or 10 he may be detained for up to 48 hours on the authority of an examining officer and thereafter, where the Secretary of State extends the detention period, for up to a further five days.

In its judgment of 29 November 1988 in the Case of *Brogan and Others*, the European Court of Human Rights held that there had been a violation of Article 5(3) in respect of each of the applicants, all of whom had been detained under Section 12 of the 1984 Act. The Court held that even the shortest of the four periods of detention concerned, namely four days and six hours, fell outside the constraints as to time permitted by the first part of Article 5(3). In addition, the Court held that there had been a violation of Article 5(5) in the case of each applicant.

Following this judgment, the Secretary of State for the Home Department informed Parliament on 6 December 1988 that, against the background of the terrorist campaign, and the over-riding need to bring terrorists to justice, the Government did not believe that the maximum period of detention should be reduced. He informed Parliament that the Government were examining the matter with a view to responding to the judgment. On 22 December 1988, the Secretary of State further informed Parliament that it remained the Government's wish, if it could be achieved, to find a judicial process under which extended detention might be reviewed and where appropriate authorised by a judge or other judicial officer. But a further period of reflection and consultation was necessary before the Government could bring forward a firm and final view.

Since the judgment of 29 November 1988 as well as previously, the Government have found it necessary to continue to exercise, in relation to terrorism connected with the affairs of Northern Ireland, the powers described above enabling further detention without charge for periods of up to 5 days, on the authority of the Secretary of State, to the extent strictly required by the exigencies of the situation to enable necessary enquiries and investigations properly to be completed in order to decide whether criminal proceedings should be instituted. To the extent that the exercise of these powers may be inconsistent with the obligations imposed by the Convention the Government has availed itself of the right of derogation conferred by Article 15(1) of the Convention and will continue to do so until further notice.

Dated 23 December 1988.

The 1989 notification

The United Kingdom Permanent Representative to the Council of Europe presents his compliments to the Secretary General of the Council, and has the honour to convey the following information.

In his communication to the Secretary General of 23 December 1988, reference was made to the introduction and exercise of certain powers under section 12 of the Prevention of Terrorism (Temporary Provisions) Act 1984, Article 9 of the Prevention of Terrorism (Supplemental Temporary Provisions) Order 1984 and Article 10 of the Prevention of Terrorism (Supplemental Temporary Provisions) (Northern Ireland) Order 1984.

These provisions have been replaced by section 14 of and paragraph 6 of Schedule 5 to the Prevention of Terrorism (Temporary Provisions) Act 1989, which make comparable provision. They came into force on 22 March 1989. A copy of these provisions is enclosed.

The United Kingdom Permanent Representative avails himself of this opportunity to renew to the Secretary General the assurance of his highest consideration.

23 March 1989.

PART II
RESERVATION

At the time of signing the present (First) Protocol, I declare that, in view of certain provisions of the Education Acts in the United Kingdom, the principle affirmed in the second sentence of Article 2 is accepted by the United Kingdom only so far as it is compatible with the provision of efficient instruction and training, and the avoidance of unreasonable public expenditure.

Dated 20 March 1952. Made by the United Kingdom Permanent Representative to the Council of Europe.

SCHEDULE 4
JUDICIAL PENSIONS

Duty to make orders about pensions

1.—(1)   The appropriate Minister must by order make provision with respect to pensions payable to or in respect of any holder of a judicial office who serves as an ECHR judge.

(2)   A pensions order must include such provision as the Minister making it considers is necessary to secure that—

(a)   an ECHR judge who was, immediately before his appointment as an ECHR judge, a member of a judicial pension scheme is entitled to remain as a member of that scheme;

(b)   the terms on which he remains a member of the scheme are those which would have been applicable had he not been appointed as an ECHR judge; and

(c)   entitlement to benefits payable in accordance with the scheme continues to be determined as if, while serving as an ECHR judge, his salary was that which would (but for section 18(4)) have been payable to him in respect of his continuing service as the holder of his judicial office.

Contributions

2.   A pensions order may, in particular, make provision—

(a)   for any contributions which are payable by a person who remains a member of a scheme as a result of the order, and which would otherwise be payable by deduction from his salary, to be made otherwise than by deduction from his salary as an ECHR judge; and

(b)   for such contributions to be collected in such manner as may be determined by the administrators of the scheme.

Amendments of other enactments

3.   A pensions order may amend any provision of, or made under, a pensions Act in such manner and to such extent as the Minister making the order considers

necessary or expedient to ensure the proper administration of any scheme to which it relates.

Definitions

4.   In this Schedule—

'appropriate Minister' means—

(a)   in relation to any judicial office whose jurisdiction is exercisable exclusively in relation to Scotland, the Secretary of State; and

(b)   otherwise, the Lord Chancellor;

'ECHR judge' means the holder of a judicial office who is serving as a judge of the Court;

'judicial pension scheme' means a scheme established by and in accordance with a pensions Act;

'pensions Act means—

(a)   the County Courts Act (Northern Ireland) 1959;

(b)   the Sheriffs' Pensions (Scotland) Act 1961;

(c)   the Judicial Pensions Act 1981; or

(d)   the Judicial Pensions and Retirement Act 1993; and

'pensions order' means an order made under paragraph 1.

CONVENTION FOR THE PROTECTION OF HUMAN RIGHTS AND FUNDAMENTAL FREEDOMS

as amended by Protocol No. 11 (Date of entry into force 1 November 1998)

The governments signatory hereto, being members of the Council of Europe,

Considering the Universal Declaration of Human Rights proclaimed by the General Assembly of the United Nations on 10th December 1948;

Considering that this Declaration aims at securing the universal and effective recognition and observance of the Rights therein declared;

Considering that the aim of the Council of Europe is the achievement of greater unity between its members and that one of the methods by which that aim is to be pursued is the maintenance and further realisation of human rights and fundamental freedoms;

Reaffirming their profound belief in those fundamental freedoms which are the foundation of justice and peace in the world and are best maintained on the one hand by an effective political democracy and on the other by a common understanding and observance of the human rights upon which they depend;

Being resolved, as the governments of European countries which a re like-minded and have a common heritage of political traditions, ideals, freedom and the rule of law, to take the first steps for the collective enforcement of certain of the rights stated in the Universal Declaration,

Have agreed as follows:

Article 1
Obligation to respect human rights

The High Contracting Parties shall secure to everyone within their jurisdiction the rights and freedoms defined in Section I of this Convention.

Section I — Rights and freedoms

Article 2
Right to life

1 Everyone's right to life shall be protected by law. No one shall be deprived of his life intentionally save in the execution of a sentence of a court following his conviction of a crime for which this penalty is provided by law.

2   Deprivation of life shall not be regarded as inflicted in contravention of this article when it results from the use of force which is no more than absolutely necessary:

   a   in defence of any person from unlawful violence;

   b   in order to effect a lawful arrest or to prevent the escape of a person lawfully detained;

   c   in action lawfully taken for the purpose of quelling a riot or insurrection.

Article 3
Prohibition of torture

No one shall be subjected to torture or to inhuman or degrading treatment or punishment.

Article 4
Prohibition of slavery and forced labour

1   No one shall be held in slavery or servitude.

2   No one shall be required to perform forced or compulsory labour.

3   For the purpose of this article the term 'forced or compulsory labour' shall not include:

   a   any work required to be done in the ordinary course of detention imposed according to the provisions of Article 5 of this Convention or during conditional release from such detention;

   b   any service of a military character or, in case of conscientious objectors in countries where they are recognised, service exacted instead of compulsory military service;

   c   any service exacted in case of an emergency or calamity threatening the life or well-being of the community;

   d   any work or service which forms part of normal civic obligations.

Article 5
Right to liberty and security

1   Everyone has the right to liberty and security of person. No one shall be deprived of his liberty save in the following cases and in accordance with a procedure prescribed by law:

   a   the lawful detention of a person after conviction by a competent court;

   b   the lawful arrest or detention of a person for non-compliance with the lawful order of a court or in order to secure the fulfilment of any obligation prescribed by law;

   c   the lawful arrest or detention of a person effected for the purpose of bringing him before the competent legal authority on reasonable suspicion of having committed an offence or when it is reasonably considered necessary to prevent his committing an offence or fleeing after having done so;

   d   the detention of a minor by lawful order for the purpose of educational supervision or his lawful detention for the purpose of bringing him before the competent legal authority;

   e   the lawful detention of persons for the prevention of the spreading of infectious diseases, of persons of unsound mind, alcoholics or drug addicts or vagrants;

f   the lawful arrest or detention of a person to prevent his effecting an unauthorised entry into the country or of a person against whom action is being taken with a view to deportation or extradition.

2   Everyone who is arrested shall be informed promptly, in a language which he understands, of the reasons for his arrest and of any charge against him.

3   Everyone arrested or detained in accordance with the provisions of paragraph 1.c of this article shall be brought promptly before a judge or other officer authorised by law to exercise judicial power and shall be entitled to trial within a reasonable time or to release pending trial. Release may be conditioned by guarantees to appear for trial.

4   Everyone who is deprived of his liberty by arrest or detention shall be entitled to take proceedings by which the lawfulness of his detention shall be decided speedily by a court and his release ordered if the detention is not lawful.

5   Everyone who has been the victim of arrest or detention in contravention of the provisions of this article shall have an enforceable right to compensation.

Article 6
Right to a fair trial

1   In the determination of his civil rights and obligations or of any criminal charge against him, everyone is entitled to a fair and public hearing within a reasonable time by an independent and impartial tribunal established by law. Judgment shall be pronounced publicly but the press and public may be excluded from all or part of the trial in the interests of morals, public order or national security in a democratic society, where the interests of juveniles or the protection of the private life of the parties so require, or to the extent strictly necessary in the opinion of the court in special circumstances where publicity would prejudice the interests of justice.

2   Everyone charged with a criminal offence shall be presumed innocent until proved guilty according to law.

3   Everyone charged with a criminal offence has the following minimum rights:

a   to be informed promptly, in a language which he understands and in detail, of the nature and cause of the accusation against him;

b   to have adequate time and facilities for the preparation of his defence;

c   to defend himself in person or through legal assistance of his own choosing or, if he has not sufficient means to pay for legal assistance, to be given it free when the interests of justice so require;

d   to examine or have examined witnesses against him and to obtain the attendance and examination of witnesses on his behalf under the same conditions as witnesses against him;

e   to have the free assistance of an interpreter if he cannot understand or speak the language used in court.

Article 7
No punishment without law

1   No one shall be held guilty of any criminal offence on account of any act or omission which did not constitute a criminal offence under national or international law at the time when it was committed. Nor shall a heavier penalty be imposed than the one that was applicable at the time the criminal offence was committed.

2   This article shall not prejudice the trial and punishment of any person for any act or omission which, at the time when it was committed, was criminal according to the general principles of law recognised by civilised nations.

Article 8
Right to respect for private and family life

1   Everyone has the right to respect for his private and family life, his home and his correspondence.

2   There shall be no interference by a public authority with the exercise of this right except such as is in accordance with the law and is necessary in a democratic society in the interests of national security, public safety or the economic well-being of the country, for the prevention of disorder or crime, for the protection of health or morals, or for the protection of the rights and freedoms of others.

Article 9
Freedom of thought, conscience and religion

1   Everyone has the right to freedom of thought, conscience and religion; this right includes freedom to change his religion or belief and freedom, either alone or in community with others and in public or private, to manifest his religion or belief, in worship, teaching, practice and observance.

2   Freedom to manifest one's religion or beliefs shall be subject only to such limitations as are prescribed by law and are necessary in a democratic society in the interests of public safety, for the protection of public order, health or morals, or for the protection of the rights and freedoms of others.

Article 10
Freedom of expression

1   Everyone has the right to freedom of expression. This right shall include freedom to hold opinions and to receive and impart information and ideas without interference by public authority and regardless of frontiers. This article shall not prevent States from requiring the licensing of broadcasting, television or cinema enterprises.

2   The exercise of these freedoms, since it carries with it dudes and responsibilities, may be subject to such formalities, conditions, restrictions or penalties as are prescribed by law and are necessary in a democratic society, in the interests of national security, territorial integrity or public safety, for the prevention of disorder or crime, for the protection of health or morals, for the protection of the reputation or rights of others, for preventing the disclosure of information received in confidence, or for maintaining the authority and impartiality of the judiciary.

Article 11
Freedom of assembly and association

1   Everyone has the right to freedom of peaceful assembly and to freedom of association with others, including the right to form and to join trade unions for the protection of his interests.

2   No restrictions shall be placed on the exercise of these rights other than such as are prescribed by law and are necessary in a democratic society in the interests of national security or public safety, for the prevention of disorder or crime, for the protection of health or morals or for the protection of the rights and freedoms of

others. This article shall not prevent the imposition of lawful restrictions on the exercise of these rights by members of the armed forces, of the police or of the administration of the State.

Article 12
Right to marry

Men and women of marriageable age have the right to marry and to found a family, according to the national laws governing the exercise of this right.

Article 13
Right to an effective remedy

Everyone whose rights and freedoms as set forth in this Convention are violated shall have an effective remedy before a national authority notwithstanding that the violation has been committed by persons acting in an official capacity.

Article 14
Prohibition of discrimination

The enjoyment of the rights and freedoms set forth in this Convention shall be secured without discrimination on any ground such as sex, race, colour, language, religion, political or other opinion, national or social origin, association with a national minority, property, birth or other status.

Article 15
Derogation in time of emergency

1   In time of war or other public emergency threatening the life of the nation any High Contracting Party may take measures derogating from its obligations under this Convention to the extent strictly required by the exigencies of the situation, provided that such measures are not inconsistent with its other obligations under international law.

2   No derogation from Article 2, except in respect of deaths resulting from lawful acts of war, or from Articles 3, 4 (paragraph 1) and 7 shall be made under this provision.

3   Any High Contracting Party availing itself of this right of derogation shall keep the Secretary General of the Council of Europe fully informed of the measures which it has taken and the reasons therefor. It shall also inform the Secretary General of the Council of Europe when such measures have ceased to operate and the provisions of the Convention are again being fully executed.

Article 16
Restrictions on political activity of aliens

Nothing in Articles 10, 11 and 14 shall be regarded as preventing the High Contracting Parties from imposing restrictions on the political activity of aliens.

Article 17
Prohibition of abuse of rights

Nothing in this Convention may be interpreted as implying for any State, group or person any right to engage in any activity or perform any act aimed at the destruction of any of the rights and freedoms set forth herein or at their limitation to a greater extent than is provided for in the Convention.

Article 18
Limitation on use of restrictions on rights

The restrictions permitted under this Convention to the said rights and freedoms shall not be applied for any purpose other than those for which they have been prescribed.

Section II — European Court of Human Rights

Article 19
Establishment of the Court

To ensure the observance of the engagements undertaken by the High Contracting Parties in the Convention and the Protocols thereto, there shall be set up a European Court of Human Rights, hereinafter referred to as 'the Court'. It shall function on a permanent basis.

Article 20
Number of judges

The Court shall consist of a number of judges equal to that of the High Contracting Parties.

Article 21
Criteria for office

1   The judges shall be of high moral character and must either possess the qualifications required for appointment to high judicial office or be jurisconsults of recognised competence.

2   The judges shall sit on the Court in their individual capacity.

3   During their term of office the judges shall not engage in any activity which is incompatible with their independence, impartiality or with the demands of a full-time office; all questions arising from the application of this paragraph shall be decided by the Court.

Article 22
Election of judges

1   The judges shall be elected by the Parliamentary Assembly with respect to each High Contracting Party by a majority of votes cast from a list of three candidates nominated by the High Contracting Party.

2   The same procedure shall be followed to complete the Court in the event of the accession of new High Contracting Parties and in filling casual vacancies.

Article 23
Terms of office

1   The judges shall be elected for a period of six years. They may be re-elected. However, the terms of office of one-half of the judges elected at the first election shall expire at the end of three years.

2   The judges whose terms of office are to expire at the end of the initial period of three years shall be chosen by lot by the Secretary General of the Council of Europe immediately after their election.

3   In order to ensure that, as far as possible, the terms of office of one-half of the judges are renewed every three years, the Parliamentary Assembly may decide,

before proceeding to any subsequent election, that the term or terms of office of one or more judges to be elected shall be for a period other than six years but not more than nine and not less than three years.

4   In cases where more than one term of office is involved and where the Parliamentary Assembly applies the preceding paragraph, the allocation of the terms of office shall be effected by a drawing of lots by the Secretary General of the Council of Europe immediately after the election.

5   A judge elected to replace a judge whose term of office has not expired shall hold office for the remainder of his predecessor's term.

6   The terms of office of judges shall expire when they reach the age of 70.

7   The judges shall hold office until replaced. They shall, however, continue to deal with such cases as they already have under consideration.

Article 24
Dismissal

No judge may be dismissed from his office unless the other judges decide by a majority of two-thirds that he has ceased to fulfil the required conditions.

Article 25
Registry and legal secretaries

The Court shall have a registry, the functions and organisation of which shall be laid down in the rules of the Court. The Court shall be assisted by legal secretaries.

Article 26
Plenary Court

The plenary Court shall
    a   elect its President and one or two Vice-Presidents for a period of three years; they may be re-elected;
    b   set up Chambers, constituted for a fixed period of time;
    c   elect the Presidents of the Chambers of the Court; they may be re-elected;
    d   adopt the rules of the Court, and
    e   elect the Registrar and one or more Deputy Registrars.

Article 27
Committees, Chambers and Grand Chamber

1   To consider cases brought before it, the Court shall sit in committees of three judges, in Chambers of seven judges and in a Grand Chamber of seventeen judges. The Court's Chambers shall set up committees for a fixed period of time.

2   There shall sit as an *ex officio* member of the Chamber and the Grand Chamber the judge elected in respect of the State Party concerned or, if there is none or if he is unable to sit, a person of its choice who shall sit in the capacity of judge.

3   The Grand Chamber shall also include the President of the Court, the Vice-Presidents, the Presidents of the Chambers and other judges chosen in accordance with the rules of the Court. When a case is referred to the Grand Chamber under Article 43, no judge from the Chamber which rendered the judgment shall sit in the Grand Chamber, with the exception of the President of the Chamber and the judge who sat in respect of the State Party concerned.

Article 28
Declarations of inadmissibility by committees

A committee may, by a unanimous vote, declare inadmissible or strike out of its list of cases an application submitted under Article 34 where such a decision can be taken without further examination. The decision shall be final.

Article 29
Decisions by Chambers on admissibility and merits

1   If no decision is taken under Article 28, a Chamber shall decide on the admissibility and merits of individual applications submitted under Article 34.

2   A Chamber shall decide on the admissibility and merits of inter-State applications submitted under Article 33.

3   The decision on admissibility shall be taken separately unless the Court, in exceptional cases, decides otherwise.

Article 30
Relinquishment of jurisdiction to the Grand Chamber

Where a case pending before a Chamber raises a serious question affecting the interpretation of the Convention or the protocols thereto, or where the resolution of a question before the Chamber might have a result inconsistent with a judgment previously delivered by the Court, the Chamber may, at any time before it has rendered its judgment, relinquish jurisdiction in favour of the Grand Chamber, unless one of the parties to the case objects.

Article 31
Powers of the Grand Chamber

The Grand Chamber shall

a   determine applications submitted either under Article 33 or Article 34 when a Chamber has relinquished jurisdiction under Article 30 or when the case has been referred to it under Article 43; and

b   consider requests for advisory opinions submitted under Article 47.

Article 32
Jurisdiction of the Court

1   The jurisdiction of the Court shall extend to all matters concerning the interpretation and application of the Convention and the protocols thereto which are referred to it as provided in Articles 33, 34 and 47.

2   In the event of dispute as to whether the Court has jurisdiction, the Court shall decide.

Article 33
Inter-State cases

Any High Contracting Party may refer to the Court any alleged breach of the provisions of the Convention and the protocols thereto by another High Contracting Party

Article 34
Individual applications

The Court may receive applications from any person, non-governmental organisation or group of individuals claiming to be the victim of a violation by one of the

High Contracting Parties of the rights set forth in the Convention or the protocols thereto. The High Contracting Parties undertake not to hinder in any way the effective exercise of this right.

Article 35
Admissibility criteria

1   The Court may only deal with the matter after all domestic remedies have been exhausted, according to the generally recognised rules of international law, and within a period of six months from the date on which the final decision was taken.

2   The Court shall not deal with any application submitted under Article 34 that

a   is anonymous; or

b   is substantially the same as a matter that has already been examined by the Court or has already been submitted to another procedure of international investigation or settlement and contains no relevant new information.

3   The Court shall declare inadmissible any individual application submitted under Article 34 which it considers incompatible with the provisions of the Convention or the protocols thereto, manifestly ill-founded, or an abuse of the right of application.

4   The Court shall reject any application which it considers inadmissible under this Article. It may do so at any stage of the proceedings.

Article 36
Third party intervention

1   In all cases before a Chamber of the Grand Chamber, a High Contracting Party one of whose nationals is an applicant shall have the right to submit written comments and to take part in hearings.

2   The President of the Court may, in the interest of the proper administration of justice, invite any High Contracting Party which is not a party to the proceedings or any person concerned who is not the applicant to submit written comments or take part in hearings.

Article 37
Striking out applications

1   The Court may at any stage of the proceedings decide to strike an application out of its list of cases where the circumstances lead to the conclusion that

a   the applicant does not intend to pursue his application; or

b   the matter has been resolved; or

c   for any other reason established by the Court, it is no longer justified to continue the examination of the application.

However, the Court shall continue the examination of the application if respect for human rights as defined in the Convention and the protocols thereto so requires.

2   The Court may decide to restore an application to its list of cases if it considers that the circumstances justify such a course.

Article 38
Examination of the case and friendly settlement proceedings

1   If the Court declares the application admissible, it shall

a   pursue the examination of the case, together with the representatives of the parties, and if need be, undertake an investigation, for the effective conduct of which the States concerned shall furnish all necessary facilities;

    b   place itself at the disposal of the parties concerned with a view to securing
a friendly settlement of the matter on the basis of respect for human rights as defined
in the Convention and the protocols thereto.
    2   Proceedings conducted under paragraph 1.b shall be confidential.

Article 39
Finding of a friendly settlement

If a friendly settlement is effected, the Court shall strike the case out of its list by
means of a decision which shall be confined to a brief statement of the facts and of
the solution reached.

Article 40
Public hearings and access to documents

    1   Hearings shall be in public unless the Court in exceptional circumstances
decides otherwise.
    2   Documents deposited with the Registrar shall be accessible to the public
unless the President of the Court decides otherwise.

Article 41
Just satisfaction

If the Court finds that there has been a violation of the Convention or the protocols
thereto, and if the internal law of the High Contracting Party concerned allows only
partial reparation to be made, the Court shall, if necessary afford just satisfaction to
the injured party.

Article 42
Judgments of Chambers

Judgments of Chambers shall become final in accordance with the provisions of
Article 44, paragraph 2.

Article 43
Referral to the Grand Chamber

    1   Within a period of three months from the date of the judgment of the
Chamber, any party to the case may, in exceptional cases, request that the case be
referred to the Grand Chamber.
    2   A panel of five judges of the Grand Chamber shall accept the request if the
case raises a serious question affecting the interpretation or application of the
Convention or the protocols thereto, or a serious issue of general importance.
    3   If the panel accepts the request, the Grand Chamber shall decide the case by
means of a judgment.

Article 44
Final judgments

    1   The judgment of the Grand Chamber shall be final.
    2   The judgment of a Chamber shall become final
    a   when the parties declare that they will not request that the case be referred
to the Grand Chamber; or
    b   three months after the date of the judgment, if reference of the case to the
Grand Chamber has not been requested; or

c   when the panel of the Grand Chamber rejects the request to refer under Article 43.

3   The final judgment shall be published.

Article 45
Reasons for judgments and decisions

1   Reasons shall be given for judgments as well as for decisions declaring applications admissible or inadmissible.

2   If a judgment does not represent, in whole or in part, the unanimous opinion of the judges, any judge shall be entitled to deliver a separate opinion.

Article 46
Binding force and execution of judgments

1   The High Contracting Parties undertake to abide by the final judgment of the Court in any case to which they are parties.

2   The final judgment of the Court shall be transmitted to the Committee of Ministers, which shall supervise its execution.

Article 47
Advisory opinions

1   The Court may, at the request of the Committee of Ministers, give advisory opinions on legal questions concerning the interpretation of the Convention and the protocols thereto.

2   Such opinions shall not deal with any question relating to the content or scope of the rights or freedoms defined in Section I of the Convention and the protocols thereto, or with any other question which the Court or the Committee of Ministers might have to consider in consequence of any such proceedings as could be instituted in accordance with the Convention.

3   Decisions of the Committee of Ministers to request an advisory opinion of the Court shall require a majority vote of the representatives entitled to sit on the Committee.

Article 48
Advisory jurisdiction of the Court

The Court shall decide whether a request for an advisory opinion submitted by the Committee of Ministers is within its competence as defined in Article 47.

Article 49
Reasons for advisory opinions

1   Reasons shall be given for advisory opinions of the Court.

2   If the advisory opinion does not represent, in whole or in part, the unanimous opinion of the judges, any judge shall be entitled to deliver a separate opinion.

3   Advisory opinions of the Court shall be communicated to the Committee of Ministers.

Article 50
Expenditure on the Court

The expenditure on the Court shall be borne by the Council of Europe.

Article 51
Privileges and immunities of judges

The judges shall be entitled, during the exercise of their functions, to the privileges and immunities provided for in Article 40 of the Statute of the Council of Europe and in the agreements made thereunder.

Section III — Miscellaneous provisions

Article 52
Inquiries by the Secretary General

On receipt of a request from the Secretary General of the Council of Europe any High Contracting Party shall furnish an explanation of the manner in which its internal law ensures the effective implementation of any of the provisions of the Convention.

Article 53
Safeguard for existing human rights

Nothing in this Convention shall be construed as limiting or derogating from any of the human rights and fundamental freedoms which may be ensured under the laws of any High Contracting Party or under any other agreement to which it is a Party.

Article 54
Powers of the Committee of Ministers

Nothing in this Convention shall prejudice the powers conferred on the Committee of Ministers by the Statute of the Council of Europe.

Article 55
Exclusion of other means of dispute settlement

The High Contracting Parties agree that, except by special agreement, they will not avail themselves of treaties, conventions or declarations in force between them for the purpose of submitting, by way of petition, a dispute arising out of the interpretation or application of this Convention to a means of settlement other than those provided for in this Convention.

Article 56
Territorial application

1   Any State may at the time of its ratification or at any time thereafter declare by notification addressed to the Secretary General of the Council of Europe that the present Convention shall, subject to paragraph 4 of this Article, extend to all or any of the territories for whose international relations it is responsible.

2   The Convention shall extend to the territory or territories named in the notification as from the thirtieth day after the receipt of this notification by the Secretary General of the Council of Europe.

3   The provisions of this Convention shall be applied in such territories with due regard, however, to local requirements.

4   Any State which has made a declaration in accordance with paragraph 1 of this article may at any time thereafter declare on behalf of one or more of the territories to which the declaration relates that it accepts the competence of the

Court to receive applications from individuals, non-governmental organisations or groups of individuals as provided by Article 34 of the Convention.

Article 57
Reservations

1   Any State may, when signing this Convention or when depositing its instrument of ratification, make a reservation in respect of any particular provision of the Convention to the extent that any law then in force in its territory is not in conformity with the provision. Reservations of a general character shall not be permitted under this article.

2   Any reservation made under this article shall contain a brief statement of the law concerned.

Article 58
Denunciation

1   A High Contracting Party may denounce the present Convention only after the expiry of five years from the date on which it became a party to it and after six months' notice contained in a notification addressed to the Secretary General of the Council of Europe, who shall inform the other High Contracting Parties.

2   Such a denunciation shall not have the effect of releasing the High Contracting Party concerned from its obligations under this Convention in respect of any act which, being capable of constituting a violation of such obligations, may have been performed by it before the date at which the denunciation became effective.

3   Any High Contracting Party which shall cease to be a member of the Council of Europe shall cease to be a Party to this Convention under the same conditions.

4   The Convention may be denounced in accordance with the provisions of the preceding paragraphs in respect of any territory to which it has been declared to extend under the terms of Article 56.

Article 59
Signature and ratification

1   This Convention shall be open to the signature of the members of the Council of Europe. It shall be ratified. Ratifications shall be deposited with the Secretary General of the Council of Europe.

2   The present Convention shall come into force after the deposit of ten instruments of ratification.

3   As regards any signatory ratifying subsequently, the Convention shall come into force at the date of the deposit of its instrument of ratification.

4   The Secretary General of the Council of Europe shall notify all the members of the Council of Europe of the entry into force of the Convention, the names of the High Contracting Parties who have ratified it, and the deposit of all instruments of ratification which may be effected subsequently.

Done at Rome this 4th day of November 1950, in English and French, both texts being equally authentic, in a single copy which shall remain deposited in the archives of the Council of Europe.

The Secretary General shall transmit certified copies to each of the signatories.

PROTOCOL [NO. 1] TO THE CONVENTION FOR THE PROTECTION OF HUMAN RIGHTS AND FUNDAMENTAL FREEDOMS, AS AMENDED BY PROTOCOL NO. 11

The governments signatory hereto, being members of the Council of Europe,

Being resolved to take steps to ensure the collective enforcement of certain rights and freedoms other than those already included in Section I of the Convention for the Protection of Human Rights and Fundamental Freedoms signed at Rome on 4 November 1950 (hereinafter referred to as 'the Convention'),

Have agreed as follows:

Article 1
Protection of property

Every natural or legal person is entitled to the peaceful enjoyment of his possessions. No one shall be deprived of his possessions except in the public interest and subject to the conditions provided for by law and by the general principles of international law.

The preceding provisions shall not, however, in any way impair the right of a State to enforce such laws as it deems necessary to control the use of property in accordance with the general interest or to secure the payment of taxes or other contributions or penalties.

Article 2
Right to education

No person shall be denied the right to education. In the exercise of any functions which it assumes in relation to education and to teaching, the State shall respect the right of parents to ensure such education and teaching in conformity with their own religious and philosophical convictions.

Article 3
Right to free elections

The High Contracting Parties undertake to hold free elections at reasonable intervals by secret ballot, under conditions which will ensure the free expression of the opinion of the people in the choice of the legislature.

Article 4
Territorial application

Any High Contracting Party may at the time of signature or ratification or at any time thereafter communicate to the Secretary General of the Council of Europe a declaration stating the extent to which it undertakes that the provisions of the present Protocol shall apply to such of the territories for the international relations of which it is responsible as are named therein.

Any High Contracting Party which has communicated a declaration in virtue of the preceding paragraph may from time to time communicate a further declaration modifying the terms of any former declaration or terminating the application of the provisions of this Protocol in respect of any territory.

A declaration made in accordance with this article shall be deemed to have been made in accordance with paragraph 1 of Article 56 of the Convention.

Article 5

Relationship to the Convention

As between the High Contracting Parties the provisions of Articles 1, 2, 3 and 4 of this Protocol shall be regarded as additional articles to the Convention and all the provisions of the Convention shall apply accordingly.

Article 6

Signature and ratification

This Protocol shall be open for signature by the members of the Council of Europe, who are the signatories of the Convention; it shall be ratified at the same time as or after the ratification of the Convention. It shall enter into force after the deposit of ten instruments of ratification. As regards any signatory ratifying subsequently, the Protocol shall enter into force at the date of the deposit of its instrument of ratification.

The instruments of ratification shall be deposited with the Secretary General of the Council of Europe, who will notify all members of the names of those who have ratified.

Done at Paris on the 20th day of March 1952, in English and French, both texts being equally authentic, in a single copy which shall remain deposited in the archives of the Council of Europe. The Secretary General shall transmit certified copies to each of the signatory governments.

PROTOCOL NO. 4 TO THE CONVENTION FOR THE PROTECTION OF HUMAN RIGHTS AND FUNDAMENTAL FREEDOMS, SECURING CERTAIN RIGHTS AND FREEDOMS OTHER THAN THOSE ALREADY INCLUDED IN THE CONVENTION AND IN THE FIRST PROTOCOL THERETO, AS AMENDED BY PROTOCOL NO. 11

The governments signatory hereto, being members of the Council of Europe,

Being resolved to take steps to ensure the collective enforcement of certain rights and freedoms other than those already included in Section 1 of the Convention for the Protection of Human Rights and Fundamental Freedoms signed at Rome on 4th November 1950 (hereinafter referred to as the 'Convention') and in Articles 1 to 3 of the First Protocol to the Convention, signed at Paris on 20th March 1952,

Have agreed as follows:

Article 1

Prohibition of imprisonment for debt

No one shall be deprived of his liberty merely on the ground of inability to fulfil a contractual obligation.

Article 2

Freedom of movement

1   Everyone lawfully within the territory of a State shall, within that territory, have the right to liberty of movement and freedom to choose his residence.

2   Everyone shall be free to leave any country, including his own.

3   No restrictions shall be placed on the exercise of these rights other than such as are in accordance with law and are necessary in a democratic society in the

interests of national security or public safety, for the maintenance of *ordre public*, for the prevention of crime, for the protection of health or morals, or for the protection of the rights and freedoms of others.

4   The rights set forth in paragraph 1 may also be subject, in particular areas, to restrictions imposed in accordance with law and justified by the public interest in a democratic society.

Article 3
Prohibition of expulsion of nationals

1   No one shall be expelled, by means either of an individual or of a collective measure, from the territory of the State of which he is a national.

2   No one shall be deprived of the right to enter the territory of the state of which he is a national.

Article 4
Prohibition of collective expulsion of aliens

Collective expulsion of aliens is prohibited.

Article 5
Territorial application

1   Any High Contracting Party may, at the time of signature or ratification of this Protocol, or at any time thereafter, communicate to the Secretary General of the Council of Europe a declaration stating the extent to which it undertakes that the provisions of this Protocol shall apply to such of the territories for the international relations of which it is responsible as are named therein.

2   Any High Contracting Party which has communicated a declaration in virtue of the preceding paragraph may, from time to time, communicate a further declaration modifying the terms of any former declaration or terminating the application of the provisions of this Protocol in respect of any territory.

3   A declaration made in accordance with this article shall be deemed to have been made in accordance with paragraph 1 of Article 56 of the Convention.

4   The territory of any State to which this Protocol applies by virtue of ratification or acceptance by that State, and each territory to which this Protocol is applied by virtue of a declaration by that State under this article, shall be treated as separate territories for the purpose of the references in Articles 2 and 3 to the territory of a State.

5   Any State which has made a declaration in accordance with paragraph 1 or 2 of this Article may at any time thereafter declare on behalf of one or more of the territories to which the declaration relates that it accepts the competence of the Court to receive applications from individuals, non-governmental organisations or groups of individuals as provided in Article 34 of the Convention in respect of all or any of Articles 1 to 4 of this Protocol.

Article 6
Relationship to the Convention

As between the High Contracting Parties the provisions of Articles 1 to 5 of this Protocol shall be regarded as additional Articles to the Convention, and all the provisions of the Convention shall apply accordingly.

Article 7
Signature and ratification

1   This Protocol shall be open for signature by the members of the Council of Europe who are the signatories of the Convention; it shall be ratified at the same time as or after the ratification of the Convention. It shall enter into force after the deposit of five instruments of ratification. As regards any signatory ratifying subsequently, the Protocol shall enter into force at the date of the deposit of its instrument of ratification.

2   The instruments of ratification shall be deposited with the Secretary General of the Council of Europe, who will notify all members of the names of those who have ratified.

In witness whereof the undersigned, being duly authorised thereto, have signed this Protocol.

Done at Strasbourg, this 16th day of September 1963, in English and in French, both texts being equally authoritative, in a single copy which shall remain deposited in the archives of the Council of Europe. The Secretary General shall transmit certified copies to each of the signatory states.

PROTOCOL NO. 6 TO THE CONVENTION FOR THE PROTECTION OF HUMAN RIGHTS AND FUNDAMENTAL FREEDOMS CONCERNING THE ABOLITION OF THE DEATH PENALTY, AS AMENDED BY PROTOCOL NO. 11

The member States of the Council of Europe, signatory to this Protocol to the Convention for the Protection of Human Rights and Fundamental Freedoms, signed at Rome on 4 November 1950 (hereinafter referred to as 'the Convention'),

Considering that the evolution that has occurred in several member States of the Council of Europe expresses a general tendency in favour of abolition of the death penalty;

Have agreed as follows:

Article 1
Abolition of the death penalty

The death penalty shall be abolished. No-one shall be condemned to such penalty or executed.

Article 2
Death penalty in time of war

A State may make provision in its law for the death penalty in respect of acts committed in time of war or of imminent threat of war; such penalty shall be applied only in the instances laid down in the law and in accordance with its provisions. The State shall communicate to the Secretary General of the Council of Europe the relevant provisions of that law.

Article 3
Prohibition of derogations

No derogation from the provisions of this Protocol shall be made under Article 15 of the Convention.

Article 4
Prohibition of reservations

No reservation may be made under Article 57 of the Convention in respect of the provisions of this Protocol.

Article 5
Territorial application

1   Any State may at the time of signature or when depositing its instrument of ratification, acceptance or approval, specify the territory or territories to which this Protocol shall apply.

2   Any State may at any later date, by a declaration addressed to the Secretary General of the Council of Europe, extend the application of this Protocol to any other territory specified in the declaration. In respect of such territory the Protocol shall enter into force on the first day of the month following the date of receipt of such declaration by the Secretary General.

3   Any declaration made under the two preceding paragraphs may, in respect of any territory specified in such declaration, be withdrawn by a notification addressed to the Secretary General. The withdrawal shall become effective on the first day of the month following the date of receipt of such notification by the Secretary General.

Article 6
Relationship to the Convention

As between the States Parties the provisions of Articles 1 to 5 of this Protocol shall be regarded as additional articles to the Convention and all the provisions of the Convention shall apply accordingly.

Article 7
Signature and ratification

The Protocol shall be open for signature by the member States of the Council of Europe, signatories to the Convention. It shall be subject to ratification, acceptance or approval. A member State of the Council of Europe may not ratify, accept or approve this Protocol unless it has, simultaneously or previously, ratified the Convention. Instruments of ratification, acceptance or approval shall be deposited with the Secretary General of the Council of Europe.

Article 8
Entry into force

1   This Protocol shall enter into force on the first day of the month following the date on which five member States of the Council of Europe have expressed their consent to be bound by the Protocol in accordance with the provisions of Article 7.

2   In respect of any member State which subsequently expresses its consent to be bound by it, the Protocol shall enter into force on the first day of the month following the date of the deposit of the instrument of ratification, acceptance or approval.

Article 9
Depositary functions

The Secretary General of the Council of Europe shall notify the member States of the Council of:

a   any signature;

b   the deposit of any instrument of ratification, acceptance or approval;

c   any date of entry into force of this Protocol in accordance with Articles 5 and 8;

d   any other act, notification or communication relating to this Protocol.

In witness whereof the undersigned, being duly authorised thereto, have signed this Protocol.

Done at Strasbourg, this 28th day of April 1983, in English and in French, both texts being equally authentic, in a single copy which shall be deposited in the archives of the Council of Europe. The Secretary General of the Council of Europe shall transmit certified copies to each member State of the Council of Europe.

PROTOCOL NO. 7 TO THE CONVENTION FOR THE PROTECTION OF HUMAN RIGHTS AND FUNDAMENTAL FREEDOMS, AS AMENDED BY PROTOCOL NO. 11

The member States of the Council of Europe signatory hereto,

Being resolved to take further steps to ensure the collective enforcement of certain rights and freedoms by means of the Convention for the Protection of Human Rights and Fundamental Freedoms signed at Rome on 4 November 1950 (hereinafter referred to as 'the Convention'),

Have agreed as follows

Article 1
Procedural safeguards relating to expulsion of aliens

1   An alien lawfully resident in the territory of a State shall not be expelled therefrom except in pursuance of a decision reached in accordance with law and shall be allowed:

a   to submit reasons against his expulsion,

b   to have his case reviewed, and

c   to be represented for these purposes before the competent authority or a person or persons designated by that authority.

2   An alien may be expelled before the exercise of his rights under paragraph 1.a, b and c of this Article, when such expulsion is necessary in the interests of public order or is grounded on reasons of national security.

Article 2
Right of appeal in criminal matters

1   Everyone convicted of a criminal offence by a tribunal shall have the right to have his conviction or sentence reviewed by a higher tribunal. The exercise of this right, including the grounds on which it may be exercised, shall be governed by law.

2   This right may be subject to exceptions in regard to offences of a minor character, as prescribed by law, or in cases in which the person concerned was tried in the first instance by the highest tribunal or was convicted following an appeal against acquittal.

Article 3
Compensation for wrongful conviction

When a person has by a final decision been convicted of a criminal offence and when subsequently his conviction has been reversed, or he has been pardoned, on the ground that a new or newly discovered fact shows conclusively that there has been a miscarriage of justice, the person who has suffered punishment as a result of such conviction shall be compensated according to the law or the practice of the State concerned, unless it is proved that the non-disclosure of the unknown fact in time is wholly or partly attributable to him.

Article 4
Right not to be tried or punished twice

1   No one shall be liable to be tried or punished again in criminal proceedings under the jurisdiction of the same State for an offence for which he has already been finally acquitted or convicted in accordance with the law and penal procedure of that State.

2   The provisions of the preceding paragraph shall not prevent the reopening of the case in accordance with the law and penal procedure of the State concerned, if there is evidence of new or newly discovered facts, or if there has been a fundamental defect in the previous proceedings, which could affect the outcome of the case.

3   No derogation from this Article shall be made under Article 15 of the Convention.

Article 5
Equality between spouses

Spouses shall enjoy equality of rights and responsibilities of a private law character between them, and in their relations with their children, as to marriage, during marriage and in the event of its dissolution. This Article shall not prevent States from taking such measures as are necessary in the interests of the children.

Article 6
Territorial application

1   Any State may at the time of signature or when depositing its instrument of ratification, acceptance or approval, specify the territory or territories to which the Protocol shall apply and state the extent to which it undertakes that the provisions of this Protocol shall apply to such territory or territories.

2   Any State may at any later date, by a declaration addressed to the Secretary General of the Council of Europe, extend the application of this Protocol to any other territory specified in the declaration. In respect of such territory the Protocol shall enter into force on the first day of the month following the expiration of a period of two months after the date of receipt by the Secretary General of such declaration.

3   Any declaration made under the two preceding paragraphs may, in respect of any territory specified in such declaration, be withdrawn or modified by a notification addressed to the Secretary General. The withdrawal or modification shall become effective on the first day of the month following the expiration of a period of two months after the date of receipt of such notification by the Secretary General.

4   A declaration made in accordance with this Article shall be deemed to have been made in accordance with paragraph 1 of Article 56 of the Convention.

5   The territory of any State to which this Protocol applies by virtue of ratification, acceptance or approval by that State, and each territory to which this Protocol is applied by virtue of a declaration by that State under this Article, may be treated as separate territories for the purpose of the reference in Article 1 to the territory of a State.

6   Any State which has made a declaration in accordance with paragraph 1 or 2 of this Article may at any time thereafter declare on behalf of one or more of the territories to which the declaration relates that it accepts the competence of the Court to receive applications from individuals, non-governmental organisations or groups of individuals as provided in Article 34 of the Convention in respect of Articles 1 to 5 of this Protocol.

Article 7
Relationship to the Convention

As between the States Parties, the provisions of Article 1 to 6 of this Protocol shall be regarded as additional Articles to the Convention, and all the provisions of the Convention shall apply accordingly.

Article 8
Signature and ratification

This Protocol shall be open for signature by member States of the Council of Europe which have signed the Convention. It is subject to ratification, acceptance or approval. A member State of the Council of Europe may not ratify, accept or approve this Protocol without previously or simultaneously ratifying the Convention. Instruments of ratification, acceptance or approval shall be deposited with the Secretary General of the Council of Europe.

Article 9
Entry into force

1   This Protocol shall enter into force on the first day of the month following the expiration of a period of two months after the date on which seven member States of the Council of Europe have expressed their consent to be bound by the Protocol in accordance with the provisions of Article 8.

2   In respect of any member State which subsequently expresses its consent to be bound by it, the Protocol shall enter into force on the first day of the month following the expiration of a period of two months after the date of the deposit of the instrument of ratification, acceptance or approval.

Article 10
Depositary functions

The Secretary General of the Council of Europe shall notify all the member States of the Council of Europe of:

a   any signature;

b   the deposit of any instrument of ratification, acceptance or approval;

c   any date of entry into force of this Protocol in accordance with Articles 6 and 9;

d   any other act, notification or declaration relating to this Protocol.

In witness whereof the undersigned, being duly authorised thereto, have signed this Protocol.

Done at Strasbourg, this 22nd day of November 1984, in English and French, both texts being equally authentic, in a single copy which shall be deposited in the archives of the Council of Europe. The Secretary General of the Council of Europe shall transmit certified copies to each member State of the Council of Europe.

PROTOCOL NO. 12 TO THE CONVENTION FOR THE PROTECTION OF HUMAN RIGHTS AND FUNDAMENTAL FREEDOMS

The member states of the Council of Europe signatory hereto,

Having regard to the fundamental principle according to which all persons are equal before the law and are entitled to the equal protection of the law;

Being resolved to take further steps to promote the equality of all persons through the collective enforcement of a general prohibition of discrimination by means of the Convention for the Protection of Human Rights and Fundamental Freedoms signed at Rome on 4 November 1950 (hereinafter referred to as 'the Convention');

Reaffirming that the principle of non-discrimination does not prevent States Parties from taking measures in order to promote full and effective equality, provided that there is an objective and reasonable justification for those measures,

Have agreed as follows:

Article 1
General prohibition of discrimination

1   The enjoyment of any right set forth by law shall be secured without discrimination on any ground such as sex, race, colour, language, religion, political or other opinion, national or social origin, association with a national minority, property, birth or other status.

2   No one shall be discriminated against by any public authority on any ground such as those mentioned in paragraph 1.

Article 2
Territorial application

1   Any state may, at the time of signature or when depositing its instrument of ratification, acceptance or approval, specify the territory or territories to which this Protocol shall apply.

2   Any state may at any later date, by a declaration addressed to the Secretary General of the Council of Europe, extend the application of this Protocol to any other territory specified in the declaration, in respect of such territory the Protocol shall enter into force on the first day of the month following the expiration of a period of three months after the date of receipt by the Secretary General of such declaration.

3   Any declaration made under the two preceding paragraphs may, in respect of any territory specified in such declaration, be withdrawn or modified by a notification addressed to the Secretary General. The withdrawal or modification shall become effective on the first day of the month following the expiration of a period of three months after the date of receipt of such notification by the Secretary General.

4   A declaration made in accordance with this article shall be deemed to have been made in accordance with paragraph 1 of Article 56 of the Convention.

5   Any state which has made a declaration in accordance with paragraph 1 or 2 of this article may at any time thereafter declare on behalf of one or more of the territories to which the declaration relates that it accepts the competence of the Court to receive applications from individuals, non-governmental organisations or groups of individuals as provided by Article 34 of the Convention in respect of Article 1 of this Protocol.

Article 3
Relationship to the Convention

As between the States Parties, the provisions of Articles 1 and 2 of this Protocol shall be regarded as additional articles to the Convention, and all the provisions of the Convention shall apply accordingly.

Article 4
Signature and ratification

This Protocol shall be open for signature by member states of the Council of Europe which have signed the Convention. It is subject to ratification, acceptance or approval. A member state of the Council of Europe may not ratify, accept or approve this Protocol without previously or simultaneously ratifying the Convention. Instruments of ratification, acceptance or approval shall be deposited with the Secretary General of the Council of Europe.

Article 5
Entry into force

1   This Protocol shall enter into force on the first day of the month following the expiration of a period of three months after the date on which ten member states of the Council of Europe have expressed their consent to be bound by the Protocol in accordance with the provisions of Article 4.

2   In respect of any member state which subsequently expresses its consent to be bound by it, the Protocol shall enter into force on the first day of the month following the expiration of a period of three months after the date of the deposit of the instrument of ratification, acceptance or approval.

Article 6
Depositary functions

The Secretary General of the Council of Europe shall notify all the member states of the Council of Europe of:

a   any signature;

b   the deposit of any instrument of ratification, acceptance or approval;

c   any date of entry into force of this Protocol in accordance with Articles 2 and 5;

d   any other act, notification or communication relating to this Protocol.

In witness whereof the undersigned, being duly authorised thereto, have signed this Protocol.

Done at ...., this .... day of .... 2000, in English and French, both texts being equally authentic, in a single copy which shall be deposited in the archives of the Council of Europe. The Secretary General of the Council of Europe shall transmit certified copies to each member state of the Council of Europe.

INDEX